Intersex Rights

Nikoletta Pikramenou

Intersex Rights

Living Between Sexes

Thank you InterAct!
Nicole

Nikoletta Pikramenou
Athens, Greece

ISBN 978-3-030-27553-2 ISBN 978-3-030-27554-9 (eBook)
https://doi.org/10.1007/978-3-030-27554-9

This Springer imprint is published by the registered company Springer Nature Switzerland AG.
The registered company address is: Gewerbestrasse 11, 6330 Cham, Switzerland

Acknowledgements

I became aware of the issues that intersex people encounter in 2014, while at a seminar on human rights and bioethics at the European Inter-University Centre for Human Rights and Democratisation in Venice, Italy. The struggle of intersex people for equal rights immediately sparked my interest, and I felt the need to contribute to their pursuit of justice by aiming to fulfil the "gap" that exists in the field of legal research and intersex rights. In 2015, when I talked with Prof. Lina Papadopoulou about intersex and elaborated on the idea to write a doctoral thesis on the topic, she was highly interested in supporting this research as the main supervisor. At that time, one of my goals was to analyse the case of Greece as despite the fact that legislation on intersex existed, nothing was ever written about it. Prof. Papadopoulou suggested to collaborate with a foreign university and the first person that I thought of was Prof. Anna Sara Lind from Uppsala University as our previous collaboration during my master's on human rights was excellent. Therefore, words cannot describe my gratitude to both Prof. Papadopoulou and Prof. Lind for believing in this project from the very beginning. Prof. Papadopoulou supported this project significantly with her invitations to present parts of my research to different audiences as she always believed in its international impact and potential. At the same time, my annual visits at Uppsala University were extremely valuable, Prof. Lind was always enormously welcoming, and I would like to thank her for her warmth and psychological support (and delicious princess tårta). At that point, I would also like to thank the medical law team at Uppsala University for their great feedback and Jameson Garland in particular for our conversations on intersex. The contribution of the third member of the supervising committee, Prof. Katerina Fountedaki, was equally important and her feedback was much appreciated. I would also like to thank the members of the examination Committee: Theofano Papazissi from the Law Faculty of Aristotle University, Rosie Harding from Birmingham Law School, Giorgos Karavokiris from the Law Faculty of Aristotle University and Neda Kanelopoulou from Panteion University.

The outcome of this research wouldn't be the same without my stays in Germany and the United States. First, my research visits at European University Viadrina and Humboldt University allowed me to comprehend the exact situation on intersex rights in Germany, the first European country that legislated on the matter. I would like to thank Prof. Eva Kocher and Prof. Carmen Thiele who invited me to Viadrina and Rebekka Manke who supported me during my research fellowship in the best possible way. At Humboldt University, I would like to thank Prof. Anja Schmidt who was delighted to learn about my research and provide her feedback. In New York, I thank Charles Whiteley, who offered me the opportunity to work at the Delegation of the European Union to the United Nations in New York and promote intersex rights. Moreover, I would like to thank Dörthe Wacker for the excellent collaboration during the organisation of the first event on intersex rights at the Delegation. I am also grateful to Kimberly Zieselman and Hanne Gaby Odiele from InterAct, for sharing their personal experience as intersex activists. In addition, I would like to thank Hayley Gorenberg from Lambda Legal and Siri May from OutRight International for their valuable inputs on intersex rights and the situation in the . I also thank Charles Radcliffe for our fruitful discussions on intersex in Australia. Lastly, I would like to thank Rinio Simeonidou for her contribution on the situation of intersex rights in Greece and Dan Christian Ghattas for his valuable comments.

Finally, I would like to acknowledge the eternal love of my parents who supported me during all these years by all means: my dad, in particular, for his scientific inputs with regard to intersex and justice. This research wouldn't have been possible without you two.

Contents

Abbreviations

AIS	Androgen Insensitivity Syndrome
ART	Assisted Reproductive Technologies
ASEAN	Association of Southeast Asian Nations
BC	Before Christ
CAH	Congenital Adrenal Hyperplasia
CEDAW	Convention or Committee on the Elimination of All Forms of Discrimination Against Women
DEVAW	Declaration on the Elimination of Violence Against Women
CoE	Council of Europe
CIDT	Cruel Inhuman or Degrading Treatment
CRC	Convention on the Rights of the Child
CRPD	Convention on the Rights of Persons with Disabilities
DNA	Deoxyribonucleic acid
DSD	Disorders of Sex Development or Disorders of Sex Differentiation or Differences of Sex Development
ECHR	European Convention on Human Rights
ECtHR	European Court of Human Rights
ECJ	European Court of Justice
ESC	European Social Charter
EU	European Union
FGM/C	Female Genital Mutilation/Cutting
FRA	European Union Agency for Fundamental Rights
ICCPR	International Covenant on Civil and Political Rights
ICESCR	International Covenant on Economic, Social and Cultural Rights
IACHR	Inter-American Commission on Human Rights
IACtHR	Inter-American Court of Human Rights
IAAF	International Association of Athletics Federations
IOC	International Olympic Committee
IVF	In Vitro Fertilisation
LGBTQ	Lesbian, Gay, Bisexual, Transgender and Queer
OHCHR	Office of the High Commissioner of Human Rights

PACE	Parliamentary Assembly of the Council of Europe
PGD	Preimplantation Genetic Diagnosis
SDGs	Sustainable Development Goals
SOGI	Sexual Orientation and Gender Identity
SOGIESC	Sexual Orientation, Gender Identity and Expression and Sex Characteristics
TFEU	Treaty on the Functioning of the European Union
TEU	Treaty on European Union
UDHR	Universal Declaration on Human Rights
UN	United Nations
UNCAT	Convention Against Torture
UNFPA	United Nations Fund for Population Activities
UNGA	United Nations General Assembly
UNHRC	United Nations Human Rights Council
UNICEF	United Nations Children's Fund
UN Women	United Nations Women
UN Aids	United Nations Aids
U.S.	United States
WHO	World Health Organization

Chapter 1
Introduction: Trapped in the Binary

1.1 Intersex and the Sex Binary

From the very beginning of our lives, human beings are called to fit in the sex binary of male and female. Contemporary society is based upon a heteronormative gender order deriving from the idea that there are two opposite sexes.[1] Then, social rules about "normal" gender and sexuality require the definition of what is "female", "male", "masculine" and "feminine" so that the "opposite sexes" are attracted to each other and eventually reproduce.[2] Consequently, "sex" results being polarised as "female" and "male", gender as "women" and "men" and "sexuality" as "homosexuality" and "heterosexuality", restricting diversity only within this rigid and dualistic system. This sex/gender binary categorisation has been a source of negative effects for both those who identify, and those who do not, with the binary.

For those who fit in the binary, the anatomical differentiation of "male" and "female" bodies is presented as a "natural" justification of the socially constructed "distinction" between the genders which leads to the establishment of patriarchy, an arbitrary dominant power of men over women.[3] The dominance of patriarchy and inequality do not benefit neither men nor women, as "human beings, (…) do not flourish when hyper-masculinity is glorified and traditionally feminine qualities (such as care, caretaking, and valuing relationships) are denigrated. Nor do human beings flourish when all males are pressured to adopt hypermasculine attributes and repress feminine ones, and all females are pressured to adopt traditionally feminine attributes and repress masculine ones".[4] When women and men do not comply with the normative role behavior that the binary dictates, their freedom of action is compromised and this is expressed through the establishment of stereotypes. Then, the

[1] Holmes (2007), p. 21.

[2] Idem.

[3] See Bourdieu (1998).

[4] Becker (1999), p. 22.

N. Pikramenou, *Intersex Rights*, https://doi.org/10.1007/978-3-030-27554-9_1

assignment of negative stereotypes can result in sexism, which is perpetuated by systems of patriarchy, as both sexism and patriarchy are rooted on the belief that "the status of female is inferior to the status of male".[5]

For those who do not identify with the binary, it can be even more complex as the binary system turns them invisible and at the same time, the existence of heteronormative patriarchy leads to oppression and marginalisation. Over the last decades, queer theorists, have been denouncing imposed binary social regulations that affect bodies, sexualities, genders and suggesting the deconstruction of the sex/gender binary as solution to the problems emerging from heteronormativity. In "Gender Trouble", which constitutes one of the founding works of queer theory, Judith Butler states that "when the constructed status of gender is theorized as radically independent of sex, gender itself becomes a free-floating artifice, with the consequence that man and masculine might just as easily signify a female body as a male one, and women and feminine a male body as easily as a female one".[6] To deconstruct traditional perceptions on sex and gender, queer theory has been also using the example of intersex people[7] who are born with sex characteristics that do not fit typical binary notions of male or female bodies[8] and therefore they are pathologised and treated as "abnormal" and "outcasts". Butler has underlined that intersex persons "live and breathe in the interstices of this binary relation, showing that it is not exhaustive; it is not necessary".[9] Anne Fausto-Sterling has also mentioned that intersex individuals "by their existence they call into question our system of gender" and added that "if we choose, to let mixed-gender bodies and altered patterns of gender-related behavior become visible, we will have chosen to change the rules of cultural intelligibility".[10]

Queer analysis has also focused on gender and its intersection with law and regulatory power. Michel Foucault has depicted the law and the juridical field as operating to manipulate and control expert knowledge to their own ends.[11] Butler, drawing from the Foucaultian scholarship on regulatory power contravenes the assertion that "gender is but the instance of a larger regulatory operation of power" and states that "gender requires and institutes its own distinctive regulatory and disciplinary regime".[12] Considering the above, the binary system of sex and gender constitutes a rigid norm that aims to control human bodies and this is depicted in the law[13] as the sex/gender dichotomy is essential for the individual's existence within legal

[5] See Lindsey (2014).

[6] Butler (1990), p. 6.

[7] See also Morland (2009) and Hester (2004a, b).

[8] Free & Equal, Factsheet "Intersex", 2015.

[9] Butler (2004), p. 65.

[10] Fausto-Sterling (2000a, b), p. 76.

[11] See Smith (2000) and Foucault (1977).

[12] Butler (2004), p. 41.

[13] See Julie A. Greenberg, "Defining Male and Female: Intersexuality and the Collision between Law and Biology", Arizona Law Review, 1999 and Julie A. Greenberg, "Intersexuality and the Law: Why Sex Matters", NYU Press, 2012.

frameworks. For instance, the issuance of binary legal documents such as birth certificates, identification documents and passports is crucial for the individual's recognition within legal frameworks and full integration in societies. This entrenchment of sex and gender based on which legal frameworks are organised, produces several negative consequences for people who fall outside this sex/gender dualism. On the one hand, the dual system legitimises and privileges those who are comfortable in the sex assigned to them at birth. On the other hand, it disadvantages and marginalises all persons whose sex and gender do not conform to social and legal expectations. To include non-binary individuals in contemporary analyses on sex and gender and achieve justice, it is essential to move beyond the binary and this involves two elements; first, the reconsideration of current distinctions between masculine/feminine and male/female, and second, the reconceptualisation of gender as strictly social and of sex as strictly biological.[14]

For decades, intersex persons used to be invisible but during the 1990s they started "coming out", addressing injustice and demanding full integration in societies and recognition under the law.[15] Among their first priorities was, and still is, the explicit ban of invasive, involuntary and harmful surgeries that target to fit them in the binary by making them "fully male" or "fully female". In other words, when an infant is born intersex, doctors will often advise parents to perform surgical and other medical interventions on intersex bodies, in order to make them conform to binary male or female characteristics even though in most cases, such interventions are not medically necessary and can have extremely negative consequences.[16] Intersex people are stigmatised and subjected to human rights violations due to their physical characteristics including violations of their rights to health and physical integrity, to be free from torture and ill-treatment, access to informed decision-making, informed consent, medical records and justice.[17] Moreover, sometimes, Preimplantation Genetic Diagnosis (PGD) is performed to prevent their birth leading to violations of the right to life of intersex embryos. Intersex people are also vulnerable to potential human rights violations during their lifetime as well, since due to the binary understanding of sex/gender that prevails in legal frameworks they cannot access identification documents, they are discriminated in numerous areas including employment and access to sports and they are denied the right to found a family.

The above human rights violations are depicted in Public Statements that intersex organisations from around the globe have issued, together with their legal demands. In 2013, the outcome of the Third International Intersex Forum was the Malta Declaration which called for the introduction of legislative reforms and measures to protect intersex rights.[18] Among the demands of the Malta Declaration were: the ban of mutilating and "normalising" practices such as genital surgeries

[14] Johnson and Repta (2012), p. 17.

[15] United Nations, Free & Equal (2015), p. 7.

[16] Ghattas (2015), p. 9. See also Karkazis (2008) and Creighton (2001).

[17] United Nations, Free & Equal (2015), p.1. See also Garland (2016) and Scherpe et al. (2018).

[18] OII Europe, Malta Declaration (1 December 2013).

through legislation means, the possibility of amending sex/gender classifications through a simple administrative procedure, the recognition of the right to full information and access to medical records which is essential for the adequate redress, reparation and access to justice of intersex, the introduction of anti-discrimination legislation and provisions that guarantee intersex people's right to marry, form a family and participate in competitive sport in accordance with their legal sex.[19] A year later, the European Intersex Meeting produced the Statement of Riga which reaffirmed the Malta Declaration and also clarified that to achieve protection against discrimination for intersex, the adoption of anti-discrimination legislation on the ground of "sex characteristics" is essential as it refers to "the chromosomal, gonadal and anatomical features of a person, which include primary characteristics such as reproductive organs and genitalia and/or chromosomal structures and hormones; and secondary characteristics such as, but not limited to, muscle mass, hair distribution, breasts and/or stature."[20] In 2017, the Vienna Statement reaffirmed the demands and objectives of the two previous statements and also called on governments to "recognise intersex people as a community that has specific and vital needs and that their human rights need protection".[21] The same year, a joint consensus statement by Australian and Aotearoa/New Zealand intersex organisations issued detailed priorities with regards to the human rights of intersex including the call for an end to genetic discrimination in insurance and employment and the introduction of the right to marry and form a family irrespective of sex characteristics.[22] Similar statements were also delivered in Asia and Africa where the Malta Statement was recalled but the specific needs of intersex in the regions were addressed as well. For instance, the Public Statement by the African Intersex Movement demanded to put an end to infanticide and killings of intersex people led by traditional and religious beliefs[23] and the Public Statement by the Asian Intersex Movement urged "to end practices that force "normalizing" surgeries on intersex children to be male as a requirement of inheritance" and to ensure that the right to inheritance of intersex people is not denied on the ground of infertility."[24]

When it comes to international human rights organisations and institutions, in 2013, the United Nations (UN) Special Rapporteur on Torture, Juan E. Mendés, declared surgeries on intersex infants as a human rights violation and urged Member States to ban them.[25] In his subsequent report in 2016, he assessed the applicability of the prohibition of torture and other cruel, inhuman or degrading treatment or punishment in international law to the unique experiences of intersex persons.[26] At the same time, the Council of Europe introduced the report "Human Rights and

[19] Idem, "Demands".

[20] Statement of Riga, 2014.

[21] Statement of the 1st European IntersexCommunity Event, Vienna, 2017.

[22] Darlington Statement, 2017, "Human rights and legal reform".

[23] Public Statement by the African Intersex Movement, 2017.

[24] Public Statement by the Asian Intersex Movement, 2018, paras. 12 and 13.

[25] A/HRC/22/53, 2013, para. 88.

[26] See A/HRC/31/57, 2016 and Sect. 2.3.

intersex people" that highlighted human rights violations that intersex individuals encounter in all spheres including their legal recognition, non-discrimination and access to justice and accountability.[27] Also at the regional level, the European Union published a detailed report on the situation of intersex in the EU and called Member States to take adequate measures.[28] Furthermore, the European Commission focused on discrimination against intersex people in the EU through its report "Trans and intersex people: Discrimination on the grounds of sex, gender identity and gender expression".

Despite all the above efforts and calls, intersex people remain invisible under current binary legal frameworks at all levels and are often victims of gross violations and injustice. According to the findings of this research, intersex surgeries and PGD are still performed, intersex people are not legally recognised, they are subjected to discrimination and they are denied the right to found a family due to the absence of non-binary legal frameworks. Intersex people are the living proof that sexes/genders are not only two and their existence stresses the need to reform outdated legal frameworks and seek for a broader understanding of sex/gender equality beyond binaries. During the past years, intersex have been treated as "problematic" and the violation of their fundamental rights through the performance of harmful "normalising" surgeries coupled with their exclusion from legal frameworks seemed as the only solution to the "problem". Nonetheless, the root of the "problem" can be detected on the foundation of societies and the laws as they are based on "preconceived notions of "normality" and maleness and femaleness, instead of, embracing diversity and respecting the autonomy of the individual".[29]

In this book, the legal demands of intersex people regarding the recognition and protection of their human rights will be initially analysed. It will also be examined how these demands have been addressed by numerous jurisdictions worldwide. In other words, this research constitutes an analysis of legal frameworks concerning intersex rights both at international and regional levels (including Africa,[30] the Americas,[31] Asia,[32] Oceania[33] and Europe[34]). Lastly, in light of this research, conclusions and recommendations will be provided on the current situation with regards to

---

[27] See Council of Europe, "Human Rights and Intersex people", 2015 and Sect. 4.5. The Council of Europe on SOGI and Intersex. Later, in 2017, the Council of Europe released the report "The Rights of Children in Biomedicine: Challenges posed by scientific advances and uncertainties" that specifically addressed human rights violations concerning intersex infants and children, See Zillén et al. (2017).

[28] European Union Agency for Fundamental Rights (FRA), "The fundamental rights situation of intersex people", 2015. European Commission, "Trans and Intersex people, Discrimination on the grounds of sex, gender identity and gender expression", 2012.

[29] Scherpe et al. (2018), p. 6.

[30] See Table 3.1. Legislation and case law on intersex people's rights in Africa.

[31] See Table 3.2. Legislation, case law, practices on intersex people's rights in Americas.

[32] See Table 3.4. Legislation, case law, practices on intersex people's rights in Asia.

[33] See Table 3.3. Legislation, case law, practices on intersex people's rights in Oceania.

[34] See Table 4.1. Explicit legislation, case law, policies on intersex people in the EU.

the protection of intersex rights and how the case of intersex can shape inclusive legal frameworks and lead to equality for all.

1.2 Research Purposes and Legal Questions

Existing legal literature on intersex has been focusing mainly on human rights violations that intersex infants and adults face due to the performance of involuntary, invasive and harmful sex reassignment surgeries. As it was already stated, in the case of intersex surgeries, the rights at stake among others are the right to life, bodily integrity and autonomy, self-determination, the right to health, the right to freedom form torture, or cruel, inhuman or degrading treatment. Legal literature on the matter, has analysed the problems of consent and decision-making with regards to intersex infants and "normalising" surgeries and the legal recognition of intersex with a focus on the designation of a legal gender on birth certificates.[35] Nonetheless, this is only one aspect of the issues that intersex people face. Even if we assume that at some point harmful and involuntary surgeries performed on intersex individuals are explicitly outlawed and birth certificates are modified to include intersex as a sex/gender, the rest of legal provisions remain based on the male/female binary. In other words, how intersex individuals' right to marry and found a family would be protected when the vast majority of frameworks include only men and women? How an intersex person who faces discrimination at work, could reach justice, when legal provisions on non-discrimination in employment do not include "intersex" or "sex characteristics" as a prohibited ground? Accordingly, the purpose of this research is to go beyond the human rights violations surrounding intersex surgeries, examine the full scope and address the main question: how intersex people can, considering that they do not fit in the female/male binary, be accommodated in legal frameworks and reach sex/gender equality beyond binaries?

This research initially highlights the disadvantage emanating out of heteronormativity and the legal binary sex/gender model (this chapter), and then identifies and examines multiple human rights violations that intersex people experience due to the sex/gender binary as depicted by intersex individuals themselves through the publication of Public Statements by intersex rights organisations (Chap. 2). Additional sources on intersex rights violations will also be consulted including reports issued by international human rights organisations and institutions such as the UN and the CoE. Afterwards, regional legal developments on intersex will be explored with the purpose to examine how these jurisdictions have accommodated intersex and to which extent those developments are effective -or not- for the recognition and protection of intersex rights (Chaps. 3 and 4). In detail, Chap. 3 focuses on the situation of intersex rights within the UN Member States and includes an

[35] See Garland (2016), Ní Mhuirthile (2015) and Scherpe et al. (2018).

analysis of intersex rights in countries in Africa,[36] Asia,[37] Oceania[38] and the Americas,[39] constituting this research the first global legal analysis of intersex rights. Then, Chap. 4 introduces the first legal comparative study within EU Member States on intersex rights. It also includes recommendations on how the EU and its Member States can recognise and safeguard intersex rights. This original presentation of the comprehensive situation on intersex rights worldwide allows the reader to grasp to which degree current binary legal frameworks violate intersex rights. Last, based on all the above findings, conclusions and recommendations will be introduced to elaborate on how intersex rights can be safeguarded under the law and at the same time reach equality for all (Chap. 5). It has to be noted that, in the last Chapter, the discussion is also focusing on the emerging legal trend of "genderless/sexless" law, permitting the reader to reflect on the evolution of the law and gender and picture future legal frameworks beyond the male/female binary.

When it comes to intersex terminology,[40] numerous texts on intersex are still failing to depathologise intersex fully since they use terms such as "disorder" or "differences".[41] In order to fully depathologise intersex, this research uses adequate terminology as suggested by intersex rights organisations.[42] This is out of respect for the human complexity and diversity and provided that human rights are universal, inalienable and indivisible,[43] it needs to be stressed that everyone is born with and possesses the same rights, regardless of their sex and gender.[44] The title also aims to break the binary by not specifying how many sexes there are.

In relation with the language applied in the text, research indicates that there are diverse relationships and intersections between the use of language and gender.[45] During the last years, there is a "push" against traditional boundaries of gender and this is reflected in "queer linguistics" which is a project that "incorporates the deconstructionist and anti-essentialist insights of queer theory with the study of language".[46] Even though this research questions the sex/gender binary, "he" and "she" will be applied as British English is the language used and the Cambridge dictionary has not yet been officially updated to include individuals who may not identify as "he" and "she".

Terminology and concepts on "sex", "gender", "sexual orientation", "gender identity", "gender expression" and "intersex" in particular will be analysed in

[36] See Table 3.1. Legislation and case law on intersex people's rights in Africa.

[37] See Table 3.4. Legislation, case law, practices on intersex people's rights in Asia.

[38] See Table 3.3. Legislation, case law, practices on intersex people's rights in Oceania.

[39] See Table 3.2. Legislation, case law, practices on intersex people's rights in Americas.

[40] See Lundberg et al. (2018) and Davis (2011).

[41] See Tamar-Mattis (2008), Garland (2016) and Cornwall (2009).

[42] See Sect. 1.4.2.

[43] See Universal Declaration of Human Rights of 1948 and Article 1 in particular and Henkin (1989).

[44] UNFPA (2005).

[45] See Speer (2004) and Hall and Bucholtz (1995).

[46] Weber (2011), p. 153. See also Morton-Brown (1999).

Chap. 1. In this Chapter, statistics on intersex as well as their pathologisation in the medical field and fundamental distinctions between intersex and Lesbian, Gay, Bisexual, Trans and Queer (LGBTQ) individuals will be explored.

All references to French, German, Greek, Portuguese and Spanish sources are translated by the author unless otherwise specified.

Taking into account the rapid developments with regards to intersex rights, it has to be noted that legal and other sources available have been consulted as of September 2018.

1.3 Sex and Gender: When Biology and Society Meet

"Assigned" sex is a label that individuals are given at birth based on medical factors, including hormones, chromosomes and genitals.[47] Some would call the sex assigned at birth "biological sex" but it is believed that this term cannot capture all variations that may occur. Others argue that it would be preferable to use "assigned male at birth" or "assigned female at birth" as this term acknowledges that someone (often a doctor) is deciding for someone else.[48]

At the same time, gender refers to all social characteristics linked to males and females.[49] Different disciplines offer a range of perspectives on gender roles. For instance, the ecological perspective suggests that gender roles are created by the interactions between individuals, communities and their environments. As a result, women have a natural affinity toward the feminine gender role and men have a natural affinity towards the masculine gender role.[50] The feminist perspective is based on the idea that gender roles are not simply about appropriate behaviour for males and females but are also related to the different levels of power that males and females hold in society.[51]

Our societies are structured on heteronormativity and legal frameworks are based on the sex/gender binary, constituting a source of human rights violations for individuals who fall out of it. Although nature and the case of intersex individuals, who are born between sexes, prove that sexes are not only two; the prevailing binary understanding of sex/gender causes significant problems. For instance, intersex people are pathologised and often treated as "outcasts" due to the fact that they don't fit into standard social, medical and legal models.[52]

This section serves as a review of basic concepts and terminologies on sex and gender and purposes to familiarise the reader with complex ideas that will later be developed. Firstly, the concepts of sex, gender, gender identity and sexual orientation

---

[47] Planned Parenthood, "Gender and Gender Identity".

[48] Idem.

[49] WHO, "Gender".

[50] Blackstone (2003), p. 337.

[51] Idem.

[52] Butler (2004).

will be clarified. Then, terminology and statistics on intersex will be explored as well as the pathologisasion of the situation of intersex people within the medical field. Last, fundamental distinctions between intersex and other sexual minorities will be explained. The above terms and concepts will be mentioned multiple times as they are used widely in reports, recommendations, legal frameworks and case-law.

As it was already mentioned, this book focuses on human rights and therefore one of its goals is to destigmatise and depathologise non-binary individuals such as intersex. It has to be pointed out that such concepts and terms may sometimes lead to stigmatisation, discrimination and marginalisation as non-binary people may be forced to "outings" or choose "labels" that do not express the complexity of their experience. Nonetheless, since sex and gender terminology are used by human rights institutions as a common point of reference to address human rights violations, these terms will be presented, explained and used later on in this research.

1.3.1 The Attempt to Define Sex and Gender

For many years, sex and gender were considered as being connected to each other. In 1955, John Money in "Hermaphroditism, gender and precocity in hyperadrenocorticism: Psychologic findings" introduced the concept of a gender role that was described as "used to signify all those things that a person says or does to disclose himself or herself as having the status of boy or man, girl or woman, respectively. It includes, but is not restricted to, sexuality in the sense of eroticism."[53] However, as it will be later analysed, John Money's theory with regards to "sex" and "gender" was proved extremely problematic and detrimental for his patients' well-being. In 1972, John Money and Anke Ehrhardt introduced the idea that sex and gender should be viewed as separate categories.[54] They claimed that sex is anatomically and physiologically determined, and they perceived gender as the internal conviction that one is either male or female and the behavioral expressions of that conviction.[55] Since then, gender literature and feminist studies in particular, distinguished the social and cultural backgrounds of the differences between the gender binary of men and women from the biological ones that are related to the sex binary of female and male.[56]

In sociology, essentialist thinkers perceive "the "natural" or real body as the basis onto which social and cultural ideas about femininity and masculinity are imposed".[57] Most feminists are never fully essentialist, reasoning that femininity is

---

[53] Money (1955), pp. 253–264.

[54] Fausto-Sterling (2000a, b), p. 3.

[55] Idem.

[56] Haig (2004), p. 87.

[57] Holmes (2007), p. 89.

a social production.[58] Feminist theories tend to follow the constructionist way of thinking which opposes essentialism and assumes that gender is about conforming to social expectations.[59] Primarily, the argument that gender is socially constructed was used as a means to resist perceptions that men were biologically superior to women[60] and to deconstruct and attack patriarchy. Simone de Beauvoir, was the first to claim that one is not born but rather becomes a woman ("On ne naît pas femme: on le devient. ").[61] This can be interpreted as a claim about gender socialisation as females become women through a process whereby they acquire feminine traits and learn feminine behavior.[62] Judith Butler, claimed that Beauvoir's formulation introduced a distinction between "sex" and "gender".[63] Queer theory, with Butler one of its core theorists, took existing gender theories to the next level by introducing an anti-normative approach that refuses dichotomies and suggests that there is a more complex explanation of gender which goes beyond the limit of feminism, considers all marginalised sexual identities and introduces the concept of "gender fluidity" by rejecting the binarism between men and women.[64] However, the commencement of queer theory is claimed to appear in Michel Foucault's assertions, that homosexuality and sexuality in general is a constructed category of knowledge rather than as a discovered identity.[65] In "Performative Acts and Gender Constitution", Butler argued that it is more valid to perceive gender as a performance that an individual agent acts in and that "the actions appropriate for men and women have been transmitted to produce a social atmosphere that both maintains and legitimises a seemingly natural gender binary".[66] In "Gender Trouble: Feminism and the Subversion of Identity", Butler debated how both terms "gender" and "sex" are socially and culturally constructed. She mentioned that feminism made a mistake in trying to make "women" a discrete group as this approach reinforces the binary view of gender relations because it allows for two distinct categories (men and women).[67]

Foucault analysed the case of intersex in his book "Herculine Barbin" who was a French intersex, he describes that Herculine was "brought up as a poor and deserving girl in a milieu that was almost exclusively feminine and strongly religious, Herculine Barbin, who was called Alexina by her familiars, was finally recognized as being 'truly' a young man. Obliged to make a legal change of sex after juridical proceedings and a modification of his civil status, he was incapable of adapting himself to a new identity and ultimately committed suicide."[68] With this words,

[58] Idem.

[59] Idem, p. 90.

[60] Idem.

[61] De Beauvoir (1949), p. 13.

[62] Stanford Encyclopedia of Philosophy, "Feminist Perspectives on Sex and Gender", 2011.

[63] Butler (1988), pp. 519–531.

[64] Piantato (2016), p. 5.

[65] See Foucault (2012a, b) and Huffer (2009).

[66] Idem.

[67] Butler (1990), Chapter 1.

[68] Foucault (1980), p. xi.

Foucault emphasises the state-enforced assignment of identity and by reading Barbin's story it its illustrated that "one's sense of self and subjectivity is not easily written onto a body".[69] Later, Butler, in her book "Undoing Gender", examines the binary gender, and how one can define oneself as human without conforming fully to what the binary dictates. To justify this, she uses the case of David Reimer, a boy who was raised as a girl after undergoing a sex reassignment at 19 months of age, and who eventually transformed himself back into a man during adolescence.[70] David's nurture was based on John Money's theory that gender is not about "nature" but "nurture".[71] Nonetheless, Butler does not center on answering this "nature vs. nurture" question of gender, but rather on her claim that David neither proves nor disproves either of these medical arguments but he stands outside every limitation of accepted gender norms, and he is no less human for doing so.[72] Butler, applies an approach that centers the wellbeing of the human being and looks at how both "constructivist" (nurture) and "essentialist" (nature) accounts of gender identity tend to reduce the worth of people to "what they have between their legs".[73]

The fundamental purpose of all the above theories is to establish that gender inequalities are the result of social processes and therefore can be challenged. Feminist and queer theories have significantly impacted the law as they triggered claims on self-determination for queer, trans and non-binary people in general. In addition, they have been contributing to shift the way legal frameworks describe and perceive "sex" and "gender". This research is mainly influenced by queer theory and seeks to apply it in law by concluding that current binary legal frameworks are outdated and must be reformed in order to include intersex as well as all non-binary individuals to achieve gender equality.[74] In the upcoming section, it will be shown how the above-mentioned theories have impacted the legal understanding of "sex" and "gender" in international legal instruments.

1.3.2 Sex, Gender and the Law

The notion of "*sex*" is mentioned in several international legal documents. The Universal Declaration of Human Rights (UDHR) in its article 2 cites that "everyone is entitled to all the rights and freedoms set forth in this Declaration, without distinction of any kind, such as race, colour, *sex*, language, religion (…)".[75] Likewise, the

---

[69] Kerry (2009), p. 2.

[70] Colapinto (2000), p. 57.

[71] See Sect. 2.2.1.

[72] Mind The Gap, "Intersexuality and Injustice: Examining Gender Identity and Reassignment via Butler and David Reimer".

[73] Butler (2004), p. 71.

[74] See Chap. 5.

[75] Universal Declaration of Human Rights, adopted by the General Assembly of the United Nations on 10 December 1948.

International Covenant on Civil and Political Rights (ICCPR) enshrines the rights of all people to non-discrimination and equality before the law. Article 2(1) of the ICCPR sets out the principle of non-discrimination and underlines that there "the rights recognised in the present Covenant, without distinction of any kind such as race, colour, *sex*, language, religion, political or other opinion, national or social origin, property, birth or other status.".[76] Article 26 of the ICCPR introduces the principle of equality as "the law shall prohibit any discrimination and guarantee to all persons equal and effective protection against discrimination on any ground such as race, colour, **sex**, language, religion, political or other opinion, national or social origin, property, birth or other status".[77] Additionally, according to article 5 of the Convention on the Elimination of All Forms of Discrimination against Women (CEDAW), States Parties shall take all appropriate measures "to modify the social and cultural patterns of conduct of men and women, with a view to achieving the elimination of prejudices and customary and all other practices which are based on the idea of the inferiority or the superiority of either of the *sexes* or on stereotyped roles for men and women".[78]

"Sex" is also mentioned in the European Convention on Human Rights[79](ECHR) and its article 14 that prohibits "discrimination on any ground such as *sex*, race, colour, language (…)". Similarly, at a European Union level, the Treaty on the Functioning of the European Union (TFEU) cites in its article 10 that "the Union shall aim to combat discrimination based on *sex*, racial or ethnic origin, religion or belief, disability, age or sexual orientation."[80] The Committee on Economic, Social and Cultural rights in its General Comment No.20 refers to the International Covenant on Economic, Social and Cultural Rights which guarantees the equal right of men and women to enjoyment of economic, social and cultural rights.[81] It adds that since the adoption of the Covenant, the notion of the prohibited ground "sex" has evolved to cover not only physiological characteristics but also the social construction of gender stereotypes, prejudices and expected roles, which have created obstacles to the equal fulfillment of economic, social and cultural rights.[82]

Given these points, "sex" is used as a ground in the non-discrimination provisions of human rights conventions and often, it is interpreted as including "gender".[83]

---

[76] International Covenant on Civil and Political Rights, Adopted and opened for signature, ratification and accession by General Assembly resolution 2200A (XXI) of 16 December 1966, entry into force 23 March 1976, in accordance with Article 49.

[77] Idem.

[78] Convention on the Elimination of All Forms of Discrimination against Women, adopted by the United Nations General Assembly on 18 December 1979 and entered into force as an international treaty on 3 September 1981.

[79] European Convention on Human Rights as amended by Protocols Nos, 11 and 14, supplemented by Protocols Nos, 1,4,6,7,12 and 13.

[80] Consolidated Version of the Treaty on the Functioning of the European Union, 26/10/2012, C 326/47.

[81] Article 3 of the Covenant and General Comment No. 16.

[82] General Comment No. 20, Committee on Economic, Social and Cultural Rights, E/C.12/GC/20. 10 June 2009.

[83] CEDAW General Recommendation no. 28, 2010, para. 5.

WHO describes "gender" as "the socially constructed characteristics of women and men – such as norms, roles and relationships of and between groups of women and men."[84] "*Gender*" as depicted in international human rights documents, refers primarily to women and this can be explained historically as the feminist movement arose earlier than the LGBTQ movements. The Convention of the Elimination of All Forms of Discrimination Against Women (CEDAW) which is a women's bill of rights and aims to protect women's rights in all spheres was an outcome of the work of Commission on the Status of Women (CSW) which was originally established in 1946 as a sub-commission of the Commission on Human Rights but quickly granted the status of full commission resulting from the pressure of women's rights activists.[85] In 1992, the General Recommendation of the United Nations Committee on the Elimination of Discrimination against Women (CEDAW Committee) established that "gender-based violence" is "violence that is directed against a woman because she is a woman or that affects women disproportionately"[86] and that it "is a form of discrimination that seriously inhibits women's ability to enjoy rights and freedoms on a basis of equality with men".[87] The Declaration on the Elimination of Violence against Women (DEVAW), the first international document that addresses explicitly violence against women, defines it as "any act of gender-based violence that results in, or is likely to result in, physical, sexual or psychological harm or suffering to women, including threats of such acts, coercion or arbitrary deprivation of liberty, whether occurring in public or in private life".[88] General Recommendation No. 35 of the Committee of the CEDAW in an effort to expand the understanding of gender-based violence and move beyond the binary, mentioned that "The Committee, in its jurisprudence, has highlighted the fact that such factors include women's ethnicity/race, (…) being lesbian, bisexual, transgender or intersex (…). Accordingly, because women experience varying and intersecting forms of discrimination, which have an aggravating negative impact, the Committee acknowledges that gender-based violence may affect some women to different degrees, or in different ways, meaning that appropriate legal and policy responses are needed."[89]

In recent years, following the developments on gender literature and the rise of the Lesbian, Gay, Bisexual, Trans (LGBT) and intersex movements, international human rights bodies have started taking steps to include non-binary individuals in the understanding of sex/gender. Yogyakarta principles, is a non-binding set of international standards that promote and protect human rights of sexual minorities, guarantee the enjoyment of all human rights without discrimination on the grounds of sexual orientation or gender identity.[90] In this document, sexual orientation and

[84] World Health Organization, "Gender".

[85] UN Women, "Short History of CEDAW Convention".

[86] See General Recommendation No. 19, Article 6, 1992.

[87] Idem, Article 1.

[88] Article 1 of the Declaration on the Elimination of Violence against Women, 1993.

[89] CEDAW/C/GC/35, para. 12.

[90] Yogyakarta Principles on the Application of International Human Rights Law in relation to Sexual Orientation and Gender Identity, Principle 2: "Discrimination on the basis of sexual orien-

gender identity are defined and protected. *Sexual orientation* is defined as "each person's capacity for profound emotional, affectional and sexual attraction to, and intimate and sexual relations with, individuals of a different gender or the same gender or more than one gender" and *gender identity*, on the other, refers to "each person's deeply felt internal and individual experience of gender, which may or may not correspond with the sex assigned at birth, including the personal sense of the body (which may involve, if freely chosen, modification of bodily appearance or function by medical, surgical or other means) and other expressions of gender, including dress, speech and mannerisms".[91] The above definitions clarify gender identity and sexual orientation as independent concepts and this amplification is crucial as often these concepts tend to be conflated. The UN has described "gender identity" as reflecting "a deeply felt and experienced sense of one's own gender. Everyone has a gender identity, which is part of their overall identity" and "sexual orientation" as a "person's physical, romantic and/or emotional attraction towards other people. Everyone has a sexual orientation, which is part of their identity".[92] The UN Committee on Economic, Social and Cultural Rights has also cited that "gender identity is recognised as among the prohibited grounds of discrimination, for example, persons who are transgender, transsexual or intersex often face serious human rights violations".[93] To date, there is no hidden exemption clause in any of international human rights treaties that might allow a State to guarantee full rights to some but withhold them from others purely on the basis of gender identity or sexual orientation.[94]

The Yogyakarta Principles Plus 10 were adopted in 2017 and added additional principles and state obligations to the previous document which was adopted in 2006. Now, Yogyakarta Principles cover also "gender expression" and "sex characteristics" as non-discrimination grounds. "*Gender expression*" is defined as "each person's presentation of the person's gender through physical appearance – including dress, hairstyles, accessories, cosmetics – and mannerisms, speech, behavioural patterns, names and personal references, and noting further that gender expression may or may not conform to a person's gender identity;" and "*sex characteristics*" are defined as "each person's physical features relating to sex, including genitalia and other sexual and reproductive anatomy, chromosomes, hormones, and secondary physical features emerging from puberty;".[95]

---

tation or gender identity includes any distinction, exclusion, restriction or preference based on sexual orientation or gender identity which has the purpose or effect of nullifying or impairing equality before the law or the equal protection of the law, or the recognition, enjoyment or exercise, on an equal basis, of all human rights and fundamental freedoms."

[91] Yogyakarta Principles on the Application of International Human Rights Law in relation to Sexual Orientation and Gender Identity, Introduction.

[92] UN, Living Free & Equal (2016), p. 18.

[93] General Comment No. 20, Committee on Economic, Social and Cultural Rights, E/C.12/GC/20.

[94] Free&Equal United Nations for LGBT Equality, "Factsheet on International Human Rights Law and Sexual Orientation & Gender Identity".

[95] Yogyakarta Principles Plus 10, Preamble.

Obviously, the term "sex" is referred and explained in several international human rights sources and documents, but it is not legally defined. There is no specific law which points out explicitly under which criteria we define men and women. The legal interpretation of "sex" follows the perception of sex dichotomy which prevails in modern societies and as there is no law to regulate who is male and who is female, doctors are the ones responsible to assign sexes when infants are born. To protect intersex individuals against human rights violation that emanate from the sex dichotomy, the ground "sex characteristics" has been introduced during the last years. At the same time, the concept of "gender" keeps on evolving as well. Years ago, gender discrimination applied tacitly only to women. Nowadays, even though discrimination against women persists, the meaning of "gender" has expanded to include "gender identity" and "gender expression". All the above terms are internationally used by official reports, legislation and jurisprudence in order to ensure full inclusion of the many ways in which gender can be felt, identified with, experienced and expressed. In this book, legal frameworks on sexual orientation, gender identity, gender expression and sex characteristics will be later presented and analysed.

1.4 Intersex Bodies

1.4.1 The Emergence and Evolution of Intersex

Intersex is mentioned in many ancient cultures, in which one of the main ideas was that human beings, males and females, were generated from primal androgynous beings.[96] When it comes to mythology, in one of the Sumerian creation myths[97]; Ninmah, who was a fertility goddess, after having created three men and one woman, fashioned one creature with neither female nor male genitalia on its body who was named "Nibru".[98] In Greek and Roman mythology, "Hermaphroditus" was the son of Aphrodite and Hermes and according to Ovid,[99] he was a remarkably handsome boy who was transformed into an androgynous being by union with the water nymph Salmacis.[100] The Greek historian Diodorus Siculus wrote that Hermaphroditus is a combination of a man and a woman as he endowed throroughly with the attributes of each parent[101] and the Greek philosopher Plato, has referred to three sexes: male, female and hermaphrodite.[102] Intersex can also be identified in

[96] Scherpe et al. (2018), p. 122.

[97] A creation myth is a symbolic narrative of how the world began and how people first came to inhabit it.

[98] The Electronic Text Corpus of Sumerian Literature, ETLCSL translation,"Enki and Ninmah".

[99] Ovid was a Roman poet who lived during the reign of Augustus.

[100] Encyclopaedia of the Hellenistic World, Asia Minor.

[101] Siculus (1935), Book IV.

[102] See Plato, "Symposium", Written 360 B.C.E. (online text).

theology where studies have questioned the sex of Jesus and discussed his maleness in light of intersex.[103]

Gender studies have been also challenging the binary sex/gender and Anne Fausto-Sterling in particular enshrined the idea of five sexes. In 1993, she published "The Five Sexes", where she suggested the existence of male, female, "male pseudohermaphrodites" called "merm" who have testes and some aspects of the female genitalia but not ovaries, "female pseudohermaphrodites" called "ferm" who have ovaries and some aspects of the male genitalia but lack testes and true hermaphrodites called "herm" who possess one testis and one ovary.[104] Her article was used to introduce the argument that sexism and heterosexism are more complex than previously presented by feminist studies.[105] Later, in her revisited publication of "The Five Sexes", she acknowledged and agreed with Suzanne J. Kessler's point: "The limitation with Fausto-Sterling's proposal is that … (it) still gives genitals… primary signifying status and ignores the fact that in the everyday world gender attributions are made without access to genital inspection… What has primacy in everyday life is the gender that is performed, regardless of the flesh's configuration under the clothes".[106] She continued by mentioning that "it would be better for intersexuals and their supporters to turn everyone's focus away from genitals. Instead, as she (Kessler) suggests, one should acknowledge that people come in an even wider assortment of sexual identities and characteristics than mere genitals can distinguish".[107] In "Sexing the Body" Fausto-Sterling declared that she is no longer using these categories because they sensationalise intersex who cannot benefit them.[108]

Feminist theory has provided the adequate framework for people who do not conform to the binary and has helped intersex persons realise how intersex medical treatments have been based on societal assumptions about sex and gender.[109] Female Genital Mutilation (FGM/C) in particular has been associated with intersex surgeries due to their strong cultural and social background. This is reflected on the fact that surgeries performed on intersex are also called "Intersex Genital Mutilation (IGM)" as according to OII Intersex Network like FGM/C, IGM "is carried out upon the genitals of newborn babies, infants and children for cultural or religious reasons. Both are forms of infant genital surgery. In the case of IGM, medical needs are also cited as a justification for the surgery but the evidence of actual need is slim at best.".[110]

---

[103] See Cornwall (2014).

[104] See Fausto-Sterling (1993).

[105] Koyama and Lisa Weasel (2001).

[106] See Kessler (1998).

[107] Fausto-Sterling (2000a, b).

[108] Fausto-Sterling (2000a, b), p. 221.

[109] Greenberg et al. (2010), p. 17.

[110] OII Intersex Network, "Intersex Genital Mutilation- IGM: The Fourteen Days of Intersex". See also Jones (2018) and Sect. 2.2.3.

Queer theorists have worked on whether queer theory can include intersex rights in its agenda.[111] Judith Butler[112] has highlighted the common ground between trans and intersex requests and stated that "although intersex and transsex sometimes seem to be movements at odds with one another, (…) it is most important to see that both challenge the principle that a natural dimorphism should be established or maintained at all costs".[113] In "Undoing Gender" she uses the case of intersex to stress the case of persons whose desires may differ from what is conceived as "normal" but still seek to be recognised in order to live even though the conditions to be recognised usually make life "unlivable". She proposes that through the interrogation of such conditions, people who challenge them, may have more possibilities of living.[114] Before "Undoing Gender", Butler never addressed the T or the I (transgender and intersex) in a sustained way and therefore according to Atticus Schoch Zavaletta, "in turning her gaze toward what is unthinkable even for many gays and lesbians, Butler has continued to push against the boundaries of the field she had a large part in creating. "Undoing Gender" constitutes a thoughtful and provocative response to the new gender politics and elegantly employs psychoanalysis, philosophy, feminism, and queer theory in an effort to pry open the future of the human."[115] It has to be noted that, many intersex people resent that they are constantly used by gender studies as an example for a theory that might be important to academia, but the same time objectifies intersex people and makes their suffering invisible.[116]

Recent intersex discussions and advocacy have been evolving to meet intersectionalities not only with feminism and queer but also with Lesbian, Gay, Bisexual, Transgender (LGBT) and disability. The interconnection between disability and intersex in theory, has been raised mostly within theology and specifically by Susannah Cornwall, an Anglican theologian who has pointed out that there is a basic affinity between intersex and disability and has intended to reconfigure intersex conditions "as physical variations akin to impairments-which may preclude particular, limited physical activity, or may simply appear as physiological difference, but in no way compromise the personhood or predetermine the gender identity of the individuals involved".[117] Cornwall draws on queer and disability theologies and seeks to render intersex "theologically meaningful".[118] In contrast to Cornwall's arguments, the official Church documents position intersex within the wider eccle-

---

[111] See Morland (2009).

[112] Judith Butler's theory has been characterised as "problematic" among the intersex community as she was at John Hopkins University at the very same time that Money developed his ideas (Ghattas 2019, personal communication, 17 July).

[113] Butler (2004), p. 6.

[114] See Butler (2004).

[115] Zavaletta Schoch (2005), p. 153.

[116] Ghattas (2019, personal communication, 17 July). See also Carpenter (2015, p. 5).

[117] Cornwall (2009), p. 217. See also Scherpe et al. (2018) and in particular Part II, Theology and Legal History, "Intersex in the Christian Tradition: Personhood and Embodiment" by Duncan Dormor.

[118] See Cornwall (2013, 2014, 2015).

sial preoccupations on gender and sexuality.[119] A typical example is the recent resolution of the Southern Baptist Convention (SBC) titled "On Transgender Identity" which states that: "We grieve the reality of human fallenness which can result in such biological manifestations as intersexuality or psychological manifestations as gender identity confusion and point all to the hope of the redemption of our bodies in Christ."[120]

Intersex advocacy has stressed the intersectionality that may occur when an individual is intersex with a disability and the importance of intersex to be allies with disability advocates.[121] In the case of intersex and the LGBT movement, the "I" is often added in the initials for several reasons: first, it is argued that intersex bodies are pathologised and erased in a similar way to how homosexuality has been treated within psychiatry and second transgender people are labeled as "suffering" from "gender identity disorder" and are treated as abnormal instead of human beings.[122] It is also believed that among the motives of the surgical treatment for intersex are homophobia, transphobia and misogyny.[123] However, among the counter-arguments with relation to the inclusion of the "I" within the LGBT initials and movement are: the fear that adding the "I" insinuates that intersex people are lesbian, gay, bisexual, and/or transgender; more conflation can be created among society on the understanding of the concepts of LGBT and intersex; and the inclusion of the "I" could degrade the specific needs of intersex individuals.[124] Maybe, including the "I" within the "LGBT" movement could be useful for advocacy reasons but intersex is about experience of body, trans about experience of gender and lesbian, gay, bisexual about sexual orientation.

1.4.2 Intersex Definitions and Terminology

The word "hermaphrodite" which derives from Greek mythology cannot be used to describe intersex because according to intersex organisations, the term "hermaphrodite" when it relates to persons, it implies that a person is both fully male and fully female and this is impossible.[125] The term "hermaphrodite" also fails to reflect modern understandings of intersex, confuses clinicians, harms patients and panics parents.[126] "Hermaphrodite" has been substituted with "intersex" which is perceived as

---

[119] See Scherpe et al. (2018) and in particular Part II, Theology and Legal History, "Intersex in the Christian Tradition: Personhood and Embodiment" by Duncan Dormor.

[120] SBC, "On Transgender Identity", Resolution 2250, 2014.

[121] See Darlington Statement, Joint Consensus Statement from the Intersex Community Retreat in Darlington, March 2017.

[122] Koyama Emi, Intersex Initiative "Adding the "I": Does Intersex Belong in the LGBT Movement?".

[123] Idem.

[124] Idem.

[125] See ISNA, "Is a person who is intersex a hermaphrodite?".

[126] Idem.

"a composite one to embrace a variety of conditions that can lead to confusion with the sex of an individual as defined in the binary sense of male or female".[127]

Different descriptions have been provided for the term "intersex" by intersex organisations. For instance, the Organization Intersex International (OII) Europe mentions that "Intersex is an umbrella term for the experience of being born with a body that does not meet the societal expectation of male or female. We are individuals born with sex characteristics that are either female and male at the same time or not quite female or male or neither female or male. Our sex characteristics and bodies are healthy variations of the human sexes".[128] InterAct describes "intersex" as a term that "refers to people who are born with any of a range of sex characteristics that may not fit a doctor's notions of binary "male" or "female" bodies. Variations may appear in a person's chromosomes, genitals, or internal organs like testes or ovaries. Some intersex traits are identified at birth, while others may not be discovered until puberty or later in life".[129]

At the international level, the Office of the United Nations (UN) High Commissioner for Human Rights has defined intersex as a "person who is born with sexual anatomy, reproductive organs, and/or chromosome patterns that do not fit the typical definition of male or female. This may be apparent at birth or become so later in life. An intersex person may identify as male or female or as neither. Intersex status is not about sexual orientation or gender identity: intersex people experience the same range of sexual orientations and gender identities as non-intersex people".[130] The Council of Europe has outlined intersex as a term that "refers to atypical and internal and/or external anatomical sexual characteristics, where features usually regarded as male or female may be mixed to some degree. This is a naturally occurring variation in humans and not a medical condition. It is to be distinguished from transsexuality, a phenomenon where someone has an evident sex, but feels as if he or she belongs to the other sex and is therefore ready to undergo a medical intervention altering his or her natural sex".[131]

In this research, the term "intersex" will be used and terms such as "intersexed" and/or "intersexuality" will be avoided due to the fact that they are often confused with the concept of "sexuality". Instead of "biological sex", the term "sex traits" will be preferred when referring to intersex people as they are born with sex traits and these may not always line up to the common perception of one's "biological sex".[132] The term "born with ambiguous genitalia" will be replaced by "born with genitalia outside of the typical male/female binary" because genitals do not determine gender, but it is up to the individual to figure out as they grow.[133] Sentences such as "born both a man and a woman" and "with both sexes/genders" will be

[127] Scherpe et al. (2018), p. 30.

[128] OII Intersex-Europe, "What is intersex?".

[129] InterAct, "What is intersex?".

[130] Free & Equal, "What is intersex?". See also Lundberg et al. (2018).

[131] Doc. 13297 of the Parliamentary Assembly, 2013.

[132] InterAct, "Tips for Intersex Inclusive Language".

[133] Idem.

avoided since they enforce the binary understading of sex/gender and be replaced with "born intersex" or "with multiple sexes/genders".[134] However, when parts from other sources are quoted that include the above language, they will not be modified.

It needs to be noted that the term "intersex" may not always reflect the experience of all people born with genitalia outside of the typical male/female binary, but it will be used in this research as a human right centered and widely accepted term is needed to elaborate on intersex rights. When it comes to legal grounds, the terms "intersex" and/or "sex characteristics" will be used.

1.4.3 Intersex in Numbers[135]

Humans are born with 46 chromosomes in 23 pairs. The X and Y chromosomes determine a person's sex and most women are 46XX while most men are 46XY.[136] According to the World Health Organization (WHO), in a few births per thousand some individuals will be born with a single sex chromosome and some with three or more sex chromosomes.[137] This signifies that there are not only females who are XX and males who are XY but there is a range of chromosome complements, hormone balances and phenotypic variations that determine sex.[138]

As estimated, one in 2000 babies are born with reproductive or sexual anatomy and/or a chromosome pattern that doesn't fit typical binary definitions of male or female.[139] These traits are sometimes grouped under the terms "intersex", and include androgen insensitivity syndrome, some forms of congenital adrenal hyperplasia, Klinefelter's syndrome, Turner's syndrome, hypospadias, Swyers' syndrome, and many others.[140] Typical examples are when a person is born appearing to be female on the outside but having mostly male-typical anatomy on the inside or a person who may be born with genitals that are in-between the usual male and female types.[141] Nevertheless, intersex anatomy doesn't always show up at birth and sometimes a person may not have realised is intersex until she/he reaches the age of

[134] Idem.

[135] This section may not provide a full picture on the statistics of intersex as all the displayed information comes from several articles and texts. Since there is still not a comprehensive academic text about the topic, this section serves to provide the reader with a general understanding on intersex statistics but still, from a non-discrimination and human rights perspective numbers don't really matter when explaining who intersex people are.

[136] World Health Organization (WHO), "Gender and Genetics, Genetic Components of Sex and Gender".

[137] Idem.

[138] Idem.

[139] InterAct, "interact FAQ".

[140] Idem.

[141] ISNA, "What is intersex?".

puberty, or finds himself/herself an infertile adult, or dies of old age and is autopsied.[142]

There are no firm population figures for people with intersex variations. The main reason for this is the lack of accurate recording of data on intersex diagnoses.[143] The most thorough existing research finds intersex people to constitute an estimated 1.7% of the population which makes being intersex about as common as having red hair.[144] This percentage was published by Blackless and others in the American Journal of Human Biology.[145] Many sources cite lower bound estimates of 1 in 1.500 or 1 in 2.000 live births[146] but it is argued that these statistics exclude intersex variations that are considered by medicine nowadays to be "Disorders of Sex Development" and they focus on a narrower range of traits where external genitalia are "ambiguous".[147] In 2002, Sax L published a response to Blackless and others and argued that the term intersex should be restricted to those conditions in which chromosomal sex[148] is inconsistent with phenotypic sex,[149] or in which the phenotype is not classifiable as either male or female and therefore, the prevalence of intersex would be about 0.018%.[150] According to the Factsheet on Intersex that was published by the United Nations in 2017, between 0.05 and 1.7% of the population is born with intersex traits.[151] In 2014, a study released by the Netherlands Institute of Social Research indicated that the total prevalence lies with 0.5078% which means that 1 person in 200 has a variation of sex characteristics.[152]

1.4.4 *Pathologisation of Intersex*

According to many physicians, the nomenclature "intersex", "hermaphrodite" and "pseudohermaphrodite" is out of date and many urologists are concerned that these terms could be perceived to be pejorative by some affected families.[153] In response to concerns regarding "outdated" and" controversial" terms, the Chicago Consensus, which was held in 2005, recommended new terminology based on the umbrella

---

142 Idem.

143 OII Australia, "On the number of intersex people".

144 OII United States, "How Common is Intersex? An Explanation of the Stats". See also United Nations Free&Equal, 2017, p. 1.

145 Blackless et al. (2000), p. 159.

146 Dorumat-Dreger (1998), pp. 24–35.

147 OII Australia, "On the number of intersex people".

148 The sex as determined by the presence of the XX (female) or the XY (male) genotype in somatic cells, without regard to phenotypic manifestations. It is called also genetic sex.

149 The visible body characteristics associated with sexual behaviors.

150 Sax (2002), pp. 174–178.

151 United Nations Free & Equal (2017, p. 1).

152 See The Netherlands Institute for Social Research (2014, p. 86).

153 Kim and Kim (2012), p. 1.

term Disorders of Sex Development (DSDs).[154] From a medical point of view, the term DSD is considered to have a comprehensive definition including any problem noted at birth in which the genitalia are atypical in relation to the chromosomes or gonads.[155] The proponents of the term DSD also refer to the fact that parents with intersex children have described terms like "intersex" and "hermaphrodite" as offensive and counterproductive, arguing that they frame individuals with atypical sex as being in between sexes, freaks of nature.[156]

Over the years, the term DSD has been controversial. In the field of academia, Morgan Holmes claims that the replacement of the word "intersex" with DSD "reinstitutionalises clinical power to delineate and silence those marked by the diagnosis".[157] She underlines that the point of her argument is not to determine which diagnostic language is superior but to retain the hard-won right to secure the ability to operate socially without the stamp of "disorder" or "disease".[158] As an alternative to the word "disorder", the word "difference" has been suggested as such a neutral term is considered as non-threatening and retains the DSD acronym.[159] Intersex organisations have opposed any terminology that pathologises intersex and avoid systematically the use of DSD.[160]

In a series of articles on Preimplantation Genetic Diagnosis (PGD) in the American Journal of Bioethics in 2013, bioethicists and related authors used the reference "intersex traits" or "intersex conditions".[161] In May 2014, the World Health Organisation (WHO) issued a joint statement on "Eliminating forced, coercive and otherwise involuntary sterilisation" with the Office of the High Commissioner for Human Rights (OHCHR), United Nations Women (UN Women), United Nations AIDS (UN Aids), United Nations Development Program (UNDP), UNFPA (United Nations Fund for Population Activities) and United Nations Children's Fund (UNICEF). This report refers to involuntary surgical "sex-normalising or other procedures" on "intersex persons".[162] Despite all these developments, on June 2018, WHO published the updated International Classification of Diseases[163] where even though it removed trans identities from the mental health chapter, intersex is still viewed as a pathology.[164]

---

[154] Idem.

[155] Idem.

[156] Reis (2007).

[157] Holmes (2011), pp. 87–114.

[158] Idem, abstract.

[159] Scherpe et al. (2018), p. 32.

[160] See InterAct, "Statement on Terminology" and ihra, "Tony Briffa writes on "Disorders of Sex Development".

[161] Nisker (2013), pp. 47–49.

[162] OHCHR, UN Women, UNAIDS, UNDP, UNFPA, UNICEF and WHO, "Eliminating forced, coercive and otherwise involuntary sterilization, An interagency statement".

[163] ICD-11 for Mortality and Morbidity Statistics (2018).

[164] OII Europe, "WHO published ICD-11- and no end in sight for pathologisation of intersex people".

1.4.5 Intersex and Sexual Minorities

According to the UN, "*transgender* (sometimes shortened to "trans") is an umbrella term used to describe people with a wide range of identities—including *transsexual* people, *cross-dressers* (sometimes referred to as "transvestites"), people who identify as third gender,[165] and others whose appearance and characteristics are perceived as gender atypical and whose sense of their own gender is different to the sex that they were assigned at birth. Trans women identify as women but were classified as males when they were born. Trans men identify as men but were classified female when they were born. Some transgender people seek surgery or take hormones to bring their body into alignment with their gender identity; others do not."[166] Intersex people differ from trans people as their status relates only to their biological makeup and is not gender related. Often, trans people are confused with intersex because they are perceived as two groups who want to have the freedom to choose their gender identity, whereas intersex is primarily about sex characteristics. However, sometimes intersex people may decide to change gender, so they might also identify themselves as trans later in their lives.[167]

There is no consensus regarding the above terminology and often it differs at regional levels. For instance, the European Commission mentions that transgender people live permanently in their preferred gender and unlike transsexuals they may not necessarily wish to or need to undergo any medical interventions.[168] The European Commission also refers to *androgyne, polygender and genderqueer* people who have a combination of masculine and feminine characteristics, are "gender fluid" and move between genders,[169] *agender people* who do not have a gender identity and refuse to be classified as male or female or in any other way, *gender variant* or *gender non-conforming people* whose gender varies from normative gender identity and the roles of the gender assigned at birth.[170]

When it comes to sexual orientation, the UN states that "*gay* men and *lesbian* women are attracted to individuals of the same sex as themselves. *Heterosexual* people are attracted to individuals of a different sex from themselves. *Bisexual* (sometimes shortened to "bi") people may be attracted to individuals of the same or different sex."[171]

---

[165] In some countries, intersex people are also included in the third gender category (See Chap. 3, Sect. 3.6.2 and Chap. 5 the cases of Austria and Germany).

[166] Living Free & Equal (2016), p. 18.

[167] ISNA, "What's the difference between being transgender or transsexual and having intersex conditions?".

[168] European Commission (2012), p. 14.

[169] Idem. Often, genderqueers use a variety of terms to describe themselves, including transboi, boyduke, third gendered, bi-gendered, multi-gendered and gender bender. Sometimes they refuse to label their gender identities at all, feeling that no word or phrase can adequately capture the complexities of how they experience gender.

[170] Idem.

[171] Living Free & Equal (2016), p. 18.

Lesbian, gay, bisexual, trans and intersex people may also be victims of intersectional discrimination based on the grounds of skin colour, ethnic origin, sex, gender, disability, age, migratory status, family status, nationality, religion, health status, income level, and on other grounds.[172] In this book, the terms gay, lesbian, trans and intersex will be used while exploring legal frameworks on sexual orientation, gender identity and sex characteristics. It has to be noted that, even though "intersex" is strictly connected with "sex characteristics", laws on sexual orientation and gender identity may impact intersex as well since they are all linked to the accommodation of "sex" and "gender" under the law. For instance, as it will be later demonstrated (Chaps. 3 and 4), intersex can benefit from laws that initially were designed for same sex couples or at the same time could be subjected to detrimental effects emanating from laws on gender identity especially in the case where there is no explicit legal procedure with regards to intersex recognition under the law.

1.5 Remarks

Intersex bodies challenge legal and societal norms, clinical procedures and medical standards of care and academic critique as they do not fit in the sex binary and therefore, they are medicalised, pathologised and treated as "abnormal" from the very beginning of their lives. Discussions surrounding "sex" and "gender" illustrate that there is no consensus on where the female/male binary ends, and other sexes and/or genders begin. In rethinking gender categories, it is essential to distinguish the concepts of "sex" and "gender". The idea that sex and gender should be viewed distinctively is quite recent and the feminist movement played a significant role in revealing that gender is a social construct and underscoring human rights violations and injustice against women that emanate from patriarchy. Then, the emergence of the LGBT movement together with queer theory shifted the focus from injustices committed within the binary by stressing that the binary itself oppresses people who do not conform with it.

Despite all the above, still, in contemporary societies, it is declared what organs are the markers of sexual identity and the idea of gender is hanged on to anatomy[173] and that, makes the concept of gender seem natural whereas it is an idea, a social construction. The existence of intersex people proves that sex is a social construct exactly as gender. For years, it has been believed that sexes are only two and are limited to female and male but "intersex children evidence the futility of the male/female binary that is imposed upon human and it illustrates the spectrum of bodies that legitimately exist in the world".[174] Accordingly, sex is not a "binary" but rather a "spectrum" consisted of diversities. Prevailing norms instead of respecting diversity and recognising intersex, they view the intersex body as unable to fit within the

---

[172] Idem, p. 19.

[173] Prerna (2013), p. 5.

[174] Matos, "Towards a Livable Mode of Existence: Judith Butler's Undoing Gender, 2013.

parameters of the normative male/female binary and thus, it is approached by the status quo as a pathology.[175] The pathologisation of intersex persons leads to the performance of harmful, invasive and non-consensual intersex surgeries which violate fundamental rights of intersex people.

According to Foucault, "power is essentially what dictates its law to sex".[176] This implies that sex is placed in a binary system such as licit and illicit or permitted and forbidden and this is translated based on its relation to the law.[177] Indeed, as it will be later discussed, most legal documents originate from the binary understanding of "sex" and "gender" and it could be assumed that whoever transgresses the binary system is "illicit" or "forbidden". International law has been adapting to recent developments and recognising the existence of individuals who do not identify with the binary. The Committee of the CEDAW through its recommendations has expanded the understanding of "gender" to go beyond "women" and include "transgender" and "intersex". Nonetheless, as it will be later analysed, the binary concept of "sex" has not yet been adequately addressed. Due to the binary understanding of "sex", intersex people, tend to cause the sex/gender system "explode" and society and the law in an effort to "normalise" them and "fit them in", violate their fundamental human rights. The UN has introduced human rights friendly terminology to describe non-binary individuals and for those who are born between sexes, the terms "intersex" and "sex characteristics" are being used. Reports that clarify the significance of different terms and concepts on non-binary individuals have been issued at international and regional levels (i.e. EU Commission) in order to highlight the diversity that exists within sexual minorities. At the same time, is it possible to depict how human beings perceive their sex and gender? There may be a need for a reference point between doctors, law practitioners, academics and activists but human nature is too complex and unique to fit into descriptive terms.

Given these points, Chap. 2 will focus on numerous possible human rights violations that an intersex individual may face including the rights to bodily integrity, self-determination, health, the access to legal recognition, the right to found a family and non-discrimination in several fields such as employment and sports. Chapters 3 and 4 will then present the situation of intersex rights at regional levels with the aim to demonstrate that in order to challenge the existing understanding of "sex" in both society and the law, intersex should be seen as a "reformative means" that will reform outdated legal frameworks and lead the way to sex/gender equality beyond binaries and justice.

---

[175] Idem.

[176] Foucault (1990), p. 83.

[177] P p. 5.

Chapter 2
Eliminating the "Abnormal"

"Normality" or "normalcy" is a broad concept and its definition varies among disciplines, scientific communities, individuals, eras, societies and circumstances. "Normality" is treated as a statistical perception according to which philosophers and society consider it as the state of being "normal" which is linked to the "most usual".[1] Several psychoanalysts use "normal" to indicate the perfect and ideal and physicians frequently use "normal" with a technical significance which implies what ought to be.[2] Attributing characteristics to an individual such as "normal" or "deviant" and "unusual" lead to "labeling". "Labeling" is based on the thesis that human identity is created through the process of interaction between an individual and the others in society.[3] Then, society based on "labeling", responds by forming prejudices and stigmatising the targeted individuals. Individuals who are victims of stigmatisation often create a negative image for themselves and face marginalisation, discrimination and human rights violations.[4]

In the case of intersex, the normative, societal and medical perceptions of "normality" are dominant. Societal structure prescribes that people should fit in the binary sex/gender model of female/male and whoever falls out of this dichotomy needs to be "fixed", initially through genital or sex "normalising" surgeries. Intersex is treated as a pathology and thus different treatments are often undertaken before and during infancy and childhood of intersex people to alter their bodies and make them conform to gendered norms.[5] It could be stated that medicine impacts significantly the modern development of societal norms as medical power is at the heart of the society of normalisation.[6] The role of the concept of "normal" within, is to create an ideal derived from cultural, historical and societal values. Hence, medicine

[1] Wellman (1958), p. 43.

[2] Idem.

[3] Skopalová (2010), p. 329.

[4] Idem.

[5] WHO (2015), p. 26.

[6] Foucault (1996), p. 197.

N. Pikramenou, *Intersex Rights*, https://doi.org/10.1007/978-3-030-27554-9_2

presents itself as the solution for those "abnormal problems" that do not meet the ideal.[7] Next, societal norms affect majorly legal norms as the evolution of societies is usually followed by the evolution of the legal systems. In our days, most legal systems picture the sex/gender binary that prevails in societies and exclude whoever falls out of the norm, including intersex people.

Existing human rights discourse and literature have been focusing only on certain aspects of intersex including invasive and harmful surgeries and legal recognition.[8] Nonetheless, this is not the only case where intersex individuals' rights are infringed. As societies are evolving to embrace sex/gender diversity and promote inclusiveness, more and more individuals are and will gradually be able to live and identify as intersex. With this in mind, the main question to be addressed would be, how current legal frameworks, which are based on the female/male binary, could accommodate the needs of intersex people and safeguard their rights. Enhancing the quality of life of intersex people requires a multipronged approach given that living as intersex in societies where the sex/gender binary is the prevailing "norm" may result to marginalisation and multiple human rights violations.

The aim of this Chapter is to investigate multiple human rights violations that intersex individuals are subjected to. The working hypothesis focuses on the fact that intersex persons face considerable human rights violations from the very beginning till the end of their lifetime and they remain unprotected under international and national human rights law, including case-law, as it will be demonstrated in Chaps. 3 and 4. Human rights violations that will be presented in this Chapter are limited to and reflect the legal demands of intersex individuals as depicted by intersex organisations in their Public Statements including the Malta Declaration, the Statement of Riga, the Vienna Statement, the Darlington Statement and the Public Statements issued by the African Intersex Movement and the Asian Intersex Forum.[9] Other reports on intersex rights will be consulted as well, in particular the ones published by the Council of Europe[10] and the United Nations.[11] The reports issued by international human rights institutions will be referred in conjunction with the Public Statements of intersex organisations as intersex individuals' legal demands need to be heard and included in legal discussions on intersex. The identification and analysis of possible human rights violations as expressed by intersex rights' and international organisations is essential prerequisite for the analysis, in order for the reader to grasp all aspects of the research topic and be able to place the analysis concerning the regional level (Chaps. 3 and 4) into the wider context. Last, the concluding Chapter will provide an overview and analysis with regards to which extent the legal demands of intersex are covered under modern legal frameworks worldwide.

---

[7] Hester (2004a, b), p. 37.

[8] See Garland (2016), Ní Mhuirthile (2015) and Scherpe et al. (2018).

[9] See Sect. 1.1.

[10] See Council of Europe, Human Rights and Intersex people (2015).

[11] See United Nations Free & Equal, "Factsheet Intersex" (2016).

In detail, even before intersex people are born, Preimplantation Genetic Diagnosis (PGD) may be used to prevent their birth.[12] In the case that intersex infants are born, often involuntary and harmful surgeries are performed to fit in the male/female binary. Later, intersex people who -operated or not- identify as such, will struggle to be integrated in modern societies since legal frameworks are binary and impose numerous obstacles to non-binary individuals: intersex are often not entitled to found a family, to access identification documents and employment and participate in sports.

The first section of this Chapter will focus on human rights abuses deriving from the performance of PGD and "normalising" surgeries including the right to life, access to justice and reparations, access to information, decision-making, informed consent, bodily integrity and individual autonomy. The second section focuses on how binary frameworks prevent intersex from enjoying the right to found a family and access Assisted Reproductive Technologies (ART), legal recognition, non-discrimination in employment, and participation in sport.

2.1 "Preventing" Intersex

Even though there is historical evidence of legal rulings that attempted to decide the status of intersex persons as either male or female in the seventeenth century, the involvement of biomedicine began in the nineteenth century.[13] It could be argued that the increasing recognition of the existence of intersex individuals relates to medical surveillance as well the emergence of several sexual rights movements that started destabilising gender/sex boundaries.[14]

Modern human rights discourse has been addressing mainly non-consensual surgeries performed on intersex individuals, but nowadays, this is not the only possible way to "fix" or "prevent" the creation of intersex bodies. Advancements in reproductive technologies over the past few decades have given parents the freedom and ability to select the sex of their children and even prevent the birth of children who are considered to fall outside the binary norm.[15] For instance, there are several techniques of sex selection such as pre-natal testing and termination of pregnancy, preimplantation genetic testing of embryos and sperm sorting—selection of sperm carrying X or Y chromosomes followed by insemination or In Vitro Fertilisation (IVF).[16] However, the most common form of reproductive technology used in the case of intersex is Preimplantation Genetic Diagnosis (PGD).

---

[12] See Sparrow (2013).

[13] Dreger (1999), p. 6.

[14] Lear (2007), p. 13.

[15] See Damiano (2011) and Sparrow (2013).

[16] Human Genetics Alert (2002), p. 1.

Obviously, all intersex treatments whether surgical or not, are rooted in the societal perception and definition of "normal" which also prevails within the medical field. Intersex bodies, falling out of the female/male binary, are immediately pathologised and ought to be "corrected" in order to fit in societal and legal standards. The Malta Declaration has called "to put an end to preimplantation genetic diagnosis, pre-natal screening and treatment, and selective abortion of intersex foetuses."[17] Moreover, the Public Statemnt by the Asian Intersex Movement requests "to put an end to preimplantation genetic diagnosis, pre-natal screening and interventions, and selective abortion of intersex fetuses" and "to inappropriate medical practices and protocols, including the administration of medication for gender selection and medical interventions on foetuses and newborn babies, as a result of lack of awareness about intersex people and intersex variations."[18] The Council of Europe in its report on the human rights of intersex people has also referred to pre-natal intervention and selective abortion of intersex fetuses.[19] In this section, the use of PGD to prevent intersex and its human rights implications will be explored.

2.1.1 Preimplantation Genetic Diagnosis (PGD) Based on Sex

Currently, the sex of a child is no longer a surprise, but rather a technological artifact. Through technology, parents in **some** countries are granted the reproductive freedom to choose the child's gender. "Sex selection" refers to the practice of using medical techniques to choose the sex of offspring and encompasses several practices including selecting embryos for transfer and implantation following IVF, separating sperm, and selectively terminating a pregnancy.[20] According to World Health Organization (WHO), "there are three core motivations for engaging in sex selection: first, medical reasons such as preventing the birth of children affected or at risk of X-linked disorders, second, family balancing reasons, where couple choose to have a child of one sex because they already have one or more children of the other sex and third, gender preference, often in favour of male offspring stemming from cultural, social, and economic bias in favour of male children and as a result of policies requiring couples to limit reproduction to one child, as in China".[21] WHO has also stressed the principal concerns surrounding sex selections and these are the

[17] OII Europe, Malta Declaration (2013), "Demands".

[18] Public Statement by the Asian Intersex Movement, paras. 6-7.

[19] Council of Europe (2015), p. 21.

[20] WHO, "Gender and Genetics: Sex selection and discrimination".

[21] Idem.

distortion of the natural sex ratio which leads to gender imbalance and the reinforcement of discriminatory and sexist stereotypes towards women.[22]

Preimplantation Genetic Diagnosis (PGD) is a technology that tests the chromosomes of an embryo to determine genetic abnormalities and sex/gender before being placed in the womb.[23] The practice was originally developed to circumvent severe genetic diseases and it provides prospective parents or parent with possibilities to select specific embryos based on an increasing number of genetic conditions and traits.[24] Specifically, the PGD process is performed during IVF: on the third day of fertilisation, blastomere cells are extracted from the embryo and their DNA is multiplied by the thousands.[25] The DNA is then used to identify specific genes, such as gender, and the embryos with the preferable DNA sequence are put back in the uterus.[26] These embryos will then be grown to full term with the hope, aided by technology, that the child will indeed be the gender the parents desired.[27]

In the case of intersex, the use of PGD depends on the intersex condition involved. In particular, "intersex" is a term that encompasses different medical conditions, including Androgen Insensitivity Syndrome (AIS), virilising Congenital Adrenal Hyperplasia (CAH), Klinefelter's syndrome, Turner's syndrome, hypospadias, bladder exstrophy, and many others.[28] Due to the above differentiations, intersex infants may have genitals that seem to be clearly male or clearly female, but are atypical in some way, such as a very large clitoris, a penis that is very small or has a urethra somewhere along the underside of the penis.[29] Others have typical male or female genitals, but they may have atypical sex chromosomes or internal sex organs (such as testes inside the abdomen of a child with female genitals), and/or they may have atypical sex development at puberty.[30] A significant number of the causes of intersex conditions are heritable and therefore PGD could be an option for the

[22] Idem. WHO also notes that "in some countries, such as India and China, it is commonly known that the practice of sex-selective abortion has resulted in distortions of the natural sex ratio, in favour of males. In addition, there is concern that sex selection involves inappropriate control over nonessential characteristics of children and may place a potential psychological burden on, and hence cause harm to, sex-selected offspring." On China and India see also Pinde and Malhotra (2006) and Zhou et al. (2011).

[23] Akchurin and Kartzke (2007), p. 21.

[24] Behrmann and Ravitsky (2013), p. 39.

[25] Idem, p. 22.

[26] Idem.

[27] Idem.

[28] Tamar-Mattis (2012), p. 2.

[29] Idem.

[30] Idem.

prospective parents or parent. For instance, Turner syndrome,[31] AIS[32] and CAH[33] have a genetic cause and could be avoided using PGD.[34] Reportedly, PGD has been used by parents with family histories of CAH and AIS.[35] The United Kingdom (UK) Human Fertilisation and Embryology Authority includes CAH and AIS inits list of conditions for which PGD is permissible.[36] In Australia, Intersex Human Rights Australia called the Australian National Health and Medical Research Council to prohibit PGD interventions on intersex stating that: "we believe that intersex traits are a normal human phenomenon, part of the diversity of human experience. We believe that de-selecting pre-embryos and embryos with intersex traits is no different from de-selection on grounds of sex, ethnicity or, should testing become available in future, sexual orientation or gender identity."[37]

Robert Sparrow has argued that "PGD to select against genes for intersex conditions that involve serious medical harms can be justified by a concern for the well-being of the future child. PGD for merely cosmetic variations in sexual anatomy might also be justified on this basis. Arguing that parents should make decisions about their children's genes on the basis of concern for the sort of society that would result if the choice were universalized commits us to a form of eugenics that is equally—if not more—problematic as the social pressures that might motivate parents to want to spare their children the social consequences of being born with a non-standard sexual anatomy. Unlike surgery, PGD will not harm the child, nor is it

---

[31] Turner syndrome is a chromosomal condition that affects development in females. The most common feature of Turner syndrome is short stature, which becomes evident by about age 5. An early loss of ovarian function (ovarian hypofunction or premature ovarian failure) is also very common. The ovaries develop normally at first, but egg cells (oocytes) usually die prematurely and most ovarian tissue degenerates before birth. Many affected girls do not undergo puberty unless they receive hormone therapy, and most are unable to conceive (infertile). A small percentage of females with Turner syndrome retain normal ovarian function through young adulthood (U.S National Library of Medicine, "Turner Syndrome").

[32] Androgen insensitivity syndrome is a condition that affects sexual development before birth and during puberty. People with this condition are genetically male, with one X chromosome and one Y chromosome in each cell. Because their bodies are unable to respond to certain male sex hormones (called androgens), they may have mostly female external sex characteristics or signs of both male and female sexual development (U.S National Library of Medicine, "Androgen Insensitivity Syndrome").

[33] Congenital adrenal hyperplasia (CAH) due to 11-beta-hydroxylase deficiency is one of a group of disorders (collectively called congenital adrenal hyperplasia) that affect the adrenal glands. The adrenal glands are located on top of the kidneys and produce a variety of hormones that regulate many essential functions in the body. In people with CAH due to 11-beta-hydroxylase deficiency, the adrenal glands produce excess androgens, which are male sex hormones. There are two types of CAH due to 11-beta-hydroxylase deficiency, the classic form and the non-classic form. The classic form is the more severe of the two types (U.S National Library of Medicine, "Congenital adrenal hyperplasia due to 11-beta-hydroxylase deficiency").

[34] Sparrow (2013), p. 31.

[35] Idem.

[36] Human Fertilisation & Embryology Authority, "PGD conditions".

[37] Intersex Human Rights Australia, "Submission on the ethics of genetic selection against intersex traits", 2014.

plausible to object on the basis of the inability of the child to consent."[38] Georgiann Davis, a sociologist who is personally and professionally connected with the intersex community answered to Sparrow's arguments and stated that the performance of PGD to select against intersex traits is mainly protecting binary ideologies about sex and its presumed correlation with gender.[39] She added that in the case of intersex, it is primarily about sex eugenics and not "gender" and "individuals with intersex traits force society to disentangle sex and gender, and in the process, open up new possibilities for embracing all sorts of human diversity".[40] Indeed, the performance of PGD for cosmetic reasons to erase intersex cannot be considered as a means to fight injustice, justice for intersex will be granted only if intersex is used as a means to shape diverse and equal societies.

2.1.2 *The Right to Life of Intersex Embryos*

PGD takes place before the placement of the embryo in the womb. Consequently, it may be considered as harmless, especially comparing to intersex surgeries as there is no "individual" involved. However, this may depend on when it is considered that life begins.

International human rights treaties protect the right to life but without defining when life begins. According to article 1 of the Universal Declaration of Human Rights "all human beings are born free and equal in dignity and rights".[41] In fact, the history of the UDHR negotiations indicates that the word "born" was used to exclude a prenatal application of the rights protected in the Declaration.[42] The Preamble of the Convention on the Rights of the Child (CRC) states that "the child, by reason of his physical and mental immaturity, needs special safeguards and care, including appropriate legal protection, before as well as after birth".[43] The Committee on the Rights of the Child, which interprets and monitors State compliance with the CRC, supports the understanding that the CRC does not protect a prenatal right to life and has not issued any documents which dictate that there is a right to life before birth.[44]

At a European level, Article 14 of the Council of Europe Convention on Human Rights and Biomedicine (ETS No. 164) prohibits discrimination on the grounds of

---

[38] Sparrow (2013), p. 36.

[39] Davis (2013), p. 51.

[40] Idem. See also Nisker (2013).

[41] Universal Declaration of Human Rights, adopted by the General Assembly of the United Nations on 10 December 1948.

[42] Center for Reproductive Rights (2012), p. 5.

[43] Convention on the Rights of the Child, Adopted and opened for signature, ratification and accession by General Assembly resolution 44/25 of 20 November 1989 entry into force 2 September 1990, in accordance with article 49.

[44] Center for Reproductive Rights (2012), p. 6.

a person's "genetic heritage" as well as the use of techniques of medically assisted procreation "for the purpose of choosing a future child's sex, except where serious hereditary sex-related disease is to be avoided".[45] The explanatory report of the convention raises concern with regard to genetic testing as it "may become a means of selection and discrimination".[46] The Parliamentary Assembly of the Council of Europe in its Resolution 1829 on "Prenatal sex selection" has condemned "the practice of prenatal sex selection as a phenomenon which finds its roots in a culture of gender inequality".[47] Earlier in 2002, the Committee of Ministers' recommendation had called on Member States to "prohibit enforced sterilisation or abortion, contraception imposed by coercion or force, and pre-natal selection by sex, and take all necessary measures to this end".[48]

In Costa and Pavan v. Italy,[49] the applicants, were healthy carriers of the genetic disease cystic fibrosis and they wanted to avoid transmitting the disease to their offspring but under Italian law, the use of PGD was possible only for sterile or infertile couples or couples in which the man suffers from a sexually transmissible viral disease (such as the HIV virus, or hepatitis B and C).[50] The Court considered the applicants' desire to be encompassed by Article 8 as a form of expression of their private and family life and found that the legislative ban amounted to an interference.[51] In other words, the Court stated that to have a healthy child "constitutes an aspect of their private and family life and comes under the protection of Article 8"[52] and therefore, the legal impossibility to achieve this infringes their right to respect for private and family life.[53] With this decision, the formulation of a new right is noted, which is the right to a healthy child, implying access to the means of selection.[54]

Another question that has been treated by the ECtHR is the beginning of life in the case of unborn children, considering that Article 2 (1) of the ECHR provides that "everyone's rights to life shall be protected by law".[55] In Vo v. France the Court elaborated that is neither desirable nor possible to answer in the abstract question

---

[45] Convention for the Protection of Human Rights and Dignity of the Human Being with regard to the Application of Biology and Medicine: Convention on Human Rights and Biomedicine, Oviedo, 4.IV.1997.

[46] See Explanatory Report to the Convention for the protection of Human Rights and Dignity of the Human Being with regard to the Application of Biology and Medicine: Convention on Human Rights and Biomedicine, Oviedo, 4.IV.1997, Article 11-Non-discrimination.

[47] Resolution 1829, 2011, para. 4.

[48] Recommendation of the Committee of Ministers to member states, 2002, para. 79.

[49] Costa and Pavan v. Italy, application no. 54270/10, final judgment 11 February 2013.

[50] European Court of Human Rights (2016), p. 25.

[51] Idem, p. 26.

[52] Costa and Pavan v. Italy, application no. 54270/10, para. 57.

[53] Idem, para. 58.

[54] See Grégor Puppinck, "Prohibition of Pre-implantation Genetic Diagnosis: The ECHR Censors the Italian Law", 2012.

[55] European Convention on Human Rights as amended by Protocols Nos, 11 and 14, supplemented by Protocols Nos, 1,4,6,7,12 and 13.

whether the unborn child is a person and it left the matter to the appreciation of the States.[56] In the judgment, the Court makes extensive reference to the Oviedo Convention on Human Rights and Biomedicine, its Additional Protocol on the Prohibition of Cloning Human Beings and its Draft Additional Protocol on biomedical research to the opinion on the ethical aspects of research involving the use of human embryo[57] and it points out that the latter Convention and protocols notably do not define the concept of "human being".[58]

According to the Council of Europe (CoE), the right to life of intersex can be violated if the performance of PGD is not justified and it is incompatible with ethics and human rights standards due to the discrimination perpetrated against intersex people on the basis of their sex characteristics.[59] In addition, Yogyakarta principles plus 10 introduced a new State obligation on non-discrimination in relation to prenatal interventions[60] and called for an end to prenatal treatments and genetic selection that discriminate against intersex people on grounds of sex characteristics.[61] Regardless, PGD still remains a complex and expensive medical procedure because it necessitates IVF which does not guarantee a successful pregnancy and it is unlikely that future parents or parent will undertake it unless there is a major concern on preventing the child from being affected by a specific condition.[62]

2.1.3 Reproductive Liberty vs Intersex Rights

WHO states that reproductive rights rest on the recognition of the basic right of all couples and individuals to decide freely and responsibly the number, spacing and timing of their children and to have the information and means to do so, and the right to attain the highest standard of sexual and reproductive health.[63] The Convention on the Elimination of All Forms of Discrimination Against Women (CEDAW) guarantees in its Article 16 women equal rights in deciding "freely and

[56] Vo v. France, judgment of 8 July 2004, para. 13.

[57] Korff (2006), p. 9.

[58] Idem, para. 84.

[59] Council of Europe (2015), p. 30.

[60] The language used in this paragraph reflects similar statements on the role of sex selection in discriminating against women. The State obligation doesn't call for prohibition of such technologies, because it is limited to existing norms in international human rights law. Recognising that human genetic modification is becoming technologically feasible, this is anticipated (See IHRA, "The Yogyakarta Principles plus 10 launched").

[61] The Yogyakarta principles plus 10, 2017, Principle 38 para L.

[62] Idem.

[63] WHO, "Gender and Reproductive rights".

responsibly on the number and spacing of their children and to have access to the information, education and means to enable them to exercise these rights". Yogyakarta principles plus 10 ensure in Principle 17 para. O the "access to a range of safe, affordable and effective contraceptives, including emergency contraception, and to information and education on family planning and sexual and reproductive health, without discrimination based on sexual orientation, gender identity, gender expression and sex characteristics". Moreover, principle 23 para. M guarantees the provision of "access to medical care and counselling appropriate to those seeking asylum, recognising any particular needs of persons on the basis of their sexual orientation, gender identity, gender expression or sex characteristics, including with regard to reproductive health (…)".

The negative enjoyment of reproductive liberty or freedom occurs when individuals avoid having offspring and involves the freedom to act to avoid the birth of biologic offspring, such as avoiding intercourse, using contraceptives, refusing the transfer of embryos to the uterus, discarding embryos, terminating pregnancies, and being sterilised.[64] In contrast, the liberty or freedom to have offspring involves the positive enjoyment of freedom to take steps or make choices that result in the birth of biologic offspring, such as having intercourse, providing gametes for artificial or in vitro conception, placing embryos in the uterus, preserving gametes or embryos for later use, and avoiding the use of contraception, abortion, or sterilisation.[65] Henceforth, PGD could be considered to fall within the sphere of reproductive liberty or freedom of prospective parents to select the sex of their offspring but it is contested among jurisdictions whether it consists of a legal right.[66]

With regards to intersex, PGD could not be justified based on social policies which enforce sex heteronormativity and sex dichotomy in societies as it could lead to a form of eugenics. Additionally, selecting against intersex to conform with the binary, is discriminatory. Given these points, whereas it is problematic to label prenatal sex selection itself as a human rights violation, the causes of prenatal sex selection may raise human rights concerns as well as their consequences which can impact on the human rights of individuals. Procreative liberty is the equivalent to assuming that parents know what is best for an unborn child and that the decision of parents should guarantee a better outcome than natural selection would.[67] The birth of intersex infants should not be avoided but rather be used as a tool to transform societies. The empowerment of formerly stigmatised and pathologised sex minorities can allow for the emergence of liberated and diverse societies. In the meantime, the ethical discussion on PGD against intersex can lead to a broader reflection on the

---

[64] Robertson (2003), p. 447.

[65] Idem.

[66] See Bayefsky (2016) and Shelby Deeney (2013).

[67] See Sect. 2.3.

way ART may intersect with the liberation of sex minorities and the promotion of moral progress and socially just and inclusive communities.[68]

2.2 "Fixing" Intersex

2.2.1 *Background of Sex/Gender "Normalising" Surgeries*

Foucault, in Herculine Barbin, explains that "In the Middle Ages, the rules of both canon and civil law were very clear (…) the designation 'hermaphrodite' was given to those in whom the two sexes were juxtaposed, in proportions that might be variable. In these cases, it was the role of the father or godfather (thus of those who 'named' the child) to determine at the time of the baptism which sex was going to be retained".[69] Before the middle of the twentieth century, most children born with genitalia that did not fit the male-female binary norm were not subjected to surgery.[70] Sex/gender "normalising" surgeries were performed between 1930 and 1960, as during that era the medical field was developing rapidly and surgery could be used as a "means" to conform to social and religious norms. Their rise is detected in the 1950s when a team of medical specialists at Johns Hopkins University developed the "optimum gender of rearing" system for treating children with intersex conditions.[71] The reasoning behind this system was that in cases of intersex infants, sex/gender assignment surgeries and hormonal treatments should be performed early, so children would be brought up to be girls and boys.[72] Gender/sex assignment surgeries on intersex infants started arising with John Money and Claude Migeon who advised on a surgical intervention which would influence the default standards of healthcare for intersex infants.[73] Based on Money's theory that infants would become the gender they were raised in, regardless of their "biological sex" (sex traits), intersex children were "corrected" surgically and then raised into an assigned gender with belief by parents and medical professionals that they could lead "normal" lives.[74] It has to be noted that, sex/gender "normalising" surgeries often have negative consequences, including the loss of sexual function and feeling

---

[68] Behrmann and Ravitsky (2013), p. 41.

[69] Foucault (1980), p. vii.

[70] Elders et al. (2017), p. 2.

[71] ISNA, "What's wrong with the way intersex has traditionally been treated?".

[72] On the medical management of intersex infants see also Garland (2016) and Scherpe et al. (2018).

[73] Human Rights Watch and Interact (2017), p. 21.

[74] ISNA, "What's wrong with the way intersex has traditionally been treated?".

in ones' genitalia.[75] The history of intersex surgeries[76] also involved stigmatisation as doctors would instruct parents to conceal the diagnosis and treatment from the child and as a result many intersex people would not learn about their conditions until they accessed their medical files as adults.[77]

John Money used to advocate that gender identity is all about nurture (upbringing), not nature (inborn traits), and that gender assignment is the key to treating all children with atypical sex anatomies, such as intersex.[78] David Reimer's story proved John Money's theories wrong. David Reimer was born as male but due to doctor's fault, his penis was accidentally burned off during circumcision. At the advice of psychologist John Money at Johns Hopkins University, David's parents agreed to have him "sex reassigned" and made into a girl via surgical, hormonal, and psychological treatments—i.e., via the system Money advocated for intersex children.[79] As soon as David discovered what happened to him, he reassumed the social identity of a boy proving intersex surgeries and nurture/nature theories wrong. Although David was not an intersex child, the case indicates that a decision to assign a child a gender identity can have disastrous consequences and it also raises questions on whether a decision to assign a gender identity can be made too early.[80]

David Reimer's case raised a lot of concerns and in 1990, a former collaborator of Money, Suzanne J Kessler published her critique, questioning that clinical practice as it was based on little research.[81] Later, several scientists started questioning intersex surgeries and the sex binary as a social construct. In 2000, Anne Fausto-Sterling expressly stated that "intersexuality, in Money's view, resulted from fundamentally ab-normal processes"[82] and that "patients required medical treatment because they ought to have become either a male or a female"[83] child.

2.2.2 *Current Medical Trends*

In 2005, during a time of controversy around sex/gender "normalising" surgeries, the Chicago Consensus[84] was introduced and it recommended very few changes to the "optimal gender policy" relative to gender assignment and medical interventions

---

[75] Thorn (2014), p. 610.

[76] See also Garland (2016), Scherpe et al. (2018), Karkazis (2008), Creighton (2001), Creighton and Minto (2001), Greenberg (2012), Morland (2006), Preves (2008) and Reis and Kessler (2010).

[77] Human Rights Watch and Interact (2017), p. 6.

[78] ISNA, "Who was David Reimer (also, sadly, known as "John/Joan")?".

[79] Idem.

[80] Australian Human Rights Commission (2009), p. 7.

[81] Kessler (1990).

[82] Fausto-Sterling (2000a, b), p. 46.

[83] Idem.

[84] Lee et al. (2006).

in infancy.[85] In other words, the Chicago Consensus did not depathologise intersex but rather proposed the term "disorders of sex development" (DSD) with the view that terms such as "intersex," "pseudohermaphroditism," "hermaphroditism," "sex reversal," and gender-based diagnostic labels are "as potentially pejorative by patients and can be confusing to practitioners and parents alike".[86] The Consensus tried to place the surgeon within the framework of a multidisciplinary team with an explicit mandate to collaborate with service users and families.[87]

Regarding the current situation of surgeries, there is presently no definitive evidence that the Chicago Consensus has had a significant impact on the number of children undergoing genital surgery.[88] There have been few audits of the implementation of the Consensus and recent publications focus more on medical literature on surgical techniques rather than reporting on patient experiences.[89] In 2016, a Global Disorders of Sex Development Update stated that there is still no consensual attitude regarding indications, timing, procedure and evaluation of outcome of sex/gender "normalising" surgery and that physicians working on the matter should be aware that the trend in recent years has been for legal and human rights bodies to increasingly emphasise on preserving patient autonomy.[90] In 2017, three former surgeons M. Joycelyn Elders, David Satcher and Richard Carmona published a paper stating that "cosmetic infant genitoplasty is not justified absent a need to ensure physical functioning".[91] This statement was based on three major points: there is insufficient evidence that growing up with atypical genitalia leads to psychosocial distress, there is little evidence that cosmetic infant genitoplasty is necessary to reduce psychological damage and these surgeries violate an individual's right to personal autonomy over their own future.[92]

Nonetheless, genital surgeries are not yet eliminated. According to a 2013 study which focused on medical attitudes towards surgeries in 12 countries, genital surgery was performed from infancy to adolescence and adulthood in all examined countries.[93] These countries are: Belgium, Germany, France, Ukraine, Turkey, Serbia, Uganda, South Africa, Taiwan, Australia, Uruguay and New Zealand. In a minority of cases there was a medical emergency in a narrow sense, but intersex individuals generally had perfectly healthy bodies. With exception of Australia and Turkey, babies/infants were most heavily affected whereas Western European coun-

[85] Garland (2016), p. 102.

[86] Lee et al. (2006).

[87] Creighton et al. (2014), p. 38.

[88] Idem, p. 41.

[89] Idem, p. 38.

[90] Lee et al. (2016), p. 177. See also Mouriquand et al. (2016) and Baratz (2016).

[91] Elders et al. (2017), p. 2.

[92] Idem, 2017, p. 3.

[93] Ghattas (2013).

tries and South Africa had a tendency towards a distribution up to adolescence.[94] No details were provided on Taiwan.[95]

There is no doubt that the outcomes of intersex surgeries are severe and irreversible.[96] Intersex surgeries terminate or permanently reduce intersex individuals' sexual and reproductive capacity. While some intersex people are born infertile, and some retain their fertility after medical treatment, many undergo removal of viable reproductive organs, leaving them with permanent, irreversible infertility and causing severe mental suffering.[97] In addition to the physical and emotional problems that can be caused by surgical intervention, many intersex individuals suffer lasting psychological effects because of repeated genital examinations in childhood such as medical display, genital photography and excessive genital exams.[98] These practices, due to their nature and lack of sufficient research on their outcomes, have also been characterised as "human experimentation".[99]

2.2.3 Intersex Surgeries and Female Genital Mutilation/ Cutting (FGM/C)

As it was already mentioned, intersex surgeries were introduced during the 1950s and they are still being performed by several physicians worldwide. The motives behind intersex surgeries are social and not medical. Even though "gender" is usually considered as a social construct, the case of intersex people proves that "sex" is also a social construct. Even though the existence of intersex shows that the sex is not binary, societies are still based on heteronormativity and cisnormativity,[100]

---

[94] Idem, p. 19.

[95] Idem.

[96] On the detrimental effects of intersex surgeries see also Garland (2016), Scherpe et al. (2018), Ittelson and Tamar-Mattis (2016), Feder and Dreger (2016), Diamond and Garland (2014) and Greenberg (2012).

[97] Tamar-Mattis (2012), p. 6.

[98] Idem, pp. 7–8.

[99] Idem, p. 8.

[100] "Cisnormativity" has been described as "the assumption that all, or almost all, individuals are cisgender. At best, cisnormativity contributes to the erasure of trans* and nonbinary experiences. At worst, it is part of a deliberate and calculated system of oppression that includes institutionalized cissexism, transphobia as well as interophobia" (The Queer Dictionary, "Definition of "Cisnormativity""). The term has appeared in several articles including the article ""We don't exist": a qualitative study of marginalization experienced by HIV-positive lesbian, bisexual, queer and transgender women in Toronto, Canada" published by the Journal of the International AIDS Society". In the article "I don't think this is theoretical; this is our lives": How erasure impacts health care for transgender people on the Journal of the Association of Nurses in AIDS Care, the term "cisnormativity" has been described as "the expectation that all people are cissexual, that those assigned male at birth always grow up to be men and those assigned female at birth always grow up to be women. This assumption is so pervasive that it otherwise has not yet been named. Cisnormative assumptions are so prevalent that they are difficult at first to even recognize.

excluding whoever falls beyond the "gender" and "sex" binary. Intersex people are surgically "corrected" in order to fit primarily in the "sex" binary and then they are expected to develop a "gender" which will conform to the sex assigned to them at birth.

Because of their social motives, intersex surgeries are often associated with Female Genital Mutilation/Cutting (FGM/C).[101] FGM/C is a social convention that is often considered a necessary part of raising a girl and a way to prepare her for adulthood and marriage.[102] Conversely, intersex surgeries are mostly based upon the social construct of the sex binary which dictates that individuals should be divided in females and males. The practices may differ, but it can be argued that they both challenge social sex/gender norms. On one hand, FGM/C challenges the role of women and girls as they are "corrected" in order to conform to patriarchal norms that impose a modest, subordinate life free of pleasure. On the other hand, intersex surgeries challenge the social fundamentals of societies which are based on the sex/gender binary and to that aim, intersex people are "fixed" to fit in the binary. In both cases, the goal is to accommodate individuals in social norms through the control of their sexual and reproductive anatomies and behaviour.

FGM/C also emanates from a strong cultural background as it is associated with cultural ideals of femininity, which include the notion that girls are clean and beautiful after removal of body parts that are considered unclean, unfeminine or male.[103] The practice is mostly carried out by traditional circumcisers, who often play other central roles in communities.[104] In many settings, health care providers perform FGM/C due to the belief that the procedure is safer when medicalised[105] Intersex surgeries derive from the cultural ideals that intersex bodies are unappealing and need to be fixed to be considered "normal". In both cases, circumcisers and/or physicians under the paternalistic authority, which prevails in close communities as well as the medical field, pathologise their "patients" and decide about their future. Especially, in the case of intersex, physicians are unconsciously enforcing the cultural categories of society, through the scientific knowledge they disseminate and the treatments they perform and convey the message that those born with intersex

---

Cisnormativity shapes social activity such as child rearing, the policies and practices of individuals and institutions, and the organization of the broader social world through the ways in which people are counted and health care is organized. Cisnormativity disallows the possibility of trans existence or trans visibility. As such, the existence of an actual trans person within systems such as health care is too often unanticipated and produces a social emergency of sorts because both staff and systems are unprepared for this reality."

[101] According to WHO, female genital mutilation/cutting comprises all procedures that involve partial or total removal of the external female genitalia, or other injury to the female genital organs for non-medical reasons (WHO, "Female genital mutilation"). The NHS defines FGM/C as the procedure where the female genitals are deliberately cut, injured or changed, but where there's no medical reason for this to be done".

[102] WHO, "Female genital mutilation".

[103] Idem.

[104] Idem.

[105] Idem.

conditions are "abnormal", "pathological", and "needing correction".[106] Then, parents, based on social and cultural pressures and prejudices, are convinced that they are dealing with an emergency that needs to be "fixed" and they consent to the performance of intersex surgeries.

Chery Chase, an intersex activist who was surgically "corrected" during infancy, examines the way human rights advocates and media condemn African practices and compares that treatment with their response to intersex surgeries[107] which is almost non-existent.[108] Indeed, the same attitude prevails in medical practice where African practices that remove the clitoris and other parts of female genitals are perceived as "harmful", whereas intersex genital cutting is perceived as "healing".[109] FGM/C is widely considered as "harmful" because it is based on cultural/traditional norms whereas intersex surgery is presented as a "medical emergency". Therefore, intersex is portrayed as a "scientific" case and this makes it more challenging to "disclose" its cultural and social motives.

When it comes to human rights violations, FGM/C violates the right to health, the rights of the child, the right to sexual and physical integrity, and the rights to be free from discrimination and free from torture, cruel, inhuman and degrading treatment. Same rights are violated when intersex surgeries are performed. However, the essential difference between the two practices is that FGM/C, in any form, is recognised internationally as a gross violation of human rights. For instance, the Convention on the Rights of the Child (CRC) which is part of binding international law, obliges Member States that are signatories to protect their own nationals from harmful practices such as FGM/C.[110] Addressing FGM/C as a violation of international human rights law places responsibility on governments who have a duty to ensure the enjoyment of human rights in their jurisdictions.

FGM/C and intersex surgeries are different practices, but they present similarities specifically regarding their socio-cultural background and their harmful outcomes that violate basic human rights.[111] The fact that FGM/C is considered as a "traditional" practice makes it easier to denounce its illegitimacy whereas intersex surgery is a more complex practice and due to its complexity, it is hard to identify all the issues that are at stake. Regardless, FGM/C discourse may serve as a means towards the international recognition and condemn of the irreversible harms of intersex surgery.

---

[106] Ehrenreich and Mark (2005), p. 120.

[107] Cheryl Chase also uses the term Intersex Genital Mutilation (IGM).

[108] Chase (2002), p. 140.

[109] Ehrenreich and Mark (2005).

[110] Convention on the Rights of the Child, article 24 para. 3 "States Parties shall take all effective and appropriate measures with a view to abolishing traditional practices prejudicial to the health of children."

[111] The UN Special Rapporteur on Health has stated that partial clitoridectomy as part of the treatment of intersex persons is a form of female genital mutilation (A/HRC/32/33 para 56).

2.3 Human Rights Implications of Intersex Surgeries

The ban of intersex surgeries has always been a top priority of intersex rights organisations due to its social motives, invasive nature and the violation of fundamental human rights including the rights to bodily integrity, physical autonomy, self-determination and health. The first demand of the Malta Declaration is "to put an end to mutilating and "normalizing" practices such as genital surgeries, psychological and other medical treatments through legislative and other means. Intersex people must be empowered to make their own decisions affecting own bodily integrity, physical autonomy and self-determination".[112] In 2014, the European Intersex Meeting which took place in Riga, underlined the need "to work towards making non-consensual medical and psychological treatment unlawful. Medical practitioners or other professionals should not conduct any treatment to the purpose of modifying sex characteristics which can be deferred until the person to be treated can provide informed consent".[113] Later, the Vienna Statement urged governments to take decisive action to "install legislative protections that ban medical interventions on children with variations of sex characteristics, on social, psychosocial, cultural or cosmetic grounds" and it continues by mentioning that "this may include installing legislative measures that penalise medical professionals that commit or assist in Intersex Genital Mutilation (IGM)".[114] The Darlington Statement called "for the immediate prohibition as a criminal act of deferrable medical interventions, including surgical and hormonal interventions, that alter the sex characteristics of infants and children without personal consent" and "for freely-given and fully informed consent b individuals (…)".[115] The African Intersex Movement and the Asian Intersex Movement in its public statements urged "to put an end to mutilating and 'normalising' practices such as genital surgeries, psychological and other medical interventions through legislative and other means. Intersex people must be empowered to make their own decisions affecting their own bodily integrity, physical autonomy and self-determination" and to end "non-consensual sterilization of intersex people".[116]

The demands of the above statements delivered by organisations comprised by intersex people are also reflected on the reports issued by the UN Special Rapporteur on Torture who has characterised intersex surgeries as a "torture", the Council of Europe, the World Health Organization, the European Union and on the wording of Yogyakarta Principles. In 2016, UN experts including the Committee against Torture, the Committee on the Rights of the Child and the Committee on the Rights of Persons with Disabilities, along with the Council of Europe Commissioner for

---

[112] OII Europe, Malta Declaration, 1 December 2013.

[113] OII Europe, Statement of Riga, 2014.

[114] OII Europe, Statement of the 1st European Intersex Community Event, Vienna, 2017.

[115] Darlington Statement, 2017, para. 7.

[116] Public Statement by the Asian Intersex Movement, 2018, paras. 5 and 8 and Public Statement by the African Intersex Movement, 2017, "Demands".

Human Rights, the Inter-American Commission on Human Rights and United Nations Special Rapporteurs called for an urgent end to human rights violations against intersex persons committed in medical settings "States must, as a matter of urgency, prohibit medically unnecessary surgery and procedures on intersex children. They must uphold the autonomy of intersex adults and children and their rights to health, to physical and mental integrity, to live free from violence and harmful practices and to be free from torture and ill-treatment. Intersex children and their parents should be provided with support and counselling, including from peers".[117]

In this section, human rights violations that are caused by the performance of intersex surgeries will be analysed including the rights to bodily integrity, individual self-determination, health, decision-making, inform consent and access to medical records and justice.

2.3.1 Torture and Cruel Inhuman or Degrading Treatment (CIDT)

Torture has enduring effects on the physical, mental, and emotional well-being of its survivors, crippling or destroying their capacity to pursue fulfillment and happiness.[118] It seeks to annihilate the victim's personality and denies the inherent dignity of the human being; therefore, it is inconsistent with basic human rights and the international and European community have condemned it and recognised it as a crime under European and international law.[119]

Internationally, torture and other cruel, inhuman or degrading treatment (CIDT) or punishment are prohibited under Article 5 of the Universal Declaration of Human Rights.[120] Moreover, Article 7 of the International Covenant on Civil and Political Rights[121] mentions explicitly the case of medical interventions: "no one shall be subjected to torture or to cruel, inhuman or degrading treatment or punishment. In particular, no one shall be subjected without his free consent to medical or scientific experimentation". Torture and CIDT are also specifically prohibited under the UN Convention against Torture and Other Cruel, Inhuman or Degrading Treatment or Punishment (UNCAT) where Article 1 para 1. of the UNCAT defines "torture" as "any act by which severe pain or suffering, whether physical or mental, is intention-

[117] United Nations Human Rights Office of the High Commissioner, Intersex Awareness Day, "End violence and harmful medical practices on intersex children and adults, UN and regional experts urge", 2016.

[118] Global Citizenship Commission, Appendix E, p. 1.

[119] OHCHR (2002), p. 3.

[120] Universal Declaration of Human Rights, adopted by the General Assembly of the United Nations on 10 December 1948 "Article 5: No one shall be subjected to torture or to cruel, inhuman or degrading treatment or punishment."

[121] International Covenant on Civil and Political Rights, entry into force 23 March 1976.

ally inflicted on a person for such purposes as obtaining from him or a third person information or a confession, punishing him for an act he or a third person has committed or is suspected of having committed, or intimidating or coercing him or a third person, or for any reason based on discrimination of any kind, when such pain or suffering is inflicted by or at the instigation of or with the consent or acquiescence of a public official or other person acting in an official capacity. It does not include pain or suffering arising only from, inherent in or incidental to lawful sanctions.". In relation to children's rights, the CRC prohibits torture in Article 37 para. a where "no child shall be subjected to torture or other cruel, inhuman or degrading treatment or punishment".[122]

In 2013, in his report to the UN Human Rights Council (UNHRC), Juan E. Mendés, the UN Special Rapporteur on torture and other cruel, inhuman or degrading treatment or punishment, condemned non-consensual surgical intervention on intersex people as a form of torture.[123] His report states that "[t]here is an abundance of accounts and testimonies of persons being … subjected to … a variety of forced procedures such as sterilisation, State-sponsored forcible … hormone therapy and genital-normalising surgeries under the guise of so-called 'reparative therapies'. These procedures are rarely medically necessary, can cause scarring, loss of sexual sensation, pain, incontinence and lifelong depression and have also been criticised as being unscientific, potentially harmful and contributing to stigma".[124] The Committee on the Elimination of Discrimination against Women (CEDAW) expressed concern about intersex women as "victims of abuses and mistreatment by health service providers".[125]

In 2016, a new report was released by the UN Special Rapporteur to the UNHRC that assesses the applicability of the prohibition of torture and other cruel, inhuman or degrading treatment or punishment in international law to the unique experiences of intersex persons. The report states that "in many States, children born with atypical sex characteristics are often subject to irreversible sex assignment, involuntary sterilisation and genital normalising surgery, which are performed without their informed consent or that of their parents, leaving them with permanent, irreversible infertility, causing severe mental suffering and contributing to stigmatisation. In some cases, taboo and stigma lead to the killing of intersex infants.".[126] This time, the Rapporteur explored the impact of entrenched discrimination, patriarchal, heteronormative and discriminatory power structures and socialised gender stereotypes and qualified human rights violations committed against persons who transgress sexual and gender norms.[127]

---

[122] Convention on the Rights of the Child, Adopted and opened for signature, ratification and accession by General Assembly resolution 44/25 of 20 November 1989 entry into force 2 September 1990, in accordance with article 49.

[123] A/HRC/22/53, 2013.

[124] Idem, para. 76.

[125] A/HRC/19/41, 2011, para. 56.

[126] A/HRC/31/57, 2016, para. 50.

[127] InterAct, "New UN Special Rapporteur on Torture Report addresses Intersex issues among others".

At European level, torture is prohibited under Article 3 of the European Convention of Human Rights.[128] In addition, the European Convention for the Prevention of Torture and Inhuman and Degrading Treatment or Punishment[129] provides for the setting up of an international committee empowered to strengthen the implementation of the existing prohibition of torture under the ECHR. Following international developments, in 2017, the Parliamentary Assembly of the Council of Europe adopted the first intersex-specific resolution of its kind from a European intergovernmental institution.[130] The resolution highlights the invasive and irreversible nature of "sex-normalising" surgeries on intersex infants and calls on Member States to prohibit such interventions and defer treatments that seek to alter the sex characteristics of intersex children until they can participate in the decision.[131] This resolution is based on a detailed report by Rapporteur Piet de Bruyn on intersex people in which he quotes the previous UN reports where intersex surgeries are explicitly qualified as a torture.[132]

All things considered, could intersex surgeries qualify as a torture? Intersex non-consensual surgeries lead to irreversible sterilisation, traumatic post-surgery physio-psychological issues and they have also been characterised as "human experimentation" due to their inhumane nature and lack of scientific data on the matter. Medical procedures performed on intersex infants fall within the sphere of torture and CIDT as they are intentional and performed for discriminatory and non-medical purposes; are performed with or without consent; can cause severe physical and psychological pain or suffering; and involve children who are powerless to refuse.[133]

2.3.2 *The Right to Bodily Integrity*

The principle of bodily integrity or physical integrity sums up the right of each human being to autonomy and self-determination over their own body and it considers an unconsented physical intrusion as a human rights violation.[134] Bodily integrity is not explicitly recognised under international law, but it has been recognised at a European level.

[128] European Convention on Human Rights as amended by Protocols Nos, 11 and 14, supplemented by Protocols Nos, 1,4,6,7,12 and 13 "Article 3 (Prohibition of torture): No one shall be subjected to torture or to inhuman or degrading treatment or punishment."

[129] Details of Treaty No.126, European Convention for the Prevention of Torture and Inhuman or Degrading Treatment or Punishment, 1987.

[130] OII, "Intersex resolution adopted by the Parliamentary Assembly of the Council of Europe".

[131] PACE, Resolution 2191, 2017.

[132] PACE, Doc. 14404, 2017, paras. 37 and 38.

[133] Tamar-Mattis (2012), p. 10.

[134] Child Rights International Network, "Bodily Integrity".

At both levels, "bodily integrity" has been interpreted to be part of the right to security of the person,[135] freedom from torture and cruel, inhuman, and degrading treatment; the right to privacy[136]; and the right to the highest attainable standard of health.[137] International general recommendations state explicitly the right to bodily integrity. For instance, general comment no. 35 on article 9 of the ICCPR mentions in its third paragraph that "Article 9 recognizes and protects both liberty of person and security of person. Liberty of person concerns freedom from confinement of the body. Security of person concerns freedom from injury to the body, or bodily integrity."[138] In relation to children, the right to bodily integrity is indirectly recognised under Article 19 of the CRC as it stipulates the obligation of Contracting States to protect the child from all forms of physical or mental violence, injury or abuse, neglect or negligent treatment.[139] In 2015, the Committee on the Rights of the Child asserted for the first time that non-consensual intersex surgeries violate physical integrity and constitute a harmful practice.[140]

Regarding the ECHR and the right to respect for private and family life mentioned above, the European Court of Human Rights has held that the person's body is an intimate aspect of his or her private life[141] and a sound mental state is an important factor for the possibility to enjoy the right to private life.[142] Measures which affect the physical integrity or mental health must reach a certain degree of severity to qualify as an interference with the right to private life under Article 8.[143] The ECtHR has also pointed out that even minor interferences with a person's physical

[135] See Article 9 of the ICCPR para. 1 "Everyone has the right to liberty and security of person. No one shall be subjected to arbitrary arrest or detention. No one shall be deprived of his liberty except on such grounds and in accordance with such procedure as are established by law." and Article 5 of the ECHR "Everyone has the right to liberty and security of person. No one shall be deprived of his liberty save in the following cases and in accordance with a procedure prescribed by law (…)".

[136] See Article 17 of the ICCPR para. 1 "No one shall be subjected to arbitrary or unlawful interference with his privacy, family, home or correspondence, nor to unlawful attacks on his honour and reputation" and Article 8 of the ECHR para. 1 "Everyone has the right to respect for his private and family life, his home and his correspondence.". See also Y.F v. Turkey, judgment of 22 July 2003, Bensaid v. the U.K, judgment of 6 February 2001 and Storck v. Germany, judgment of 16 June 2005.

[137] See Article 12 para 1 of the ICESC "1. The States Parties to the present Covenant recognize the right of everyone to the enjoyment of the highest attainable standard of physical and mental health." And Article 11 of the European Social Charter (ESC) "With a view to ensuring the effective exercise of the right to protection of health, the Parties undertake, either directly or in cooperation with public or private organisations, to take appropriate measures designed inter alia (…)".

[138] CCPR/C/107/R.3, 2015.

[139] Convention on the Rights of the Child, Adopted and opened for signature, ratification and accession by General Assembly resolution 44/25 of 20 November 1989 entry into force 2 September 1990, in accordance with article 49.

[140] CRC/C/CHE/CO/2-4, 2015, paras. 42-43.

[141] Y.F v. Turkey, judgment of 22 July 2003 para. 33.

[142] Bensaid v. the U.K, judgment of 6 February 2001, para. 47.

[143] Idem, para. 46.

integrity may fall within the scope of article 8 if they are against the person's will.[144] In addition, when physical integrity is involved, Article 8 might overlap with Article 3. In its case-law, the Court has been distinguishing the fields of application of Articles 3 and 8 according to the gravity of the interference.[145] In other words, "while Article 3 is considered lex specialis, if grave interferences with a person's well-being are in question, the right to private life is applied when the interference does not reach the threshold required to qualify it as torture or inhuman treatment.".[146]

In relation to human rights and medicine, the Oviedo Convention protects bodily integrity under Article 1 and it guarantees to everyone, without discrimination, the respect for their integrity and other rights and fundamental freedoms with regard to the application of biology and medicine.[147] Moreover, at European Union level, the EU Charter of Fundamental Rights mentions in its Article 3 that "everyone has the right to respect for his or her physical and mental integrity" and that "in the fields of medicine and biology, the following must be respected in particular[148]".[149] In its judgment of 9 October 2001 in Case C-377/98 Netherlands v European Parliament and Council, the Court of Justice confirmed that a fundamental right to human integrity is part of Union law and encompasses, in the context of medicine and biology, the free and informed consent of the donor and recipient.

Non-therapeutic and unconsented surgeries violate the right to bodily integrity including practices such as 'corrective' genital surgery performed on intersex children and gender reassignment surgery. Yogyakarta principles recognise explicitly the right to bodily and mental integrity in relation to intersex people: "no one shall be subjected to invasive or irreversible medical procedures that modify sex charac-

---

[144] Storck v. Germany, judgment of 16 June 2005, para. 143.

[145] In Bensaid v. UK, the Court mentions in para. 34: "While it is true that Article 3 has been more commonly applied by the Court in contexts in which the risk to the individual of being subjected to any of the proscribed forms of treatment emanates from intentionally inflicted acts of the public authorities or non-State bodies in the receiving country (e.g. the Ahmed v. Austria judgment, loc. cit., § 44), the Court has, in light of the fundamental importance of Article 3, reserved to itself sufficient flexibility to address the application of that Article in other contexts which might arise". Then, in para. 46 the Court clarifies the scope of Articles 3 and 8: "Not every act or measure which adversely affects moral or physical integrity will interfere with the right to respect to private life guaranteed by Article 8. However, the Court's case-law does not exclude that treatment which does not reach the severity of Article 3 treatment may nonetheless breach Article 8 in its private life aspect where there are sufficiently adverse effects on physical and moral integrity (see the Costello-Roberts v. the United Kingdom judgment of 25 March 1993, Series A no. 247-C, § 36)".

[146] Hembach Legal, "Physical and psychological integrity pursuant to article 8 ECHR". See also Y.F v. Turkey, judgment of 22 July 2003, Bensaid v. the U.K, judgment of 6 February 2001 and Storck v. Germany, judgment of 16 June 2005.

[147] Convention for the Protection of Human Rights and Dignity of the Human Being with regard to the Application of Biology and Medicine: Convention on Human Rights and Biomedicine, 4. IV.1997.

[148] Charter of Fundamental Rights of the European Union, 2000/C 364/01.

[149] It should be noted that, in its judgment of 9 October 2001 in Case C-377/98 Netherlands v European Parliament and Council, the Court of Justice confirmed that a fundamental right to human integrity is part of Union law and encompasses, in the context of medicine and biology, the free and informed consent of the donor and recipient.

teristics without their free, prior and informed consent, unless necessary to avoid serious, urgent and irreparable harm to the concerned person."[150] Especially intersex children are vulnerable to such practices, as they are unable to defend themselves, or consent.

During the last years, there has been a tendency to recognise the right to genital autonomy as well, which emanates from the general right of bodily integrity, as a fundamental human right. It can be argued that the right to bodily integrity subsumes any right to genital autonomy and should provide the legal framework for rights-based arguments deployed to minimise the non-consensual genital alteration of children or adults.[151] A typical example of violation of one's genital autonomy is FGM/C,[152] which is often related to intersex surgeries. Nevertheless, male genital cutting is neither internationally condemned nor associated with intersex surgeries. This could be explained, as there are findings on male genital cutting and its benefits for a man's health. According to WHO, there is compelling evidence that male circumcision reduces the risk of heterosexually acquired HIV infection in men by approximately 60%.[153] However, in 2012, a court in Cologne was among the first to criminalise male genital cutting as it was held that boys do have a right to genital autonomy/integrity and sexual self-determination.[154]

As can be seen, this disparate treatment of different forms of genital cutting performed on children suggests that any right to genital autonomy recognised by States or international actors is not a universal human right but, rather, a right belonging only to girls, children and women.[155] Additionally, bodily integrity has not been explicitly codified as an international human right and relying only upon it to elaborate human rights violations resulting from intersex surgeries, could lead to a "cumbersome legal path".[156] As a result, it is best to use the right to bodily integrity in conjunction with other rights, which are already explicitly recognised.

2.3.3 *The Right to Individual Self-determination*

The principle of self-determination means that the individual, as a person who owns a fundamental right of freedom, must be able to determine all the choices that do not involve damage to others, and that the State cannot interfere with the exercise of that freedom.[157] In other words, everyone has full ownership of his/her body and life,

---

[150] Yogyakarta principle 32, 2007.

[151] DeLaet (2012), p. 556.

[152] See Sect. 2.2.3.

[153] WHO, "Male circumcision for HIV prevention".

[154] See Landgericht Köln, 151 Ns 169/11.

[155] DeLaet (2012), p. 557.

[156] Idem, p. 556.

[157] Macioce (2011), p. 2.

and no one else, not even the State, can interfere with the exercise of that ownership.[158]

The right to individual self-determination is a vital element of the "inherent dignity" which according to the Preamble of the UDHR constitutes the foundation of freedom, justice and peace in the world.[159] In the case of intersex, the right to self-determination goes in hand with the right to physical integrity. In his last HRC report, the UN Special Rapporteur mentions that practices of gender reassignment "are rooted in discrimination on the basis of sexual orientation and gender identity, violate the rights to physical integrity and self-determination of individuals and amount to ill-treatment or torture".[160]

The ECtHR considers self-determination to be quite close with "personal autonomy" and therefore it falls within the sphere of the right to private life. In Pretty v. the United Kingdom, the Court held that "though no previous case has established as such any right to self-determination as being contained in Article 8 of the Convention, the Court considers that the notion of personal autonomy is an important principle underlying the interpretation of its guarantees".[161] Later, the right to self-determination was further explored in relation to trans people. In Van Kück v. Germany, the Court discerned that the domestic proceedings "touched upon the applicant's freedom to define herself as a female person, one of the most basic essentials of self-determination".[162] Furthermore, the Court held that the facts complained not only deprived the applicant of a fair hearing, "but also had repercussions on a fundamental aspect of her right to respect for private life, namely her right to gender identity and personal development".[163] The Court added to this that gender identity is one of the most intimate areas of a person's private life.[164] Thereupon, this case shows that within the principle of personal autonomy, a hierarchy can be made, with the freedom to define one's sex as one of the most basic essentials of self-determination.[165]

Yogyakarta principle 32 recognises that "everyone has the right to bodily and mental integrity, autonomy and self-determination irrespective of sexual orientation, gender identity, gender expression or sex characteristics"[166] highlighting that non-consensual intersex surgeries are cosmetic, harmful and constitute a violation of self-determination as intersex individuals do not have the freedom to have full ownership of their body. Doctors and the State, especially in the case of public hos-

---

[158] Idem.

[159] Universal Declaration of Human Rights, Adopted by the General Assembly of the United Nations on 10 December 1948.

[160] A/HRC/31/57, 2016, para. 49.

[161] Pretty v. the UK, judgment of 29 April 2002, para. 61.

[162] Van Kück v. Germany, judgment of 12 June 2003, para. 73.

[163] Idem, para. 75.

[164] Idem, para. 56.

[165] Koffemena (2010), p. 46.

[166] Yogyakarta principles, 2007.

pitals and the welfare State,[167] act as if they "own" intersex bodies and interrupt the exercise and enjoyment of the most fundamental rights of intersex persons in the most violent way. Therefore, the right to self-determination of intersex people is usually connected with their body and the fact that through invasive surgeries others decide about their sex. However, could intersex surgeries be considered as a violation of gender identity as well?

It was already mentioned that gender identity refers to each person's deeply felt internal and individual experience of gender, which may or may not correspond with the sex assigned at birth. The right to gender identity is also a part of the individual's self-determination as the individual is free to choose his/her gender identity and for this reason, his/her gender identity does not have to conform to his/her sex traits. The fact that the right to self-determination entails the right to gender identity is also depicted in academia as there is literature referring to "gender self-determination". It is believed that in the case trans people, "gender self-determination" opens space for multiple embodiments and their expressions by collectivising the struggle against both interpersonal and State violence.[168] In addition, it must be noted that, gender identity is influenced by the biological makeup of the individual but also by society's expectations for that sex.[169]

In the case of intersex, doctors, by assigning a sex to intersex infants without their consent and for non-medical purposes but rather societal, choose their sex characteristics and at the same time they assign to intersex individuals a gender identity. Then, the intersex infant ought to grow up with a different sex than the one he/she was born with and to adjust the development of his/her gender identity accordingly. Albeit human rights discourse focuses on gender identity violations in relation to trans people, intersex people's gender identity is also violated from the very first moment of their birth as gender identity development is altered when their sex traits are undetermined. Therefore, performance of intersex surgeries violates both the right to self-determination and the right to gender identity.

2.3.4 *The Right to Health*

The right to health is an economic, social and cultural right that sets a universal standard of health to which all human beings are entitled. It is described by WHO as the enjoyment of the highest attainable standard of health and it is one of the fundamental rights of every human being.[170] The right to health is protected under

---

[167] See Sect. 2.3.4.

[168] Stanley (2014), p. 91.

[169] Jones (2009), abstract.

[170] Constitution of the World Health Organization, Preamble, Basic Documents, Forty-fifth edition, Supplement, October 2006.

several international documents such as the UDHR,[171] the International Covenant on Economic, Social and Cultural Rights (ICESCR)[172] and the CRC.[173] Under international law, States are obliged to respect, protect and fulfil the right to health. The obligation to respect requires States to refrain from interfering directly or indirectly and the obligation to fulfil requires States to adopt appropriate legislative, administrative, budgetary, judicial, promotional and other measures towards the full realisation of the right to health.[174] The obligation to protect requires States to take measures that prevent third parties from interfering with article 12 of the ICESCR guarantees and the obligation to fulfil contains obligations to facilitate, provide and promote.[175] Failure to respect, protect, or fulfill responsibilities relating to health are construed explicitly in terms of the accountability of the State.[176] Within the European framework, the right to health is guaranteed under the revised European Social Charter[177] and the European Charter of Fundamental Rights.[178] The universality of the right to health implies that it is also applied to intersex people even though they are not explicitly mentioned under international nor European law.

The right to health is interrelated with other rights, and especially in the case of intersex people, the rights to human dignity, life, non-discrimination, equality, the prohibition against torture, privacy and access to information.[179] Hence, health-related impact of discrimination based on sex characteristics prevents intersex people from enjoying other economic, social, cultural, civil and political rights. In turn, the infringement of other human rights impacts the realisation of the right to health.

---

[171] Article 25 para. 1 "(1) Everyone has the right to a standard of living adequate for the health and well-being of himself and of his family, including food, clothing, housing and medical care and necessary social services, and the right to security in the event of unemployment, sickness, disability, widowhood, old age or other lack of livelihood in circumstances beyond his control.".

[172] Article 12 para. 1 "1. The States Parties to the present Covenant recognize the right of everyone to the enjoyment of the highest attainable standard of physical and mental health.".

[173] Article 24 para. 1 "1. States Parties recognize the right of the child to the enjoyment of the highest attainable standard of health and to facilities for the treatment of illness and rehabilitation of health. States Parties shall strive to ensure that no child is deprived of his or her right of access to such health care services.". See also CRC/C/GC/15, 2013.

[174] CESCR General Comment No. 14: The Right to the Highest Attainable Standard of Health (Art. 12), 2000, para. 33.

[175] Idem.

[176] Yamin (2005), p. 1157.

[177] Article 11 "Everyone has the right to benefit from any measures enabling him to enjoy the highest possible standard of health attainable." and Article 13 "Anyone without adequate resources has the right to social and medical assistance."

[178] Article 35 "Everyone has the right of access to preventive health care and the right to benefit from medical treatment under the conditions established by national laws and practices. A high level of human health protection shall be ensured in the definition and implementation of all Union policies and activities.".

[179] CESCR General Comment No. 14: The Right to the Highest Attainable Standard of Health (Art. 12), 2000, para. 3.

Recent developments in public international law stress the right to health as one of the core rights to be considered in line with "human dignity".[180]

Intersex people's right to health is violated from the very beginning of their lives as intersex surgeries prevent them from enjoying the "highest attainable standard of health" they are entitled to. Medically unnecessary intersex surgeries cause irreversible harm to children and even though some would argue that procedures may have evolved and improved in recent years, there remains no evidence that these surgeries are necessary or that the ostensible medical benefits outweigh the harms.[181] Intersex surgeries are often presented as a violation of the right to health committed by the physicians who operate them. Current human rights frameworks, such as the CRC and the Convention on Human Rights and Biomedicine, have been criticised as failing to protect children's rights "in relation to medical experimentation and scientifically risk-laden or uncertain treatment outside of research settings.".[182]

It has to be noted that intersex people may experience violations of their right to health during their lifetime as well, as they need to be guaranteed access to general health services that are appropriate, adequate and respectful of their bodily diversity.[183] They may face discrimination and stigma in the health system, in many cases being subjected to lack of quality of care, institutional violence and forced interventions throughout their lifetime.[184] The importance of access of intersex people to healthcare services has been highlighted by the Special Rapporteur on Torture who stated that "intersex persons are frequently denied medical treatment and subjected to verbal abuse and public humiliation, psychiatric evaluations, forced procedures such as sterilization, "conversion" therapy, hormone therapy and genital-normalizing surgeries under the guise of "reparative therapies. The criminalization of same-sex relationships and pervasive discrimination against intersex persons lead to the denial of health care, information and related services, including the denial of HIV care, in clear violation of international human rights".[185] The Committee on the Elimination of Discrimination against Women has expressed concerns about intersex women as "victims of abuses and mistreatment by health service providers".[186] The Special Rapporteur on Torture has called health-care providers to "be cognizant of, and adapt to, the specific needs of intersex persons"[187] and the States to "undertake appropriate training sessions and community-level gender-sensitization campaigns to combat discriminatory gender stereotypes underlying discrimination and abuses in the provision of health-care intersex persons".[188] Within academia, the impor-

---

[180] Lind (2011), p. 76.

[181] Human Rights Watch and Interact (2017), p. 142. See also Carpenter (2016) and Garland (2016).

[182] Zillén et al. (2017), p. 80.

[183] Council of Europe (2015), p. 32.

[184] WHO (2015), p. 26.

[185] A/HRC/31/57, para. 48.

[186] A/HRC/19/41, para. 56.

[187] A/HRC/22/53, para. 38.

[188] A/HRC/31/57, para. 72 (g).

tance of human rights in the medical field and the interdependence of human rights and medical law has been stressed by Jameson Garland: "as the medical profession is clearly coming to terms with the scientific uncertainties in practice, consciousness of the human rights at stake in current practice should mandate openness to considering the value of rights in medicine, especially in any medical context where the scientific support for treatment is substantially lacking".[189]

The accountability in relation to the violation of the right to health of intersex people may vary, especially in the case of welfare States. At its core, the welfare State is variously described as a government protected social minimum established as a political right and as that part of government activity concerned with securing minimum standards of income, health, nutrition, housing, and education for all citizens as a matter of legal right.[190] In modern welfare States, the provision of right to health to their citizens is also linked with social justice and the construction of a functional democracy. In that case, discrimination and disparities have a significant impact not just in relation to health status but also to laws, policies, and practices that limit popular participation in decision-making and, in turn, the establishment of a genuinely democratic society.[191] "Welfare societies" require levels of pluralistic democracy participation and commitment to fundamental values such as individual rights and gender equality.[192]

Under those circumstances, in the case of denial of healthcare services and/or unnecessary intersex surgeries in welfare States, physicians may violate patient's fundamental rights but at the same time, the State fails to provide the right to health to its intersex citizens and protect them from direct violations, such as the systemic discrimination based on sex within the health system.[193] Moreover, welfare States, by not providing special protection to individuals belonging to marginalised groups such as intersex, not only refrain individuals from the enjoyment of their right to health but they also strip them of their human dignity and jeopardise the proper functioning of democratic societies.

---

[189] Garland (2016), pp. 442–443.

[190] Kahn (2002), p. 190. See also Van Kersbergen and Vis (2014) and Kuhnle and Sander (2010).

[191] Yamin (2005), p. 1157.

[192] Kahn (2002), p. 193.

[193] Yamin (2005), p. 1157. See also Lane and Mæland (1998), Skillen (1985) and Fujimura (2000).

2.4 When Others Decide for Intersex Persons

2.4.1 Parents/Physicians vs Intersex: Decision-Making and Informed Consent

There are only few known studies which consider the experiences of parents whose child has been diagnosed with an intersex condition. These studies have shown that parents reported devastation, disbelief, confusion and all the parents talked about their experience of grief on finding out about their child's condition.[194] The above findings designate that parents may take decisions about their intersex child's future that are not rational but emotional.[195] Moreover, the physicians' expertise does not allow parents to process and question the situation.[196] Kessler's research indicates that even doctors are not sure about the surgeries and they feign confidence to keep patients and parents assured of their expertise.[197] Physicians and parents avoid giving forthright information to the intersex "patient" due to paternalistic desire to avoid inflicting confusion and pain.[198] At the same time, emphasis is placed on the newborn's ability to pass for one sex or the other, thus meeting social expectations, rather than on the child's best interests[199] and welfare.[200]

There are four levels in decision-making: to be informed; to express an informed view; to have that view considered when decisions are made; to be the main decision maker about proposed interventions, if competent to do so and potentially subject to supervision of the courts.[201] It is often argued that children cannot and should not make major decisions, for reasons linked to the four levels listed above. However, when children are involved in health care, several acts of trust may be signified by parental consent to care if a child such as parental trust in clinicians, institutional trust in both parents and clinicians to make decisions in the best interests of the child and child's reliance on all these parties for protection.[202] If information related to intersex surgeries is neither freely shared nor trustworthy, how can one suggest that decisions made by parents on behalf of their children will not undermine their future and can be of "informed consent"?[203]

---

[194] Gough et al. (2008), p. 495. See also Crissman et al. (2011).

[195] See also Steuli et al. (2013); Dayner et al. (2004); Daaboul and Frader (2001); Greenberg (2012).

[196] See also Ittelson and Tamar-Mattis (2016) and Greenberg (2012).

[197] Kessler (1990).

[198] Hester (2004a, b), p. 22.

[199] Article 3 para. 1 of the CRC "In all actions concerning children, whether undertaken by public or private social welfare institutions, courts of law, administrative authorities or legislative bodies, the best interests of the child shall be a primary consideration".

[200] Council of Europe (2015), p. 20.

[201] Alderson (2007), p. 2279.

[202] Garland (2016), p. 291.

[203] Hester (2004a, b), p. 22.

The Convention on the Rights of the Child recognises children's involvement in decision-making and of sharing information, without any age barrier. The central rights regarding the assessment of children's competency for consenting to treatment are the Articles 3 and 12 CRC. Article 3 represents the principle of the child's best interest and states that in all actions concerning children, the best interest of the child shall be a primary consideration. Furthermore, according to Article 12, the child should, in all matters affecting the child, be able to express his or her views freely and these should be given due weight in accordance with the age and maturity of the child. Article 24 para. 2 e of the CRC elaborates that children are entitled to be informed, have access to information and be supported in the use of basic knowledge of child health so that they may enjoy their right to health. The ECHR does not state rights for children, but the rights included in the convention are naturally applicable on both adults and minors. In M.A.K. and R.K. v. the United Kingdom,[204] the Court found an interference with a 9-year-old girl's private life and a breach of article 8 ECHR because medical interventions took place without the mother's approval. In addition, preventing the father from visiting his daughter on the night of her admission to hospital constituted a breach of both applicants' rights to respect of their family life.[205] The right to informed consent is also safeguarded under Article 5 of the Oviedo Convention: "an intervention in the health field may only be carried out after the person concerned has given free and informed consent to it".[206]

The extent of parental involvement and whether it is direct or indirect are important variables in the field of healthcare and can distinguish between a paternalistic approach to the child's healthcare, where the adults decide what is best for the child, and a rights-based approach, where the child is heard and involved in the process.[207] Since intersex surgeries are painful and high-risk with no proven medical benefits, a more child centered approach should be applied, and special attention should be paid to the rights to information and consent of the intersex child. In its latest report on the rights of children in biomedicine, the Committee of Bioethics of the Council of Europe has stressed that parental consent has been proven as "problematic" and there is no evidence that children benefit from these interventions.[208] During the past years, there has been a shift towards a more child centered perspective and several international human rights authorities[209] have called on all nations to either "repeal laws" that permit these procedures or "take measures" to prohibit gender "normalis-

[204] M.A.K. and R.K. v. the United Kingdom, judgment of 23 June 2010.

[205] European Court of Human Rights (2015), p. 12.

[206] See also Salako (2011).

[207] Kilkelly and Donnelly (2006), p. 11.

[208] Zillén et al. (2017), p. 44. See also Garland (2016), Hester (2004a, b) and Ford (2001).

[209] See United Nations: Human Rights Council, A/HRC/19/41, 2011 and A/HRC/29/23, 2015, Report of the Special Rapporteur on Torture to the UN General Assembly A/HRC/22/53, 2013 and A/HRC/31/57, 2016. See also Council of Europe: Parliamentary Assembly of the Council of Europe (PACE), Resolution 1952, 2013 and Resolution 2191, 2017.

ing" treatments that are not necessary for the physical health of the child without the child's free and informed consent.[210] In the case of intersex surgeries, parental informed consent is void and contrary to morals due to the non-therapeutic nature of these procedures which do not target to save the child's life but rather to impose the child's integration in the male/female binary.[211] As a result, when it comes to informed consent, the right of the child to be heard is the most crucial and it requires a delay of any procedures until the child can give the input necessary to ensure that the interventions match the child's gender, sexual interests and other wishes of their bodies.[212]

All the above suggest that with regards to unnecessary gender-related procedures, the focus should be moved from adults to intersex children and their best interests, as these procedures are extremely invasive, and it would be best to be postponed. Changing the narrative[213] from a parent-centered approach towards a child-centered one also constitutes a way to address the inequalities that intersex children face in their access to their own right to be cared for, including by healthcare and their parents.

2.4.2 *Intersex vs Parents/Physicians: Access to Medical Records and Justice*

Freedom of information can be defined as the right to access information held by public bodies.[214] It is an integral part of the fundamental right of freedom of expression, and it is recognised under Article 19 of the UDHR, which states that the fundamental right of freedom of expression encompasses the freedom "to seek, receive and impart information and ideas through any media and regardless of frontiers".[215] In 2016, the UN Special Rapporteur on Torture stated that the denial of information and related services to intersex individuals constitutes a clear violation of international human rights standards such as the Yogyakarta Principles on the Application of International Human Rights Law in relation to Sexual Orientation and Gender Identity.[216] Principle 37 of the Yogyakarta Principles elaborate on rights established to combat impunity, including a right to the truth about individuals' medical histories and access to redress, reparations and restorative treatments; and rights to preserve memory and guarantee the right to know.[217]

---

[210] Zillén et al. (2017), p. 44.

[211] See Fountedaki (2004).

[212] Idem.

[213] On new perspectives on the management of intersex see also Feder (2014) and Hermer (2002).

[214] UNESCO, "Communication and Information".

[215] Universal Declaration of Human Rights, adopted by the General Assembly of the United Nations on 10 December 1948.

[216] A/HRC/31/57, 2016, para. 48.

[217] The Yogyakarta Principles plus 10, Additional Principles And State Obligations On the Application of International Human Rights Law in Relation to Sexual Orientation, Gender Identity,

In relation to access to information and medical records at a European level, the Recommendation of the Committee of Ministers of the Council of Europe No. R (97) 5, recognises that every person shall be enabled to have access to his/her medical data and this access may be refused, limited or delayed only if the law provides for this and if this constitutes a necessary measure in a democratic society in the interests of protecting State security, public safety etc.[218] According to the ECtHR case law, the right to obtain information may be based on Article 2 of the ECHR (right to life), Article 6 (fair trial), Article 8 (the right to private and family life) and Article 10 (freedom of expression).[219] The ECtHR in K.H. and Others v. Slovakia found a violation of Article 8 of the Convention as the applicants had not been allowed to photocopy their medical records[220] and therefore they had not full access to their medical history. The Court also linked the access to medical records with the access to a fair trial under Article 6 of the ECHR by underlining that "the limitations on access to the files created a disproportionate burden on the individual in trying to develop an effective case for litigation and therefore Article 6 § 1 had been violated".[221] In 2015, the Council of Europe in its report on intersex peoples' rights clarified that medical protocols need to ensure that intersex people have the right to full information about treatments and have access to their own medical records and history.[222] Intersex people, who have been operated during their infancy, are often denied access to their medical records, which at the same time leads to the restriction of their access to justice. A typical case is Cheryl Chase, who at age 21 succeeded in gaining access to her medical records as doctors had consulted her parents to never disclose to her that she was operated.[223] Accordingly, intersex people, especially those who are victims of non-consensual surgeries, ought to have access to their medical records and be able to access justice, address impunity and claim reparations.

2.5 Living As Intersex

Living as intersex under binary legal frameworks remains a challenge as intersex individuals are often not legally recognised and their right to found a family is not guaranteed. The legal recognition of intersex including sex/gender markers on birth certificates, identification documents and passports has been also of major

Gender Expression And Sex Characteristics to Complement the Yogyakarta Principles, as adopted on 10 November 2017.

[218] Council of Europe, Committee of Ministers, Recommendation No. R (97) 5 on the Protection of Medical Data, 1997, paras. 8.1 and 8.2.

[219] Tiilika (2013), p. 79.

[220] K.H. and Others v. Slovakia, judgment of 28 April 2009, para. 68.

[221] Idem, para. 64-65.

[222] Council of Europe (2015), p. 33.

[223] Chase (1998), pp. 303–304.

importance to intersex rights activists. Intersex organisations have demanded officially through the Malta Statement "to register intersex children as females or males, with the awareness that, they may grow up to identify with a different sex or gender" and "to ensure that sex or gender classifications are amendable through a simple administrative procedure after the request of the individuals concerned. All adults and capable minors should be able to choose between female (F), male (M), non-binary or multiple options. In the future, as with race or religion, sex or gender should not be a category on birth certificates or identification documents for anybody".[224] The Public Statements by the African Intersex Movement and the Asian Intersex Movement confirm this position.[225] The Vienna Statement proposed to "install an easy administrative process to facilitate gender/sex marker change on the basis of self-determination and self-declaration. A neutral marker should be made available".[226] The Darlington Statement added also the problematic of the introduction of a "third gender" and intersex, that will be analysed in the subsequent Chapters, and stated that: "Regarding sex/gender classifications, sex and gender binaries are upheld by structural violence. Additionally, attempts to classify intersex people as a third sex/gender do not respect our diversity or right to self-determination. These can inflict wide-ranging harm regardless of whether an intersex person identifies with binary legal sex assigned at birth or not".[227] In addition, the Statement underlined that the fact that emphasising only on how to classify intersex people rather than how they are treated constitutes a form of structural violence and the larger goal is not end legal classification systems and the hierarchies that lie behind them.[228] To this aim, "(a) as with race or religion, sex/gender should not be a legal category on birth certificates or identification documents for anybody. While sex/gender classifications remain legally required, sex/gender assignments must be regarded as provisional (b) given existing social conditions, we do not support the imposition of a third sex classification when births are initially registered (c) recognising that any child may grow up to identify with a different sex/gender, and that the decision about the sex of rearing of an intersex child may have been incorrect, sex/gender classifications must be legally correctable through a simple administrative procedure at the request of the individual concerned (d) individuals able to consent should be able to choose between female (F), male (M), non-binary, alternative gender markers, or multiple options".[229]

When it comes to the right to found a family, the Darlington Statement under its "Human rights and legal reform" section called "for all adults to have the right to marry and form a family irrespective of their sex characteristics".[230] The Public

---

[224] Idem.

[225] Public Statement by the African Intersex Movement, 2017, "Demands" and Public Statement by the Asian Intersex Movement, 2018, para. 31.

[226] OII Europe, Statement of the 1st European Intersex Community Event, Vienna, 2017.

[227] Darlington Statement, 2017, para. 8.

[228] Idem.

[229] Idem.

[230] Darlington Statement, 2017, para. 12.

Statement by the Asian Intersex Movement demanded to "ensure equal and non-discriminatory legal protection for intersex people in marriage and adoption laws".[231] In the next sections, the rights to legal recognition and to found a family of intersex people will be explored.

2.5.1 Access to Identification Documents

The societal classification of humankind into two sex/gender categories and their entrenchment in identification documents, expose intersex people to human rights violations. Intersex people face two main issues regarding their access to identification documents: the registration of sex on birth certificates and the assignment of their legal sex/gender.

The issuance of identification documents is directly linked to the scrutiny of the State and therefore even though there are developments at a regional level, it is hard to legislate on the matter at an international and European level. To date, human rights developments have mostly dealt with gender recognition in relation to trans people. The United Nations High Commissioner for Human Rights has mentioned that "in many countries, transgender persons are unable to obtain legal recognition of their preferred gender, including a change in recorded sex and first name on State-issued identity documents. As a result, they encounter many practical difficulties, including when applying for employment, housing, bank credit or State benefits, or when travelling abroad.".[232] The ECtHR in A.P., Garçon and Nicot v. France stated that France, refusing to allow two applicants to change their gender marker with the motivation that they had not irreversibly transformed their appearance, violated Article 8.[233] The Court noted that the consent given to medical treatment, which would have in high probability lead to sterility, forming a mandatory prerequisite to legal gender recognition was invalid, as it forced trans people to choose between their right to bodily integrity and their right to the recognition of gender identity.[234]

Intersex and trans people's legal recognition differ significantly as intersex people are discriminated on the grounds of sex/sex characteristics and trans people are discriminated on the grounds of gender/gender identity. Nonetheless, few common points could be identified. First, trans individuals often need to go through gender consensual reassignment surgeries that usually lead to sterilisation to be legally recognised. Intersex individuals are often operated during infancy as physicians and parents need to fill in binary birth certificates. Intersex surgeries also lead to sterilisation as in the case of gender reassignment surgeries, but they are non-consensual. In other words, albeit trans people must choose between their right to bodily integ-

[231] Public Statement by the Asian Intersex Movement, 2018, para. 19.

[232] A/HRC/19/41, 2011, para. 71.

[233] A.P., Garçon and Nicot v. France, judgment of 6 April 2017, para. 135.

[234] Transgender Europe, Trans Network Balkan, ILGA Europe, Subversive Front, 2017, para. 11.

rity and their right to legal recognition, intersex individuals do not have the right to choose between their bodily integrity and legal recognition, but they are forcibly operated after birth. Second, non-operated intersex individuals who identify as male or female, in the absence of legal frameworks on intersex rights, may probably have to go through the same procedure as trans individuals to be legally recognised in binary identification documents. Consequently, intersex individuals in many States are completely invisible in law because even if they identify as male/female or intersex, there is no explicit intersex legal recognition framework as in the case of trans. There are few States that have explicitly legislated on the matter by issuing third or blank classifications for intersex and those case studies will be later analysed.

The Council of Europe has called for non-binary gender classifications to be available on a voluntary, opt-in basis and for greater consideration of the implications of new sex classifications on intersex people.[235] Furthermore, it has acknowledged concerns about the recognition of third and blank classifications, stating that these may lead to forced outings and an increase in pressure on parents of intersex children to decide in favour of one sex.[236] Specifically, Mauro Cabral, indicated that any recognition outside the female/male dichotomy needs to be adequately planned and executed with a human rights point of view, noting that: "People tend to identify a third sex with freedom from the gender binary, but that is not necessarily the case. If only trans and/or intersex people can access that third category, or if they are compulsively assigned a third sex, then the gender binary gets stronger, not weaker".[237] Last, Yogyakarta Principles stipulate that "everyone has the right to obtain identity documents, including birth certificates, regardless of sexual orientation, gender identity, gender expression or sex characteristics. Everyone has the right to change gendered information in such documents while gendered information is included in them.".[238]

Legal recognition of intersex people may be a complex and long debated issue and therefore more reflection may be needed on non-binary legal identification and securing intersex people's legal recognition. In the subsequent Chapters, regional developments on the issue will be examined and further comments and recommendations will be provided on how intersex could be recognised under the law while guaranteeing their fundamental rights.

[235] Council of Europe (2015), pp. 37–40.

[236] Idem.

[237] Idem, p. 40.

[238] The Yogyakarta Principles plus 10, As adopted on 10 November 2017, para. 31.

2.5.2 *Families Beyond the Binary*

Article 16 (1) of the Universal Declaration of Human Rights stipulates that "men and women of full age, without any limitation due to race, nationality or religion, have the right to marry and to found a family". Furthermore, Article 16 (3) describes the family as a "natural and fundamental group unit of society and is entitled to protection by society and the State". Article 23 of the International Covenant on Civil and Political Rights, in its first and second paragraphs defines the right to family in a similar way to the UDHR, limiting the enjoyment of this right only to men and women.

The notion of family is internationally recognised as a fundamental unit of society, which performs valuable functions for its members and for the community as whole. International standards do not prescribe a specific concept of family as it may vary depending on the concrete historical, social, cultural and economic make-up of the community and of the life circumstances of family members.[239] The absence of a universal concept provides a wide margin of appreciation to States, as they can define the concept of family in national legislation, taking into consideration the various legal systems, religions, customs or traditions within the country.[240] At the same time, the protection of families under international law is linked to the principle of equality, including gender equality, and to the protection of their individual members against all kinds of discrimination.[241] To that aim, the Committee on Economic, Social and Cultural Rights has stated that the concept of family must be understood "in a wide sense".[242] Even though the international human rights instruments and the Human Rights Council enforce heteronormativity by limiting the concept of family between men and women and leave a wide margin of appreciation to the Member States, the ECtHR has moved from the idea of "the family" as a nuclear unit of opposite-sex married parents and their legitimate offspring. In detail, the ECtHR has focused on the interpretation of three articles of the Convention in relation to family life: Article 8 on the right to respect for private and family life, Article 12 on the right to marry and to found a family and Article 14 on prohibition of discrimination. In Christine Goodwin v. the United Kingdom,[243] the Court departed from the traditional concept of marriage between persons of opposite sex and the interdependence between the 'right to marry' and the "right to found a family" in Article 12, and observed that the latter was not a precondition of the former.[244] The Court also stated that Article 12 must no longer always refer to a determination of gender by purely biological criteria, considering that there had

[239] A/HRC/31/37, 2016, para. 22.

[240] Idem, para. 26.

[241] Idem, para. 23.

[242] Committee on Economic, Social and Cultural, General comment No. 4, para. 6, General comment No. 4, para. 6.

[243] Christine Goodwin v. U.K., judgment of 11 July 2002.

[244] Valleala (2014), p. 34.

been major social changes in the institution of marriage since the adoption of the Convention as well as dramatic changes brought by about developments in medicine and science in the field of transsexuality.[245] Last, the Court noted that in the Article 9[246] of the European Union Charter of Fundamental Rights, the reference to a man and a woman had been deliberately removed.[247]

It is essential to note that, texts such as the UDHR and the ICCPR were adopted in 1948 and 1966 where intersex people were still invisible. These texts depict family as a 'natural' unit and the right to marry and found a family is granted only to men and women. Intersex people who are born with natural variations in sex characteristics prove that the concept of 'natural' or 'biological' has significantly evolved during the years. Nonetheless, the right to marry and found a family is still reserved to men and women discriminating against intersex people and refraining them from the full enjoyment of their fundamental rights. As it was already mentioned, the ECtHR has noted that the institution of marriage has significantly changed over the years and therefore the right to marry must no longer refer to the biological determination of gender. This reasoning implies that gender is a social construction using the typical example of trans people who experience "gender identity" issues. On the other hand, intersex people prove that nature is not only about being born as female or male and the sex binary is an outdated social construction exactly as gender. Therefore, the right to marry can no longer refer to the traditional biological determination of neither sex and/or gender as this dichotomy violates the fundamental rights of a significant part of the population that falls outside the binary.

Intersex people's right to found a family is violated from the very beginning of their lives, as often they may be subjected to non-consensual sex/gender "normalising" surgeries that lead to their sterilisation. The Council of Europe in its report on intersex people's rights notes that "such sterilisation practices violate fundamental human rights, including the right to decide on the number and spacing of children, the right to found a family and the right to be free from discrimination".[248] At the same time, the Yogyakarta Principles focus only on the right of intersex people to access surrogacy by stating that surrogacy, where legal, should be provided without discrimination, based on sex characteristics.[249]

Considering the above, the problematic could also focus on whether a sterilised intersex individual, should be offered the same options of Assisted Reproductive Technologies (ART) as any infertile person. During the last years, the advancement of reproductive technologies has offered a wide range of options to infertile people but there is no international nor European consensus concerning the regulation of access to reproductive technologies, and there are no enforceable, international

---

[245] Idem.

[246] "The right to marry and the right to found a family shall be guaranteed in accordance with the national laws governing the exercise of these rights."

[247] Christine Goodwin v. U.K., judgment of 11 July 2002, para. 100.

[248] Council of Europe (2015), p. 25.

[249] The Yogyakarta Principles plus 10, Relating to the right to found a family (Principle 24).

obligations for States to allow equal access to reproductive technologies in their healthcare systems.[250]

Since Assisted Reproductive Technologies include a variety of reproductive options, the ECtHR has been adopting a case-to-case approach on the matter. For instance, the Court treated differently Costa and Pavan v. Italy,[251] which concerned Preimplantation Diagnosis (PID) and homologous insemination, and S.H. and Others v. Austria,[252] which concerned access to donor insemination. In addition, in the field of reproductive rights, the Court has used widely the margin of appreciation doctrine leaving discretionary power to States to make best choice decisions as it is a field where diverse cultural, legal traditions and diverse societal norms among different States prevail.[253] Still, the reasoning in Costa and Pavan v. Italy, where the Court held that there had been a violation of Article 8 due to the inconsistency in Italian law that denied a couple to access embryo screening,[254] has demonstrated the increasing willingness of the Court to limit the margin of appreciation the States possess in legislative matters concerning ethically controversial areas. Theoretically, restricting intersex people's access to ART could constitute a discrimination on the grounds of sex. But practically, it would be impossible to pronounce over the right of an intersex individual to access ART from a legal point of view due to the absence of a consensus and the highly controversial nature of the reproductive field.

2.5.3 Discrimination Against Intersex People

Since intersex people are considered individuals with a "disorder" or "difference", they are discriminated against and treated as outcasts worldwide.[255] The principles of equality and non-discrimination are part of the foundations of the rule of law and the international human rights legal framework contains numerous instruments to combat specific forms of discrimination including discrimination based on sex and gender but[256] no specific provision refers to intersex people. It could be argued that "the rights contained in international human rights treaties apply to all people, and thus to intersex people through the conventions' open-ended non-discrimination clauses".[257] Indeed, the UN Committee on Economic Social and Cultural Rights (CESCR), with regard to the ICESCR has stated that "other status" as recognised in Art. 2(2) includes "gender identity [...] as among the prohibited grounds of discrimination", adding that "persons who are transgender, transsexual or intersex

---

[250] Arora (2017), p. 5.

[251] See Costa and Pavan v. Italy, application no. 54270/10, final judgment 11 February 2013.

[252] See S.H. and Others v. Austria, application no. 57813/00, 1 April 2010.

[253] Arora (2017), p. 3.

[254] See Costa and Pavan v. Italy, application no. 54270/10, final judgment 11 February 2013.

[255] See Ghattas (2013).

[256] United Nations and the Rule of Law, "Equality and Non-discrimination". See also Sect. 1.3.2.

[257] Agius (2015), p. 19.

often face serious human rights violations, such as harassment in schools or in the workplace."[258]

The Convention on the Elimination of All Forms of Discrimination Against Women (CEDAW) is designed to protect rights exclusively related with sex and gender but its binary understanding implies that only women's rights are covered: Article 1 prescribes the term "discrimination against women" as "any distinction, exclusion or restriction made on the basis of sex which has the effect or purpose of impairing or nullifying the recognition, enjoyment or exercise by women, irrespective of their marital status, on a basis of equality of men and women, of human rights and fundamental freedoms in the political, economic, social, cultural, civil or any other field.". However, Meghan Campbell mentions that "there is an implicit commitment to address all forms of oppression and disadvantage women experience, including intersectional discrimination".[259] Truly, the Committee on the Elimination of All Forms of Discrimination Against Women (CEDAW) has issued recommendations and developed jurisprudence[260] on intersectional discrimination and has explicitly mentioned "intersex". General recommendation No. 33 states that "In addition, discrimination against women is compounded by intersecting factors that affect some women to a different degree or in different ways than men and other women. Grounds for intersectional or compounded discrimination may include ethnicity/race, indigenous or minority status, colour, socio-economic status and/or caste, language, religion or belief, political opinion, national origin, marital and/or maternal status, age, urban/rural location, health status, disability, property ownership, and being lesbian, bisexual, transgender women or intersex persons".[261] General recommendation No. 35 reaffirms that "discrimination against women is inextricably linked to other factors that affect their lives".[262] The problem that is posed by the Committee's approach is that it treats "intersex" as an additional "factor" and does not aim to expand the binary understanding of the text to cover all non-binary individuals or at least, introduce the ground "sex characteristics". Still, the United Nations has urged governments to "ban discrimination on the basis of sex characteristics, intersex traits or status, including in education, health care, employment, sports and access to public services, and consult intersex people and

[258] E/C.12/GC/20, 2009, para. 32.

[259] Campbell (2015), p. 487.

[260] See Jallow v. Bulgaria, 2012; S.V.P. v. Bulgaria, 2012; Kell v. Canada, 2012; A.S. v. Hungary, 2006; R. P. B. v. the Philippines, 2014; M.W. v. Denmark, 2016, among others and inquiries (in particular, concerning Mexico (2005) and Canada (2015)).

[261] CEDAW/C/GC/33, 2015, para. 8. See also other general recommendations relevant to intersectional discrimination: general recommendation No. 15 on women and AIDS, No. 18 on women with disabilities, No. 21 on equality in marriage and family relations, No. 24 on women and health, No. 26 on women migrant workers, No. 27 on older women and protection of their human rights, No. 30 on women in conflict prevention, conflict and post-conflict situations, No. 31 on harmful practices, No. 32 on the gender-related dimensions of refugee status, asylum, nationality and statelessness of women and No. 34 on the rights of rural women.

[262] CEDAW/C/GC/35, 2017, para. 12.

organizations when developing legislation and policies that impact their rights".[263] At a European level, the ECHR protects everybody including intersex as it contains an open-ended list of prohibited grounds of discrimination and the ECtHR case law has interpreted its articles to cover sexual minorities so far.[264] Moreover, in its report on the human rights of intersex people, the Council of Europe acknowledged that intersex people are extremely vulnerable to discrimination due to "their invisibility and the general lack of knowledge about intersex issues in society that can result in the perpetration of discrimination with impunity especially in the absence of specific non-discrimination guarantees.".[265]

Intersex people are discriminated from the beginning till the end of their lives and for this reason, intersex organisations have been aiming to end discrimination. The Malta Declaration demands "to build intersex anti-discrimination legislation in addition to other grounds, and to ensure protection against intersectional discrimination".[266] The Public Statement by the African Intesex Movement also highlighted the need for protection against intersectional discrimination.[267] The Statement of Riga recommends that "the adoption of anti-discrimination legislation on the ground of sex characteristics – regardless of the specific appearance or configuration of these characteristics."[268] The Darlington Statement also calls for the introduction of "sex characteristics" as a ground for non-discrimination.[269] The Vienna Statement suggests that "if adding a new ground ("sex characteristics") is not an option "sex characteristics" should be included explicitly in the ground of "sex". Intersex people must benefit from the same rights and protections given to other citizens."[270]

All the above statements have highlighted discrimination against intersex that emanates basically from the performance of intersex surgeries and the lack of legal recognition, but intersex people may also be discriminated in other areas. The Darlington Statement has addressed discrimination in employment and called for the ban of "genetic discrimination, including in insurance and employment".[271] The Malta Statement, the Darlington Statement, the Public Statement by the African Intersex Movement and the Asian Intersex Movement have all called for equal participation and access in sports. Therefore, in the upcoming sections discrimination against intersex in employment and in sports will be explored. It has to be noted that discrimination in education will not be analysed as intersex organisations' demands in relation with education concern mostly policy-making and this research focuses on the analysis of legal matters.

---

[263] United NatIons Free & Equal, Fact Sheet "Intersex".

[264] See Sect. 4.2.

[265] Council of Europe (2015), p. 43.

[266] OII Europe, Malta Declaration, 2013, "Demands".

[267] Public Statement by the African Intersex Movement, 2017, "Demands".

[268] OII Europe, Statement of Riga, 2014, para. 2.

[269] Darlington Statement, 2017, para. 9.

[270] OII Europe, Statement of the 1st European Intersex Community Event, 2017.

[271] Darlington Statement, 2017, para. 11.

2.5.3.1 Employment

Discrimination in employment may deprive intersex people of their voice at work and their ability to fully participate. It also accentuates social and gender inequalities and is the basis for social exclusion and poverty.[272] The UDHR recognises that "everyone has the right to work, to free choice of employment, to just and favorable conditions of work and to protection against unemployment" and the right to equal pay for equal work without any discrimination.[273] Article 7 of the ICESCR establishes that everyone has the right to just and favorable conditions of work, fair wages, and equal remuneration for work of equal value; in particular, women are guaranteed conditions of work not inferior to those enjoyed by men.[274]

In 2000, the United Nations launched the UN Global Compact, the world's largest corporate responsibility initiative, to encourage companies to respect universal principles and contribute to a more sustainable and inclusive global economy.[275] In 2017, a paper was launched by the UN Human Rights Office of the High Commissioner on the Standards of Conduct for companies on how to respect and support the rights of LGBT and Intersex people in the workplace, marketplace and community. According to this paper, as of the start of 2017, only 67 out of 193 countries had banned discrimination in employment on grounds of sexual orientation, 20 offered explicit protection on grounds of gender identity or expression and only 3 countries[276] protected intersex persons against discrimination.[277] Growing quantitative evidence has showed that the more patriarchal and male-dominated a society, the more intolerant it will be toward LGBT and Intersex people.[278] In that case, LGBT and Intersex people may face specific vulnerabilities driven by strict gender norms.

Although the ECHR does not itself contain a right to employment, Article 8 has under certain circumstances been interpreted to cover the sphere of employment. A landmark decision of the Court on gender identity and employment is the Christine Goodwin v. UK, where the applicant also complained of the lack of legal recognition of her changed gender in terms of employment. The Court attached major importance "to the clear and uncontested evidence of a continuing international trend in favour not only of increased social acceptance of transsexuals but of legal

[272] ILO, 10. Gender Equality and Non-Discrimination.

[273] Universal Declaration of Human Rights, 1948, Article 23 paras 1 and 2.

[274] International Covenant on Economic, Social and Cultural Rights, 1966, Article 7.

[275] United Nations Human Rights Office of the High Commissioner (2017), p. 3.

[276] Australia and Malta explicitly prohibit discrimination in employment on grounds of sexual orientation, gender identity and sex characteristics (or intersex status, in the case of Australia) through specific legislation. South Africa, through legislative acts broadened the definition of the term "sex" in its anti-discrimination legislation and it should be read to include intersex (See the OHCHR booklet, "Living Free and Equal").

[277] Idem, p. 29.

[278] The World Bank (2016), pp. 14–15.

recognition of the new sexual identity of postoperative transsexuals".[279] The Court clarified that "the current situation of post-operative transsexuals is not sustainable and that in the twenty first century the right of transsexuals to personal development and to physical and moral security in the full sense enjoyed by others in society cannot be regarded as a controversy".[280]

Combating discrimination against intersex in employment is not only about the safeguard of intersex rights but it is about the benefit of societies as a "whole". Securing intersex non-discrimination in employment is an essential part of promoting decent work, tackling gender inequalities and fighting against poverty.

2.5.3.2 Access to Sports

The UN Inter-Agency Task Force on Sport for Development and Peace defines sport, as "all forms of physical activity that contribute to physical fitness, mental well-being and social interaction, such as play, recreation, organized or competitive sport, and indigenous sports and games".[281] Article 24 of the UNDHR grants "the right to rest and leisure", Article 31 of the CRC states that "the right of the child to rest and leisure, to engage in play and recreational activities" and Article 30 of the Convention on the Rights of Persons with Disabilities (CRPD) recognises the right of persons with disabilities to take part on an equal basis with others in leisure and sport. In a human rights and development context, sport is a means by which other ends, such as gender equality, racial equality, health promotion, education development, and social cohesion, can be achieved.[282]

In 2009, Caster Semenya, won the women's world 800 metres world title. Almost immediately some of the other competitors called her victory into question, claiming that she was a man. She was not permitted to compete in any other events by the International Association of Athletics Federation (IAAF) until July 2010 by which time she had fully received adequate medical therapy.[283] Later, four women were found to have testosterone levels and after further investigation, it was concluded that they were intersex.[284]

In 2011, the IAAF and International Olympic Committee (IOC) introduced regulations instituting eligibility regulations on women athletes with naturally-elevated testosterone levels.[285] The IAAF regulations cause female athletes with endogenous

[279] Christine Goodwin v. U.K., judgment of 11 July 2002, para. 85.

[280] Idem, para. 90.

[281] United Nations, Office on Sport for Development and Peace.

[282] Ireland-Piper and Weinert (2014), p. 7.

[283] Newbould (2016), p. 256.

[284] Idem.

[285] See International Association of Athletics Federations. IAAF Regulations Governing Eligibility of Females With Hyperandrogenism to Compete in Women's Competitions and International Olympic Committee. IOC Regulations on Female Hyperandrogenism.

testosterone levels above 10 nmol/L[286] to be suspended or to be banned from competition unless they undergo medical intervention to lower their testosterone levels. Consequently, the need to undergo castration and other surgical and medical interventions is imposed on those women discriminating them from women who pursue other careers.

The IOC/IAAF policy has been characterised as motivated by a misguided sense of "fairness" where policymakers seem to believe that some natural qualities in women are significantly associated with outstanding athletic performance that, unlike other naturally occurring variations that may affect performance, they must be diagnosed by testing and reduced or eliminated by medical intervention to create "fairness" in athletic competition.[287] The concept of "fairness" and eligibility in sports based on "gender" has been in the core of debates for a long time and it has mainly involved binary distinctions that are challenged by doped athletes and the eligibility of trans women to compete with women. Some argue that there is a parallel between athletes who use steroids and trans athletes[288] and others argue that advantages that trans athletes possess differ substantially from the advantages of doped athletes.[289] Knox and Anderson conclude that even though trans women may challenge the rule of "fairness", "sport is rife with inequities, including those arising from the genetic lottery that results in some of us being very short and others very tall. This gives weight to the argument that we should allow trans-women with high levels of testosterone to compete against cis women."[290] All the above show that there is no consensus on whether "fairness" in sports depends strictly on biological factors as there is no sufficient research, therefore "given the impact of decisions relating to transgender and intersex athletes, there is now an urgent need to determine not only what physical advantages transgender women carry but also what effect these advantages may have on transgender women competing against cisgender women in a variety of different sports."[291] It should be noted that, medical intervention could mean sacrificing fertility as a male for a trans woman, although this is usually not the case for intersex women since testicular tissue in this context has typically lost fertility.[292]

To date, the application of the IAAF regulations remains suspended after the Court of Arbitration for Sport released in an "Interim Award"—a decision suspend-

---

[286] IAAF Regulations Governing Eligibility of Females with Hyperandrogenism to Compete in Women's Competitions para. 6.5 The Expert Medical Panel shall recommend that the athlete is eligible to compete in women's competition if: (1) she has androgen levels below the normal male range; or (2) she has androgen levels within the normal male range but has an androgen resistance such that she derives no competitive advantage from having androgen levels in the normal male range.

[287] Sonksen et al. (2015), p. 825.

[288] See Devine (2018).

[289] See Teetzel (2006).

[290] Taryn Knox and Lynley Anderson, "Fairness and Inclusion: Is it time to replace the gender binary in elite sport?".

[291] Pitsiladis et al. (2016), p. 387.

[292] Newbould (2016), pp. 257–258.

ing the IAAF's Hyperandrogenism Regulations and invited the IAAF to submit further written evidence and expert reports addressing the concerns expressed regarding those regulations.[293] According to Women's Sports Foundation, eligibility standards for women's sports that require an athlete to demonstrate particular hormone levels promote the policing of gender by medical means, leading to the unwarranted invasions of privacy not only for intersex athletes, but any athlete whose femininity is questioned.[294] Compulsory medical interventions on intersex women athletes keeps on constituting a violation of their right to bodily integrity and personal autonomy and the "source" of the problem is the same as in the case of intersex surgeries: intersex individuals fall outside the strict dichotomy of sex and therefore are excluded from elite athletic competition. To fit in the binary norm, intersex women athletes are forced to undergo medical interventions that directly violate their human rights. Women's foundation considers any policy that singles out women's sports for eligibility based on hormone levels discriminatory. Those policies transmit the message that female athletes are uniquely vulnerable and in need of special protection from "the normal, natural variation in size, skill, and athletic ability that exists among members of either sex".[295]

The UN Special Rapporteur on Health has referred to the participation of intersex people in sports: "In the recent past, women athletes have undergone chromosomal testing, only to discover that they do not possess two X chromosomes. This has led to stigmatization and to spurious exclusion from competitive sport. Recently, certain international and national sporting federations have instead introduced policies banning women with testosterone levels exceeding a certain threshold from participating in competitive sport. However, there is insufficient clinical evidence to establish that those women are afforded a "substantial performance advantage" warranting exclusion. Although currently suspended, following the interim judgement in Chand v. Athletics Federation of India and the International Association of Athletics Federations, these policies have led to women athletes being discriminated against and forced or coerced into "treatment" for hyperandrogenism."[296] In addition, the Rapporteur called sporting organisations to "implement policies in accordance with human rights norms and refrain from introducing policies that force, coerce or otherwise pressure women athletes into undergoing unnecessary, irreversible and harmful medical procedures in order to participate as women in competitive sport" and urged States to "adopt legislation incorporating international human rights standards to protect the rights of intersex persons at all levels of sport, given that they frequently report bullying and discriminatory behaviour, and should take steps to protect the health rights of intersex women in their jurisdiction from interference by third parties".[297]

---

[293] Court of Arbitration for Sport, "The application of the IAAF Hyperandrogenism Regulations remains suspended".

[294] Women's Sports Foundation, p. 1.

[295] Idem.

[296] A/HRC/32/33, 2016, para. 55.

[297] Idem, para. 57.

Several alternative solutions have been proposed aiming to combat discriminatory practices against intersex women practices. For instance, it could be possible to devise a system in which gender categories are abolished but in which athletes are streamed based on any biological parameter, such as height or weight or a combination of them.[298] Another alternative would be to form the two groups on testosterone level rather than gender or men and women could be permitted to compete in accordance with their self-identification, and gonadectomy could be voluntary and not enforced.[299]

2.6 Remarks

From the beginning of their lifetime, intersex people are treated as "abnormal" and are subjected to multiple human rights violations to fit in the binary of male/female. Intersex is the "living" proof that sex is a spectrum and its conception as exclusively "blue" and "pink" constitutes a social construct which aims to dichotomise, divide and categorise individuals into two sexes. In addition, the strictly male/female binary understanding of "sex" allows patriarchy, paternalism, heteronormativity and cisnormativity to prevail in modern societies leading to the implicit "legitimisation" of human rights violations committed against intersex individuals.

Even before intersex lives begin, prospective parents or parent may have the option to use ART and prevent the birth of an intersex infant. Then, often, when an intersex infant is born, is subjected to different treatments and surgeries to become either male or female and fit in the sex binary. The impact of social, cultural and traditional beliefs on sex and gender within the medical field leads to a direct intersectional discriminatory treatment of intersex people based on their sex and gender. The non-consensual assignment of the male or female sex to the intersex infant directly impacts the free development of his/her gender identity, gender expression and sexual orientation. The human dignity of intersex people is violated in order to preserve and sustain non-inclusive societies which promote homogeneity by violating fundamental rights and freedoms and sacrificing the individual well-being.

Intersex surgeries deny the full-ownership of intersex bodies and interfere with the spheres of individual freedoms such as the right to bodily integrity, personal autonomy and self-determination, private life, information, healthcare and the freedom from torture. Intersex surgeries also constitute a form of gender-based violence. General Recommendation No. 35 of the Committee on the Elimination of Discrimination against Women expanded the understanding of gender-based violence to include violations of women's sexual and reproductive rights and called attention to the particular vulnerability to gender-based violence of women who faced intersecting forms of discrimination, including intersex women.[300] The next step would be to expand gender-based violence to intersex people as a whole to

[298] Newbould (2016), p. 258.

[299] Idem.

[300] CEDAW/C/GC/35, para. 12.

preserve their human rights and protect them against non-consensual surgeries that lead to enforced sterilisation.

To eliminate human rights violations that intersex infants face due to the performance of sex/gender "normalising" surgeries there has been a shift towards a more child-centered approach.[301] Nevertheless, this shift will require reformulations of legal rules to guarantee all rights associated with health care and bodily integrity. Treatment protocols will have to ensure access to the highest attainable standard of care for intersex children as well as their involvement in decision-making and access to identification documents will require protections for intersex infants i.e. the inclusion of an alternative sex/gender option for intersex children; or the option of delayed registration in order to allow intersex children to choose a sex/gender in accordance with their gender development.[302]

Despite the fact that intersex surgeries have been widely condemned by human rights institutions and physicians have started managing intersex cases with a more human rights centered approach, it seems challenging to accommodate non-operative intersex individuals in current international and European legal frameworks. Current frameworks are built upon the dichotomy of male/female depriving intersex people from the enjoyment of their human rights in all spheres. The right to family is strictly guaranteed to men and women as the unit of family is perceived as "natural" and "nuclear". Discrimination against intersex people in employment and sports is a missing ground and therefore they remain unprotected in case of breach of their rights. Perhaps a wider interpretation of sex in existing legal documents could safeguard intersex peoples' rights to some degree but still this seems more possible in the case of "open" lists of discrimination grounds such as the ECHR.

When it comes to identification documents and access to healthcare, the State sets limits to the realisation of intersex rights. Especially in the case of identification documents, intersex individuals may have to undergo gender-normalising surgeries to be able to modify their official documents. In those circumstances, the States instead of violating intersex bodily integrity and personal autonomy could introduce alternative human rights centered solutions such as the introduction of alternative classifications to prevent the jeopardy of the rights of intersex citizens within societies. Certainly, assuring respect for rights will also require the continued development of stable societies and of the commitment to constitutionalism as even though societies are receptive to basic rights and human needs of people who fit in the binary,[303] non-binary rights such as intersex rights that question societal, cultural and traditional foundations meet deep resistance.

The accommodation of intersex people within international and European legal frameworks will happen only if the current legal perception of "sex" and "gender" expands to cover all individuals. If the understanding of the above terms extends to embrace the whole spectrum of sex and gender, the universality of human rights will be guaranteed, and no one will be left behind.[304]

---

[301] See Magritte (2012).

[302] Zillén et al. (2017), p. 45.

[303] Henkin (1989), p. 10.

[304] See the United Nations 2030 Agenda for Sustainable Development.

Chapter 3
Towards Intersex Legal Protection Beyond Europe

3.1 SOGI and Intersex Rights in the United Nations

Human rights have been institutionalised globally through the United Nations system and the connections between the development of international human rights institutions, frameworks and policies.[1] At the same time, the development of international human rights law and policy have been influenced by regionalism.[2] Regional human rights bodies monitor, promote and protect human rights around the world. Furthermore, regional human rights systems play a significant role in protecting human rights among their Member States, including by deciding States' responsibility for violations alleged in complaints submitted by individuals.[3] Different theories on the relationship between international and regional human rights law and mechanisms have been advanced over the years. For instance, a growing literature emphasises the extent to which international human rights norms are incorporated into domestic legal systems and how this internalisation affects political actors.[4] Other schools of literature evaluate the empirical relationship between country participation in human rights treaties and country performance on different measures of human rights in practice.[5]

During the last decades, several steps have been taken for the human rights protection of LGBT[6] and intersex people. The UN Charter promotes and encourages "(…) respect for human rights and for fundamental freedoms for all without distinction (…)"[7] and the UDHR states that "everyone is entitled to all the rights and

[1] Engstrom (2017).

[2] Idem.

[3] International Justice Resource Center, "Regional Systems".

[4] See Koh (1997).

[5] See Hathaway (2002), Goodliffe and Hawkins (2006) and Vreeland (2007).

[6] See Harding (2011) and Scherpe (2015).

[7] United Nations Charter, Article 1 (3).

N. Pikramenou, *Intersex Rights*, https://doi.org/10.1007/978-3-030-27554-9_3

freedoms set forth in this Declaration, without distinction of any kind".[8] Despite the broad language of the UN foundational documents, it took years for the UN Member States to start discussing the rights of sexual minorities both at international and regional levels. In April 2003, the Brazilian delegation to the United Nations Commission on Human Rights introduced "a historic and unexpected resolution prohibiting discrimination on the basis of sexual orientation to the United Nations Commission on Human Rights".[9] This resolution elicited strong opposition from a number of countries, including the Vatican, Zimbabwe, Pakistan, Malaysia, Saudi Arabia, and Bahrain.[10] Support for the resolution came from Japan and the European Union, along with a diverse array of many Latin American and Central and Eastern European countries.[11] Three years later, Norway presented a joint statement on human rights violations based on sexual orientation and gender identity on behalf of 54 states.[12]

The first resolution on sexual orientation and gender identity was led by South Africa in 2011 and requested that the UN High Commissioner for Human Rights drafts a report "documenting discriminatory laws and practices and acts of violence against individuals based on their sexual orientation and gender identity".[13] The first ever UN report released in 2011 and detailed the worldwide manifestations of discrimination based on sexual orientation, noting that violence against LGBT persons relies on historical hate-motivated violence and can lead to discrimination in work, health care, education, detention and torture.[14] Consequently, the year of 2011 was marked by two historical events: 85 countries signed on to a statement calling for the decriminalisation of homosexuality and the resolution initiated by South Africa was passed and became the first UN resolution calling for support of LGBT rights.[15]

A second resolution followed in 2014, led by Brazil, Chile, Colombia and Uruguay, requested the UN High Commissioner for Human Rights to update the 2011 report in order to share "good practices and ways to overcome violence and discrimination, in application of existing international human rights law and standards".[16] In 2016, the UN adopted a third resolution on sexual orientation and gender identity as it decided "to appoint, for a period of three years, an Independent Expert on protection against violence and discrimination based on sexual orientation

[8] Universal Declaration of Human Rights, Article 2.

[9] United Nations Human Rights Commission, Campaign Dossier, p. 3.

[10] Idem.

[11] Idem.

[12] See 2006 Joint Statement, 3rd Session of the Human Rights Council, Ambassador & Permanent Representative of Norway to the United Nations Office in Geneva.

[13] HRC RES 17/19 HR, para. 1.

[14] See Annual report of the United Nations High Commissioner for Human Rights and reports of the Office of the High Commissioner and the Secretary-General, A/HRC/19/41, "Discriminatory laws and practices and acts of violence against individuals based on their sexual orientation and gender identity".

[15] Gary and Rubin, 2012.

[16] A/HRC/RES/27/32, para. 2.

and gender identity" with the mandate to "assess the implementation of existing international human rights instruments with regard to ways to overcome violence and discrimination against persons on the basis of sexual orientation or gender identity (...)".[17] Notwithstanding all the efforts on behalf of the UN and its Member States, according to the latest report of the International, Lesbian, Gay, Bisexual, Trans and Intersex Association (ILGA) there are still 72 States where same-sex sexual relations are de facto severely outlawed and in 45 of these States the law is applied to women as well as men.[18] In addition, according to Transgender Europe (TGEU), of 114 mapped countries, in 57, trans people are criminalised and/or prosecuted.[19]

Intersex rights have not been fully discussed at the UN level. The first efforts made by the UN to raise awareness on intersex can be identified in 2014 where a number of UN agencies published an interagency statement where they condemned forced, coercive and involuntary sterilisation on intersex individuals.[20] In 2015, as a part of its Free & Equal campaign, the UN focused on the meaning of intersex and the multiple human rights violations that arise from sex reassignment surgeries on intersex people.[21] The same year, the Member States of the United Nations General Assembly (UNGA) reached an agreement to end inequality by 2030 and adopted the 2030 Agenda for Sustainable Development which includes the 17 Sustainable Development Goals (SDGs).[22] The new Agenda, which is grounded in the Universal Declaration of Human Rights and international human rights treaties, seeks to complete what the previous Millennium Development Goals did not achieve. Even though LGBT and intersex rights are not explicitly mentioned in the text, there is broad language with regards to the inclusion and sexual and reproductive health and rights that encompasses LGBT and intersex issues.

First, the resolution in its preamble mentions that "no one will be left behind", embracing people such as intersex who are marginalised because of their sexual orientation, gender identity and expression, and sex characteristics (SOGIESC). Then, Goal 3[23] "ensures healthy lives and promote well-being for all at all ages"[24] encompassing non-consensual medical procedures on intersex people which violate their bodily integrity, physical autonomy and well-being.[25] Goal 5[26] aims to "achieve gender equality and empower all women and girls"[27] encompassing intersex persons

[17] A/HRC/RES/32/2, para. 3 (a).

[18] Carroll and Mendos, 2017, p. 8.

[19] TGEU, map on "Criminalisation and Prosecution of Trans People", 2018.

[20] See OHCHR, UN Women, UNAIDS, UNDP, UNFPA, UNICEF, WHO, "Eliminating forced, coercive and otherwise involuntary sterilization" An interagency statement, 2014.

[21] See Free & Equal United Nations for LGBT Equality, Factsheet: Intersex, 2015.

[22] United Nations A/RES/70/1, 2015, p. 1.

[23] See also Targets 3.7 and 3.8.

[24] Idem, p. 16.

[25] The Global Forum on MSM & HIV & OutRight Action International (2017), p. 28.

[26] Targets 5.1 and 5.2.

[27] A/RES/70/1, 2015, p. 18.

who identify as "women", "girls" or as "intersex women" and "intersex girls". Target 10.2[28] promotes the social, economic and political inclusion of all irrespective of sex and target 10.3 reduces inequalities imposed by discriminatory laws, policies and practices. Discrimination against intersex people is often reinforced by laws, policies and practices as they exclude them and fail to take their needs into account. As a result, these laws reinforce negative social attitudes such as interphobia. Last, Goal 16[29] promotes "inclusive societies" encouraging modern sex/gender normative societies to recognise and fully integrate non-binary individuals.

The UN Special Rapporteur has released two reports, the first in 2013 and the second in 2016, condemning medical interventions on intersex infants and calling for the prohibition of surgeries that lead to irreversible harm.[30] It seems that a possible next step would be on behalf of the UN Member States to pass a resolution on the prohibition of involuntary sex reassignment surgeries on intersex infants. Nonetheless, the violation of intersex rights is not only limited within the medical field and the pathologisation of intersex bodies. As it was already mentioned in the previous chapter, intersex individuals experience multiple human rights violations in all aspects of their lives that still need to be addressed by the UN Member States both at international and regional level.

As international developments affect directly regional developments and vice versa, the purpose of this Chapter is to analyse regional developments of UN Member States regarding the protection of intersex rights. The aim of this analysis is to provide the reader with a complete understanding of the current situation of intersex rights worldwide and especially across Africa,[31] Asia,[32] Oceania[33] and the Americas (Tables 3.1, 3.2, 3.3 and 3.4).[34] In addition, as the next Chapter focuses on the situation of intersex rights in Europe and within the European Union in particular, the reader will acquire a more comprehensive approach which will help him/her familiarise and deepen in issues regarding intersex rights protection. It is important to realise that, international and regional developments in human rights law are interconnected and interrelated, particularly when States are Member States of the same human rights institutions such as the UN. Besides, during the modern era which is characterised by globalisation, it is crucial to adopt a holistic approach in relation with human rights, as they are universal and essential to all human beings.

In the previous Chapter, human rights violations against intersex were analysed as depicted by the Public Statements of intersex organisations, the UN and the

[28] See Targets 10.2 and 10.3.

[29] A/RES/70/1, 2015, p. 25.

[30] See Human Rights Council A/HRC/22/53, "Report of the Special Rapporteur on torture and other cruel, inhuman or degrading treatment or punishment, Juan E. Méndez", 2013 and Human Rights Council A/HRC/31/57, "Report of the Special Rapporteur on torture and other cruel, inhuman or degrading treatment or punishment", 2016.

[31] See Table 3.1. Legislation and case law on intersex people's rights in Africa.

[32] See Table 3.4. Legislation, case law, practices on intersex people's rights in Asia.

[33] See Table 3.3. Legislation, case law, practices on intersex people's rights in Oceania.

[34] See Table 3.2. Legislation, case law, practices on intersex people's rights in Americas.

Table 3.1 **Legislation** and/or case law on intersex people's rights in Africa

Country Jurisdiction	Physical integrity and bodily autonomy	Modification or Access to identification documents	Third gender or sex classifications	Anti-discrimination protection	Right to marry
Kenya		X			
South Africa		X		X	X
Uganda		X			

Council of Europe. In this Chapter, several countries will be examined with the purpose to deduce to which extend regional jurisdictions have dealt with the intersex legal demands. This study is not comparative, and it will be limited only to countries that have legislated, developed case-law and introduced practices with the aim to recognise and guarantee intersex rights and are members of the United Nations but not of the European Union. Each section of this Chapter will be divided into two subsections. The first subsection will elaborate on sexual orientation and gender identity (SOGI) rights situation in the country and the second on intersex rights. While it is already cited that SOGI should not be confused with intersex, developments on the SOGI field may affect directly intersex rights. As it will be later demonstrated, both sexual orientation and gender identity legal frameworks and case-law rely primarily on the accommodation of "sex" and "gender" and therefore, they often overlap with legal issues surrounding intersex. Moreover, both

Table 3.2 **Legislation**, case law, **practices** on intersex people's rights in Americas

Country Jurisdiction	Physical integrity and bodily autonomy	Modification or Access to identification documents	Third gender or sex classifications	Anti-discrimination protection	Right to marry
Argentina		X			
Chile	X *condemned surgeries under Circular 18 before the new Circular 7 that pathologises intersex	X *pending legislation	X	X	X
Colombia	X	X			
United States	X *State level (resolution)		X *State level		

LGBT and intersex persons are considered as sexual minorities and may be victims of the same human rights violations. In that case, laws on SOGI and intersex may function as complementary. Last, the efficiency of intersex practices, legal frameworks and case-law will be observed.

This Chapter provides the reader with the situation of intersex rights in Africa, Americas, Oceania and Asia and prepares her/him adequately for the following

Table 3.3 **Legislation,** case law, **practices** on intersex people's rights in Oceania

Country Jurisdiction	Physical integrity and bodily autonomy	Modification or Access to identification documents	Third gender or sex classifications	Anti-discrimination protection	Right to marry
Australia		X *State laws	X *Federal policies for passports	X *Commonwealth law	X
New Zealand		X *the Citizenship and Passport Offices have also introduced policies	X *Passports		X

Chapter where the situation of intersex rights within the EU Member States is analysed. The main purpose of both Chaps. 3 and 4 is to illustrate the exact and full situation of intersex rights globally. Finally, the remarks provided in this Chapter will serve as a basis for the recommendations on the best protection of intersex rights which will be explored in the last Chap. 5.

3.2 Africa

SOGI rights in Africa could be considered as limited, considering the fact that 33 African States outlaw same-sex sexual acts.[35] There is also a lack of research on trans issues and populations in Africa, and it is possible that the invisibility of

[35] Illegal same-sex sexual acts in Africa (33 States: 24 of which apply to women): Algeria, Angola, Botswana, Burundi, Cameroon, Comoros, Eritrea, Ethiopia, Gambia, Ghana, Guinea, Kenya, Liberia, Libya, Malawi, Mauritania, Mauritius, Morocco, Namibia, Nigeria, Senegal, Sierra

Table 3.4 **Legislation**, case law, **practices** on intersex people's rights in Asia

Country Jurisdiction	Physical integrity and bodily autonomy	Modification or Access to identification documents	Third gender or sex classifications	Anti-discrimination	Right to marry
Bangladesh			X		
India		X	X		
Nepal		X	X		
Pakistan			X	X	
Philippines		X			
Viet Nam		X			

transgender people in epidemiological data is related to the criminalisation of same-sex behaviour in many countries and the subsequent fear of negative repercussions from participation in research.[36] Alternatively, trans people may be being overlooked in research due to confusion among researchers about how to ask questions about gender identity.[37]

Intersex persons have been referred to as "hermaphrodites" or persons with "disorders of sexual development" (DSD), no research has been done in Africa to establish the number of intersex persons and there is misconception around intersex, sexual orientation and gender identity.[38] The main challenges faced by intersex people are coerced, uninformed and unnecessary genital normalising surgeries on minors, infanticide and dumping of intersex children, lack of appropriate legal recognition and poor birth registration and other civil status administrative processes, unfair discrimination in schools resulting in school drop-outs, and discrimination in healthcare facilities, competitive sports, work place, and places of detention.[39]

The African Charter on Human and Peoples' Rights entered into force on October 21, 1986 and guarantees individuals many of the same civil, political, social, and economic rights as the ICCPR and ICESCR.[40] Article 2 of the African Charter underlines that the rights in the Charter may be invoked "without distinction of any kind such as race, ethnic group, color, sex, language, religion, political or any other opinion, national or social origin, fortune, birth or other status". The use of the "such as" and "or other status" shows that the list of grounds for non-discrimination is non-exhaustive.

The African Commission on Human and Peoples' rights has explicitly included sexual orientation and gender identity in its soft law instruments. The 275 Resolution on Protection against Violence and other Human Rights Violations against Persons on the basis of their real or imputed Sexual Orientation or Gender Identity condemns the acts of violence, discrimination and other human rights violations committed on individuals in many parts of Africa because of their actual or imputed sexual orientation or gender identity.[41] Furthermore, the Commission's General Comment No. 4 notes that anyone, regardless of their gender, may be a victim of sexual and gender-based violence that amounts to torture or ill-treatment. And in

---

Leone, Somalia, South Sudan, Sudan, Swaziland, Tanzania, Togo, Tunisia, Uganda, Zambia and Zimbabwe. See ILGA, "State-Sponsored Homophobia, A World Survey of Sexual Orientation Laws: Criminalisation, Protection and Recognition", 11th Edition, Updated to October 2016.

[36] Jobson et al. (2012), p. 160.

[37] Idem.

[38] SOGIE Unit, "Fact sheet on intersex persons".

[39] Idem.

[40] African (Banjul) Charter on Human and Peoples' Rights Adopted 27 June 1981, OAU Doc. CAB/LEG/67/3 rev. 5, 21 I.L.M. 58 (1982), entered into force 21 October 1986.

[41] 275: Resolution on Protection against Violence and other Human Rights Violations against Persons on the basis of their real or imputed Sexual Orientation or Gender Identity, Adopted at the 55th Ordinary Session of the African Commission on Human and Peoples' Rights in Luanda, Angola, 28 April to 12 May 2014.

this regard, "lesbian, gay, bisexual, transgender and intersex persons are of equal concern.".[42]

In 2017, the First African Intersex Meeting took place in Johannesburg, South Africa where the "Public Statement by the African Intersex Movement" was drafted. The Statement calls to "end the infanticide and killings of intersex people led by traditional and religious beliefs"; put an end to mutilating and "normalising" practices such as genital surgeries through legislative means as intersex people must make their own decisions affecting their own bodily integrity, physical autonomy and self-determination; "ensure that sex or gender classifications are amendable through a simple administrative procedure and all adults and capable minors should be able to choose between female, male, intersex or multiple options"; "ensure that intersex people have the right to full information and access to their medical records and history"; "acknowledge the suffering and injustice caused to intersex people"; "to build intersex anti-discrimination legislation in addition to other grounds, and ensure protection against intersectional discrimination"; "to ensure the provision of all human rights and citizenship rights to intersex people, including the right to marry and form a family".[43]

In this section, Kenya, South Africa and Uganda will be analysed as they are the only jurisdictions in Africa that have introduced legislation and case-law on intersex.

3.2.1 Kenya

3.2.1.1 Situation of SOGI Rights

Homosexuality in Kenya is criminalised by the Penal Code under sections 162 and 165. These provide that any person who has carnal knowledge of any person against the order of nature or permits a male person to have carnal knowledge of him or her against the order of nature is guilty of a felony and is liable to imprisonment for 21 years and 14 years respectfully.[44] There are no specific provisions on lesbian relationships. The attempts to decriminalise homosexuality have in the recent past faced a lot of resistance from government and the citizens of Kenya.[45] There are arguments that the Constitution of Kenya 2010 provides an opportunity for safeguarding the rights of sexual minorities. Those arguments are based on the fact that the

[42] General Comment No. 4 on the African Charter on Human and Peoples' Rights: The Right to Redress for Victims of Torture and Other Cruel, Inhuman or Degrading Punishment or Treatment (Article 5), Adopted at the 21st Extra-Ordinary Session of the African Commission on Human and Peoples' Rights, held from 23 February to 4 March 2017 in Banjul, The Gambia, para. 59.

[43] Astraea Lesbian Foundation for Justice, "Public Statement by the African Intersex Movement".

[44] See Penal Code, Section 162 "Unnatural offences".

[45] Kenya National Commission on Human Rights, 2012, p. 92.

Constitution provides for international law being part of the laws of Kenya.[46] The rights guaranteed in the Kenyan Constitution apply to all sexual minorities. Specifically, on the right to marry, Article 45 (2) of the Constitution provides that "Every adult has the right to marry a person of the opposite sex, based on the free consent of the parties". This means that the Constitution forbids same sex marriages but does not specify same sex relationships as forbidden thus sexual minorities are restricted from formalising their relationships into marriages.[47] The Constitution accords everyone including sexual minorities the right to life (Article 26), the right to equality and non-discrimination (Article 27 (4)), the right to human dignity (Article 28), the right to privacy (Article 31), freedom and security of person (Article 29), freedom of expression (Article 33), access to information (Article 35) freedom of association (Article 36), freedom of movement (Article 39), the right to health including reproductive health, right to housing, food, security and education (Article 43).

3.2.1.2 Intersex Rights

For most communities in Kenya, an intersex child is deemed to be a curse and is either abandoned or killed by the community. Most parents of an intersex child do not know that they can opt to have their child go through reconstructive surgery.[48] Intersex children are raised in unsupportive environments where they are hardly given information on their conditions. They grow up in a society that treats them as "freaks" of nature and uses derogatory terms such as "hermaphrodites" to refer to them.[49] In cases of intersex births, the Ministry of Health lacks guidelines directing families and medical practitioners on how to facilitate a child's genuinely informed consent.[50] Most intersex individuals are taken through unnecessary corrective surgeries when they are born or simply assigned a gender role and raised as such without being given a chance to choose their gender or undergo a surgery when they are of age.[51] There are no medical provisions or policies for intersex persons who choose to undergo gender reassignment therapy.[52]

In Kenya, there are some provisions on intersex under the Persons Deprived of Liberty Act of 2014, where Article (3) stipulates that "intersex persons deprived of liberty have the right to decide the sex of the person to do a body search on them." and Article 12 (3) (e) states that "intersex persons deprived of liberty are held sepa-

[46] Article 2 (5) of the 2010 Constitution "The general rules of international law shall form part of the law of Kenya" and Article 2 (6) "Any treaty or convention ratified by Kenya shall form part of the law of Kenya under this Constitution".

[47] Kenya National Commission on Human Rights, 2012, p. 102.

[48] The Kenya Human Rights Commission, 2011, p. 25.

[49] Idem, p. 43.

[50] Idem.

[51] The Kenya Human Rights Commission, 2011, p. 42.

[52] Idem, p. 40.

rate from other persons". The above provisions can be explained as during the last years there have been great developments in Kenyan jurisprudence on intersex.

In 2010, the High Court of Kenya ruled that Richard Muasya, was a victim of inhuman and degrading treatment while he was being held in prison. Muasya, was born intersex and his parents gave him a male name but, as a result of his non-binary sex/gender, he did not obtain a birth certificate and thus could not acquire an identity card or passport.[53] The petitioner was charged with robbery and held in prison. During a routine physical search, the prison officers discovered his "ambiguous genitalia" and could not decide whether to house him in a male or female cell. It was alleged that while he was in prison he was subjected to invasive body searches, mockery and abuse because of his condition.[54]

The petitioner sought the recognition of a third gender and damages for inhuman and degrading treatment. The Court first elaborated on the definition of "intersex" and concluded that "intersex is a term describing an abnormal condition of varying degrees with regard to the sex constitution of a person. The term intersex and the term hermaphrodite may therefore be used interchangeably. It appears however, that the current preference is for the term intersex rather than the term hermaphrodite.".[55] Then, the Court accepted that the petitioner had indeed been inhumanely treated by State officials, under the Constitution and Article 5 of the UDHR and this treatment revealed a lack of respect for the petitioner's human dignity and constituted a violation of his constitutional rights.[56] Furthermore, the Court found that at birth, the petitioner's external genitalia and dominant physiological characteristics fit more with the male sex and that he therefore could have been registered as male under the Births and Deaths Registration Act. As a result, the Court rejected the petitioner's contention that he suffered from a lack of legal recognition based on an inability to have his birth registered and did not agree with the petitioner's assertion that, in order to provide intersex with equal protection of the law, the term "sex" in the Constitution should be interpreted widely to include a third category of gender.[57]

Later, in Baby "A" (Suing through the Mother E.A) & another v Attorney General & 6 others, the High Court ruled that the petitioner, an infant who had been found to have both male and female genitalia, had suffered from the lack of legal recognition and that differential treatment was not on account of discrimination.[58] First, the Court determined that the petitioner was an intersex person, thus recognising that such a category of individuals existed, contrary to the finding in the

[53] International Commission of Jurists, "Richard Muasya v. the Hon. Attorney General, Hight Court of Kenya (2 December 2010).

[54] Idem.

[55] Richard Muasya v. the Hon. Attorney General, Hight Court of Kenya Petition No. 705 of 2007, para. 106.

[56] Idem, paras. 160–170.

[57] International Commission of Jurists, "Richard Muasya v. the Hon. Attorney General, Hight Court of Kenya (2 December 2010) and paras. 119–133.

[58] National Gay and Lesbian Human Rights Commission, Network for Adolescent and Youth of Africa, Gay and Lesbian Coalition of Kenya, East Africa Trans & Advocacy Network, 2017, p. 6.

Richard Muasya case.[59] Second, the Court ordered "appropriate relief" for the petitioner by compelling the Attorney General to file a report identifying the status of a statute addressing intersex persons as well as guidelines and regulations on "corrective surgery" for this group.[60] On May 26, 2017, the Government of Kenya gazetted a taskforce on policy, legal, institutional and administrative reforms regarding intersex persons in Kenya in an effort to implement the decision in the Baby 'A" Case.[61]

The Baby "A" case should be seen as a progressive continuation of the Richard Muasya case as it "broke" cultural norms about sex in relation to intersex. Back in 2010, Justice Sitati, had written that "the Kenyan society is predominantly a traditional African society in terms of social, moral and religious values. We have not reached the stage where such values involving matters of sexuality can be rationalised or compromised through science.".[62] In contrast, Justice Lenaola in the Baby "A" decision stated that "time is now ripe for the development of rules and guidelines on corrective surgeries for intersex children especially minors such as Baby A."[63]

The most important way in which the Baby "A" case differed significantly from the Richard Muasya case is that while the reasoning in the first case was tantamount to erasing persons with intersex conditions by rigidly affirming the male/female binary, the Court in the Baby "A" case departed from this traditional understanding of the meaning of sex as only encompassing the male/female binary.[64] In addition, in the baby "A" case the Court recognised persons with intersex conditions as a class whose rights needed protection.[65] Therefore, though the conclusion of the case did appear to be unfavourable for Baby A as an individual, the petition was successful in raising awareness about the rights of persons with intersex conditions generally.[66] Last, in both cases, the Courts found that the petitioners had not brought evidence of discrimination and this leaves room for further public interest litigation if a petitioner could bring concrete evidence of how lack of legal recognition violates rights including the right to non-discrimination.[67] Nonetheless, despite all these developments, intersex children in Kenya remain unprotected. As it was already mentioned, children who are born intersex are exposed to corrective

[59] Idem and Baby 'A' (suing through the Mother E.A.) & another v. Attorney General & 6 others [2014] eKLR, petition no. 266 of 2013, paras. 51–53.

[60] Idem and paras. 54–67.

[61] The Kenya Gazette, May 26 2017.

[62] Richard Muasya v. the Hon. Attorney General, Hight Court of Kenya Petition No. 705 of 2007, para. 148.

[63] Baby 'A' (suing through the Mother E.A.) & another v. Attorney General & 6 others [2014] eKLR, petition no. 266 of 2013, para. 66.

[64] Kangaude et al. (2017), p. 132.

[65] Baby 'A' (suing through the Mother E.A.) & another v. Attorney General & 6 others [2014] eKLR, petition no. 266 of 2013, para. 61.

[66] Kangaude et al. (2017), p. 132.

[67] Idem.

surgeries and even infanticide. Further legislative structure is needed that will protect intersex children from irreversible surgeries that violate their fundamental rights.

3.2.2 *South Africa*

3.2.2.1 Situation of SOGI Rights

In 1996, the South African government, in addition to ending de jure apartheid, approved a new Constitution that was the first in the world to protect the rights of homosexuals.[68] The Constitution, under Section 9 (3), provides that "The state may not unfairly discriminate directly or indirectly against anyone on one or more grounds, including race, gender, sex, pregnancy, marital status, ethnic or social origin, colour, sexual orientation, age, disability, religion, conscience, belief, culture, language and birth.". During the following decade, emerging jurisprudence and legislation recognised several rights and freedoms to LGBT individuals.

In the 1998 National Coalition for Gay and Lesbian Equality et al. v Minister of Justice et. Al., the Constitutional Court of South Africa overturned the offence of sodomy.[69] In the 2015 decision of Minister of Home Affairs v Fourie, the Constitutional Court ruled that it was unconstitutional for the State to deny to same-sex couples the ability to marry.[70] Later, the Civil Union Act, 2006 came into force which despite its title, recognises same-sex marriages as well.[71]

The Constitutional Court's ruling in Du Toit v Minister of Welfare and Population Development gave same-sex partners the same adoption rights as married spouses.[72] Then, the Children's Act, 2005, allowed adoption by spouses and by partners regardless of sexual orientation.[73] Furthermore, the Alteration of Sex Description and Sex Status Act allows people to apply to have their sex status altered to receive identity

[68] Ilyayambwa (2012), p. 51.

[69] Para. 133 "This judgment holds that in determining the normative limits of permissible sexual conduct, homosexual erotic activity must be treated on an equal basis with heterosexual, in other words, that the same-sex quality of the conduct must not be a consideration in determining where and how the law should intervene (…)".

[70] See Minister of Home Affairs and Another v Fourie and Another (CCT 60/04) [2005] ZACC 19; 2006 (3) BCLR 355 (CC); 2006 (1) SA 524 (CC) (1 December 2005).

[71] Preamble: "And noting that the family law dispensation as it existed after the commencement of the Constitution did not provide for same-sex couples to enjoy the status and the benefits couples with the responsibilities that marriage accords to opposite-sex couples, be it therefore enacted by the Parliament of the Republic of South Africa as follows (…)".

[72] See Du Toit and Another v Minister of Welfare and Population Development and Others (CCT40/01) [2002] ZACC 20; 2002 (10) BCLR 1006; 2003 (2) SA 198 (CC) (10 September 2002).

[73] See Children's Act 38, 2015, Section 231 "Persons who may adopt child".

documents and passports indicating their new sex and it applies to both trans and intersex individuals.[74]

This progressive legislation in relation to SOGI and intersex rights, however, does not reflect the attitudes of most South Africans, who do not support LGBT rights and it appears that there is a gap between South African tolerant laws and the conservative social attitudes of its citizens.[75] Negative public attitudes towards homosexual and transgender communities couple with the State's failure to enforce legal and constitutional protections have led to a pattern of discrimination, violence and extreme prejudice.[76] The main reason for this discrimination is strong societal bias that arises from cultural and gender norms. This prejudice and social stigma against sexual minority groups, is not only perpetuated by general society but also by officers of the State, who are charged with protecting these rights.[77] It is believed that one of the main sources of these gender norms is the previous apartheid state which was characterised by rigid patriarchal norms expressed in dominant, violent and authoritarian forms of masculinity.[78]

3.2.2.2 Intersex Rights

The Judicial Matters Amendment Act, 2005 amended the Promotion of Equality and Prevention of Unfair Discrimination Act, 2000 and includes intersex within its definition of sex. The Act stipulates that ""intersex" means a congenital sexual differentiation which is atypical, to whatever degree; "sex" includes intersex".[79] According to the Act, discrimination based on "sex" causes systemic disadvantage, undermines human dignity and affects the equal enjoyment of a person's rights and freedoms. Considering that the South African law recognises that the spectrum of "sex" includes intersex, it can be argued that the Civil Union Act, 2006 applies to intersex individuals as well and therefore all couples can marry regardless of their characteristics. In addition, the Prevention and Combating of Hate Crimes and Hate Speech Bill condemns hate crimes against intersex: "any person who intentionally publishes, propagates or advocates anything or communicates to one or more persons in a manner that could reasonably construed to demonstrate a clear intention to be harmful or to incite harm or to promote or propagate hatred based on (…) sex, which includes intersex or sexual orientation, is guilty of the offence of hate speech.".[80]

---

[74] See Alteration of Sex Description and Sex Status Act, 2003 enacted by the Parliament of South Africa.

[75] Ilyayambwa (2012), p. 51.

[76] Rosenbloom (2014), p. 55.

[77] Scheepers and Lakani (2017), p. 141.

[78] Rosenbloom (2014), p. 55.

[79] Amendment of section 1 of Act 4 of 2000.

[80] Prevention and Combating of Hate Crimes and Hate Speech Bill, Clause 4, 3.4.1.

The Alteration of Sex Description and Sex Status Act, 2003 allows intersex people to change the sex recorded on their official documents. The applicant must submit a report prepared by a medical practitioner corroborating that the applicant is intersex and a report prepared by a qualified psychologist or social worker corroborating that the applicant is living and has lived stably and satisfactorily, for an unbroken period of at least 2 years, in the gender role corresponding to the sex description under which he or she seeks to be registered.[81] While the country recognises the right of intersex persons to change their sex description, the change is limited to one of two binary categories of male or female and intersex persons can change their sex description only if they live as their "preferred" sex for an uninterrupted period of 2 years.

South Africa may be considered as most progressive when it comes to intersex rights in Africa, but corrective surgeries are still performed on intersex children violating their physical integrity and bodily autonomy. The Committee on the Rights of the Child on its 2016 concluding observations on the second periodic report of South Africa expressed its concerns regarding the high prevalence of harmful practices including violent or harmful initiation rites and intersex genital mutilation.[82] The Committee called South Africa to "guarantee the bodily integrity, autonomy and self-determination of all children, including intersex children, by avoiding unnecessary medical or surgical treatment during infancy and childhood".[83] South African law understands the concept of "evolving capacity" in children and the age of consent for medical procedures begins at 12 years of age for children.[84] This may be interpreted to mean that non-consensual and cosmetic surgeries may not be done on an infant until they are over the age of 12 years and can, with the assistance of their parent, guardian or caregiver, make an informed decision and give full consent.[85] This proposed interpretation is in line with the principle of the best interests of the child and would go a long way in limiting the cases of corrective surgeries which result in forced sterilisation.[86]

Concluding, infanticide needs to be condemned and banned explicitly in the country as in other African countries as well. Some cultures in South Africa believe that intersex infants are "bad omens", a sign of witchcraft, a punishment from God and a curse on the family they are born into. In these instances, it is often understood to be preferable to kill the child and birth parents are often told that their child was

---

[81] Section "Application for alteration of sex description", (2) (d).

[82] CRC/C/ZAF/CO/2*, para. 39.

[83] Idem, para. 40 (d).

[84] Section 129(2) of the Children's Act provides; "A child may consent to his or her own medical treatment or the medical treatment of his or her child ifa. The child is over the age of 12 years; and b. The child is of sufficient maturity and has the mental capacity to understand the benefits, risks, social and other implications of the treatment." Section 129(3) provides similarly in relation to surgical operations and additionally stipulates that a parent, guardian or caregiver may "duly assist".

[85] National Intersex Meeting Report 2018, pp. 21–22.

[86] Idem.

stillborn and not to ask further questions.[87] However, it is not only infants that are being killed. If an intersex child survives birth but is later found to be intersex by rural or traditional communities, this can also put the child's life in danger. In informal research carried out by Northern Cape LGBTI organisation LEGBO between 2008 and 2010 it was discovered that of the 90 traditional birth attendants and midwives interviewed 88 admitted to having 'gotten rid of' ostensibly intersex children after their birth.[88]

3.2.3 Uganda

3.2.3.1 Situation of SOGI Rights

Sexual minorities in Uganda are not significantly protected under the law. The Constitution prohibits marriage between persons of the same sex.[89] According to sections 145 and 146 of the Penal Code, "carnal knowledge of any person against the order of nature" is punishable with up to life imprisonment.[90] As it is hard to prosecute the offence of unnatural offences, the Penal Code has other provisions that can be used against sexual minorities. These are the offences of indecent practices,[91] common nuisance,[92] being idle and disorderly,[93] being rogue and vagabond[94] and personation.[95] The Penal Code does not refer to women, but the Sexual Offences Bill 2015 expands criminalisation of "unnatural offences" to women.[96]

In late 2009, a Ugandan member of Parliament introduced the Anti-Homosexuality Bill that sought to increase punishments for homosexuality as well as the "promotion of homosexuality".[97] The Bill imposed new criminal penalties for "aiding and abetting homosexuality"[98] and failing to report homosexuals to the police. The Bill also allowed Uganda to nullify any of its international and regional commitments that it deemed contradictory to the spirit and provisions enshrined in this Act. After reducing the death penalty provision[99] to life imprisonment, the Parliament passed

[87] Idem, p. 14.

[88] Idem.

[89] Government of Uganda, Constitution of Uganda, 2005, Section 31 Article 2a.

[90] Government of Uganda, Penal Code Act 1950, chapter 120.

[91] Idem, Penal Code Act 1950, Section 148.

[92] Idem, Section 160.

[93] Idem, Section 167.

[94] Idem, Section 168.

[95] Idem, Section 381.

[96] Bill No. 35, Sexual Offences Bill, 2015, Part II, Section 16 (c).

[97] Human Rights first, p. 1.

[98] Bill No. 18, The Anti Homosexuality Act, 2009, Part I, Section 7.

[99] Idem, See Section 3 and (2) "A person who commits the offence of aggravated homosexuality shall be liable on conviction to suffer death".

the bill in December of 2013[100] and the new law was promulgated in February 2014.[101] Critics explicitly connected the timing of the Anti-Homosexuality Bill with other policies such as the Non-Governmental Organisation Registration (Amendment) Bill, which would allow the NGO Board to dissolve any organisation for any reason "necessary for the public interest", or The Public Order Management Act of 2013, which gives the police wide powers to issue orders to disperse public meetings.[102]

When the Act was put to vote by the Parliament, members of Parliament, most notably the Prime Minister, twice asserted that there was not a quorum present, as required under the Uganda Constitution.[103] On 1st August 2014, in the case of Prof J. Oloka Onyango & 9 Others v Attorney General, the Constitutional Court found that the Anti-Homosexuality Act, 2014 was enacted when there was no quorum. This was unconstitutional and rendered the Act null and void.[104] This case is significant for the LGBT and intersex community in Uganda as it annulled the Act. An opportunity was therefore missed when the Court avoided determining the substantive human rights issues. Its decision on this would have created further opportunities to bring the matter before regional or international tribunals or courts, depending on the outcome in the national court.[105] Following the annulment of the Act, The Prohibition of Promotion of Unnatural Sexual Practices Bill was circulated by members of the ruling party in October 2014 but there is no indication that it has been put before parliament.[106]

Nonetheless, the violation of human rights of sexual minorities persists. Openly LGBT Ugandans confront stigma, discrimination, legal restrictions, harassment, intimidation, violence and death threats.[107] Ugandan families have been known to discriminate against and disown LGBT family members whose sexual orientation or gender identities (SOGI) are exposed. A Pew Research Center survey in June 2013 reported that 96 percent of Ugandans disapprove of homosexuality.[108]

Members of the police have arrested LGBT and intersex persons without following due process and without giving them the details of their arrests. In many cases, those arrested are subjected to lengthy pre-trial detention.[109] Further, police officers in Uganda are responsible for the widespread application of public order laws in a discriminatory and selective fashion against LGBT and intersex individuals.[110]

---

[100] McKayl and Angotti (2016).

[101] CNN, "Uganda's President Museveni signs controversial anti-gay bill into law".

[102] McKayl and Angotti (2016).

[103] Kangaude et al. (2017), p. 140.

[104] Prof J. Oloka Onyango & 9 Others v Attorney Gerneral (Constitutional Petition No. 08 of 2014) [2014[UGCC 14 (1 August 2014), Answer to question 2 (i) and (ii).

[105] Kangaude et al. (2017), p. 142.

[106] Independent Advisory Group on Country Information, 2017, p. 14.

[107] Thapa (2015), p. 1.

[108] Idem.

[109] Civil Society Coalition on Human Rights and Constitutional Law et al. (2014), p. 19.

[110] Idem.

Discrimination, transphobia and homophobia reach deeply into personal lives as members of sexual minority groups often are evicted from their homes due to their sexual orientation or gender identify.[111] Ugandan school officials discriminate against students because of their sexual orientation or gender expression, sometimes leading to their being expelled, while LGBT students report that they are bullied and harassed by their classmates.[112] Last, there are numerous instances where Ugandan media have published the names, photographs, and contact details for individuals who are reported to be LGBT and intersex with dangerous consequences for the persons named.[113]

3.2.3.2 Intersex Rights

In Uganda, due to superstition it is often believed that intersex children are witches, or victims of witchcraft and their birth is mostly seen as a punishment of the mother who will in many cases be excluded from society. To protect themselves from that treatment, many parents kill or abandon their intersex infants shortly after their birth.[114] Other children are forced to live a secret life; they are often forced to live in a small hut far from their families to not pass on their "curse".[115]

Many intersex children are also forced to undergo involuntary surgical procedures and mutilation which leads in most cases to long mental and physical scars.[116] This is also dictated by the law, as Section 38 of the Registration of Persons Act 2015 provides that "if a child born a hermaphrodite, after being registered, through an operation, changes from a female to a male or from a male to a female and the change is certified by a medical doctor, the registration officer shall, with the approval of the Executive Director of the Authority upon application of the parents or guardian of that child update the particulars of the child, which appear on the register.". Intersex persons in Uganda are still called "hermaphrodites" which is an outdated and non-human rights friendly term. Even though they are able to modify their identification documents, they need to be operated in order to become "male" or "female". This violates their fundamental rights and forces them to be accommodated within the binary. In reality, they continue to be "invisible" under the law as legal recognition is granted to them only if they follow binary legal frameworks.

In relation to intersex adults, many intersex people experience significant stigma and discrimination in Uganda such as humiliation, ostracism, exploratory rape, evictions from accommodation facilities due to superstitions, lack of access to healthcare, employment, and education to exclusion from community and family

[111] Idem, p. 27.

[112] Idem, p. 30.

[113] Idem, p. 37.

[114] Support Initiative for Persons with Congenital Disorders, 2016.

[115] Idem.

[116] Idem.

life.[117] Intersex persons face unique circumstances and concerns, but these are often confused with issues concerning gender identity and sexual orientation.[118] The UN Committee on Economic, Social and Cultural Rights has expressed its concern that "(…) intersex persons (were) being denied access to health care (…)" and urged Uganda to "investigate and deter acts of discrimination against (…) intersex people, bring perpetrators to justice and provide compensation to victims".[119] Furthermore, the Committee "expressed concern about the lack of comprehensive antidiscrimination legislation and recommended taking steps to combat and prevent discrimination and societal stigma, in particular against (…) intersex individuals, and ensure access to housing, employment, social security, health care and education".[120]

3.3 Americas

During the past years, there has been remarkable progress on SOGI and intersex rights in the Americas. In some countries such as Argentina, Uruguay and Brazil the legal status of SOGI rights is significant with same-sex marriage or civil unions, strong anti-discriminatory law, hate-crime laws and powerful courts and movements defending LGBT rights.[121]

In 2015, the Inter-American Commission on Human Rights (IACHR) released a report on violence against LGBT and intersex persons. The Commission expressed its concerns about human rights violations carried out against intersex persons "because their bodies do not physically conform to the medically and culturally defined standards for "female" and "male" bodies. These include sex assignment and genital surgeries that are performed without informed consent of intersex persons. Most of these procedures are reported to be irreversible in nature and aimed at attempting to "normalize" the appearance of the person's genitals. Such surgeries and procedures have been reported to cause intersex children and adults great harm, including—but not limited to—chronic pain, lifelong trauma, genital insensitivity, sterilization, and diminished or lost capacity for sexual pleasure. Often these surgeries result in forced or coerced sterilization. According to the information received, these interventions are standard practice in countries across the Americas. The IACHR also noted that there is limited access to justice for intersex persons and their families."[122] The Commission recommended that Member States "make necessary amendments to law and policy to prohibit medically unnecessary medical procedures on intersex children and adults, when it is administered without their prior, free, and informed consent, except in cases of medical risk or necessity.

[117] Finnish Immigration Service (2015), pp. 91–91.

[118] Idem.

[119] A/HRC/WG.6/26/UGA/2, 2016, para. 24.

[120] Idem, para. 25.

[121] Corrales (2015), p. 54.

[122] OAS/Ser.L/V/II.rev.1, 2015, Chapter 4 para. 10.

Non-medically necessary surgeries and other medical intervention should be delayed until intersex persons can decide for themselves."[123]

The Inter-American Court of Human Rights (IACtHR) in its jurisprudence, has interpreted the provisions of the American Convention on Human Rights in the light of LGBT rights and of trans rights in particular. The Court has interpreted the right to privacy guaranteed under the American Convention as "a series of factors associated with the dignity of the individual, including, for example, the ability to develop his or her own personality and aspirations, to determine his or her own identity and to define his or her own personal relationships".[124] The right to privacy is inextricably linked to identity, which has been defined by the Court as "the collection of attributes and characteristics that allow for the individualization of the person in a society, and in that sense, encompasses a number of other rights according to the subject it treats and the circumstances of the case".[125]

Article 64 of the American Convention on Human Rights provides that any Member State of the Organization of American States (OAS) may request an advisory opinion from the IACtHR regarding the protection of human rights and the compatibility of its domestic laws with the Convention. On May 18, 2016, Costa Rica requested an advisory opinion on whether parties to the Convention must recognise name-change and identity information of persons according to their preferred gender identity. They also asked for an opinion on whether parties must recognise economic rights derived from a relationship between people of the same sex.[126] Later, the Inter-American Court of Human Rights, in a landmark advisory opinion affirmed that the American Convention on Human Rights requires countries to allow same-sex couples to access civil marriage and asserted that governments should allow people, through a fast, easy and cost-free process, to change their name and gender marker on official documents in accordance with their self-perceived gender identity.[127] The advisory opinion mentioned explicitly intersex rights especially with regards to the problem of heteronormativity and discriminatory norms that "impact negatively the quality of health care services and can lead to denial or to the absence of services that correspond to the specific health needs of LGBTI people and intersex".[128]

---

[123] Idem, para. 11.

[124] Atravia Murillo et al. (In Vitro Fertilization) v. Costa Rica, Preliminary objections, merits, reparations and costs, Judgment, Inter-Am. Ct. H.R., (ser C) No. 257, 2012, para. 143.

[125] Gelman v. Uruguay, Merits and Reparations, Judgment, Inter-Am. Ct. H. R. (ser C) No. 221, 2011, para. 122.

[126] Library of Congress, Global Legal Monitor "Costa Rica/OAS: Inter-American Court of Human Rights Declares Right to Marry Should Be Extended to Same-Sex Couples".

[127] Ramirez, "Latin America Could Lead the Way for LGBT Rights in 2018" and See I/A Court H.R. Gender identity, and equality and non-discrimination with regard to same-sex couples. State obligations in relation to change of name, gender identity, and rights deriving from a relationship between same-sex couples (interpretation and scope of Articles 1(1), 3, 7, 11(2), 13, 17, 18 and 24, in relation to Article 1, of the American Convention on Human Rights). Advisory Opinion OC-24/17 of November 24, 2017. Series A No. 24 (available in Spanish).

[128] Opinión consultiva OC-24/17 de 24 de Noviembre de 2017 solicitada por la república de Costa Rica Identidad de género, e igualdad y no discriminación a parejas del mismo sexo obligaciones

This section will be focusing on Argentina, Chile, Colombia and the United States as legal developments on intersex have taken place. It has to be noted that from the four countries that will be later analysed, the United States has signed but not ratified the American Convention on Human Rights.[129]

3.3.1 Argentina

3.3.1.1 Situation of SOGI Rights

In 2010, Argentina became the first country in Latin America to recognise the right to marry for same-sex couples at a national level.[130] Article 2 of Law 26.618 on Equitable Marriage (Ley 26.618 Matrimonio Igualitorio) established that "marriage shall have the same effects, regardless of whether the parties are of the same or different sex"[131] granting equal rights to all individuals irrespective of their sex. The Equitable Marriage Law also grants equal adoption rights and pension benefits to same sex couples.[132] The new Civil and Commercial Code of the Nation (Código Civil y Comercial de la Nación) which came into force in 2015 recognises that "no norm can be interpreted nor applied in the sense of limiting, restricting, excluding or suppressing the equality of rights and obligations of the parties of marriage, and the effects that this produces, be constituted by two people of different or same sex".[133]

The Law No 26.862 on Medically Assisted Reproduction (Ley 28.862-Reproducción Medicamente Asistida y Reglementación) establishes that "all persons of legal age can access medically assisted reproduction services without requirements or limitations that imply discrimination or exclusion based on sexual orientation or marital status".[134] On 27 February 2009, Argentina's Parliament

estatales en relación con el cambio de nombre, la identidad de género, y los derechos derivados de un vínculo entre parejas del mismo sexo (interpretación y alcance de los artículos 1.1, 3, 7, 11.2, 13, 17, 18 y 24, en relación con el artículo 1 de la Convención Americana sobre derechos humanos), para. 39.

[129] American Convention on Human Rights "Pact of San Jose, Costa Rica", Signatories and Ratifications.

[130] Identidad & Diversidad, Ley 26.618-Matrimonio Igualtorio (2010).

[131] Articulo 2° — Sustitúyese el artículo 172 del Código Civil, el que quedará redactado de la siguiente forma: Artículo 172: El matrimonio tendrá los mismos requisitos y efectos, con independencia de que los contrayentes sean del mismo o de diferente sexo.

[132] See Ley 26.618-Matrimonio Igualitario (2010).

[133] Libro Segundo, Relaciones de Familia, Titulo I, Matrimonio, Capitulo 1, Principios de libertad y de igualdad, Artículo 402.- interpretación y aplicación de las normas. Ninguna norma puede ser interpretada ni aplicada en el sentido de limitar, restringir, excluir o suprimir la igualdad de derechos y obligaciones de los integrantes del matrimonio, y los efectos que éste produce, sea constituido por dos personas de distinto o igual sexo.

[134] Ley 28.862: Reproducción Médicamente Asistida "Que la Ley No 26.862 establece que pueden acceder a las prestaciones de reproducción médicamente asistida todas las personas mayores de

passed a Military Reform Act (Ley 26.394 Justicia Militar) and allowed gay and lesbians to serve in the military and banned discrimination on the basis of sexual orientation within the armed forces.[135] In 2012, Law 26.791(Ley 26.791) amended the Penal Code and added life imprisonment to hate crimes based on sexual orientation and gender identity or expression.[136] In relation to trans individuals, the Gender Identity Law (Ley 26.743 Identidad de Genero) grants adults sex reassignment surgery and hormone therapy as a part of their public or private health care plans and allows for changes to gender, image or birth name on civil registries without the approval of a doctor or a judge.[137]

Despite all the progressive developments, there is no legal framework addressing discrimination based on sexual orientation and gender identity as Law 23.592 on Discrimination Acts does not refer to these grounds (Ley 23.592 Actos Discriminatorios). In 2017, the United Nations Independent Expert on the protection against violence and discrimination based on sexual orientation and gender identity called on Argentina to reform laws and policies which might lead to violence and discrimination, and to prevent laws on public decency and anti-drugs measures from being used to discriminate against people based on their sexual orientation or gender identity.[138]

3.3.1.2 Intersex Rights

In Argentina, there are several harmful misconceptions about intersex that prevail in public, notably if intersex is counterfactually described as being the same as or a subset of LGBT or SOGI, if intersex and/or intersex status are represented as a sexual orientation, and/or as a gender identity, as a subset of transgender, or as a form of sexual preference.[139]

Intersex surgeries are still practiced in Argentina, parents and children are misinformed and do not have access to appropriate support.[140] Most intersex children are deprived from their provinces to be treated at few hospitals located in Buenos Aires city.[141] Some doctors are slowly considering their approach to certain harmful

---

edad sin que se pueda introducir requisitos o limitaciones que impliquen discriminación o exclusioón fundandas en la orientación sexual o el estado civil (…).”

[135] Ley 26.394 Justicia Militar, Derógasnse el Código de Justicia Militar y todas las normas, resoluciones y disposiciones de carácter interno que lo reglamentan. Modifícanse el Código Penal y el Código Procesal Penal de la Nación.

[136] Artículo 80 4o: “Por placer, odio racial, de género o a la orientación sexual, identidad de género o su expression.”

[137] Ley 26.743 Identidad de Género, Establécese el derecho a la identidad de género de las personas, Sancionada: Mayo 9 de 2012, Promulgada: Mayo 23 de 2012.

[138] United Nations Human Rights Office of the High Commissioner, “UN expert commends Argentina’s “progressive laws and policies” but urges action to stop attacks on LGBT people”.

[139] Justicia Intersex and StopIGM.org/Zwischengeschlecht.org, 2017, p. 7.

[140] Idem, p. 3.

[141] Idem, p. 9.

practices, but others continue being performed.[142] Provisions on patient and children's rights are not applied to intersex persons and relevant institutions are supportive of unnecessary medical interventions or indifferent to them.[143] According to the National Institute Against Discrimination, Xenophobia and Racism the rights of intersex people to bodily integrity, decisional autonomy and health must be guaranteed. To that aim, it is important to provide psycho-social support instead of pathologising intersex bodies and subjecting them to unnecessary surgeries or other medical treatments. It is fundamental to ensure the right to integrity and self-determination of one's body and intersex people's integrity is already violated before they have the ability to decide.[144]

The National Institute highlights that medical treatments and interventions-when necessary- must respect intersex people's rights to health and decision-making. Therefore, it is necessary to work to reduce the violence that emanates from the binary system, support diversity and create safe environments for intersex people and their families.[145] The Institute also condemns some practices regarding the management of intersex cases such as revealing the name of the person born and their parents as well as the address and family photographs. This attitude violates the right of all people and in particular of children to the preservation of their family life and privacy. It may also undermine the principle of non-discrimination since the revelation of personal sensitive data as in the case of intersex, can constitute a source of discrimination.[146]

In Argentina, the Gender Identity Law removed all requirements that were demanded for accessing legal recognition of gender identity such as sterilisation, hormonal treatment, surgical procedures, psychiatric diagnosis and replaced them with a simple administrative procedure. This law made Argentina the first country to allow people to change their gender identity without any kind of medical intervention or certification. The law defines gender identity as "the internal and individual way in which gender is perceived by persons, that can correspond or not to gender assigned at birth, including the personal experience of the body".[147] The law guarantees voluntary access to hormonal and surgical procedure on an informed consent basis under its article 2 that allows sex reassignment interventions "through pharmacological, surgical or other means, always provided that it is freely chosen".[148] It appears that, according to the report of the National Institute on intersex, the

---

[142] Idem, p. 8.

[143] Idem.

[144] Instituto Nacional contra la Discriminación, la Xenofobia y el Racismo, 2015, p. 49.

[145] Archivo Prensa INADI, "Intersexualidad: el INADI contra la violencia del Sistema binario de sexo y de género".

[146] Archivo Prensa INADI, "Intersexualidad: el INADI contra la violencia del Sistema binario de sexo y de género".

[147] TGEU, English Translation of Argentina's Gender Identity Law as approved by the Senate of Argentina on May 8, 2012.

[148] Articulo 2o- […] a través de medios farmacológicos, quirúrgicos o de otra índole, siempre que ello sea libremente escogido […].

Gender Identity Law is applied to intersex people as well and gives them the possibility to modify freely their sex on identification documents.[149] However, this freedom of choice is limited as in the case of minors the principles and requirements of Article 5 are applied, which stipulates that for persons under the age of 18 a legal representative is needed. In addition, the Gender Identity Law reinforces the binary model instead of eradicating it as individuals still have to choose between "female" and "male".

3.3.2 Chile

3.3.2.1 Situation of SOGI Rights

Chile has introduced non-discrimination provisions on the basis of sexual orientation and gender identity in the majority of sectors. Law 20.609 (Ley 20.609) condemns acts of discrimination on the basis of race, ethnicity, nationality, marital status, disability, sex, sexual orientation, gender identity and personal appearance. Citizens can file anti-discrimination lawsuits and the State ought to develop public policies to end discrimination.[150] Law 20.940 (Ley 20.940) modified the Labor Code to explicitly prohibit discrimination based on sexual orientation and gender identity.[151] The School Inclusion Law 20.845 (Ley 20.845 de Inclusión Escolar) guarantees non-discrimination based on sexual orientation and gender identity mentioning the Law 20.609 on non-discrimination.[152] The Anti-torture law (Ley 20.968) which was introduced in 2016, criminalised physical, psychological abuse and sexual violence including sexual orientation and gender identity as protected grounds.[153] After a petition[154] processed by the Inter-American Commission of Human Rights regarding the lack of access to civil marriage by three same-sex couples in Chile, the government introduced a Bill that recognised marriage equality. The Bill amended the definition of marriage as established under the Civil Code and replaced the phrase that described it as the union "between a man and a woman" by the "union between two people". The sentence "between two people" gives space for broader interpretation since it does not refer to individuals based on their sex but rather on their "personhood" encompassing all sex and gender diversities including intersex. The Bill also recognised the right to adoption and filiation for same-sex couples.[155]

[149] Instituto Nacional contra la Discriminación, la Xenofobia y el Racismo, 2015, pp. 50–51.

[150] See Ley Número 20.609, Establece Medidas Contra La Discriminación.

[151] Ley Número 20.940, Artículo 1o (1).

[152] Ley 20.845, Artículo 1, 7 (c).

[153] Ley Número 20.968, Artículo 1 (3).

[154] See Acuerdo de Solución Amistosa, Caso P-946-12.

[155] See Legislatura 365, Modifica diversos cuerpos legales para regular, en igualdad de condiciones, el matrimonio de parejas del mismo sexo and Rehbein Consuelo, "Conoce los detalles de la ley matrimonio igualitario".

Regarding trans rights, since 2001, the Civil Register allows trans individuals to obtain their identity documentation without having to change their appearance.[156] The Ministry of Health approved Circular No 34 in 2011 which obliged to call and register trans people by their social name in all care centres within Chile.[157] In 2016, a Bill on System of Guarantees of Rights of the Childhood (Sistema de Garantías de Derechos de la Niñez: Proyecto informado por la Comisión de Familia y Adulto Mayor) recognised the right to children and adolescents to develop their gender identity. In 2018, after 4 years of debate, the Chilean Congress approved a bill that would allow trans adults to legally change their name and gender without surgery or a court order.[158] On 13 September 2018, the Chilean House of Deputies passed the Gender Identity Bill which allows anyone over the age of 14 to self-identify their gender.[159] The Congress took that step after the publication of the advisory opinion OC-24/17 of the Inter-American Court of Human Rights on Gender Identity, and Equality and Non-Discrimination of Same-Sex Couples. The IACtHR ruled that several rights under the Convention, including article 18 (right to a name), article 3 (right to legal personality), article 7.1 (right to personal liberty), and article 11 (right to privacy), encompass the right to change one's name and have one's personal identity information reflect the gender one prefers.[160] The Court ruled that parties to the Convention are obliged to establish appropriate procedures under articles 1.1 and 24 to respect and guarantee rights without discrimination and under article 2 to adopt domestic law to the rights provided for under the Convention.[161]

Despite all the above measures, in Chile, children and adolescents whose sexual orientation and/or gender identity does not match the expectations of their families and society, often find their rights flouted and little protection is provided from the State.[162] The 2017 Annual Report on the Situation of Human Rights in Chile (Informe Anual de Derechos Humanos) observed that structural discrimination affects trans people since childhood and intersex since birth and identifies discrimination in access to education and health as main areas of concern.[163]

---

[156] See Biblioteca del Congreso Nacional de Chile, "Cambio de sexo registral en Chile: procedimiento legal y jurisprudencia".

[157] Circular No 34, 2. Registros en ficha clínica "Todos los registros derivados de la atención de salud deben contemplar en primer lugar el nombre legal de la persona y en segundo lugar el nombre social con el cual dicha persona se identifica. Esto aplica tanto para la ficha clínica como para la solicitud de exámenes, procedimientos, perescripción de medicamentos y brazaletes de identificación. Se insiste en que la identificación verbal debe ser a través de su nombre social".

[158] Washington Blade, "Chilean House of Deputies approves transgender rights bill".

[159] Gaystarnews, "Trans people in Chile can now change their name and gender, without surgery".

[160] Advisory Opinion OC-24/17 of November 24, 2017, *supra*, para. 118.

[161] Washington Blade, "Chilean House of Deputies approves transgender rights bill".

[162] Observatorio de Derechos Humanos –Chile (Andrés Rivera Duarte) International Gay and Lesbian Human Rights Commission (IGLHRC) (2015), p. 2.

[163] MOVILH (2017), p. 28.

3.3.2.2 Intersex Rights

The first case that shed light on intersex births in Chile was the Bejamín-Maricarmen case. In 1993, a baby who was born with genitalia outside of the typical male/female binary, named Maricarmen, suffered an irreversible surgical intervention. Following doctors' recommendations, after surgery, Maricarmen had to transition to become Benjamín, change her official documents and go through medical treatments and physical and psychiatric examinations.[164] In 2005, the mother filed a lawsuit against the Maule Health Service which ended up at the Supreme Court. In 2012, the Court condemned the Maule Health Service for "lack of service" and compensations for moral and psychological damages.[165] The ruling states that the hospital should have performed examinations that would allow the parents and the victim to "decide about the removal of these organs and the condition of man or woman which they would face life and society".[166]

According to a study that was published in 2001 the rate of prevalence of intersex births only in the Maternity Clinic of the Clinical Hospital of the University of Chile (la Maternidad del Hospital Clínico de la Universidad de Chile) in the last 18 years was 4.7 per 10,000 births.[167] Other maternity hospitals in the county such as the Guillermo Grant Benavent Hospital of Conception reported 1.9 out of 10,000 births and the Regional Hospital of Valvidia 2.6 intersex births out of 10,000 births.[168]

In 2015, the UN Committee on the Rights of the Child recommended to Chile to "expedite the development and implementation of a rights-based health-care protocol for intersex children that sets the procedures (…) to ensure that no one is subjected to unnecessary surgery or treatment during infancy or childhood, protect the rights of the children concerned to physical and mental integrity, autonomy and self-determination, provide intersex children and their families with adequate counselling and support, including from peers, and ensure effective remedy for victims, including redress and compensation".[169] Later this year, Circular 18 on "Instructions on aspects of health care to intersex children" (Instruye sobre ciertos aspectos de la atención de salud a niños y niñas intersex) was published and instructed the ceasing of "unnecessary normalisation" treatment of intersex children, including irreversible genital surgeries, until they are old enough to decide about their bodies".[170] The same paragraph recognised the need to assign a gender in the birth registration of an intersex infant, stating that no surgery would be tolerated. The Circular by instructing that harmful and unnecessary medical procedures must be banned in intersex

[164] Centro de Derechos Humanos et al. (2016), pp. 346–347.

[165] Idem.

[166] Gabriela García, "Identidad Forzada".

[167] Centro de Derechos Humanos et al. (2016), p. 344.

[168] Idem, p. 345.

[169] CRC/C/CHL/CO/4-5, 2015, para. 49.

[170] Circular No 18, "Se instruye que se se detengan los tratamientos innecesarios de "normalización" de niños y niñas intersex, incluyendo cirugias genitales irreversibles hasta que tengan edad suficiente para decider sobre sus cuerpos".

infants, children and adolescents, protected the right to autonomy and bodily integrity of intersex children. In addition, the Sentence RIT P-598-2015 (Sentencia RIT P-598-2015) was a historic step towards the protection of intersex children's rights as the judge Susan Sepúlveda found that the rights of an intersex child had been violated as it had been subjected to corrective surgeries. The judgment established that by virtue of Circular 18 of the Ministry of Health, the case should be analysed not only from a medical perspective but also with a focus on rights and gender.[171]

A year later, Circular 7 turned out to be a step back to intersex children's rights, as it stated that the earlier "recommendation not to perform unnecessary genital surgeries does not apply to "pathologies" where sex can be clearly determined (…)"[172] revoking Circular 18. In detail, Circular 7 pathologises intersex and characterises intersex cases as a social emergency which can be solved through medical interventions. One of the main setbacks is the Fourth Section where it is stated that "the possibility should be explained of deferring a surgery to an age where the patient may manifest or demonstrate tendencies of a sexual identity".[173] No human rights recommendation states that surgeries should be deferred based on the awareness of the sexual identity of an intersex person. Rather, surgeries must be deferred until the individual is able to consent or deny such procedures, in order to preserve their right to self-determination as quoted by the CRC in their observations to the Chilean State.[174] The prevailing issue in Circular 7 is that the Ministry of Health links intersex surgeries to gender identity or "sexual identity" instead on focusing on the human rights that are at stake such as the right of a patient to physical integrity, the right to bodily autonomy, the right to be informed and to decide freely.[175] Under the same token, Circular 7, following a non-patient's rights centered approach, does not specify that the patient should be entitled to health care and must be guided on options to move forward but prioritises the will of doctors and legal representatives.

Intersex in Chile can change their name and sex in identification documents following the same procedure as trans according to the Civil Registry. In addition, the Civil Registry allows for birth certificates available with the option "indeterminate" sex if it is not possible to assign a sex at birth upon request through the Civil Tribunals.[176] According to a recent study conducted by the Civil Registry as a part of the Program of Equity of Gender 2017, 269 intersex infants have been registered under the category of "indeterminate sex" on official records from 2006 till 2017.[177]

---

[171] Centro de Derechos Humanos et al. (2016), pp. 353–354.

[172] Circular No 7, Segundo: "La recomendación que alude a no realizer cirugías inecesarias, no se refiere a patologías en que existe un sexo claramente determinado (…)".

[173] Circular No 7, Cuarto: "Se debe explicitar la posibilidad de diferir la cirugía hasta una edad en que el paciente pueda manifestar o demonstrar tendencias de identidad sexual".

[174] Inter Laura and Aoi Hana (2017), p. 6.

[175] Idem.

[176] See Ordinario Circular No 1297/2012, Guía Técnica, "Peritaje de Sexología Forense para Personas Trans e Intersex".

[177] See Registro Civil e Identificación, Programa Equidad de Género 2017, "Datos Registrales con Enfoque de Género".

Moreover, Circular No 21 that Reiterates instruction on the care of trans people in the health care network (Reitera instrucción sobre la atención de personas trans en la red asistencial), established the duty of officials in health care services to respect gender identity and the social name of both trans and intersex people. It explains that "intersex people or those born with ambiguous genitalia, may also manifest a similar situation (as trans), when genital sex does not correspond to the gender identity that the person is developing".[178] Circular No 1297/2012 instructs compliance with the expert technical guide of forensic sexology for trans and intersex cases (instruye cumplimiento de Guía Técnica Pericial de Sexología Forense para casos de personas trans e intersex). The goal of the Circular is to safeguard human dignity of trans and intersex people. To that aim, trans and intersex persons should not be subjected to invasive expert reports and they must be called by their social name or the one that the person prefers.[179]

In 2017, the Bill on System of Guarantees of Rights of the Childhood (Ley de Garantías y Derechos de la Niñez) was passed that protects intersex children from discrimination. Article 9 states that "no child shall be arbitrarily discriminated against because of their sexual orientation, gender identity, gender expression and sex characteristics".[180]

3.3.3 Colombia

3.3.3.1 Situation of SOGI Rights

Colombian legal frameworks do provide the LGBT community with a robust protection of their rights. The Anti-discrimination Law No.1482 of 2011 (Ley No. 1482 de 2011) established imprisonment of 1–3 years and fines for people who discriminate against different groups and the LGBT community.[181] The law also promulgates that penalties are increased when discrimination is committed in a public space, carried out through mass media or by a public official and when discriminatory acts deprive someone of labour rights or the provision of a public service.[182]

The Colombian Constitutional Court has developed a wide jurisprudence which is human-rights centered and guarantees several rights to sexual minorities. In 2007, the Court changed its precedence and recognised the legal existence of same-sex

---

[178] Circular No 21, "las personas intersex o que nacen con ambigüedad genital, también pueden llegar a manifestar una situación similar, cuando el sexo genital, no se corresponde con la identidad de Género que la persona va desarrollando".

[179] See Ordinario Circular No 1297/2012, Guía Técnica, "Peritaje de Sexología Forense para Personas Trans e Intersex" paras. 1 and 3.

[180] MOVILH, "Cámara de Diputados aprueba incorporar a niños y niñas LGBTI en proyecto de ley sobre derechos de la infancia".

[181] See Ley No. 1482 de 2011, Artículo 134 A.

[182] Idem.

couples granting them common-law marriage property and inheritance rights that were previously denied.[183] With this decision, the Court could have achieved an entire transformation of the Colombian legal system so that all frameworks that regulate marriage could be applied to same-sex couples.[184] Even though this ruling did not have this effect, it opened the way for a series of rulings concerning the rights of same-sex couples: C-811/2007, C-336/2008, C-798/2008, T-856/2007 and T-1241/2008 confirmed that same-sex couples may constitute de facto marital unions and extended several rights and responsibilities of same-sex couples[185] such as social security and pension benefits. The Court also granted full same-sex adoption rights in a series of rulings.[186] Last, in a major ruling in the C-029/2009 case, that arised from a lawsuit that challenged the constitutionality of 26 legal norms differentiating unfairly between same-sex and heterosexual couples, the Court signaled that this set of legal norms aiming at heterosexual couples is constitutional only if it also applies to same-sex couples.[187]

The main line of the case-law developed by the Colombian Constitutional Court is the premise that members of same-sex couples are subjects of law and therefore entitled to an important set of individual rights and obligations.[188] It has to be noted that all rulings are based on three legal pillars: human dignity, free development of personality and equality. In other words, the Court elaborates on the fact that dignity is an attribute that arises as a consequence of the autonomy of a human and guarantees the basic equality of all human beings. The Court claims that this attribute is in itself a constitutional principle that forms the premise from which fundamental rights are deduced.[189] The principle of dignity has a negative and positive dimension. On one hand, the State has the duty to refrain from any action that violates the autonomy of human beings and on the other hand it has the duty to ensure the minimum material conditions that allow for autonomy to be exercised.[190] Moreover, the free development of personality summarises, promotes and protects the principle of human dignity.[191]

In the same vein and following the three main legal pillars applied in the case of same-sex couples, the Constitutional Court developed a wide jurisprudence with regards to gender identity and trans rights. In T-063/15, T-918/12 and T-231/13 the Court recognised that transgender people have the right reassign their gender,

[183] See Sentencia C-075 de 2007 Regimen Patrimonial de Compañeros Permanentes-Pareja homosexuals/Parejas Homosexuales y Union Marital de Hecho-Protección patrimonial/Parejas Homosexuales-Vulneración de la dignidad humana y libre desarrollo de la personalidad al excluirlos de regimen de protección patrimonial.

[184] Bonilla (2016), p. 185.

[185] Pierceson et al. (2013), p. 113.

[186] See C-683/15, C-071/15 and T-276/12.

[187] Idem, p. 114.

[188] Idem.

[189] Idem.

[190] Idem.

[191] Idem, p. 115.

provided that they have the medical or psychological evidence and the State must guarantee access to these alterations in a dignified manner. In T-876/12 and T-918/12 the Court recognised the rights to sexual identity and health to trans. In these judgments, the sex reassignment surgery was considered as vital for trans people because otherwise it would constitute a violation of their dignity based on the fact that it is impossible for them to live a proper life otherwise.

On the matter of protection from discrimination, the Court in T-063/15 determined that the State must guarantee that people of all sexual orientations and gender identities can live with dignity and respect.[192] It mentioned the example of trans and intersex people to elaborate on the fact that "sex" can no longer be understood as an attribute that is exclusively linked to the biological characteristics of a person at the moment of birth.[193] The ruling recognised that trans people suffer several human rights violations such as their right to gender identity, access to employment, education and political participation and for that reason, they enjoy special constitutional protection.[194] In its earlier jurisprudence, the Constitutional Court had established the "presumption of discrimination" ("presunción de discriminación") that establishes that when the transgender person receives unequal treatment, it is up to the person who is accused of committing it, to prove the absence of discrimination.[195]

The Court in T-392/17 highlighted that transgender people are exposed to social prejudices and discriminatory acts for expressing their identity to society, generally through physical transformations.[196] It also interpreted Article 13 of the Constitution[197] to stress the duty of all inhabitants of the national territory and public authorities to respect and guarantee the dignity, autonomy and free development of the personality of transgender people.[198]

[192] See T-063/15, para. 5.1.

[193] Idem, para. 5.2.

[194] Idem, para. 5.4.

[195] See T-805/14, para. 5 and 5.1.

[196] See T-392/17, para. 28.

[197] Acticle 13 of the Colombian Constitution as translated by Marcia W. Coward, Peter B. Heller, Anna I. Vellve Torras, and Max Planck Institute: "All individuals are born free and equal before the law, will receive equal protection and treatment from the authorities, and will enjoy the same rights, freedoms, and opportunities without any discrimination on account of gender, race, national or family origin, language, religion, political opinion, or philosophy. The State will promote the conditions so that equality may be real and effective and will adopt measures in favor of groups that are discriminated against or marginalized. The State will especially protect those individuals who on account of their economic, physical, or mental condition are in obviously vulnerable circumstances and will sanction the abuses or ill-treatment perpetrated against them."

[198] See T-392/17, para. 29.

3.3.3.2 Intersex Rights

Even though Colombia does not prohibit harmful practices on intersex infants, they are regulated through a series of decisions by the Constitutional Court relating to bodily autonomy of intersex infants and children. First, in T-477/95, the Court considered the case of a teenager who had been accidentally castrated as an infant and then subjected to sex reassignment surgery and raised as a girl,[199] like David Reimer in the "John/Joan" case.[200] When the applicant discovered about the operation, sued the doctors and the hospital. The Court ruled that the sex of a child could not be altered without the child's informed consent.[201] It also held that sex operations, without consent, violate an individual's right to develop his/her own sexual identity and established that only the individual whom gender assignment surgery will be performed can give consent to the surgery, regardless of the age of the individual.[202]

In SU-337/99, the midwife declared the infant to be female and was raised as a girl but at the age of three a doctor diagnosed the child as a "pseudohermaphroditic" male. A medical team recommended genital-conforming surgery but then refused to perform it because the Constitutional Court had already held that parental permission could not be substituted for the permission of the child and that the child could not make such a decision until the age of majority. The plaintiff (mother of the child) sought permission from the Court to substitute the plaintiff's consent since the child was still a minor and "could not make decisions for herself", contending that, if the medical team were to wait for the child to have "the capacity to decide, it would be too late and would prevent normal psychological, physical, and social development".[203]

The Court noted that there was little jurisprudence on intersex issues and that almost all cases referring to sexual identity dealt with homosexuality and transgender issues. Nevertheless, it emphasised that determining consent in intersex surgical cases was important because about 15,000–37,000 intersex persons lived in Colombia.[204] The Court elaborated on the fact that consent is central to medical autonomy because individuals must decide how they want to approach personal health as free moral agents and that it was a part of the constitutional rights to personal development. At that time, the child was 8 years old and therefore, the Court found that a child of that age had a sense of autonomy, and prior cases established that the need to protect the right of free development grew as a child became more

---

[199] International Commission of Jurists, SOGI Casebook: "Chapter six: Intersex".

[200] See Sect. 2.2.1.

[201] See T-477/95, Part B "Consentimiento de Tratamiento Médico en el Caso de Menores", Section 13.

[202] Idem, Sections 15 and 15.1.

[203] International Commission of Jurists, "Sentencia SU 337/99, Constitutional Court of Colombia (12 May 1999)".

[204] Idem.

self-aware.[205] Then the Court concluded that, constitutionally, consent could not be substituted if a child had a full cognitive, social, and emotional understanding of his or her body and a gender identity firmly in place.[206] The Court stated that "intersexuality appeals to our capacity for tolerance and challenges our ability to accept difference. Public authority, the medical community and citizens in general have a duty to open a space for the people [who have been] silenced up till now".[207]

Later in 1999, the Court ruled in the case T-551/99 that parents could give permission for the performance of an intersex surgery as long as the informed consent was "qualified and persistent".[208] The consent can be considered as "qualified and persistent" when parents are given detailed information about the advantages and disadvantages of intersex surgeries, are allowed ample periods of time to consider the alternatives to intersex surgery and make decisions in consideration of their child's best interests.[209] In that case, the parents had not examined alternative options to surgery and they were led to believe that intersex surgery was the only option. Afterwards, in T-912/08, the Court held that the child and parents had to be fully informed about the surgery, its implications and concerns and then they could together give a joint consent. But if the child's decision did not accord with that of the parents, then no surgery could be performed until the child had reached the age of majority and could make an independent decision.[210]

In its most recent judgment, the T-450A/13 case, the infant's sex was not identified at birth and as a result, was not registered by the officials of the Civil Registry. Due to that event, the Hospital refused the provision of health services and the authorities had to intervene. The Court considered that the indeterminacy of sex cannot constitute an obstacle to the exercise of the right to legal personality, which is inherent to the human being by the mere fact of existing.[211] Considering the principle of human dignity and the right to equality, there is no reason to justify that infants and children whose sex cannot be identified at birth, are not registered and remain "invisible" for the State and society.[212] The Court ruled that authorities are obliged to register intersex children and an interdisciplinary team of experts is responsible for the decision on the assignment of sex.[213]

---

[205] Idem.

[206] Idem.

[207] SU-337/99, Aclaraci6n final.

[208] See T-551/99, para. 29.

[209] White (2014), p. 801.

[210] See T-912/08 para. 2.4.3. and International Commission of Jurists, SOGI casebook:" Chapter six: intersex".

[211] See T-450A/13, para. 6.2.

[212] Idem.

[213] Idem, para. 6.3.

3.3.3.3 The Particular Case of "Judicial Activism" in Colombia

In 1991, Colombia enacted a new Constitution that established the Constitutional Court to decide all constitutional law issues. Since its creation, the Court has been at the centre of controversy due to its revolutionary decisions involving issues of fundamental rights and freedoms.[214] The ground-breaking approach taken by the Court in a series of decisions especially with regards to ethically sensitive and debated matters has led to describe the justices' work as "judicial activism".

"Judicial activism" has been explained as "an approach to the exercise of judicial review, or a description of a particular judicial decision, in which a judge is generally considered more willing to decide constitutional issues and to invalidate legislative or executive actions".[215] Greg Jones has mentioned that "at the broadest level, judicial activism is any occasion where a Court intervenes and strikes down a piece of duly enacted legislation".[216] The Colombian Constitutional Court represents a radical departure from the traditional model of separation of powers and assumes a more active and aggressive role.[217] It appears that the Colombian system places confidence in the justices and "assigns" them the task to declare the validity of the acts or omissions of the political branches.[218] In its Article 241, the Colombian Constitution prescribes that the Constitutional Court is "the guardian of the Constitution".[219] According to it, the Court has the power to declare unconstitutional multiple and diverse normative bodies and political decisions such as constitutional amendments, laws, plebiscites, and executive orders enacted by the President at exercising extraordinary powers, international treaties approbatory laws, among others.[220] The Colombian justices assume jurisdiction by using principles of law and determine what is best for the common well-being. By doing so, the outcomes in the decisions appear as judge-made law.[221]

Nowadays, the Colombian Court is considered as one of the key institutions within the Colombian institutional mainstream.[222] The Court has succeeded to envisage the Constitution as a dynamic document that is "under an ongoing construction progress" which is "refueled" by the Court's interpretations and adjudications.[223] One of the strengths of the Constitutional Court, is its ability to turn "traditionally invisible cases" visible and integrate them "into the public agenda", thus unveiling them as "public issues" subject to judicial protection.[224] In the case of

[214] Nagle-Ortiz (1995), Introduction.

[215] Roosevelt Kermit, "Judicial Activism".

[216] Jones (2001), p. 143.

[217] Nagle-Ortiz (1995), p. 82.

[218] Idem.

[219] Constitución Política de Colombia, Actulizada con los Actos Legislativos, 2016.

[220] Gonzalez, p. 2.

[221] Idem.

[222] Gonzalez, p. 1.

[223] Idem, p. 5.

[224] Idem, p. 6.

sexual minorities, the Court has achieved their destigmatisation and depathologisation. In its decisions, it considers sexual minorities as individuals and subjects of law entitled to individual rights and obligations. At the same time, the Court clarifies that the State must guarantee that sexual minorities live with dignity and respect.[225]

Regarding intersex people in particular, the Court departs from the mainstream concept of "sex" and highlights that it is no longer exclusively linked to the principles of biology. It places intersex people within the broader context of Colombian society and grants them visibility by demedicalising and depathologising their "indeterminate" sex. The Colombian Constitutional Court also introduces a "duty" for Colombian authorities to register intersex infants as they are entitled to the right to legal personality and their "indetermination" of sex cannot be considered as a valid justification to violate their fundamental rights.

3.3.4 United States

3.3.4.1 Situation of SOGI Rights

On June 26 of 2003, the United States (U.S.) Supreme Court ruled in Lawrence v. Texas that a Texas state law criminalising intimate sexual conduct between two consenting same-sex consenting adults was against the Constitution.[226] In declaring the Texas "homosexual conduct" law unconstitutional, the Court overturned the 1986 Supreme Court decision in Bowers v. Hardwick,[227] which upheld state laws making homosexual sex a criminal offense.[228] The amicus brief argued that the principles of privacy and equal protection being examined by the Court should be interpreted in light of the rulings of foreign and international courts of nations with similar histories, legal systems, and political cultures.[229] In the Court ruling, Justice Anthony M. Kennedy referred to a series of ECtHR case-law to elaborate on the right to privacy in relation with same-sex couples: "(…) the reasoning and holding in Bowers have been rejected elsewhere. The European Court of Human Rights has followed not Bowers but its own decision in Dudgeon v. United Kingdom. Other nations, too, have taken action consistent with an affirmation of the protected right of homosexual adults to engage in intimate, consensual conduct.".[230]

---

[225] See also Scherpe et al. (2018) and Part IV, "Colombia (The Colombian Constitutional Court)" by Ruth Rubio-Marín and Stefano Osella in particular.

[226] See Lawrence v. Texas, 539 U.S. 558, 2003. See also Garland (2006).

[227] See Bowers v. Hardwick, 478 U.S. 186, 1986.

[228] Human Rights Watch, "Lawrence v. Texas, Constitutional right to privacy of gays and lesbians in the United States".

[229] Idem.

[230] See Lawrence v. Texas, 539 U.S. 558, 2003, [576].

After a decade, in 2013, in Windsor v. United States, the plaintiff sued to recover the tax payment she paid after inheriting her same-sex spouse's estates and being denied the estate tax exemption for surviving spouses due to Section 3 of the Defense of Marriage Act that forbade the recognition of same-sex marriages as its definitions of "marriage" and "spouse" excluded same-sex couples.[231] The Court found the federal statute invalid as it violated the Fifth Amendment of the Constitution and based its reasoning on the fact that "no legitimate purpose overcomes the purpose and effect to disparage and to injure those whom the State, by its marriage laws, sought to protect in personhood and dignity".[232]

Later, in 2015, in the landmark decision Obergefell v. Hodges, the Court ruled that state bans on same-sex marriages are unconstitutional as they violate the equal protection clauses of the Fourteenth Amendment to the U.S. Constitution.[233] Justice Anthony M. Kennedy explained that liberties protected by the fourteenth Amendment extend to "intimate choices that define personal identity and beliefs"[234] and he mentioned that "the Constitution promises liberty to all (…) to define and express their identity".[235] The reference to "identity" can be interpreted as an indirect victory for the trans community since one possible interpretation could be that "sex" or "gender" cannot determine the eligibility of a person to marry. Therefore, it can be argued that Obergefell does not only recognise same-sex couples' right to marry but examines the potential to help eliminate obstacles that trans people face by supporting their constitutional rights.[236]

Despite the fact that Obergefell v. Hodges is a significant step towards SOGI rights recognition and marriage equality across the U.S., lawmakers in several States proposed laws and bills allowing those with religious or moral objections to refuse or decline to provide a range of services to same-sex couples.[237] These laws and bills vary, some allow people to refuse to participate or to provide goods and services to same-sex wedding ceremonies and others allow child welfare agencies, health providers and others to refuse service to LGBT people.[238] For instance, Mississippi enacted a law that prevents the government from taking "any discriminatory action" against religious organisations or persons that discriminate in a variety of ways against LGBT individuals "consistent with a sincerely held religious belief or moral conviction".[239] The listing in this Section is very broad and covers the provision of wedding-related services, the rental or sale of housing, child placement services, health care and particularly fertility and transition-related services.[240]

[231] See Windsor v. United States, No. 12-307. Argued March 27, 2013, Decided June 26, 2013.

[232] Windsor v. United States, No. 12-307, pp. 25–26.

[233] See Obergefell v. Hodges, No. 14-556. Argued April 28, 2015, Decided June 26, 2015.

[234] Obergefell v. Hodges, No. 14-556, p. 10.

[235] Idem, p. 2.

[236] Cruz (2015–2016), Abstract.

[237] Human Rights Watch (2018), p. 6.

[238] Idem, p. 2.

[239] Mississipi House Bill 1523, 2016, Section 3.

[240] Idem.

Other States may have not enacted such a broad legislation, but they pose restrictions in selected spheres. For example, in relation with health care, Tennessee enacted a law that states that "no counselor or therapist providing counseling or therapy services shall be required to counsel or serve a client as to goals, outcomes, or behaviors that conflict with a sincerely held religious belief of the counselor or therapist; provided, that the counselor or therapist coordinates a referral of the client to another counselor or therapist who will provide the counseling or therapy."[241] As specified by a recent survey, respondents who oppose religious freedom laws view LGBT individuals as a group facing potential mistreatment based on social prejudices and in need of protection. They view religious freedom legislation as threatening the freedom of LGBT people to fully participate in public life.[242] On the other hand, people who favour religious freedom exemption laws view business owners as potentially harmed if they are unable to exercise their religion in making business decisions, placing the rules of "free market" and capitalism above individual rights.[243]

Religious freedom and liberty in the U.S are used to discriminate "legitimately" against LGBT people surpassing human rights limitations set out by international human rights instruments. The Human Rights Committee has emphasised that Article 18 of the ICCPR on freedom of thought, conscience and religion "does not permit any limitations whatsoever on the freedom of thought and conscience or on the freedom to have or adopt a religion or belief of one's choice" but recognising that religious exercise may affect others, does permit limited restrictions on the freedom to manifest one's religion or beliefs.[244] According to Article 29 (2) of the Universal Declaration of Human Rights "in the exercise of his rights and freedoms, everyone shall be subject only to such limitations as are determined by law solely for the purpose of securing due recognition and respect for the rights and freedoms of others and of meeting the just requirements of morality, public order and the general welfare in a democratic society". Article 29 of the UDHR is further reinforced by Article 19 (3) of the International Covenant on Civil and Political Rights.[245]

Religious exemptions aiming to "legitimise" discrimination against LGBT individuals in the provision of a wide range of services cannot be justified under international human rights principles since they do not fall within the scope of morality, public order and the welfare in a democratic society. In contrast, this kind of religious exercise imposed by such legal frameworks affects sexual minorities negatively and prevents them from enjoying basic human rights. Given this point, religious exemptions not only impinge upon the rights of LGBT individuals to equal treatment, they also jeopardise the enjoyment of several other rights such as the

[241] Tennessee Senate Bill 1556, 2016, Section 1(a).

[242] Kazyak et al. (2018), p. 14.

[243] Idem.

[244] Human Rights Committee, General Comment 22, paras. 3–4.

[245] "(...) respect for the rights and reputations of others, and protection of national security, public order, public health or morals".

right to health.[246] Of course, such laws do not only affect LGBT individuals but intersex people as well since they are also considered as a sexual minority and may be denied the provision of services based on religious exemptions.

3.3.4.2 Intersex Rights

According to a recent report launched by InterAct and Human Rights Watch, despite the absence of nationwide data on intersex surgeries, available data sources show that doctors continue to perform unnecessary intersex surgeries in the U.S.[247] Most practitioners interviewed by Human Rights Watch said they observed a general decrease in surgeries on intersex infants and they linked this trend both to changes in societal attitudes and changes in medical practice.[248]

The first case in the U.S. that addressed legally the harm caused by an intersex surgery performed on an infant was M.C. v. Aaronson.[249] M.C. was born intersex and he was in the legal custody of the South Carolina Department of Social Services. In 2006, M.C. was subjected to an unnecessary intersex surgery and 4 months later he was adopted. M.C.'s adoptive parents filed an action alleging there was inadequate informed consent for the surgery and alleging that the South Carolina Department of Social Services was grossly negligent in facilitating the recommended surgery.[250] In 2015, the Court of Appeals for the Fourth Circuit reversed the previous decision of the District Court of South Carolina and dismissed the complaint while stating that "it did not mean to diminish the severe harm that M.C. claims to have suffered" based on the assumption that a reasonable official in 2006 did not have fair warning from then-existing precedent that performing sex assignment surgery violated M.C. constitutional rights.[251] The Court did not rule whether or not the performance of the intersex surgery constituted a violation of M.C.'s constitutional rights. After 4 years of litigation, the Parties agreed that it was mutually beneficial to amicably resolve the case with no admission of liability on the part of the Medical University of South Carolina.[252] The M.C. case offered the opportunity to the U.S. to denounce intersex surgeries and show that it is time for the law to abandon the deduction that children are psychosexually neutral and that unnecessary surgeries on intersex infants are not harmful.[253] In 2018, California State Legislature approved a resolution denouncing medically unnecessary surgeries on intersex infants and "calling upon stakeholders in the health professions to foster the well-being of children born with variations of sex characteristics through the

[246] Human Rights Watch (2018), p. 35.

[247] Human Rights Watch and Interact (2017), p. 48.

[248] Idem, p. 50.

[249] See SPLC Southern Poverty Law Center, "M.C. v. Aaronson".

[250] Idem.

[251] See M.C. v. Aaronson, No. 13-2178, United States Court of Appeals for the Fourth Circuit.

[252] SPLC Southern Poverty Law Center, "M.C. v. Aaronson".

[253] White (2014), p. 820.

enactment of policies and procedures that ensure individualized, multidisciplinary care".[254] This can be considered as a small first step towards the ban of intersex surgeries since it is not a change of statute and does not ban the practice.

In May 2016, the United States Department of Health and Human Services issued a statement on Section 1557 of the Affordable Care Act stating that the Act prohibits "discrimination on the basis of intersex traits or atypical sex characteristics" in publicly-funded healthcare.[255] InterAct stated that this was the first time a government regulation specifically stated that a ban on sex discrimination includes discrimination against intersex people, and it constitutes precedent for Courts interpreting similar rules in the future.[256]

On October 26, 2015, Lamba Legal filed a federal discrimination lawsuit against the U.S. State Department on behalf of Dana ZZyym[257] who are intersex and were denied a U.S. passport because they could not choose either male of female on the application form.[258] The District Court of Colorado ruled in favor of Dana and Judge R. Brooke Jackson stated that there was "no evidence that the (State) Department followed a rational decision-making process in deciding to implement its binary-only gender passport".[259] In 2017, California passed Senate Bill No. 179 and in its Section 2 (c) states that "an option of a nonbinary gender designation on state-issued identification documents would allow intersex people, like transgender and nonbinary people, to be able to use state-issued identification documents that accurately recognize their gender identification as female, male, or nonbinary.".[260] In 2014, New York City eased requirements for gender marker change applications. The new code allows a gender marker change on a birth certificate to be processed upon receipt of an affirmation or affidavit written by a licensed medical or mental health provider.[261] In 2016, New York City issued the first birth certificate with "intersex" in the gender field.[262]

Intersex persons in the U.S. remain unprotected under federal law. Unnecessary intersex surgeries are being performed and are not yet outlawed. The case of M.C. also highlights the fact that American justices have not yet followed recent human rights developments at international level that condemn intersex surgeries based on the fact that they lead to a gross violation of fundamental rights. At a State level, some States have started recognising intersex people when it comes to identification

[254] Senate Concurrent Resolution No. 110, Introduced by Senator Wiener.

[255] Section 1557: Protecting Individuals Against Sex Discrimination.

[256] InterAct, "Federal Government Bans Discrimination Against Intersex People in Health Care".

[257] Dana uses gender-neutral pronouns "they", "them" and "their".

[258] Lambda Legal, "Lambda Legal Sues U.S. State Department on Behalf of Intersex Citizen Denied Passport".

[259] Zzyym v. Pompeo (formerly Zzyym v. Tillerson & Zzyym v. Kerry), In the United States District Court for the District of Colorado, Judge R. Brooke Jackson, Civil Action No. 15-cv-02362-RBJ. See also Scherpe et al. (2018) and Part IV, "United States" by Julie A. Greenberg in particular.

[260] SB-179 Gender identity: female, male or nonbinary, Senate Bill No. 179, Chapter 853.

[261] CNN, "Hundreds have changed genders on NYC birth certificates".

[262] Idem.

documents but still intersex rights are non-existent in other fields such as employment, education, access to healthcare. The current existing conflict on LGBT rights and religious freedom jeopardises intersex peoples' rights and makes it harder for them to become visible and claim their rights.

3.4 Oceania

In Oceania, the situation of SOGI rights varies significantly among countries. The British colonial laws are still apparent in the Cook Islands, Kribati, Papua New Guinea, Samoa, the Solomon Islands, Tonga and Tuvalu as they still criminalise same-sex activity.[263] Some Pacific states have indicated that they may repeal these laws, but others such as Papua New Guinea have signaled the opposite, and the discussion is ongoing in Tonga.[264] Gender identity is not protected in Papua New Guinea, Solomon Islands, Vanuatu, Kiribati, Nauru, Palau, Cook Islands and Tokelau.[265]

In the contrary, as it will be later explored, Australia and New Zealand have repealed colonial laws and they have introduced legislation on SOGI and intersex rights. With regards to intersex rights, in 2017, Australian and Aotearoa/New Zealand intersex organisations published the Darlington Statement which is a joint consensus that sets out priorities in relation with-among others- human rights and legal reforms. The Statement characterises medical interventions on intersex as "criminal acts" and calls for their prohibition. It also underlines the importance of "fully informed consent by individuals, with individuals and families having mandatory independent access to funded counselling".[266] On sex/gender classifications, the Statement mentions that sex and gender binaries are upheld by structural violence and therefore attempts to classify people as a third sex/gender do not respect intersex diversity and self-determination.[267] The goal is not to obtain new classifications but to end legal classifications and the hierarchies imposed by them. The Statement offers certain recommendations: sex/gender should not be a legal category on birth certificates or identification documents, sex/gender assignments in birth certificates must be regarded as provisional and be legally correctable through a simple administrative procedure, individuals able to consent should be able to choose between female (F), male (M), non-binary, alternative gender markers or multiple options.[268] Furthermore, the Statement calls for effective legislative protection from discrimination on grounds of sex characteristics in all areas and the

[263] ILGA, 2017, pp. 141–147.

[264] Harriet Smith, "Australia's marriage-equality debate reverberates through the Pacific".

[265] Equaldex, "LGBT Rights in Oceania".

[266] Darlington Statement, 2017, para. 7.

[267] Idem.

[268] Idem, para. 8 a,b,c,d.

recognition of the right to marry and form a family irrespective of sex characteristics.[269]

3.4.1 *Australia*

3.4.1.1 Situation of SOGI Rights

The Sex Discrimination Act 1984 was amended in 2013[270] to include sexual orientation, gender identity and intersex status as prohibited grounds of discrimination. The purpose of the Amendment Bill was "to foster a more inclusive society by prohibiting unlawful discrimination against LGBT and intersex people and promoting attitudinal change in Australia".[271] The Sex Discrimination Amendment extended the previous ground of "marital status" to "marital or relationship status" to provide protection from discrimination for same-sex de facto couples.[272] Furthermore, the amendments prohibit discrimination in all areas of life such as employment, education, provision of goods and services, accommodation, land, clubs and administration of Commonwealth laws and programs. Another aim of this Bill was to align with international human rights standards and guarantee the enjoyment of fundamental human rights to sexual minorities such as the rights in work, the right to an effective remedy, the right to a fair hearing, the right to freedom of thought, conscience and religion or belief, and the right to freedom of association.[273]

The Same-Sex Relationships (Equal Treatment in Commonwealth Laws-General Law Reform) Act 2008 and the Same-Sex Relationships (Equal Treatment in Commowealth Laws-Superannuation) Act 2008 amended 85 other existing federal laws to equalise the treatment of same-sex couples, and any children raised by those couples, in a range of areas including taxation, superannuation, health, social security, aged care and child support, immigration, citizenship and veterans' affairs.[274] The Marriage Amendment Act 2017 amended the Marriage Act 1961 to remove the restrictions that limited marriage to the union of "a man and a woman" and allow "two people" the freedom to marry regardless of their sex or gender.[275] The sentence

---

[269] Idem, paras. 9, 10, 11, 12, 13.

[270] See Sex Discrimination Amendment (Sexual Orientation, Gender Identity and Intersex Status) Act 2013, No. 98, 213, An Act to amend the Sex Discrimination Act 1984, and for related purposes.

[271] The Parliament of the Commonwealth of Australia, House of Representatives, Sex Discrimination Amendment (Sexual Orientation, Gender Identity and Intersex Status) Bill 2013, Explanatory Memorandum.

[272] Idem.

[273] Idem.

[274] Australian Government Attorney General's Department "Same-sex reforms: Overview of the Australian Government's same-sex law reforms".

[275] The Parliament of the Commonwealth of Australia, House of Representatives, Marriage Amendment (Definition and Religious Freedoms) Bill 2017, Explanatory Memorandum.

"two people" can be considered as groundbreaking since it allows for a broad interpretation based on the whole sex and gender spectrum including trans and intersex people. Since 2018, same-sex couples can also adopt children and Northern Territory became the last State to pass an adoption equality bill.[276]

Currently, in several States, trans people must undergo "sexual reassignment surgery", be unmarried and over the age 18 to apply for a new birth certificate.[277] However, as a result of the legalisation of same-sex marriage, many States have started removing the requirement of divorce. As of 2017, the Australian Capital Territory[278] and South Australia[279] were the only jurisdictions to allow a person to change the sex recorded on their birth certificate without a requirement to undergo sex reassignment surgery or divorce if married. In 2018, Victoria,[280] Queensland[281] and New South Wales[282] passed legislation removing the forced divorce requirement.

As it was already mentioned, after the amendment of the Marriage Act and the legalisation of same-sex marriages, States have started gradually omitting "divorce" as a requirement for trans people to modify their sex on birth certificates. At that point it should be noted that according to the federal legal system that is applied in Australia and Article 109 of the Constitution, "when a Law of a State is inconsistent with a law of the Commonwealth, the latter shall prevail, and the former shall, to the extent of the inconsistency, be invalid".[283] In addition, the Sex Discrimination Act prohibits discrimination based on gender identity in the area of "services"[284] and the term "services" includes "services of the kind provided by a government, a government authority or a local government body".[285] As a result, it can be argued that requirements imposed by certain States to trans applicants concerning their marital status or age limits constitute discrimination based on the ground of "gender identity" in relation with the provision of services provided by offices and registries that issue birth certificates, considering the fact that people who identify as "men" or "women" would not have to follow the same requirements.

---

[276] Human Rights Law Center, "Australia now has adoption equality".

[277] McAvan Emily, "Why Australia's gender recognition laws need to change".

[278] ABC News, "ACT to make it easier for transgender people to alter birth certificate".

[279] Sainty Lane, "A Tale of Two Bills: SA Passes Trans Reform, Victoria Cans It".

[280] Jones Jesse, "Victoria Moves to End Forced Divorce for Trans People under Marriage Equality".

[281] The Guardian, "Queensland scraps law forcing married transgender people to divorce".

[282] Human Rights Law Centre, "NSW delivers marriage equality for trans people".

[283] Commonwealth of Australia Constitution Act (The Constitution), This compilation was prepared on 4 September 2013 considering alterations up to Act No. 84 of 1977.

[284] Sex Discrimination Act 1984-SECT 3.

[285] Idem-SECT 4 Interpretation.

3.4.1.2 Intersex Rights

The Sex Discrimination Act, which aims to protect sexual minorities who fall outside of the binary, prescribes that it is unlawful to discriminate against a person on the grounds of "intersex status" in several contexts such as work, education, provision of services and accommodation.[286] "Intersex status" is defined as "the status of having physical, hormonal or genetic features that are: (a) neither wholly female nor wholly male; (b) a combination of female and male; or (c) neither female nor male".[287] The Act contains two exemptions. The first is a religious exemption that applies to the internal appointment, training or practices within religious bodies.[288] The second concerns sports in certain instances but it is not applicable to activities involving children aged less than 12 years old, or persons participating in coaching, refereeing, or administering sporting activities.[289]

Despite the above developments, it has been stated that Australian protections on "intersex status" are often incorrectly imputed to offer protections on grounds of identity or legal classification even though they refer to a purely biological definition irrespective of sex classification, gender identity or sexual orientation.[290] Intersex organisations have commented on the attribute of "intersex status", which is considered to be based on a model of deficit since it implies that intersex people may lack of something and it is broad enough to include many acquired characteristics as well as innate characteristics.[291] Therefore, it is best to use the term "sex characteristics" which is universally accepted and utilised by the UN. In 2013, the Australian Senate Community Affairs References Committee reported that sex "normalising" surgeries are a reality in Australia and they are often performed on infants and young children.[292] The Committee introduced some recommendations such as the requirement of authorisation from a civil and administrative tribunal or the Family Court for intersex medical interventions on children and adults without the capacity to consent.[293]

Later, in 2016, the Australian Family Court in the case of Re: Carla judged that a family can consent to the sterilisation of their intersex child.[294] The child was raised as a girl since birth and 2 years before the case, Carla was subjected to sex reassignment surgery. The Court's reasoning was impacted by gender stereotyping and the

[286] Idem-SECT 3 (b). See also Scherpe et al. (2018) and Part IV National Legal Developments, "Australia" by Claire Fenton-Glynn in particular.

[287] Idem-SECT 4 Interpretation.

[288] Idem-SECT 37 Religious Bodies.

[289] Idem-SECT 42.

[290] Intersex Human Rights Australia, "The Yogyakarta Principles+10 launched".

[291] Idem.

[292] See The Parliament of Australia, Second Report "Involuntary or coerced sterilisation of intersex people in Australia", Chapter 3 "Surgery and the assignment of gender".

[293] See Idem, Chapter 5, "Intersex: protection of rights and best practice in health", The role of the courts and tribunals in the healthcare of intersex people, Recommendation 6.

[294] See Re: Carla (Medical procedure) [2016] FamCA 7 (20 January 2016), para. 15 (c).

pathologisation of intersex. For instance, it commented that Carla had “a range of interests/toys and colours, all of which were stereotypically female, for example, having pink curtains, a Barbie bedspread and campervan, necklaces, lip gloss and ‘fairy stations’… She happily wore a floral skirt and shirt with glittery sandals and Minnie Mouse underwear and had her long blond hair tied in braid…”.[295] The Court referred mainly to outdated medical evidence provided by doctors who lead to the pathologisation of the child and failed to interpret correctly the 2013 Australian Senate’s report on the risks that Carla was facing.[296] It did not refer to international studies on intersex surgeries and human rights documents such as the reports of the UN. Alieen Kennedy stated that in that case, judges and doctors can be considered as “accomplices”: “there is complicity between the medical and the legal construction of variations of sex development as pathological disorders in urgent need of correction. The tension between the medical and judicial responses to variations of sex development has disappeared”.[297]

The binary system of sex categorisation on identification documents was challenged in 2013 with the “Norrie” case,[298] the first explicit judicial recognition in Australia of a nonbinary concept of sex.[299] Norrie, who had undergone a “sex affirmation procedure”, applied to the Registrar to register both a change of sex to “non-specific” and a change of name.[300] The High Court of Australia stated that the Births, Deaths and Marriages Registration Act 1995 of New South Wales recognises that a person may be other than male or female and therefore permits the registration of a person’s sex as “non-specific”’.[301] Australian government policy from 2003 since 2011 was to issue passports with an “X” marker to people who could present a birth certificate that noted their sex as indeterminate.[302] In 2011, the Department of Foreign Affairs & Trade (DFAT) revised the policy to allow more people to obtain an “X” passport, including non-binary trans as well as non-binary intersex people, on the basis of a simple letter signed by a medical doctor.[303] From 2013, federal guidelines enable all people to identify gender as male, female or “X” on federal

---

[295] Idem.

[296] Idem, “Why the need for the proposed surgery?”.

[297] Kennedy (2016), p. 834.

[298] NSW Registrar of Births, Deaths and Marriages v Norrie [2014] HCA 11 2 April 2014 S273/2013.

[299] Kennedy (2016), p. 829.

[300] High Court of Australia, NSW Registrar of Births, Deaths and Marriages v Norrie [2014] HCA 11, Judgment Summary.

[301] See NSW Registrar of Births, Deaths and Marriages v Norrie [2014] HCA 11 2 April 2014 S273/2013.

[302] See Australian Human Rights Commission, “Sex Files: the legal recognition of sex in documents and government records”, 2009.

[303] Intersex Human Rights Australia, “Ten years of “X” passports, and no protection from discrimination”.

documents, including passports. Documentary evidence must be witnessed by a doctor or psychologist, but medical intervention is not required.[304]

3.4.2 New Zealand

3.4.2.1 Situation of SOGI Rights

The Marriage (Definition of Marriage) Amendment Act 2013 amended the Marriage Act 1955 and included a definition of marriage to allow marriages for all sexual minorities as it defines marriage as: "marriage means the union of 2 people, regardless of their sex, sexual orientation or gender identity".[305]

The Human Rights Act 1993 prohibits discrimination on the grounds of sexual orientation, but the wording is limiting: "sexual orientation, which means a heterosexual, homosexual, lesbian or bisexual orientation".[306] People's rights who identify with a sexual orientation beyond this definition i.e. "asexual" are not explicitly covered. The Act does not explicitly mention the whole spectrum of gender including gender identity and therefore trans people remain unprotected. In 2004, the Human Rights Commission stated that it would accept complaints from trans people within the definition of "sex"[307] under the Act.[308] The same year, the Human Rights (Gender Identity) Amendment Bill was introduced as a parliamentary private member's bill. The bill's purpose was to add "gender identity" as a prohibited ground of discrimination.[309] In response to the bill, the Crown Law Office concluded that trans people were already protected under the ground of "sex" and the bill was withdrawn.[310]

In 2007, the Human Rights Commission in its report concluded that "trans people would be better protected by a specific reference to gender identity in the Human Rights Act 1993 so a consistent, non-discriminatory definition of a person's sex applies across all laws".[311] In 2014, Louisa Wall submitted a Supplementary Order Paper which was "seeking an amendment that means section 21(1)(a) would read "sex, which includes gender identity, pregnancy and childbirth".[312] It seems that both suggestions could lead to a broader confusion since they are seeking the inclusion of gender identity under the umbrella of "sex" whereas "sex" and "gender identity" are two different concepts. In addition, other grounds such as "gender

[304] Australian Government, "Australian Government Guidelines on the Recognition of Sex and Gender".

[305] Marriage (Definition of Marriage) Amendment Act 2013, Section 2 amended (Interpretation).

[306] Human Rights Act 1993, 21 Prohibited grounds of discrimination, 1 (m).

[307] The current definition of sex under the Act is: "sex, which includes pregnancy and childbirth".

[308] New Zealand Parliament, Wall, Louisa, 2014.

[309] New Zealand Parliament, Human Rights (Gender Identity) Amendment Bill.

[310] Attorney-General, "Crown Law opinion on transgender discrimination", 2006.

[311] Human Rights Commission, 2007, p. 4.

[312] New Zealand Parliament, Wall, Louisa, 2014.

expression" and "sex characteristics" still remain unprotected. It would be more suitable if the Act was amended to protect "sex" and "gender" and it is interpreted to cover the whole spectrum of both "sex" and "gender".

Section 28 of the Births, Deaths, Marriages and Relationships Registration Act 1995 allows an eligible adult to apply to the Family Court for a declaration that his or her birth certificate should show the sex specified in the application.[313] According to this Act, to change "sex" on birth certificates, the applicant must show that they have undergone medical intervention to give them "physical confirmation" of their gender.[314] The Internal Affairs Department has issued more detailed information on whether or not an individual has to undergo a gender reassignment to change his/her "sex" on birth certificates and it has clarified that a case to case approach is followed: "every applicant does not have to go through full reconstructive surgery to meet the test, although some may do. The level of surgery required for each person will be particular to that person based on what their medical advisors are recommending, and what that individual personally feels is required to be comfortable with their gender identity. So there is no 'tick-box' list of treatments to reach the level of "permanent physical change" required. It will vary for every person and cannot be detailed any further because there are an infinite range of circumstances that may arise".[315] The Human Rights Commission has reported that that "test" is rather confusing and trans people still do not know what it means in practice.[316]

The Citizenship and Passport offices have introduced policies that have simplified the process for transgender individuals. Applicants need to complete an application form, along with a statutory declaration of their gender identity and all other usual requirements.[317]

3.4.2.2 Intersex Rights

The Human Rights Commission has received submissions from intersex people and there are concerns about medical procedures performed on intersex children and young people.[318] Limited access to medical records compounds the invisibility, secrecy and shame that many intersex people experience.[319] Non-governmental organisations have made submissions stating that legal frameworks "while rightly

[313] The Department of Internal Affairs, "Information for Transgender Applicants".

[314] Births, Deaths, Marriages, and Relationships Registration Act 1995, Section 28 "Declarations of Family Court as to sex to be shown on birth certificates issued for adults", 3 (c) (i) (A) (B) (C).

[315] Internal Affairs, "General information regarding Declarations of Family Court as to sex to be shown on birth certificates", p. 3.

[316] Human Rights Commission, 2007, p. 69.

[317] See Identity and Passports, "Information about Changing Sex/Gender Identity" and The Department of Internal Affairs "Information for Transgender Applicants".

[318] See Human Rights Commission, Human Rights in New Zealand 2010, Section Four-Rights of Specific Groups "19. Rights of Sexual and Gender Minorities".

[319] Human Rights Commission, 2010, p. 320.

prohibiting female genital mutilation, allow similar surgical interventions on intersex girls".[320] They also mentioned that intersex surgeries "are regarded as being medically beneficial or therapeutic".[321] In 2016, the UN Committee on the Rights of the Child issued observations on practices in New Zealand, including recommendations to ensure "that no one is subjected to unnecessary medical or surgical treatment during infancy or childhood, guaranteeing the rights of children to bodily integrity, autonomy and self-determination".[322]

Discrimination is prohibited only on the grounds of "sex" and the New Zealand Human Rights Commission accepts complaints of unlawful discrimination against intersex under the ground of "sex".[323] There has been attempts to include "gender identity" among the prohibited grounds but this would still not protect intersex people. New Zealand could either follow the international developments and introduce "sex characteristics" or interpret "sex" in a broad way to include intersex people.

The New Zealand's Marriage Act has clarified that a marriage is between two people so an intersex person is free to marry someone of any sex and the legality of the marriage cannot be questioned because of either partner's intersex status.

In 2008, the Family Court held that the word "indeterminate" should have been recorded on an intersex person's original birth entry and this correction was made under section 85 of the Births, Deaths and Marriages Registration Act 1995.[324] Currently, passports are issued in the applicant's preferred sex which may be "M" (male), "F" (female) or "X" (indeterminate/unspecified).[325]

3.5 Asia

In Asia, some human rights are referenced in the ASEAN Charter which is a constituent instrument of the Association of Southeast Asian Nations (ASEAN). The Member States of the Association are Brunei Darussalam, Cambodia, Indonesia, Lao PDR, Malaysia, Myanmar, Philippines, Singapore, Thailand and Viet Nam.[326] In 2009, the ASEAN established the ASEAN Intergovernmental Commission on Human Rights to promote human rights and by mid-2012 the Commission drafted

---

[320] See OII Australia, Submission to the Australian Human Rights Commission: Sexual Orientation, Gender Identity and Intersex Rights Snapshot Report, February 2015; Intersex Trust Aotearoa New Zealand, Alternate NGO Submission on the sixth periodic report to the United Nations on the Convention against Torture and Other Cruel, Inhuman or Degrading Treatment or Punishment from New Zealand, January 2015.

[321] See New Zealand Crimes Act 1961, s. 204A; Attorney General's Department, Review of Australia's Female Genital Mutilation Legal Framework – Final Report, 2013.

[322] Human Rights Commission, 2016, p. 4.

[323] Human Rights Commission, 2010, p. 311.

[324] Human Rights Commission, 2010, p. 313.

[325] Identity and Passports, "Information about Changing Sex/Gender Identity".

[326] Charter of the Association of Southeast Asian Nations, The ASEAN Charter.

the ASEAN Human Rights Declaration.[327] The first five Articles guarantee human rights to "every person" and the next Articles affirm all the civil, political, economic, social and cultural rights. The ASEAN Human Rights Declarations covers a broader range of rights that the Universal Declaration as it guarantees explicitly the right to water and sanitation (Art. 28 e), the right to a safe environment (Art. 28 f), the right to development (Art. 36) and the right to peace (Art. 30).[328]

Nonetheless, the ASEAN Declaration and the work of the ASEAN Commission on Human Rights have been severely criticised. The UN High Commissioner has highlighted elements in the Declaration that are not in line with the international standards such as the lack of inclusive and meaningful consultation with civil society.[329] The U.S. Department of State has stated that "we are deeply concerned that many of the ASEAN Declaration's principles and articles could weaken and erode universal human rights and fundamental freedoms as contained in the UDHR. Concerning aspects include: the use of the concept of "cultural relativism" to suggest that rights in the UDHR do not apply everywhere; stipulating that domestic laws can trump universal human rights; incomplete descriptions of rights that are memorialized elsewhere; introducing novel limits to rights; and language that could be read to suggest that individual rights are subject to group veto."[330] The ASEAN human rights regional mechanism may be considered as a controversial but it still is a promising effort towards human rights protection in the region even though it applies only to its Member States.

Terminology in Asia when it comes to people who fall outside the binary may differ comparing to other continents. In South Asia, there are identities that are described as "third gender" such as hijra in India and Bangladesh, thirunangai and aravani in India, khwaja sira in Pakistan and meti in Nepal.[331] In South East Asia, terms used by transgender women are kathoey in Thailand, waria in Indonesia and the reclaimed term mak nyah in Malaysia.[332] In the Philippines, the term bakla is often used to describe people assigned a male sex at birth who identify as a third gender or are effeminate.[333] Many transgender women prefer the term transpinay, because it is a term introduced by their community. In East Asia, a term used in Hong Kong is kwaa-sing-bit.[334] In some parts of Asia, including Nepal and the Philippines, the terms "third gender" and "third sex" refer to all lesbian, gay, bisexual and transgender people. This terminology often leads to the invisibility of some communities, particularly lesbians and bisexual women, transgender men and

---

[327] ASEAN Human Rights Declaration and the Phnom Penh Statement on the Adoption of the ASEAN Human Rights Declaration (AHRD).

[328] Idem.

[329] UN News, "UN Official welcomes ASEAN commitment to human rights, but concerned over declaration wording".

[330] U.S. Department of State, "ASEAN Declaration on Human Rights".

[331] Asia Pacific Forum, 2016, p. 15.

[332] Idem.

[333] Idem.

[334] Idem.

intersex people.[335] Despite the limited information about intersex rights in the region, it has been reported that "sex-normalising" surgeries and other medical interventions are identified in Indonesia, China, Viet Nam, Hong Kong and Thailand.[336]

In February 2018, the First Asian Intersex Forum took place in Bangkok, Thailand and during the Forum, participants founded Intersex Asia, the first regional network of Asian human-rights-based intersex organisations and intersex activists working for the rights of intersex people, communities and movements.[337] The outcome of the Forum is reflected in the Public Statement that recalled and affirmed the principles of the Malta Declaration, the Intersex Statement of the Intersex Pre-Conference at ILGA-Asia 2017, and extended the demands "aimed at ending discrimination against intersex people, promoting and protecting the human rights of intersex people in Asia, and to ensure the rights to life, bodily integrity, physical autonomy and self-determination."[338]

This section will examine Asian countries that have legislated on intersex including Bangladesh, India, Nepal, Pakistan, Philippines and Viet Nam.

3.5.1 *Intersex and "Hijras"*

"Hijra" is a term that encompasses trans as well as intersex people in South Asia. A Nepali branch of knowledge claims that the word Hijra derives from the Persian "hiz" which meant one who is "effeminate" "disdains women", "a catamite".[339] Some persianists suggest that the origin of hijra was "hich", from the word "hich-gah" meaning "nowhere",[340] implying a person who has no identity. The tradition of hijrahood includes both Hinduism and Islam, although many argue that hijra has shown a special bias towards Islam.[341] It is believed that the religious role of the hijras has derived from Hinduism, but their historical role has derived from the eunuchs in the Muslim courts.[342] Thus, it can be assumed that the spiritual, religious and cultural aspect of "hijras" makes them socially acceptable. While worldwide, many societal, cultural or religious structures do not accept gender divirsities, the Hindu mythology has been supporting the hijra identity. The more obvious support from Hindu mythology stems from the God Ram who acknowledged and blessed "intersexed".[343]

---

[335] Idem, p. 16.

[336] Idem, p. 69.

[337] Intersex Day, "Statement of Intersex Asia and Asian intersex forum".

[338] See Statement of Intersex Asia and Asian intersex forum, 2018.

[339] Shawkat (2016), p. 7.

[340] Idem.

[341] Stenqvist (2015), p. 10.

[342] Idem, p. 11.

[343] Hahm (2010), p. 11.

Most hijras are born male or intersex and some may undergo a ritual emasculation operation, which includes castration[344] but this varies among regions. Hijras are regarded as a third gender and most of them see themselves as "neither man nor woman". Many South Asians believe that they have the power to bless or curse, and hijras trade off this ambivalence.[345] They cannot accurately be described as eunuchs or intersex or transgender, because these are Western terms.[346] Therefore, it is hard to specify the exact diversity of hijras and apply it to international terms and standards, but it could be argued that they include transgender and intersex people. Hijras occupy a paradoxical position: on the one hand they are accepted which allows for a degree of social inclusion and legal recognition. On the other, they live marginalised with limited economic opportunities, and depend on "gurus" for protection.[347] During the last decade they have been granted legal status in Nepal, India, Pakistan, as well as Bangladesh. This section aims to analyse the legal developments regarding "hijras" and their association with intersex rights.

3.5.1.1 Bangladesh

In Bangladesh, there are no laws prohibiting discrimination on the grounds of sexual orientation and/or gender identity. There is no legal recognition of same sex civil unions and/or marriages and same-sex couples are not allowed to adopt children.[348] Section 377 of the Penal Code criminalises same-sex sexual activity with regards to gay and bisexual men.[349] In 2013, the government granted hijras legal status as members of a "third gender", meaning that they are entitled to identify their gender as "hijra" in national documents such as passports and identity cards rather than "male" or "female".[350] Despite the legal recognition of hijras, there are continuing issues about ways to legally recognise and protect the rights of those who identify as third gender.[351] In 2015, the government of Bangladesh unveiled a series of special measures for hijras, including jobs and loans but implementation of the job

[344] Home Office, 2017, p. 21.

[345] New York Times, "The Peculiar Position of India's Third Gender".

[346] Idem.

[347] Human Rights Watch (2016), p. 4.

[348] Carroll and Mendos, 2017, pp. 47, 68, 71, 73.

[349] Section 377: Unnatural offences: Whoever voluntary has carnal intercourse against the order of nature with man, woman, or animal, shall be punished with imprisonment for life, or imprisonment of either description for a term which may extend to 10 years, and shall also be liable to fine. Explanation: penetration is sufficient to constitute the carnal intercourse necessary to the offence described in this section.

[350] Home Office, 2017, p. 6.

[351] Asia Pacific Forum, 2016, p. 58.

quota scheme has been ineffective.[352] During the recruitment process some hijras were victims of humiliation and discrimination.[353]

3.5.1.2 India

Section 377 of the Indian Penal Code[354] criminalises same-sex sexual activities but in 2009, the Delhi High Court in Naz Foundation v. Government of NCT of Delhi found that the criminalisation of same-sex sexual activities is in direct violation of fundamental rights provided by the Indian Constitution.[355] Prior to that decision, the Indian Supreme Court had ruled that "An order passed on writ petition questioning the constitutionality of a Parliamentary Act whether interim or final keeping in view the provisions contained in Clause (2) of Article 226 of the Constitution of India, will have effect throughout the territory of India subject of course to the applicability of the Act."[356] attributing to the ruling of the Delhi High Court a major significance for LGBT rights. In 2013, the Supreme Court ruled in favor of the criminalisation of same-sex sexual activities and overturned the 2009 Delhi High Court ruling[357] but later in 2018 the Supreme Court agreed to reexamine Section 377 after a 2017 decision that stated that India's LGBT community had a fundamental right to express their sexuality since sexual orientation is covered under clauses of the Indian Constitution that relate to liberty.[358] Last, in 2018, the Supreme Court decriminalised same-sex sexual activities in a landmark ruling.[359] Although same-sex marriages are not legally recognised, the Gurgaon Court invoked a prior judgment which was aiming to "ensure help and assistance to runaway couples" and granted legal recognition to a same-sex marriage between two women.[360]

---

[352] Asia Pacific Forum, 2016, p. 53.

[353] Idem.

[354] 377. Unnatural offences. Whoever voluntarily has carnal intercourse against the order of nature with any man, woman or animal, shall be punished with 1*[imprisonment for life], or with imprisonment of either description for a term which may extend to 10 years, and shall also be liable to fine. Explanation. Penetration is sufficient to constitute the carnal intercourse necessary to the offence described in this section.

[355] The Court stated: "We hold that sexual orientation is a ground analogous to sex and that discrimination on the basis of sexual orientation is not permitted by Article 15. Further, Article 15(2) incorporates the notion of horizontal application of rights. In other words, it even prohibits discrimination of one citizen by another in matters of access to public spaces. In our view, discrimination on the ground of sexual orientation is impermissible even on the horizontal application of the right enshrined under Article 15."

[356] M/S. Kusum Ingots & Alloys Ltd. vs Union of India And Anr on 28 April, 2004.

[357] The Telegraph, "India's top court upholds law criminalising gay sex".

[358] Independent, "India's supreme court could be about to decriminalize gay sex in major victory for LGBT rights".

[359] Independent, "India's Supreme Court rules gay sex is no longer a crime in historic Section 377 judgment".

[360] The Times of India, "In a first, Gurgaon court recognizes lesbian marriage".

In 2014, India's Supreme Court, in a landmark decision, ruled that the Centre and State governments must grant legal recognition of gender identity as male, female or third gender.[361] In the decision, intersex people are perceived that belong to a "wide range of transgender related identities".[362] Intersex are called "eunuchs" and even though they seem to belong in the same category as "hijras", they also differ. According to the Court, "hijras can be considered as the western equivalent of transgender/transsexual (male-to female) persons but Hijras have a long tradition/culture and have strong social ties formalized through a ritual called "reet".[363] At the same time, "eunuch" refers to an emasculated male and intersexed to a person whose genitals are ambiguously male-like at birth, but this is discovered the child previously assigned to the male sex, would be recategorized as intesexed – as a Hijra".[364] Therefore, the decision covers "transgender people as a whole"[365] and following the reasoning of the Court, intersex people are included.

The Court noted that the transgender community-including the "eunuchs"—has faced prejudice and disadvantage and declared that numerous steps were necessary in order to comply with the constitutional rights to life, equality before the law, non-discrimination and freedom of expression.[366] The Court considered gender identity as an integral part of the personality and one of the most basic aspects of self-determination, dignity and freedom.[367] It added that no one can be forced to undergo medical procedures, including sex reassignment surgery, sterilisation or hormonal therapy as a requirement for legal recognition of their gender and rights have to be protected irrespective of chromosomal sex, genitals, assigned birth sex, or implied gender role.[368] Despite the fact that the Court used international legal documents to elaborate on its reasoning, the terminology used to describe the diversity of sex and gender differs significantly from the one that prevails in the international human rights community. This can be explained considering the fact that gender diversities constitute inherent part of the Indian tradition and culture and play a particular role in the society especially comparing with other countries where transgender—and intersex—people do not enjoy the same "unique" status. In 2015, the Delhi High Court reinforced the ruling, emphasising that "everyone has a fundamental right to

[361] National Legal Services Authority v Union of India and Others (Writ Petition No. 400 of 2012 with Writ Petition No. 604 of 2013), Case summary. See also Scherpe et al. (2018) and Part IV National Legal Developments, "India" by Smita Shah in particular.

[362] National Legal Services Authority v Union of India and Others (Writ Petition No. 400 of 2012 with Writ Petition No. 604 of 2013), para. 44.

[363] Idem.

[364] Idem.

[365] Idem, para. 45.

[366] National Legal Services Authority v Union of India and Others (Writ Petition No. 400 of 2012 with Writ Petition No. 604 of 2013), Case summary.

[367] Idem.

[368] Idem.

be recognized in their gender" and that "gender identity and sexual orientation are fundamental to the right of self-determination, dignity and freedom".[369]

Currently, intersex people's rights are covered under the "third gender" but it remains unclear who is exactly considered as intersex. Serena Nanda writes on intersex in India: "There is a widespread belief in India that hijras are born intersex and are taken away by the hijra community at birth or in childhood, but I found no evidence to support this belief among the hijras I met, all of whom joined the community voluntarily, often in their teens".[370]

3.5.1.3 Nepal

SOGI and intersex rights in Nepal have significantly evolved since the restoration of multiparty democracy in May 2006 and the promulgation of an Interim Constitution.[371] The new Interim Constitution protects explicitly gender diversities and sexual minorities in several articles, for instance Article 18 withholds language in the old Constitution that emanates from the sex binary and replaces "male and female" and "son or daughter" with gender-neutral terminology.[372] In 2012, in Rajani Shahi v. National Women's Commission the Supreme Court recognised a live-in relationship between a lesbian couple and stated that: "Individuals can decide as to choosing their ways of living either separately or in partnership together with homosexuals or heterosexuals – with or without solemnizing marriage. Although in the prevailing laws and tradition "marriage" denotes legal bond between heterosexuals (male and female), the legal provisions on the homosexual relations are either inadequate or mute [sic] by now".[373]

In April 2007, LGBT organisations filed a writ petition based on the Interim Constitution of Nepal seeking recognition of transgender individuals as a third gender, a law prohibiting discrimination on the basis of sexual orientation and gender identity, and reparations by the State to victims of State violence and discrimination.[374] The Court found that the writ petition fell within the category of public interest litigation because it concerned a matter of social justice[375] and stated that it was a "constitutional duty and responsibility of the state to make the deprived and socially backward classes and communities"[376] able to enjoy their rights as others

[369] See Shivani Bhat v. State of NCT of Delhi and Ors., Delhi High Court on 5 October, 2015.

[370] Nanda (1999), p. xx.

[371] UNDP, USAID (2014), p. 29.

[372] See The Constitution of Nepal, Date of Publication in Nepal Gazette, 20 September 2015 (2072.6.3).

[373] Rajani Shah v. National Women Commission et al., Supreme Court of Nepal, April 11, 2013.

[374] International Commission of Jurists, Sunil Babu Pant and Others/ v. Nepal Government and Others, Supreme Court of Nepal (21 December 2007).

[375] Idem.

[376] Sunil Babu Pant and Others/ v. Nepal Government and Others, Supreme Court of Nepal (21 December 2007), p. 266.

did. The Court then noted that the Interim Constitution's rights were "vested in the third gender people as human beings. The homosexuals and third gender people are also human beings as other men and women are, and they are the citizens of this country as well."[377] It also stated that sexual activity relied on the right to privacy and an individual's choice of sexual partner fell within the right to self-determination.[378] Last, the Court concluded that since sexual minorities are "natural persons" it is "the responsibility of the state to create an appropriate environment and make legal provisions accordingly for the enjoyment of such rights".[379]

In its ground-breaking decision, the Court established a "third gender" category and included intersex people in it: "there should be a declaration for full fundamental human rights for all sexual and gender minorities-lesbian, gay, bisexual, transgender, and intersex citizens" and "legal provisions should be made to provide for gender identity to the people of transgender or third gender, under which female third gender, male third gender and intersexual are grouped, as per the concerned person's self-feeling".[380] In an effort to describe the "third gender", the Court seems to create a confusion as it does not make a clear distinction between sexual orientation, gender identity and sex characteristics. Rather, it places all sexual minorities in one category without recognising the diversities existing within. In addition, it should be noted that even though the Court recognised intersex individuals as "citizens" and it highlighted that their rights should be acknowledged and respected, it failed to depathologise intersexuality when it stated that "it is a simple belief is that a child generally is born normal at birth. However, sometimes abnormal children such as having more than five fingers in a hand or blind or Siamese twins or handicapped are also born. Similarly, on the basis of genitals, intersex children, other than the male and female, having both genitals may also born".[381] With the above sentences, the Court characterises implicitly intersex infants as "abnormal" although later it links the sex binary with the perceptions of a "traditional society".

3.5.1.4 Pakistan

Article 377 of the Pakistan Penal Code[382] criminalises same-sex sexual activities but the government rarely prosecutes cases and lesbian, gay, bisexual, male transgender, and intersex persons "rarely revealed their sexual orientation or gender identity".[383] As in other South Asian countries, transgender women, eunuchs, and

[377] Idem, para. 4, p. 278.

[378] International Commission of Jurists, Sunil Babu Pant and Others/ v. Nepal Government and Others, Supreme Court of Nepal (21 December 2007).

[379] Sunil Babu Pant and Others/ v. Nepal Government and Others, Supreme Court of Nepal (21 December 2007), p. 284.

[380] Idem, p. 281.

[381] Idem, para. 4, p. 278.

[382] Pakistan Penal Code (XLV of 1860) 6th October, 1860.

[383] U.S. State government report, 2017, p. 45.

intersex persons, are collectively referred to as "hijras". However, some transgender individuals view the term "hijras" as pejorative and prefer the term "khwaja serra".[384]

In 2008, Lahore High Court allowed a woman to change her sex and undergo surgery after medical experts agreed that she was suffering from "gender identity disorder".[385] A year later, a constitutional petition was filed on behalf of hijras before the Supreme Court and specific problems that hijras face were identified in several areas such as inheritance, registration of identity, voting, employment and schooling.[386] The Pakistan Supreme Court in a landmark decision recognised the human rights violations that hijras encounter accepting that "this class of the society has been neglected on account of gender disorder in their bodies, otherwise they are entitled to enjoy all the rights granted to them by the Constitution (…)".[387] The Court addressed the violations of the right to inherit and to vote. Concerning voting, it stated that whereas registration sheets previously had columns only for male or female, they were to include a column for "eunuchs" which would be confirmed by medical tests.[388] It also examined the right to education that is guaranteed under the Constitution and noted that there were no provisions in place to ensure the access of eunuchs to education.[389] Last, the Court underlined that the provinces remained quiet concerning the protection of eunuchs from harassment or the prevention of non-eunuchs from using this status to commit crimes.[390]

In 2010, the Supreme Court ordered the full recognition of the trans community, including the provision of free medical and educational facilities, microcredit schemes and job quotas in every government department.[391] Seven years later, the Lahore High Court issued the order to the government, National Database and Registration Authority, and the interior ministry to include trans people in its 2017 national census.[392]

In 2018, the National Assembly in Islamabad passed the Transgender Persons (Protection of Rights) Act. The act defines "transgender person" as "an intersex (Khunsa) with mixture of male and female genital features or congenital ambiguities" or a male who "undergoes genital excision or castration", or "any person whose gender identity and/or gender expression differs from the social norms and cultural expectations based on the sex they were assigned at the time of their

---

[384] Idem.

[385] ZeeNews, "Pakistan court allows woman to change sex".

[386] International Commission of Jurists, Khaki v. Rawalpindi, Supreme Court of Pakistan (12 December 2009), Case summary.

[387] Khaki v. Rawalpindi, Supreme Court of Pakistan, Constitution Petition No. 43 of 2009, para. 2.

[388] International Commission of Jurists, Khaki v. Rawalpindi, Supreme Court of Pakistan (12 December 2009), Case summary.

[389] Idem.

[390] See Khaki v. Rawalpindi, Supreme Court of Pakistan, Constitution Petition No. 43 of 2009, paras. 3–5.

[391] Pakistan Today, "Don't we count? Transgender Pakistanis feel sidelined by census".

[392] Reuters, "Pakistan counts transgender people in national census for first time".

birth".[393] The law recognises the identity of transgender persons "a transgender person shall have a right to be recognized as per his or her self-perceived gender identity"[394] and guarantees access to identification documents such as driving licenses and passports.[395] It bans discrimination against transgender people in employment and outlaws harassment in public places or at home[396] and recognises several rights such as the right to inherit, the right to education, the right to employment, the right to vote, the right to hold public office, the right to health, the right to assembly, the right of access to public spaces and the right to property.

It is obvious that in Pakistani's case law and law there is a confusion as to what is intersex, where it starts and where it ends. The terminology used in Pakistan does not reflect the one used in international human rights documents due to the fact that gender diversities are directly connected with the Pakistani culture and tradition. Although the terminology used may result to confusion especially for readers who are not aware of the Pakistani cultural and traditional background, the new Law guarantees some major rights to intersex—and trans—people that maybe no other jurisdictions have managed to attempt. For instance, the Transgender Persons (Protection of Rights) Act guarantees the right to hold public office, transforming intersex people and all sexual minorities from a marginalised group to active citizens.

3.5.2 Philippines

3.5.2.1 Situation of SOGI Rights

In the Philippines, the terms "third gender" and "third sex" are used interchangeably to refer to all lesbian, gay, bisexual and transgender and this perpetuates the invisibility of some communities, particularly lesbians and bisexual women, transgender men and intersex people.[397] Human rights in general are restricted when it comes to sexual orientation and gender identity.

Same-sex sexual activities between two adults are legalised only when they are noncommercial and in private as the Revised Penal Code criminalises "any person who shall offend against decency or good customs".[398] Article 46 of the Family Code includes homosexuality/lesbianism as a ground for annulling marriages and the Republic Act (RA) 9262 portrays LGBT people negatively because their sexual

[393] See Transgender Persons (Protection of Rights) Act, 2018, para. n (i) (ii) (iii).

[394] Idem, Chapter II, para. 3 (1).

[395] Idem, (3).

[396] Independent, "Pakistan passes law guaranteeing transgender rights" and Transgender Persons (Protection of Rights) Act, 2018 Chapter III.

[397] Asia Pacific Forum, 2016, p. 16.

[398] The Revised Penal Code of the Philippines, An Act Revising the Penal Code and Other Penal Laws, Art. 200.

orientation and gender identity is associated as "socially bad or psychologically detrimental".[399] Since there is no national legislation on LGBT rights, some ordinances in local government units mandate protection from discrimination on the basis of SOGI.[400] Quezon City passed an ordinance banning employment-related discrimination while anti-discrimination ordinances were passed in the cities of Angeles, Cebu, Bacolod and Davao.[401]

In relation with trans rights, the RA 9048 (Clerical Error Law of 2001) condemns the modification of the first name and sex in the birth certificates for trans persons stating that "no correction must involve the change of nationality, age, status or sex of the petitioner".[402] In 2007, the Supreme Court in Rommel Jacinto Dantes Silverio v. Republic of the Philippines, denied the right of a trans individual to legally change gender identity. The Court elaborated on several aspects of trans rights and focused on the defitions of "sex" and "marriage". On "sex", the Court stated that "the sex of a person is determined at birth, visually done by the birth attendant (the physician or midwife) by examining the genitals of the infant. Considering that there is no law legally recognizing sex reassignment, the determination of a person's sex made at the time of his or her birth, if not attended by error, is immutable."[403] Then, the Court specified that "sex" can strictly be "female" or "male" reinforcing the binary and making "no room" for persons who are not born as such: "Female is "the sex that produces ova or bears young" and male is "the sex that has organs to produce spermatozoa for fertilizing ova." Thus, the words "male" and "female" in everyday understanding do not include persons who have undergone sex reassignment."[404] It appears that the Court also denied the access of the trans petitioner to legally change gender identity because of the "serious and wide-ranging legal and public policy consequences"[405] that would emanate from this change. Furthermore, the Court used a "nuclear" definition of marriage, making it "accessible" only to men and women "the petition was but petitioner's first step towards his eventual marriage to his male fiancé. However, marriage, one of the most sacred social institutions, is a special contract of permanent union between a man and a woman".[406]

In this decision the Court limits itself in the sex binary living no space for individuals who do not fit in it although in the end of its reasoning recognises that sexual

[399] UNDP-USAID, 2014, p. 22.

[400] Idem, p. 23.

[401] Idem.

[402] Republic Act No. 9048 March 22, 2001, An Act Authorizing the City or Municipal Civil Registrar or the Consul General to Correct a Clerical or Typographical Error in an Entry and/or Change of First Name of Nickname in the Civil Register without Need of a Judicial Order, Section 2 (3).

[403] See Rommel Jacinto Dantes Silverio v. Republic of the Philippines, Section "No Law Allows the Change of Entry in the Birth Certificate As To Sex On the Ground of Sex Reassignment".

[404] Idem.

[405] Idem, Section "Neither May Entries in the Birth Certificate as to First Name or Sex Be Changed on the Ground of Equity".

[406] Idem.

minorities' lives may be an "ordeal" due to the fact that they do not belong in the sex/gender binary. It also relies a lot on "biology", "medicine" as well as "religion". The Court accepts that physicians are the ones responsible for the determination of one's gender and that marriage is "sacred"; therefore, it is only restricted to men and women. The reasoning of the Supreme Court shows that it has failed to follow the international developments with regards to gender identities and the boundaries of "sex" and "gender". It has also been highlighted that Philippine courts often confuse concepts of sexual orientation and gender identity. In previous decisions, the Supreme Court has used "LGBTs" and "homosexuals" interchangeably giving the impression that it views lesbians, gay, bisexuals, and transgender as categories of sexual orientations and showing ignorance of their diverse gender identity aspects.[407]

3.5.2.2 Intersex Rights

Despite the fact that there are not significant developments on intersex rights in the Philippines, the Supreme Court confirmed the right of an intersex person to change the sex marked on his birth certificate from female to male in Republic of the Philippines v. Jennifer Cagandahan. The plaintiff was registered at birth as female but developed secondary male characteristics over time. He stated that "he thought of himself" and lived as a male person and asked for his birth certificate sex to be changed to male.[408] A medical expert testified that the plaintiff was genetically female but because of the plaintiff's condition, his female organs had not developed "normally".[409]

First, the Court defined and analysed "intersexuality" and used Wikipedia as a source of reference. Then it elaborated on the "power of nature" in relation with "sexes": "The current state of Philippine statutes apparently compels that a person be classified either as a male or as a female, but this Court is not controlled by mere appearances when nature itself fundamentally negates such rigid classification."[410] Then, the justices mentioned that they "are of the view that where the person is biologically or naturally intersex the determining factor in his gender classification would be what the individual, like respondent, having reached the age of majority, with good reason thinks of his/her sex."[411] The Court considered that the plaintiff "let nature take its course and has not taken unnatural steps to arrest or interfere with what he was born with".[412] It concluded that the plaintiff, should have "the primordial choice of what courses of action to take along the path of his sexual development

[407] Ocampo (2011), p. 195.

[408] International Commission of Jurists, Republic of the Philippines v. Jennifer Cagandahan, Supreme Court of the Philippines, Second Division, 12 September 2008, Case summary.

[409] Idem.

[410] Republic of the Philippines v. Jennifer Cagandahan, Supreme Court of the Philippines, Second Division, 12 September 2008.

[411] Idem.

[412] Idem.

and maturation" and "in the absence of evidence to show that classifying respondent as a male will harm other members of society",[413] and as a result it allowed that person to determine his own gender.

This can be considered as a "rare" Court decision since the justices perceive "sexes" as a strictly natural matter and they do not support society's and medicine's efforts to accommodate intersex within the two sexes. They pronounce against medical interventions and they are proponents of the natural development of intersex bodies. Although they did not refer to credible international human rights documents but rather to Wikipedia, they aimed to depathologise intersex and based their arguments on nature. The paradox is that in Rommel Jacinto Dantes Silverio v. Republic of the Philippines, they did not recognise the right of a trans petitioner to modify her legal gender. It seems that the significant difference between the two decisions is that according to the justices, "transgenderism" does not fall within the sphere of "the power of nature". Trans individuals are born male or female whereas intersex are born intersex or they may develop intersex traits overtime. Even though in the Republic of the Philippines v. Jennifer Cagandahan, the plaintiff claimed that he also "feels" male and that is also an argument used by trans individuals, in the case of "transgenderism" or "gender dysphoria" the role of nature and biology is still questionable.[414] Consequently, it was easier for the Court to depathologise an intersex individual since nature made him/her that way than a trans individual whose arguments are merely based on the way he/she perceives his/her gender.

3.5.3 Viet Nam

3.5.3.1 SOGI and Intersex Rights in "Confusion"

Same-sex sexual activities are not criminalised in Viet Nam and it is believed that they have never been criminalised in the country.[415] In 2013, the Decree 110/2013/ND-CP removed administrative fines with regards to the realisation of same-sex weddings.[416] The Law on Marriage and Family was amended in 2014 and even though it does not recognise same-sex marriage, it removed language contained in

[413] Idem.

[414] Scientists have not yet concluded if "gender dysphoria" is a purely biological matter: "Two decades of brain research have provided hints of a biological origin to being transgender, but no irrefutable conclusions." See Reuters, "Born this way? Researchers explore the science of gender identity" and Online Psychology "How Does Science Explain Transgenderism?".

[415] See ILGA, "State-Sponsored Homophobia A world survey of sexual orientation laws: criminalization, protection and recognition", 11th Edition, Updated to October 2016 and ILGA: Carroll Aengus and Mendos Lucas Ramón "State Sponsored Homophobia 2017: A world survey of sexual orientation laws: criminalisation, protection and recognition", 2017.

[416] Previously, Article 8 (f) of Decree 87/2001/ND-CP stipulated that "a fine between VND 100,000 and 500,000 shall be imposed for…marriage between persons of the same sex".

Article 10 of the previous Law on Marriage and Family of 2000 which stated that "marriage is forbidden…between people of the same sex".[417]

In 2015, the National Assembly passed the new Civil Code which allows sex change as well as gender marker change. The new Civil Code has two articles: Article 36 on the right to re-determine gender identity, which is open for interpretation and can extend to both trans and intersex persons: "An individual has the right to re-determine his/her gender identity. The re-determination of the gender identity of a person is implemented where the gender of such person is subject to a congenital defect or has not yet been accurately formed and requires medical intervention in order to identify clearly the gender.(…)" and Article 37 which refers explicitly to trans individuals "(…)Each surged transgender has the right and obligation to apply for change of civil status affairs as prescribed in law on civil status affairs and has the personal rights in conformity with the transformed gender as prescribed in this Code and relevant laws."[418]

Under the previous Civil Code, sex reassignment surgery was available only for intersex people and prohibited for transgender people who had to travel to Thailand to be operated.[419] The new provisions give access to transgender people to sex reassignment surgeries and the right to apply for change of their civil status. According to Human Rights Watch, "the requirement for surgical procedures as a precondition for legal gender recognition imposes a burden on transgender people that is at odds with their fundamental rights to be recognised in the gender with which they identify".[420]

Although the word "intersex" is not explicitly mentioned, Article 36 can be interpreted to include intersex individuals. Accordingly, intersex persons who wish to modify their civil status have to go through sex reassignment surgery. Even though it is clear that Article 36 covers intersex people[421] there is a confusion with regards to intersex and "gender identity". The Article states that "the gender identity of a person is implemented where the gender of such person is subject to congenital defect or has not yet been accurately formed". As it was already mentioned, gender is a social construct encompassing gender identity and gender expression. Trans individuals encounter issues emanating from their gender, but intersex usually do not suffer from gender identity issues but from issues deriving from their sex characteristics. It remains unknown if the goal of the legislator was to protect intersex

---

[417] Article 10 of The Marriage and Family Law, No. 22/2000/QH10 of June, 2000.

[418] Viet Nam Civil Code No. 91/2015/QH13 of November 24, 2015.

[419] Human Rights Watch, "Vietnam: Positive Step for Transgender Rights Vietnamese parliament adopts new transgender legislation".

[420] Idem.

[421] The Institute for Studies of Society, Economics and Environment (iSEE) that operates in Viet Nam mentions in its website under the section "10 things you need to know about the recognition of transgender rights in Viet Nam": "1. Who is obligated for the sex change? The new Civil Code has two articles: Redefine sex (Article 36) and Sex change (Article 37). Redefine sex applies to people who are born not clearly male or female (intersex people) and sex change applies to those wishing to change their sex assigned at birth. So, basically, any people can change their sexes as they wish".

individuals or to protect only trans and due to the wording of the text which allows for a broader interpretation there is confusion and at the same time, intersex rights are partially protected. The aim of the sentence "partially protected" is to highlight the fact that although access to identification documents for intersex is essential, medical interventions and surgeries remain a major violation of intersex rights. In addition, intersex people will still have to fit into the binary as they need to become physically fully male or female and identify as such.

3.6 Remarks

3.6.1 The Impact of SOGI Rights on Intersex Persons

From the countries that have been examined in this Chapter it can be concluded that developments in SOGI rights law may impact intersex rights both negatively and positively:

(a) **Negative impact of sexual orientation law on intersex**: a major problem that is posed to intersex rights by legal frameworks on sexual orientation is the recognition of same-sex marriages or civil unions. Most legal frameworks use the wording "same-sex" and usually in the explanatory note it is described as the union between a man with a man and a woman with a woman. This definition of sex excludes intersex people who do not fit in the binary system of man and woman. Therefore, it could be argued that legal frameworks on same-sex marriages and unions reinforce the sex binary nature of marriage and "legitimise" harmful medical interventions on intersex people to make them, as Gina Wilson has stated, "marriage ready" or "marriage compliant".[422]

    A peculiar situation is the one in the U.S. where the recognition of same-sex marriages by the Supreme Court caused the "resistance" of some States where religious freedom and liberty are used to escape the implementation of the Supreme Court ruling and discriminate against LGBT. The provisions target especially same-sex couples and restrict their access to a multiple range of services. However, this "backlash" in LGBT rights can easily affect intersex as often the language of the restrictive legal frameworks is broad and can be interpreted to affect all sexual minorities.

(b) **Positive impact of sexual orientation law on intersex**: Australia and New Zealand have passed laws that recognise marriage between "two individuals" or "two persons" departing from the traditional view of marriage and making it accessible to intersex people and in general to people who may not identify as "man" or "a woman".

[422] Intersex Human Rights Australia (IHRA), "Intersex people and marriage, an analysis by Gina Wilson".

(c) **Negative impact of gender identity law on intersex**: in some cases, intersex people will have to go through the same process as trans to alter their identification documents. For instance, in Argentina, Gender Identity Law is applied to intersex as well. This can be problematic as trans and intersex are not the same. Trans aim to "transition" and become fully male or fully female whereas intersex may want to just identify as intersex. Provisions introduced for trans people usually provide them with the option to identify as female or male and not as intersex. Too often, trans people will have to go through reassignment operations to change their gender on certificates and if the same frameworks apply to intersex then their right to bodily integrity is again at stake. As a result, intersex people remain unprotected and a confusion is created among authorities, legislators and justices between the concepts of "gender identity" and "intersex".

It has to be clarified that "recognition before the law means having legal personhood and the legal protections that flow from that. For intersex people, this is neither primarily nor solely about amending birth registrations or other official documents. Firstly, it is about intersex people who have been issued a male or a female birth certificate being able to enjoy the same legal rights as others (…) Some intersex people seek to amend their sex or gender details on official documents because those details were either inaccurate at birth and/or no longer reflect their sex or gender identity."[423] Consequently, trans provisions when applied on intersex, should recognise the specific experiences of intersex people and should not be framed solely around transgender people and the process of transitioning. According to Gina Wilson, "the view of intersex through a trans lens is mistaken. Intersex people do not seek transition, sex/gender binary certainty within the confines of a sex binary paradigm, even though the outcomes of intersex choices might look like that. Intersex people actually seek the right to self- determination, and autonomy; the right to sex roles that intersex people are comfortable with, and the right to freely given, prior and fully informed consent – especially in respect of medical interventions and lived sex roles."[424]

(d) **Positive impact of gender identity law on intersex**: gender identity issues have gained visibility within societies during the last decade whereas intersex issues are not yet significantly raised or recognised. As a result, discussion on gender identity law may sometimes be beneficial since questioning the binary can be a major step that can lead to further legal developments. In most cases, when trans legislation is at place intersex legislation or discussions on intersex will sooner or later follow.

[423] Asia Pacific Forum of National Human Rights Institutions, 2016, p. 80.

[424] Intersex Human Rights Australia (IHRA), "Intersex people and marriage, an analysis by Gina Wilson".

3.6.2 Opening the Pandora's Box: Intersex and the "Third Gender"

Since 2003, passports and identification documents in Australia and New Zealand have adopted the third option "X" for people who do not fit in the binary. Since 2012, U.S. States have also recognised third options in identification documents. In Asia, a "third gender" is officially recognised in numerous countries. Nonetheless, to which extend could the introduction of a third gender be positive to intersex people?

The introduction of a "third gender" differs significantly between regions. In the case of Australia, New Zealand and the U.S. a third gender was established to safeguard non-binary people's rights and provide them with a legal personhood. On the other hand, in South Asia, people who identify as a third gender have been always existed in societies as it is directly related with tradition, culture, history and religion. Thus, the "third gender" is a very abstract and fluid concept that cannot be specified due to its strong cultural character. In most of South Asian states, SOGI rights might be extremely limited or non-existent, but non-binary individuals are granted rights because they reserve a "unique" place in society.

The adoption of a "third gender" category may indeed grant some rights to non-binary individuals, but it also reinforces the male and female binary and the unequal relation of powers that it contains. The "third gender" implies that there is also a "first" and a "second" gender. This hierarchy can be associated with patriarchal attitudes that perceive the female sex/gender as a "second sex/gender" and therefore inferior to the "male sex/gender". Of course, another interpretation could be that the "female sex/gender" could be the first gender and "male sex/gender" could be second. Nonetheless, hierarchy in that case is established which can lead to inequalities between sexes and genders. Moreover, the concept of the "third gender" creates categorisation and labelling as it accommodates all individuals in one single category erasing the diversities that exist within groups of people who do not fit in the binary.

Introducing a "third gender" to guarantee intersex people's rights may not be a safe option as it does not reflect the needs of intersex people. Intersex people want primarily their sex to be recognised. Their existence proves that there are not only two sexes and that nature is that diverse that cannot fit only in male and female categories and "boxes". Second, "it is important to clarify that recognition before the law for intersex people is not about creating a third, separate category for the registration of people born with an intersex trait. To do so would risk segregating and potentially stigmatising intersex people and it would also remove their right to determine their own sex or gender."[425]

[425] Asia Pacific Forum of National Human Rights Institutions, 2016, p. 80.

3.6.3 Recognising Intersex Rights Through "Cherry-Picking"

In this Chapter, legal developments regarding intersex on different countries across four continents were examined. Considering this analysis, it can be concluded that progress on intersex rights depends on factors that are not purely legal but rather social, traditional, cultural, religious and historical. Especially in case-law, the reasoning of the justices usually was not based on international human rights sources but on what they perceive as "right" or "wrong" at the period of time of the verdict. In Kenya, for example, the first intersex case for legal recognition was rejected and justice Sitati stated that the Kenyan society was not ready to accept values involving matters of sexuality but later in the Baby "A" decision justice Lenaola concluded that the Kenyan society was "now ready to accept this kind of developments".[426] In South Asian countries case-law on intersex is directly influenced by tradition, culture and religion: in India the Court underlined the unique status of "hijras" based on the fact that they "have a long tradition/culture and have strong social ties formalized through a ritual called "reet".[427] In Philippines, justices accepted to grant legal recognition to an intersex person but not to a trans person as they stated that in the case of intersex, nature decides.

It can be observed that a strong relationship exists between the personal acceptance of the justices and legal inclusiveness. The justices as members of the society themselves, are strongly influenced by social, traditional, cultural, religious and patriarchal norms that instead of grounding their reasoning on credible facts, they mainly use their empirical experience. This is also clear when it comes to terminology on sex and gender; in many cases, the justices use most terms falsely, showing that they have not followed international developments. As a result, due to ignorance, they fail to digest the whole spectrum of sex and gender and the violations that intersex people may encounter. In addition, all the countries examined are members of the UN and as members of the UN, they are signatory to various international covenants promoting human rights such as the International Covenant on Economic, Social and Cultural Rights (ICESCR), the International Covenant on Civil and Political Rights (ICCPR), the Convention Against Torture (CAT), the United Nations Convention on the Rights of the Child (UNCRC). It was extremely rare to find decisions where justices would interpret these covenants and apply them to the case of intersex people. Especially with regards to intersex surgeries, the UN has developed soft-law that prohibits explicitly their performance and condemns them as a major violation of basic human rights. Nonetheless, in none of the above jurisdictions, intersex surgeries are explicitly outlawed. Even in Australia and New Zealand, where essential intersex rights' developments can be identified, harmful and involuntary surgeries on intersex infants are still being performed.

---

[426] Baby 'A' (suing through the Mother E.A.) & another v. Attorney General & 6 others [2014] eKLR, petition no. 266 of 2013, para. 66.

[427] Idem.

As can be seen, it seems that there is a tendency to grant rights to intersex people through "cherry-picking" since jurisdictions' main goal is to "fix" intersex rights violations only when they occur and usually this happens when a case is brought to the Court. Accordingly, there are jurisdictions that may grant legal personhood to intersex individuals but there is still an absence of comprehensive legal frameworks that will allow intersex to enjoy the same rights as people who identify as "men" and "women". Moreover, sometimes, intersex people are granted legal personhood only if they undergo through unnecessary medical interventions and become fully "male" and fully "female". These legal frameworks instead of safeguarding intersex rights, they reinforce the binary and do not treat intersex as human beings but as outcasts who need to be "fixed" and then integrated in the binary to be able to enjoy equal rights.

On the whole, the current situation highlights the fact that including intersex in legal frameworks or granting them rights is not enough. Legal developments on intersex ought to have a human-rights centered perspective which will "demedicalise" and "depathologise" intersex and treat them as visible citizens and subjects of rights. This can be succeeded primarily through the gathering of disaggregated data on intersex and the status of the law in relation to them. Data collection must then be used as a tool by legislators and justices to transform current frameworks that segregate individuals and place them in the visible "majority" of "men" and "women" and the invisible "minorities" of non-binary individuals. Only then, the appropriate conditions will be created for intersex to enjoy their rights and shape inclusive and just societies.

Chapter 4
Intersex in Europe

Over the last two decades, the European Union (EU) has been introducing legislation for the active promotion of SOGI rights. Some of the rights of sexual minorities in the EU are protected under the European Union's treaties and law. The Treaty on the Functioning of the European Union (TFEU)[1] and the Charter on Fundamental Rights[2] condemn discrimination based on sexual orientation. In the field of employment, the Council Directive 2000/78/EC called Employment Equality Framework Directive[3] combats discrimination on the ground of sexual orientation. The adoption of the Employment Directive obliges all Member States to introduce legislation banning discrimination in employment on sexual orientation.[4] Gender identity may not be incorporated in EU law but the European Court of Justice (ECJ) has provided some protection by interpreting discrimination on the basis of "sex".[5] Despite all the progress in SOGI rights, intersex have not yet received the same attention as the rest of sexual minorities in the EU.

Intersex rights are not included in EU legal frameworks and no case on intersex has reached the European Court of Justice to date. Intersex issues have progressively emerged as relevant to fundamental rights protection and they are still largely treated as primarily medical issues.[6] European societies are based on norms derived from the simplistic idea of a dichotomy of two mutually exclusive and biologically

[1] See Articles 10 and 19, Consolidated versions of the Treaty on European Union and the Treaty on the Functioning of the European Union 2012/C 326/01.

[2] Article 21 on Non-discrimination, Charter of Fundamental Rights of the European Union, 2000/C 364/01.

[3] See Articles 1 and 2, Council Directive 2000/78/EC of 27 November 2000 establishing a general framework for equal treatment in employment and occupation.

[4] ILGA Europe, "European Union and LGBT rights".

[5] See P v. S and Cornwall County Council, Case C-13/94, judgment of 30 April 1996. As it is already mentioned in Chap. 2, "since the equal treatment directives of the European Union operate with closed lists of discrimination grounds, the sex ground was simply the only applicable ground in this instance in the absence of a specific ground of transsexuality or gender identity in EU law".

[6] European Union Agency for Fundamental Rights (2015), p. 2.

N. Pikramenou, *Intersex Rights*, https://doi.org/10.1007/978-3-030-27554-9_4

defined sexes[7] and in the absence of EU regulations on non-binary individuals such as intersex, people who do not easily fit these norms remain unprotected. The "working definitions" introduced by the Council of the European Union in 2013, confirmed that traditional notions of maleness and femaleness are culturally established in the EU.[8] The existence of intersex people in most EU Member States is not recognised and healthy intersex bodies are treated as a "medical problem" and a "psycho-social emergency" that needs to be fixed through harmful and involuntary medical interventions.[9]

In a 2016 report of the European Commission, it was cited that several Member States were reviewing their laws and policies in relation to sex characteristics and this included examples of states "developing medical and legal protocols to deal with intersex aspects from birth; ensuring equal treatment on the ground of sex characteristics in the field of employment, vocational training or occupation; including intersex issues in the mandate of a national human rights institution; or initiating research into the extent and nature of problems intersex individuals face".[10] In 2017, the first European Intersex Community Event produced the Vienna Statement. In this Statement, intersex activists from all over Europe called governments to take decisive action to introduce legislative protections that ban medical interventions on intersex children, ensure that intersex people are protected from discrimination and suggested "sex characteristics" as an option that should be explicitly included in the ground of "sex".[11] In addition, the Statement calls on governments to ensure access of intersex people to medical records and reparations in case they have endured medically unnecessary or degrading treatment and to install simple administrative procedures which facilitate gender/sex marker change on the basis of self-determination and self-declaration and make available a neutral marker.[12]

According to the European Union Agency for Fundamental Rights (FRA), many Member States still legally require births to be certified as either male or female and in at least 21 Member States, sex "normalising" surgery is performed on intersex infants including Austria, Belgium, Bulgaria, the Czech Republic, Denmark, Estonia, Finland, France, Germany, Hungary, Ireland, Italy, Latvia, Lithuania, Malta, the Netherlands, Poland, Slovakia, Spain, Sweden and the United Kingdom.[13] Bearing in mind that this situation cannot be considered as acceptable in a legal union such as the European Union whose founding Treaty is established on respect for human dignity and human rights, including the rights of persons belonging to minorities,[14] the purpose of this Chapter is to conduct a comparative study on the

---

[7] European Commission, 2011, p. 9.

[8] Council of the European Union, 2013, p. 4.

[9] Ghattas (2015), p. 9.

[10] European Commission, 2016, p. 5.

[11] OII Europe, STATEMENT of the 1st European Intersex Community Event (Vienna, 30–31st of March 2017).

[12] Idem.

[13] European Union Agency for Fundamental Rights (2015), p. 7.

[14] European Commission, 2011, p. 9.

situation of intersex rights within the EU Member States. In the first section of this Chapter the values of the EU and the notions of sexual orientation, gender identity and intersex in the EU will be explored. Then, since the Treaty on the Functioning of the European Union (TFEU) stipulates that the EU and the European Convention on Human Rights are directly related,[15] sexual orientation, gender identity and intersex as reflected in the European Convention on Human Rights (ECHR) and as interpreted by the European Court of Human Rights (ECtHR) will be analysed as well.

In the previous Chapter, the situation of intersex rights in countries that are members of the UN but not of the EU was presented. The aim of the previous analysis was not to introduce a comparative study among legal frameworks but to provide the reader with the full picture of intersex rights around the globe and prepare him/her for the EU comparative study that follows in this Chapter. Accordingly, in the subsequent sections, a comparative study on intersex rights between the EU Member States will be introduced. The goal of this comparison is to answer the main question as to which extend current developments on intersex within the EU Member States promote the fundamental values of the EU as guaranteed under the Treaty of Lisbon and the Charter on Fundamental Rights. To that aim, EU Member States' developments on intersex will be divided into two main categories: (a) EU countries that explicitly promote intersex rights through laws and case-law and (b) EU countries that implicitly promote intersex rights, and this usually occurs when there are regulations on gender and gender identity that may also expand to intersex. Considering that different laws on gender in the EU Member States could be interpreted in multiple ways to protect -or not- intersex, the section on the countries that implicitly protect intersex will be limited to those that are indicated by the reports of the European Union and the Fundamental Rights Agency in particular. The division of EU countries is important in order to deepen in the examination of intersex rights and at the same time, it will allow the reader to digest the exact situation on intersex rights within the EU Member States. To illustrate the full picture of the situation on intersex rights in the EU, countries that have introduced anti-discrimination laws under the ground "other" will be briefly presented and observed. In addition, significant developments on intersex in France will be explored. It has to be noted that the comparative study will be limited only between the EU countries that have

[15] Article 6 of the TFEU: "1. The Union recognises the rights, freedoms and principles set out in the Charter of Fundamental Rights of the European Union of 7 December 2000, as adapted at Strasbourg, on 12 December 2007, which shall have the same legal value as the Treaties. The provisions of the Charter shall not extend in any way the competences of the Union as defined in the Treaties. The rights, freedoms and principles in the Charter shall be interpreted in accordance with the general provisions in Title VII of the Charter governing its interpretation and application and with due regard to the explanations referred to in the Charter, that set out the sources of those provisions. 2. The Union shall accede to the European Convention for the Protection of Human Rights and Fundamental Freedoms. Such accession shall not affect the Union's competences as defined in the Treaties.3. Fundamental rights, as guaranteed by the European Convention for the Protection of Human Rights and Fundamental Freedoms and as they result from the constitutional traditions common to the Member States, shall constitute general principles of the Union's law."

explicitly legislated on intersex and those that provide implicit protection for intersex individuals.

4.1 The Fundamental Values of the EU and the Protection of SOGI

As stated by Article 2 of the Treaty on the Functioning of the European Union (TFEU) "The Union is founded on the values of respect for human dignity, freedom, democracy, equality, the rule of law and respect for human rights, including the rights of persons belonging to minorities. These values are common to the Member States in a society in which pluralism, non-discrimination, tolerance, justice, solidarity and equality between women and men prevail".[16] In detail, human dignity is inviolable and must be respected, protected and constitutes the real basis of fundamental rights; individual freedoms such as the respect for private life; the functioning of the EU is founded on representative democracy; equality is about equal rights for all citizens before the law. However, the principle of gender equality in the EU is currently applied only to men and women; the EU is based on the rule of law, the EU countries gave final jurisdiction to the European Court of Justice which judgements have to be respected by all; human rights are protected by the EU Charter of Fundamental Rights.[17]

The Charter of Fundamental Rights of the European Union safeguards human dignity,[18] the right to life,[19] the right to the integrity of the person where Article 3 refers specifically to the field of medicine and calls for the respect of the free and informed consent of the person concerned and Article 4 prohibits torture and inhuman or degrading treatment or punishment.[20] With regards to individual freedoms, the Charter guarantees the right to marry and the right to found a family and even though it is an open provision, as it is not explicitly limited to "men" and "women", the enjoyment of this right has to be "in accordance with the national laws governing the exercise of these rights".[21] Article 21 of the Charter introduces the principle of non-discrimination, but through a closed list of several prohibited grounds that do not allow for a broad interpretation. The grounds related to sexual minorities are mainly "sex" and "sexual orientation". The rights of the child are guaranteed under Article 24 with a focus on their well-being and best interests. With regards to gender equality, Article 23 guarantees equality only between women and men excluding

[16] Consolidated version of the Treaty on European Union.

[17] European Union, The EU in brief "Goals and values of the EU". See also Weatherill (2016) and Oshri et al. (2016).

[18] Charter of Fundamental Rights of the European Union, Article 1.

[19] Idem, Article 2. See also Wilms (2017).

[20] Charter of Fundamental Rights of the European Union, 2016/C 202/02.

[21] Idem, Article 9.

individuals who may not identify as such: "equality between women and men must be ensured in all areas, including employment, work and pay".[22]

Primarily, in the Treaty establishing the European Economic Community (EEC), only one provision[23] was included to combat gender discrimination on grounds of sex and it focused on the principle of equal pay between men and women for equal work or work of equal value. The purpose behind this provision was originally purely economic; Member States wanted to eliminate distortions in competition that could have arisen from cheaper female labour in different Member States but in practice, Member States were unable or unwilling to transpose the equal-pay provision into their national laws,[24] until the adoption of the Directive on equal pay for men and women.[25] Later, the Treaty of Amsterdam enshrined the promotion of equality between men and women by introducing the obligation of gender mainstreaming so that both the Community and the Member States ought to implement the objective of equality between men and women when introducing laws and regulations.[26] The Treaty of Lisbon introduced further developments in EU gender equality law. Article 10 of the Treaty on the Functioning of the European Union (TFEU) guarantees that "in defining and implementing its policies and activities, the Union shall aim to combat discrimination based on sex, racial or ethnic origin, religion or belief, disability, age or sexual orientation". In Article 6, the Lisbon Treaty inserts a reference to the Charter of Fundamental Rights of the European Union making it legally binding. As it was already mentioned, the Charter recognises some major rights especially in relation with gender equality. To promote its fundamental values and achieve gender equality, the EU has introduced several directives such as the Directive on equal treatment in employment and occupation (2000/78) and the Directive on equal treatment of men and women engaged in a self-employed activity (2010/41). In general, the EU Directives on gender equality are focusing only on certain areas including mainly the fields of employment and social security.

It is remarkable that a "clash" could be identified between the fundamental values of the EU in theory and in practice. Equality is understood as granting equal rights to all citizens but at the same time the Treaties and Directives focus explicitly only to men and women leaving behind individuals who may not identify as such,

[22] Idem, Article 23.

[23] Article 119 EEC Treaty; the latter of which became Article 141 EC Treaty upon the entry into force of the Treaty of Amsterdam in 1999; and presently Article 157 of the Treaty on the Functioning of the European Union (TFEU).

[24] Wikigender, "Gender Equality Law in the European Union" and See also Burri, S. and Prechal, S., European Network of Legal Experts in the field of Gender Equality,"EU Gender Equality Law – update 2010", 2010 and Arribas and Carrasco (2003).

[25] See Council Directive 75/117/EEC of 10 February 1975 on the approximation of the laws of the Member States relating to the application of the principle of equal pay for men and women.

[26] The Treaty of Amsterdam amending the Treaty of the European Union, the Treaties establishing the European Communities and certain related acts, signed on 2 October 1997, and entered into force on 1 May 1999. See also Defeis (1999).

but they are also EU citizens. Thus, how could democracy, human rights and the rule of law prosper if equal rights are denied to a group of EU citizens?

4.1.1 Sexual Orientation Under EU Law

The Amsterdam Treaty is the first international treaty to explicitly recognise and protect sexual orientation. Article 13 (now Article 19 TFEU) stipulates that "the Council, acting unanimously on a proposal from the Commission and after consulting the European Parliament, may take appropriate action to combat discrimination based on sex, racial or ethnic or ethnic origin, religion or belief, disability, age or sexual orientation".[27] The Council Directive 2000/78/EC of 27 November 2000 established a general framework for equal treatment in employment and occupation. In this directive, it is reiterated that "in implementing the principle of equal treatment, the Community should (…) aim to eliminate inequalities, and to promote equality between men and women, especially since women are often victims of multiple discrimination".[28] The Framework Directive is binding upon the current Member States, while the Accession States are required to have completed national implementation of the Directive before joining the EU.[29] Directive 2004/58/EC on the rights of citizens of the EU and their family members to move and reside freely within the territory of the Member States, acknowledges an obligation of the Member States to implement this Directive without discrimination on grounds such as sex and sexual orientation.[30] Moreover, the Charter of Fundamental Rights expressly prohibits discrimination on the ground of sexual orientation: "Any discrimination based on any ground such as sex, race, color, ethnic or social origin, genetic features, language, religion or belief, political or other opinion, membership of a national minority, property, birth, disability, age or sexual orientation shall be prohibited".[31]

The European Court of Justice has developed a wide jurisprudence on sexual orientation especially with regards to social and employer benefits, blood donation, residence permits and asylum.[32] With regards to social and employer benefits, in Tadao Maruko v Versorgungsanstalt der deutschen Bühnen, Mr Maruko was refused

[27] Treaty of Amsterdam Amending the Treaty on European Union, the Treaties Establishing the European Communities and Certain Related Acts, 1997. See Mos (2013).

[28] Council Directive 2000/78/EC of 27 November 2000, (3). See also, Waaldijk and Bonini-Baraldi (2006) and Walters (2007).

[29] EqualJus, p. 20.

[30] Directive 2004/58/EC of the European Parliament and of the Council of 29 April 2004 on the right of citizens of the Union and their family members to move and reside freely within the territory of the Member States amending Regulation (EEC) No 1612/68 and repealing Directives 64/221/EEC, 68/360/EEC, 72/194/EEC, 73/148/EEC, 75/34/EEC, 75/35/EEC, 90/364/EEC, 90/365/EEC and 93/96/EEC.

[31] Charter of Fundamental Rights of the European Union, 2016/C 202/02.

[32] See also Papadopoulou (2019).

a survivor's pension because he was not married to his partner and as there was no evidence that such pension has been granted to other individuals in similar situations, it was raised that there had been no direct discrimination. The Court considered the fact that German law places partners and spouses in a comparable situation concerning survivor's benefit and concluded that such refusal was a discriminatory and unjustified conduct.[33] The Advocate General Ruiz-Jarabo Colomer had stated in his opinion that "refusal to grant a pension on the grounds that a couple has not married, where two persons of the same sex are unable to marry and have entered into a union which produces similar effects, constitutes indirect discrimination based on sexual orientation, contrary to Article 2 of Directive 2000/78".[34] In the Römer case, a man who was engaged in a life partnership with another man requested his former employer to recalculate the amount of his retirement based on a land law which allowed married people to be granted a more favourable amount of pension. His employer refused it relying on the fact that the land law was applicable only to married couples but not to couples in a partnership. The Court concluded that "there is direct discrimination on the ground of sexual orientation because, under national law, that life partner is in a legal and factual situation comparable to that of a married person as regards that pension."[35]

In relation with health services and blood donation in particular, the Court pronounced on Geoffrey Léger v Ministre des Affaires sociales, de la Santé et des Droits des femmes and Établissement français du sang and addressed the compatibility of national measures permanently banning blood donations by men who had or have sexual relations with other men with EU law. The Court found that these health policies could be justified in some circumstances and stated that "although the permanent deferral provided for in French law helps to minimise the risk of transmitting an infectious disease to recipients and, therefore, to the general objective of ensuring a high level of human health protection, the principle of proportionality might not be respected".[36] Commentators have argued that in this case the Court the EU missed a timely occasion to explain why both legally and politically such health policies are discriminatory and humiliating.[37]

On residence permits and asylum the ECJ has pronounced in several decisions. In A, B, C v Staatssecretaris van Veiligheid en Justitie,[38] the Court ruled that the

[33] See Case C-267/06, Tadao Maruko v. Versorgungsanstalt der deutschen Bühnen, Judgment of the Court (Grand Chamber) of 1 April 2008.

[34] Opinion of Advocate General Ruiz-Jarabo Colomer, delivered on 6 September 2007, Case C-267/06, Tadao Maruko v. Versorgungsanstalt der deutschen Bühnen, para. 102.

[35] Case C-147/08, Jürgen Römer v. Freie und Hansestadt Hamburg, Judgment of the Court (Grand Chamber) of 10 May 2011, para. 67 (2).

[36] Court of Justice of the European Union, Press Release No. 46/15, "The permanent deferral from blood donation for men who have had sexual relations with another man may be justified, having regard to the situation prevailing in the Member State concerned".

[37] Uladzislau Belavusau and Ivana Isailović, "Gay Blood: Bad Blood? A Brief Analysis of the Léger Case [2015] C-528/13".

[38] Joined Cases C-148/13 to C-150/13, requests for a preliminary ruling under article 267 TFEU, from the Raad van State (Netherlands), made by decision of 20 March 2013, received at the Court

submission of asylum seekers to possible "tests" in order to demonstrate their homosexuality would of its nature infringe human dignity, the respect of which is guaranteed by the Charter. Moreover, considering the sensitive nature of information on a person's personal identity which includes his sexuality, the conclusion of a lack of credibility cannot be reached merely because, "due to his reticence in revealing intimate aspects of his life, that person did not declare his homosexuality at the outset".[39] In its recent landmark ruling on Coman and others v. Romania, the Court ruled that all EU countries must recognise residency rights of same-sex spouses regardless of national same-sex marriage laws.[40] In its reasoning, the Court answered the question of the Romanian Constitutional Court whether the term "spouse" in Article 2 (2) a of the Citizen's Directive includes a non-EU national. In its answer, the Court highlighted that "the term 'spouse' within the meaning of Directive 2004/38 is gender-neutral and may therefore cover the same-sex spouse of the Union citizen concerned.",[41] approaching "marriage" in a narrow scope and opening the way for broader interpretations which could also include non-binary individuals. This decision seeks to ensure that same-sex couples' rights are protected within the EU especially in times "where certain Member States are introducing a constitutional ban on and others are legalising such marriages, the Court in Coman served as a forum for political battles that crystallise a clear divide within the EU".[42] These "political battles" within EU Member States also disclose the cultural, traditional, religious and ethical aspect that surrounds all topics related to "sex" and "sexual orientation". Consequently, this ruling could be translated as an effort on behalf of the Court to unite EU Member States despite their diversities.

It needs to be added that although discrimination based on "sexual orientation" may seem to be directly linked with "sexual preference", the legal questions that rise with regards to same-sex "marriage" and/or "civil unions" in particular, emerge from discrimination grounded on "sex".[43] For instance, as mentioned above, in

---

on 25 March 2013, in the proceedings, A (C-148/13), B (C-149/13), C (C-150/13) v Staatssecretaris van Veiligheid en Justitie, Judgment of the Court (Grand Chamber), 2 December 2014.

[39] EqualRightsTrust, Joined cases A (C-148/13), B (C-149/13), C (C-150/13) v Staatssecretaris van Veiligheid en Justitie Preliminary ruling under article 267 TFEU, from the Raad van State (Netherlands), Case Summary.

[40] See Case C- 673/16, Coman and others v. Romania, Judgment of the Court (Grand Chamber) 5 June 2018, para. 45: "the obligation for a Member State to recognise a marriage between persons of the same sex concluded in another Member State in accordance with the law of that state, for the sole purpose of granting a derived right of residence to a third-country national, does not undermine the institution of marriage in the first Member State, which is defined by national law and, as indicated in paragraph 37 above, falls within the competence of the Member States. Such recognition does not require that Member State to provide, in its national law, for the institution of marriage between persons of the same sex. It is confined to the obligation to recognise such marriages, concluded in another Member State in accordance with the law of that state, for the sole purpose of enabling such persons to exercise the rights they enjoy under EU law."

[41] Idem, para. 35.

[42] Beury Manon, "The CJEU's judgment in Coman: a small step for the recognition of same-sex couples underlying European divides over LGBT rights".

[43] See Koppelman (1995).

Coman and others v. Romania, the Court pronounced on the rights of same-sex spouses since marriage is an institution that discriminates primarily on the grounds of "'sex". In other words, "when a person marries, he or she enters into a legal contract with another person. The sex of the person is decisive, since it must be different from the sex of the person that he or she wants to enter into the contract with".[44] With this in mind, it is imperative to also analyse in this research, legal frameworks that are related with sexual orientation as they rely heavily on "sex" and as it will be later shown, intersex persons' rights can be impacted as well.

4.1.2 Gender Identity Under EU Law

Although EU law does not include the ground of "gender identity", the notion of sex has been broadly interpreted by the Court to go beyond the biological differences between men and women and include the notion of gender identity.[45]

In 1996, in the landmark decision of P v. S and Cornwall County Council, the Court extended the scope of sex equality to include discrimination against transsexuals. The applicant had had gender-reassignment procedure while on sick leave and when she returned to her work, she was dismissed even though she was not prohibited from working in her "female gender role".[46] She complained to a tribunal that she had been discriminated against on grounds of "sex". The Court held that the Equal Treatment Directive was violated and elaborated on the extent of the provision in relation with the definition and interpretation of "sex": "the scope of the directive cannot be confined simply to discrimination based on the fact that a person is of one or other sex. In view of its purpose and the nature of the rights which it seeks to safeguard, the scope of the directive is also such as to apply to discrimination arising, as in this case, from the gender reassignment of the person concerned. Such discrimination is based, essentially if not exclusively, on the sex of the person concerned. Where a person is dismissed on the ground that he or she intends to undergo, or has undergone, gender reassignment, he or she is treated unfavourably by comparison with persons of the sex to which he or she was deemed to belong before undergoing gender reassignment. To tolerate such discrimination would be tantamount, as regards such a person, to a failure to respect the dignity and freedom to which he or she is entitled, and which the Court has a duty to safeguard. Dismissal of such a person must therefore be regarded as contrary to Article 5(1) of the directive".[47] The Advocate General in his opinion, elaborated on the traditional

---

[44] Papadopoulou (2001–2002), p. 252.

[45] See also Papadopoulou (2019).

[46] EqualRightsTrust, Case Summary: P v. S and Cornwall County Council, Case C-13/94, [1996] IRLR 347.

[47] Case C-13/94, P v S and Cornwall County Council. - Reference for a preliminary ruling: Industrial Tribunal, Truro - United Kingdom. - Equal treatment for men and women - Dismissal of a transsexual, Judgment of the Court of 30 April 1996.

dichotomous definition of "sex which prevails both in societies and the law. He mentioned that "while it is quite true that the directive prohibits any discrimination whatsoever on grounds of sex, it is equally indisputable that the wording of the principle of equal treatment which it lays down refers to the traditional man/woman dichotomy".[48] Then he underlined the necessity "to go beyond the traditional classification and recognize that, in addition to the man/woman dichotomy, there is a range of characteristics, behaviour and roles shared by men and women, so that sex itself ought rather to be thought of as a continuum."[49] Considering this point, he clarified that "it would not be right to continue to treat as unlawful solely acts of discrimination on grounds of sex which are referrable to men and women in the traditional sense of those terms, while refusing to protect those who are also treated unfavourably precisely because of their sex and/or sexual identity."[50] With his wording, the Advocate General, created the adequate space for the inclusion and recognition of rights of all non-binary individuals including intersex.

In two more decisions, in 2004 and 2006 the ECJ confirmed that equal treatment must be applied on the basis of acquired gender and not on the sex assigned at birth. In the first case, K.B. v. National Health Service Pensions Agency and Secretary of State for Health, a transsexual partner who had undergone gender reassignment surgery was not entitled to a survivor's spouse pension. A clear distinction was made by the Advocate General regarding the P. v. S. case and the K.B. v. National Health Service Pensions Agency and Secretary of State for Health and it focused on the fact that "the discrimination at issue does not directly affect enjoyment of a right protected by the Treaty but rather one of the preconditions of such enjoyment. The discrimination is not focused on the award of a widow(er)'s pension; it arises merely by virtue of a necessary precondition: the capacity to marry".[51] He added that "until the United Kingdom adopts the necessary legislation enabling transsexuals to marry, the national court — which is also a Community court — must ensure, in accordance with national law, that the discrimination to which transsexuals are subject does not have any repercussions for the rights which they derive from the Treaty."[52] The Advocate here highlighted the fact that EU Member States maintain their sovereignty but at the same time, they ought to respect EU legal frameworks. With this in mind, provisions that restrict the enjoyment of human rights as set by the Treaty must be interpreted adequately so they are compatible with EU law and safeguard the fundamental rights of EU citizens. This could be achieved through several paths: "possible solutions range from interpreting the terms man and woman in such a way that transsexuals are entitled to marry, to creating a notional marriage there and then

[48] P. v S. and Cornwall County Council, Opinion of Advocate General Tesauro delivered on 14 December 1995, para. 16.

[49] Idem, para. 17.

[50] Idem.

[51] Opinion of Advocate General Ruiz-Jarabo Colomer delivered on 10 June 2003 K.B. v National Health Service Pensions Agency and Secretary of State for Health Reference for a preliminary ruling: Court of Appeal (England & Wales) (Civil Division) - United Kingdom, para. 74.

[52] Idem, para. 78.

or to establishing a separate, more flexible link, which would enable transsexuals to have access to a pension following the death of the person who would have been their spouse had that not been prohibited by unfair rules."[53]

Later, in Richards v Secretary of State for Work and Pensions, the ECJ ruled that a trans woman was discriminated against because she was refused a state pension due to the fact that she was treated as a man.[54] The Court reiterated that "sex" under the Equal Treatment Directive should be interpreted in a way to include individuals who do not align with the binary "the scope of Directive 79/7 cannot be confined simply to discrimination based on the fact that a person is of one or other sex. In view of its purpose and the nature of the rights which it seeks to safeguard, the scope of that directive is also such as to apply to discrimination arising from the gender reassignment of the person concerned".[55]

The interpretation of "sex" by the ECJ/CJEU as well as the progressive reasoning of the Advocate Generals clearly open the path for non-binary individuals to claim their rights before the European Court of Justice. In the future, the CJEU could possibly broaden the meaning of "sex" to include intersex.

4.1.3 Intersex in the EU

In 2013, the EU adopted the first ever EU policy document explicitly referring to intersex people. The guidelines recognise that intersex people are particularly vulnerable to gender-based violence as well as sexual violence.[56] On March 2017, the Vienna Statement[57] was issued reaffirming the Malta Declaration[58] and its objectives formulated previously in 2013 and 2014. According to the Vienna Statement, more than 50 times UN bodies, regional and national human rights bodies have already called on governments, policy makers and stakeholders to put an end to human rights violations faced by intersex people including taking the necessary legislative, administrative and other measures to guarantee respect for intersex rights.[59]

---

[53] Idem.

[54] See Case C-423/04, Sarah Margaret Richards v Secretary of State for Work and Pensions.
Reference for a preliminary ruling: Social Security Commissioner—United Kingdom, Judgment of the Court (First Chamber) of 27 April 2006.

[55] Idem, para. 24.

[56] Council of EU Guidelines, 2013, para. 36.

[57] OII Europe, Statement of the 1st European Intersex Community Event (Vienna, 30–31st of March 2017).

[58] OII Europe, Malta Declaration (1 December 2013).

[59] OII Europe, Statement of the 1st European Intersex Community Event (Vienna, 30–31st of March 2017).

In a national level, there are few European countries which have introduced legislation that expressly mention intersex. For instance, Malta[60] was the first country in the world to legally ban non-consensual medically unnecessary surgeries on intersex infants. The absence of non-explicit legal frameworks in the EU is putting intersex people in an uncertain legal situation as they are not protected against discrimination on the ground of their sex characteristics.[61] Existing developments in a national level will be later analysed.

Even though the European Union has started shedding light on intersex rights,[62] it has focused mainly on discrimination and the issues arising from intersex people's "medicalisation" and "pathologisation" of their bodies. It was already mentioned that the ground of "sex characteristics" is not included in EU law and no case on intersex rights has reached the ECJ so far. Through the existing ECJ case-law on gender identity it could be assumed that a broader interpretation of "sex" to include "sex characteristics" in the future could be possible. The European Commission in its 2012 report on discrimination against sexual minorities, dedicated a brief part on discrimination against intersex people. It confirmed the words of Schiek, Waddington and Bell who have stated that there is "a close relation between intersex and gender or sex, for which reason it would not be illogical to classify distinctions based on intersex as being gender based" and they supported their argument on P. v. S. in which the Court broadened the scope of "sex" of the Directive.[63] Still, the difference between discrimination against intersex and trans is underlined in the report: "discrimination against intersex people is more directly linked to sex discrimination than discrimination on the grounds of gender identity and gender expression".[64] Accordingly, it can be argued that since discrimination against intersex is linked to discrimination based on sex and not on gender, it would be even more logical for the Court to link intersex discrimination to the ground of "sex". In that case, the Court, through purposive interpretation could follow societal developments and interpret the ground "sex" as a spectrum to cover all EU citizens including intersex. Moreover, the EU Charter protects several human rights that can be applied to intersex including the right to life, to integrity of the person, the rights of the child, the right of access to health care, to marry and found a family and prohibits torture and inhuman or degrading treatment.[65]

In 2015, the European Union Agency for Fundamental Rights published a report focusing on the situation of intersex in the EU and its Member States. The report reaffirms the fact that discrimination against intersex is related with "sex": "unequal treatment of intersex people has been frequently addressed in EU policies and advocacy as part of discrimination on the ground of sexual orientation and/or gender

[60] See the "Gender Identity Gender Expression and Sex Characteristics Act", (Malta, 2015).

[61] ILGA Europe, "Intersex".

[62] See European Union Agency for Fundamental Rights, "The fundamental rights situation of intersex people", 2015.

[63] Schiek et al. (2007), p. 79.

[64] European Commission (2012), p. 82.

[65] See Charter of Fundamental Rights of the European Union (2000/C 364/01) and Chap. 3.

identity. However, such treatment can better be addressed as discrimination on the ground of sex, as it is linked to the sex assigned to a person at birth and its direct consequences."[66] In addition, according to the European Union Agency for Fundamental Rights, intersex people can benefit from protection from discrimination on the ground of sex under Article 21 of the EU's Fundamental Rights Charter on non-discrimination and "regarding secondary EU law, the Lunacek Report[67] has called on the European Commission, together with relevant agencies to "issue guidelines specifying that transgender and intersex persons are covered under "sex" in Directive 2006/54/EC [Gender Equality Directive (recast)]".[68] The Lunacek Report was issued by the European Parliament and it was conducted by the rapporteur Ulrike Lunacek, it addressed the gaps existing in the EU on the effective protection of sexual minorities. The report called the Commission to issue guidelines on intersex as mentioned above, to "mainstream issues specific to intersex people throughout the relevant EU policies" and to "address current lack of knowledge, research and relevant legislation on the human rights of intersex people".[69] It also urged the Member States to "ensure equality bodies are informed and trained about the rights of, and specific issues pertaining to, intersex people".[70]

With regards to birth certificates, as of 2015, 18 EU Member States allowed a certain delay in the registration of births: within a week in Austria, Belgium, Bulgaria, France, Luxembourg and Slovakia; longer in Cyprus, Denmark, Greece, Hungary, Ireland, Italy, Malta, Portugal, Romania, Slovenia, Spain and the United Kingdom.[71] Moreover, sex (re)assignment surgery was performed on intersex children, and young people, in at least 21 EU Member States including Austria, Belgium, Bulgaria, the Czech Republic, Denmark, Estonia, Finland, France, Germany, Hungary, Ireland, Italy, Latvia, Lithuania, Malta, the Netherlands, Poland, Slovakia, Spain, Sweden and the United Kingdom,[72] in 8 Member States, a legal representative could consent to sex reassignment surgeries regardless of the child's ability to decide and 18 Member States required patient consent provided the child had the ability to decide.[73] In its report, the European Union Fundamental Rights Agency concluded that (1) legal and medical professionals should be better informed of intersex rights (2) gender markers in identity documents and birth certificates should be reviewed to protect the needs of intersex people and (3) Member States should avoid non-consensual "sex-normalising" medical treatments on intersex infants.[74] A

[66] European Union Fundamental Rights Agency, 2015, p. 3.

[67] Committee on Civil Liberties, Justice and Home Affairs, Report on the EU Roadmap against homophobia and discrimination on grounds of sexual orientation and gender identity, Rapporteur: Ulrike Lunacek.

[68] Idem.

[69] European Parliament, 2014, para. G.

[70] Idem.

[71] European Union Fundamental Rights Agency, 2015, p. 4.

[72] Idem, p. 7.

[73] Idem, p. 1.

[74] Idem.

year later, in 2016, the summary report published by the European Commission stated that several Member States were reviewing their laws and policies in relation to sex characteristics, but it only mentioned Greece which was in the process to pass a bill on equal treatment including sex characteristics.[75]

From all the reports introduced by the EU on intersex, the Fundamental Rights Agency report is the only report that depicts the exact situation of EU intersex citizens across Member States. Although it presents some crucial information such as the point that intersex people should be considered as discriminated on the basis of their "sex" and not on other grounds involving "gender" and the problems arising from intersex surgeries and binary identification documents, it only touches upon one aspect of the human rights violations that intersex individuals are encountering. Surely, it is important for Member States to introduce "intersex friendly" practices when it comes to surgeries and identification documents but what will that mean in practice? Assuming that Member States follow the key conclusions of the European Commission's reports, intersex individuals will be then free to identify as "intersex". How could their rights as "intersex" in all fields i.e. family, employment be safeguarded if EU law is still binary? Thus, it can be held that all the guidelines suggested by the European Union so far, may constitute a first step towards intersex rights protection but there is still a lot to be done to achieve justice and equality.

4.2 The Council of Europe on SOGI and Intersex

Article 6 para. 2 of the TFEU stipulates that "the Union shall accede to the European Convention for the Protection of Human Rights and Fundamental Freedoms. Such accession shall not affect the Union's competences as defined in the Treaties". In addition, para. 3 states that "fundamental rights, as guaranteed by the European Convention for the Protection of Human Rights and Fundamental Freedoms and as they result from the constitutional traditions common to the Member States, shall constitute general principles of the Union's law". The close relationship between the EU and the CoE is highlighted in those articles as the Treaty of Lisbon provides for a duty of the EU to accede to the ECHR.[76] Recent discussions on the EU accession to the European Convention on Human Rights also underline the fact that the EU and the ECHR share common values and ideals when it comes to human rights recognition and protection.[77] Considering all the above, it is essential to include in this section a presentation of SOGI and intersex rights within the Council of Europe and the ECtHR. Furthermore, the EU Member States that will be later analysed are also members of the Council of Europe.

---

[75] European Commission, 2016, p. 5.

[76] See Daukšienė and Grigonis (2015) and Kosta et al. (2014).

[77] See Greer et al. (2018).

4.2.1 Sexual Orientation

Article 14 of the European Convention on Human Rights (ECHR) provides an open-ended list of grounds of discrimination and they are also repeated in Protocol No. 12. None of these instruments mention explicitly sexual orientation or gender identity as prohibited grounds but the commentary on the provisions of the Protocol instructs that the list of non-discrimination grounds is non-exhaustive.[78] Although sexual orientation is not expressly included in Article 14 of the ECHR, it falls under "other status" which provides for an extension of the list of the protected grounds.[79]

The ECtHR was the first international body to find that sexual orientation criminal laws violate human rights and has the longest and largest jurisprudence on the matter.[80] In 1999, the European Court of Human Rights confirmed that sexual orientation is amongst the prohibited discrimination grounds.[81] Since then, the Court has pronounced on sexual orientation in numerous cases including the right to respect for private and family life and the right to marry. The ECtHR, through its case-law, has pronounced on the lack of legal recognition of same-sex couples in several Member States. It has been held that it is required for Member States to provide legal recognition under the European Convention on Human Rights, but the Court has not yet opened the way to same-sex marriages. In Schalk and Kopf v. Austria, the Court considered for the first time whether a same-sex couple can claim the right to marry under the ECHR. It noted that Article 12 grants the right to marry to "men and women" but the "institution of marriage has undergone major social changes since the adoption of the Convention".[82] The Court also underlined that Article 9 of the Charter of Fundamental Rights departs from Article 12 of the ECHR and indeed according to the explanations provided on Article 9: "this Article is based on Article 12 of the ECHR. The wording of the Article has been modernised to cover cases in which national legislation recognises arrangements other than marriage for founding a family. This Article neither prohibits nor imposes the granting of the status of marriage to unions between people of the same sex. This right is thus similar to that afforded by the ECHR, but its scope may be wider when national legislation so provides."[83] The Court concluded that the right to marry of Article 12 must not only be limited to marriage between two people of different sex and based its reasoning on the fact that the Convention is a living instrument and therefore it follows the societal developments. In addition, it stated that there is no European consensus regarding same-sex marriage and conferred a certain "margin of appreciation" to

[78] See Explanatory report to Protocol No. 12 to the 1950 Convention for the Protection of Human Rights and Fundamental Freedoms, entered into force on 1 April 2005.

[79] Icelandic Human Rights Centre, "An overview of the case law on the prohibition of discrimination of the ECJ and the ECtHR", p. 8.

[80] University of Minnesota, Study Guide: Sexual Orientation and Human Rights.

[81] See Mouta v. Portugal, Application No. 33290/96, judgment of 21 December 1999.

[82] Schalk and Kopf v. Austria, application no. 30141/04, final judgment 22/11/2010, para. 52.

[83] See Official Journal of the European Union C 303/17 – 14.12.2007.

Member States with regards to the legal recognition of same-sex marriages. Last, the Court considered it artificial to maintain its view in previous case-aw that same-sex couples cannot enjoy "family life" under Article 8.[84]

In 2010, the Parliamentary Assembly of the Council of Europe adopted Resolution 1728 on sexual orientation according to which "under international law, all human beings are born free and equal in dignity and rights. Sexual orientation and gender identity are recognised as prohibited grounds for discrimination. According to the European Court of Human Rights, a difference in treatment is discriminatory if it has no objective and reasonable justification. Since sexual orientation is a most intimate aspect of an individual's private life, the Court considers that only particularly serious reasons may justify differences in treatment based on sexual orientation."[85] The Court has issued several judgments on alleged discrimination on grounds of sexual orientation and in these cases, it has severely limited the margin of appreciation of states stressing that "differences in treatment related to this ground require particularly weighty reasons to be legitimate under the Convention".[86]

In 2013, in Vallianatos and Others v. Greece, the Court held that excluding same-sex couples from civil unions violates the Convention. For one more time, the Court based its reasoning also on the emerging trends among the Council of Europe's Member States. It reaffirmed that "although there is no consensus among the legal systems of the Council of Europe member States, a trend is currently emerging with regard to the introduction of forms of legal recognition of same-sex relationships".[87] Later, Oliari and Others v. Italy extended the interpretation of ECHR and established a positive obligation upon the Council of Europe Member States to provide legal recognition for same-sex couples.[88] For that reason, this decision of the Court has been characterised as a "cutting-edge judgment" as it moved forward with the line of reasoning previously followed in Shalk and Kopf v. Austria and Vallianatos and Others v. Greece.[89] Nonetheless, in this judgment, the Court failed to make progress on the right to marry, considering that the Chamber declared the claim under article 12 inadmissible, whereas in Shalk and Kopf deemed it admissible and then found no violation.[90] In Chapin and Charpentier v.France, the Court confirmed its previous jurisprudence and held that denying access to same-sex marriage does not violate the Convention. In detail, the Court confirmed the traditional concept of

[84] See Schalk and Kopf v. Austria, application no. 30141/04, final judgment 22/11/2010.

[85] Parliamentary Assembly, Resolution 1728 (2010), para. 2.

[86] See Karner v. Austria, Application No. 40016/98, judgment of 24 July 2003, para. 37, E. B. v France, Application No. 43546/02, judgment of 22 January 2008, para. 91 and Schalk and Kopf v. Austria, Application No. 30141/04, judgment of 24 June 2010, para. 97.

[87] Vallianatos and Others v. Greece, Applications nos. 29381/09 and 32684/09, judgment of 7 November 2013, para. 91.

[88] See Oliari and Others v. Italy, Applications nos. 18766/11 and 36030/11, final judgment 21/10/2015.

[89] Giuseppe Zago, "Oliari and Others v. Italy: a stepping stone towards full legal recognition of same-sex relationships in Europe".

[90] Idem.

marriage and that Article 12 "does not impose an obligation on the governments of the Contracting States to grant same-sex couples access to marriage".[91] The Court reiterated that States are free to restrict access to marriage to different-sex couples preserving their margin of appreciation.[92]

It is obvious that the question of same-sex marriage pushes the Court to the limits of its ability to interpret the Convention[93] and although it seeks to apply the Convention to the evolution and emerging trends of the European societies, it has not still challenged the "foundations" of the institution of marriage. This situation creates a "paradox": since the Convention is a living instrument directly impacted by social developments, how can the Court still interpret marriage by limiting it to only "men" and "women"? First, the right to marry may be guaranteed under the ECHR but it still subject to the national laws of the contracting States. Second, considering the fact that over the last decades, the binary has been repeatedly challenged at both European and regional levels, it can be argued that in the case of marriage, the problem is not the challenge of the binary but of the whole institution of "marriage" which has cultural, social, traditional and religious origins. It seems "impossible" for the Court to interfere in the deep foundations of the European societies, therefore it attempts to strike a balance between the rights of sexual minorities and the power of tradition and religion.

4.2.2 Gender Identity

In 2015, the Parliamentary Assembly of the Council of Europe (PACE)[94] adopted the Resolution 2048 on "Discrimination against transgender people in Europe". Its purpose was to complement the already existing work of the Council of Europe on gender identity -and sexual orientation- as reflected on the PACE Resolution 1728[95]

[91] Chapin and Charpentier v. France, Application no. 40183/07, final judgment 09 September 2016, para.38.

[92] Idem, paras. 45-52.

[93] Grégor Puppinck, "The ECHR Unanimously Confirms the Non-existence of a Right to Gay Marriage".

[94] A series of Recommendations have been adopted by the Parliamentary Assembly on sexual orientation and gender identity. See Recommendation 1915 (2010) of the Parliamentary Assembly on Discrimination on the basis of sexual orientation and gender identity; Resolution 1728 (2010) of the Parliamentary Assembly on Discrimination on the basis of sexual orientation and gender identity; Recommendation 1635 (2003) of the Parliamentary Assembly on Lesbians and gays in sport; Recommendation 1474 (2000) of the Parliamentary Assembly on situation of lesbians and gays in Council of Europe member states; Recommendation 1470 (2000) of the Parliamentary Assembly on Situation of gays and lesbians and their partners in respect of asylum and immigration in the member states of the Council of Europe; Recommendation 1117 (1989) of the Parliamentary Assembly on the condition of transsexuals; Recommendation 924 (1981) of the Parliamentary Assembly on Discrimination against homosexuals; Resolution 756 (1981) of the Parliamentary Assembly on discrimination against homosexuals.

[95] See Resolution 1728 (2010) on "Discrimination on the basis of sexual orientation and gender identity".

and Recommendation 2021[96] and the Committee of Ministers Recommendation 5 on creating a right to gender identity.[97] Besides, the PACE Resolution 2048 fulfilled the ECtHR case-law by introducing a proof of an emerging consensus in Europe on the abolition of the required conditions for obtaining the legal recognition of a new gender and of the obligation to dissolve or transform an existing marriage into a civil partnership to legally recognise gender reassignment.[98]

The main approach taken by the ECtHR on gender identity can be primarily described as human rights rather than equal treatment based. Non-discrimination and equality are transversal principles underpinning human rights.[99] Both the human rights and equality treatment approaches can be grounded on the fundamental principles enunciated in the Universal Declaration of Human Rights which highlights equality in dignity and rights.[100] The ECtHR has addressed several issues regarding gender identity including discrimination, gender reassignment surgery, legal recognition of post-operative gender identity, the rights to marriage for post-operative persons. The most famous case of the ECtHR on gender identity is Christine Goodwin v. the United Kigndom. Ms Goodwin was married to a woman and underwent a male to female reassignment surgery. She complained the fact that she was denied legal recognition by the authorities as well as to get married with her new male-partner.[101] The Court found that Articles 8 and 12 of the Convention were violated. In detail, it pronounced on the conflict that trans individuals have to face when legal developments do not follow social reality.[102] The judges considered medical and scientific evidence on transsexualism and also referred to the case of intersex: "the Court notes that with increasingly sophisticated surgery and types of hormonal treatments, the principal unchanging biological aspect of gender identity is the chromosomal element. It is known however that chromosomal anomalies may

[96] See Recommendation 2021 (2013) on "Tackling discrimination on the grounds of sexual orientation and gender identity".

[97] See Recommendation CM/Rec (2010)5 of the Committee of Ministers to member states on measures to combat discrimination on grounds of sexual orientation and gender identity. The recommendation invites the member states to ensure that the stipulated principles and measures are applied in national legislation, policies and practices relevant to the protection of the human rights of LGBT persons. The recommendation covers a wide range of areas including hate crime, freedoms of association, expression and peaceful assembly, respect for family life and private life, employment, education, health, housing, sports, asylum, national human rights structures and discrimination on multiple grounds. While it is not a legally binding instrument, all Council of Europe member states should implement this recommendation (Council of Europe Publishing, 2011, p. 38).

[98] European Centre for Law & Justice, "Council of Europe Adopted Resolution Creating New Controversial Rights on Gender Identity".

[99] Oxford Human Rights Hub (2013), "Equality v Human Rights?: Same sex marriage and religious liberty".

[100] Lauri (2011), p. 12.

[101] Icelandic Human Rights Centre, "An overview of the case law on the prohibition of discrimination of the ECJ and the ECtHR", p. 7.

[102] Christine Goodwin v. the United Kingdom, Application no. 28957/95, judgment of 11 July 2002, para. 77.

arise naturally (for example, in cases of intersex conditions where the biological criteria at birth are not congruent) and in those cases, some persons have to be assigned to one sex or the other as seems most appropriate in the circumstances of the individual case."[103] Then, it continued by elaborating on the notion of "public interest" and since transsexuals do not pose any detriment to the public interest, society is expected to tolerate a certain inconvenience to enable all individuals to live in dignity.[104] The Court concluded that Article 8 on the right to private and family life was violated and continued by finding no justification for barring the applicant from enjoying the right to marry under Article 12. The justices went beyond the restriction of marriage to men and women as imposed by the Convention: "it is true that the first sentence refers in express terms to the right of a man and woman to marry. The Court is not persuaded that at the date of this case it can still be assumed that these terms must refer to a determination of gender by purely biological criteria. There have been major social changes in the institution of marriage since the adoption of the Convention as well as dramatic changes brought about by developments in medicine and science in the field of transsexuality."[105]

The Christine Goodwin case should be seen as a major contribution not only to the trans community but to non-binary individuals as a whole. Even though it fails to depathologise trans and intersex (the word "anomalies" is repeated several times) it acknowledges the fact that the Convention is a living instrument and its main goal is to protect European citizens' rights through its broad interpretation. The Court recognises the right to marry to a trans woman although in the case of same-sex marriages, as already mentioned in the above section, it limits itself only to the recognition of civil unions. While the Court has been repeatedly underlining that the Convention is a living instrument which has to be interpreted in present-day conditions, it needs to be noted that it uses that approach to develop its jurisprudence where it has already perceived a convergence of standards among Member States.[106] In Christine Goodwin v. the United Kingdom the Court had considered the fact that a majority of Contracting States permitted such marriages. In contrast, in the absence of a consensus between Member States on same-sex marriage, the States enjoy a particularly wide margin of appreciation.[107] Accordingly, if a case on the right of an intersex individual to marry reaches the Court in the future, the outcome will also depend on Member States' attitude on intersex since the Convention may set basic human rights obligations, but the ECtHR builds on the reciprocal relationship between the respect of human rights and State sovereignty.

In Van Kück, the applicant was refused reimbursement of her costs for gender reassignment surgery from her medical insurance company on the grand that the surgery was not necessary.[108] The Court described the applicant's freedom to define

[103] Idem, para. 82.

[104] Idem, para. 93.

[105] Idem, para. 100.

[106] Silvis (2014), p. 33.

[107] Idem.

[108] Icelandic Human Rights Centre, "An overview of the case law on the prohibition of discrimination of thc ECJ and thc ECtIIR", p. 8.

herself as a female person as one of the most basic essentials of self-determination[109] and stated that gender identity is one of the most intimate aspects of a person's private life.[110] In this context, the Court reached the conclusion "that no fair balance was struck between the interests of the private health insurance company on the one side and the interests of the individual on the other".[111] Concerning gender reassignment and trans legal recognition, in Y.Y. v. Turkey, the ECtHR held that Turkey's refusal to authorise gender reassignment surgery because the applicant remained capable of procreating was a violation of the right to private life under Article 8.[112] The Court considered again the prevailing trends across the Member States on trans individuals and their legal recognition and it compared policies and frameworks that both require or not sterilisation. It decided that the requirement of sterilisation is contrary to the Convention and noted that what is at stake is the freedom to define one's gender identity which is a crucial component of the right to self-determination.[113] The Court succeeded to depathologise transsexualism by focusing on the major values of the Convention such as the individual autonomy, freedom, dignity and self-determination, establishing a human-rights centered precedence which coulld serve as a "tool" for the depathologisation of non-binary individuals including intersex. According to commentators, this decision also raises bigger questions as to the role of medical expertise in legal decision-making since in order to obtain legal recognition trans individuals need to convince medical experts that they suffer from a mental condition.[114] As a result, law is relying on criteria and assumptions set by the medical community instead of determining this issue according to legal principles.[115] As it was already discussed in the previous Chapter, often, when it comes to cases that challenge the binary, the justices rely on medical assumptions and/or their own empirical experience, disregarding legal instruments.

With the Identoba judgment the Court clarified that all trans people are protected against discrimination on grounds of gender identity under art. 14 of the Convention[116] and strengthened its case-law on trans legal recognition and the requirement of sterilisation in A.P., Garçon and Nicot v. France where it ruled that the condition of sterilising gender reassignment surgeries or treatments violated Article 8.[117] The Court reiterated that "elements such as gender identity or identification, names, sexual orientation and sexual life fall within the personal sphere protected by Article 8 of the Convention"[118] and that the right to respect for private life "applies fully to

[109] Van Kuck v. Germany, application no. 35968/97, judgment of 12 June 2003, para. 73.

[110] Idem, para. 75.

[111] Idem, para. 84.

[112] Y.Y. v. Turkey, Application no. 14793/08, final judgment 10 June 2015.

[113] Idem, para. 102.

[114] Ivana Isailovic, "The Y.Y. v. Turkey case and trans individuals' gender recognition".

[115] Idem.

[116] Identoba and Others v. Georgia, judgment of 12 May 2015.

[117] A.P., Garçon and Nicot v. France, Applications nos. 79885/12, 52471/13 and 52596/13, judgment of 6 April 2017.

[118] Idem, para. 92.

gender identity, as a component of personal identity"[119] holding true for all individuals. Last, it found a violation of Article 8 in respect of the second and third applicants, based on the irreversible nature of the change in their appearance. It has been argued that in its decision, the Court recognised the stigmatisation that lies behind the medicalisation of trans individuals, but "it did not end the societal and legal pathologisation of trans since it upheld the conidition of diagnosis of transsexuality to acquire legal recognition".[120] In addition, "the Court relied on a broad margin of appreciation for the State, which was supported by the fact that the international materials did not seem to explicitly condemn such requirement" disregarding the Resolution 2048(2015) which calls for the abolition of any medical condition and diagnosis for legal gender recognition and the Yogyakarta Principles.[121]

4.2.3 Intersex Rights

Even though no case on intersex rights has reached the ECtHR so far, the Court's precedence especially on gender identity could have a positive impact on intersex. The Court may have not explicitly depathologised trans, but it has condemned medical surgeries or treatments that lead to sterilisation (intersex surgeries also lead to sterilisation) since they violate fundamental human rights such as individual autonomy, dignity and self-determination. The Parliamentary Assembly of the Council of Europe (PACE) passed a resolution on the bodily integrity of intersex children in 2013. The resolution urges to ensure that no intersex person is subjected to unnecessary medical or surgical treatment that is cosmetic rather than vital and to guarantee bodily integrity, autonomy and self-determination to intersex individuals.[122] In the same fashion, the Assembly of the Council of Europe adopted Resolution 2191, the first intersex-specific resolution in the history of European intergovernmental institutions which was based on a detailed report by rapporteur Piet de Bruyn. The report presented recent trends in several Council of Europe member States with regards to surgeries on intersex infants. For instance, the Swiss National Advisory Commission on Biomedical Ethics has found that "all (non-trivial) sex assignment treatment decisions which have irreversible consequences but can be deferred should not be taken until the person to be treated can decide for him/herself, except where a medical intervention is urgently required to prevent severe damage to the patient's body or health".[123] In France, "it has been recognised that in the past, intersex situations were presented to parents as pathologies requiring treatment, but that parents were neither well informed nor in a position to decide on behalf of their children

[119] Idem, para. 95.

[120] Pieter Cannoot, "A.P., Garçon and Nicot v. France: the Court draws a line for trans rights".

[121] Idem.

[122] PACE Resolution 1952, 2013, para. 7.5.3.

[123] See Swiss National Advisory Commission on Biomedical Ethics,On the management of differences of sex development: Ethical issues relating to "intersexuality", Opinion No. 20/2012, 2012.

regarding such treatment".[124] Therefore, the French Senate has recommended that medical teams involve intersex children to the extent possible in any decision making concerning them.[125] The report stressed that it is crucial to ensure that the law deals with issues affecting intersex people in a way that makes their lives easier and "this includes ensuring that intersex people who do not identify as male or female have access to the legal recognition of their gender identity, and that where their gender has not been correctly recorded at birth, rectifying this is simple. Anti-discrimination laws also need to be amended to ensure that the situation of intersex people is effectively covered".[126]

The Resolution 2191 calls for the prohibition of "medically unnecessary sex "normalising" surgeries, sterilisation and other treatments practiced on intersex children without their informed consent"[127] except in cases where the life of the child is at risk.[128] It also urges for intersex people's effective access to health care and their medical records. When it comes to the civil status and gender recognition of intersex, it calls for the introduction of laws and practices on birth registrars to allow sufficient flexibility in the case of intersex infants and to ensure that a range of options are available for all non-binary people including intersex who do not identity as male or female.[129] The Resolution goes beyond sex/gender legal recognition of intersex and notes that it is crucial to "ensure that, in accordance with the right to respect for private life, intersex people are not prevented from entering into a civil partnership or marriage or from remaining in such a partnership or marriage as a result of the legal recognition of their gender".[130] On discrimination against intersex people, the Resolution suggests that it should be ensured that "anti-discrimination legislation effectively applies to and protects intersex people, either by inserting sex characteristics as a specific prohibited ground in all anti-discrimination legislation, and/or by raising awareness among lawyers, police, prosecutors, judges and all other relevant professionals, as well as intersex people, (…) the possibility of dealing with discrimination against them under the prohibited ground of sex, or as an "other" (unspecified) ground where the list of prohibited grounds in relevant national anti-discrimination provisions is non-exhaustive".[131]

Prior to all the above developments, the Council of Europe Commissioner of Human Rights issued a paper in 2015 on the human rights of intersex people analysing human rights violations that intersex people face in all aspects of their lives.[132] The Commissioner also refers to hate crime against intersex and recom-

---

[124] See Défenseur des droits, Opinion No. 17-04, 20 February 2017.

[125] See Sénat, rapport d'information no 441 (2016-2017), footnote 8 above, recommendations 3, 4, 5 and 8.

[126] Doc. 14404 of the Parliamentary Assembly, 2017, para. 75.

[127] Resolution 2191 (2017) of the Parliamentary Assembly, para. 7.1.1.

[128] Idem, para. 7.1.2.

[129] Idem, para. 7.3.3.

[130] Idem, para. 7.3.5.

[131] Idem, para. 7.4.

[132] See Council of Europe, "Human Rights and Intersex people", Issue paper published by the Council of Europe Commissioner for Human Rights, first edition April 2015.

mends that hate crime legislation should be reviewed to ensure that it protects intersex by including "a specific ground in equal treatment and hate crime legislation or the ground of sex/gender should be authoritatively interpreted to include sex characteristics as prohibited grounds of discrimination".[133] According to the Commissioner's recommendations, violations that intersex people have faced in the past should be addressed, investigated and remedied. In addition, "ethical and professional standards, legal safeguards and judicial control should be reinforced to ensure future human rights compliance".[134] In 2017, the Council of Europe, in an effort to demedicalise intersex children, issued a report on the Rights of Children in Biomedicine and exposed all issues and human rights violations that intersex children face due to the performance of medically unnecessary treatments.[135]

All the above, make the Council of Europe the only human rights organisation in both international and European levels to have addressed through its soft-law almost the whole spectrum of human rights violations that intersex people face. This is of major importance for two main reasons. First, bearing in mind that the relationship between the Council of Europe and its Member States is reciprocal, any Resolutions or Recommendations issued by the Council of Europe set guidelines that Member States should consider. Accordingly, Member States following those guidelines create "trends" that are used by the European Court of Human Rights especially when it has to deliberate on a controversial topic. If during the next years, Member States keep on developing positive trends with regards to intersex rights, it is highly possible that if an intersex individual reaches the Court, the outcome will be positive. Second, as it was already mentioned in the previous Chapter, human rights are universal and should be approached holistically, meaning that developments in the Council of Europe and its Member States directly impact developments internationally.[136]

4.3 EU Countries That Explicitly Protect Intersex Rights

In 2015, two reports were launched concerning the situation of intersex rights in the EU. The European Union Agency for Fundamental Rights (FRA) published "The fundamental rights situation of intersex people" and ILGA Europe and OII Europe together with the support of the EU, published "Standing up for the human rights of intersex people- how can you help?". Based on the information provided by those reports, intersex people are invisible in the EU as most European states recognise people as either male or female and therefore, intersex individuals experience fundamental rights violations ranging from discrimination to medical interventions

[133] Council of Europe, 2015, para. 4, p. 9.

[134] Idem, para. 8, p. 9.

[135] See Zillén et al. (2017).

[136] See Higgins (2012) and Voeten (2017).

without their consent.[137] So far, apart from Malta, no other European country has enacted a comprehensive legal framework to ensure that intersex rights are protected in all areas.[138] The above reports also mention Germany as the first EU country that introduced a third option on birth certificates.[139] Since the publication of these reports, Austria, Greece and Portugal have passed legislation on intersex as well. This section constitutes the first part of the comparative study that will be conducted between explicit and implicit EU frameworks on intersex rights. Its aim is to analyse explicit legislation on intersex and its effects on other areas.

As it was already demonstrated in Chap. 3, legal developments on sexual orientation and gender identity impact directly intersex as they tend to accommodate "sex" and "gender" under the law. Therefore, sexual orientation and gender identity frameworks will be explored in this Chapter in order to show how they impact intersex peoples' rights. For instance, the introduction of a third gender in Germany and Austria has impacted the whole understanding of "sex" and "gender" under the law. Consequently, this thorough analysis will be divided into three sections: section one examines sexual orientation laws, section two examines gender identity laws and section three examines legal developments on intersex (Table 4.1).

4.3.1 Austria

4.3.1.1 Sexual Orientation

Since 2010, registered partnerships have been legal for same-sex couples in Austria under the Registered Partnership Act (Eingetragene Partnerschaft-Gesetz – EPG). On December 31st, 2018, the Constitutional Court ordered the legalisation of same-sex marriage. The Court compared the status and effects of registered partnerships to marriage and concluded that same-sex couples were discriminated: "The resulting discriminating effect is reflected in the fact that on account of the different terms used to designate a person's marital status ('married' vs. 'living in a registered partnership'), persons living in a same-sex partnership have to disclose their sexual orientation even in situations in which it is not and must not be of any significance and, especially against the historical background of this issue, they are at risk of being discriminated against."[140] The Court therefore concluded that "The distinction of the law between opposite-sex and same-sex relationships as two different legal institutions violates the principle of equal treatment, which forbids any discrimination of individuals on grounds of personal characteristics, such as their sexual

[137] European Union Agency for Fundamental Rights, 2015, p. 1.

[138] ILGA Europe, OII Europe, 2015, p. 14.

[139] European Union Agency for Fundamental Rights (2015), p. 5.

[140] Verfassungsgerichtshof Österreich, "Distinction between marriage and registered partnership violates ban on discrimination".

Table 4.1 Explicit legislation, case-law, policies on intersex people in the EU

Country/ Jurisdiction	Physical integrity and bodily autonomy	Reparations	Anti-discrimination protection	Access to identification documents	Changing gender on identification documents	Third gender classifications	Right to marry
Austria						X	X and adoption
Germany		X				X	X and adoption
Greece			X		X		X Civil unions
Malta	X		X	X	X	X	X and adoption and ART
Portugal			X		X		X and adoption
Regional							
Spain only in Basque Country			X				
UK only in Scotland			X				

orientation."[141] The repeal refers to the phrase "of different sex" in the General Code of Civil Law on marriage and the Registered Partnership Act which limit registered partnerships to same-sex couples.[142]

Following the ECtHR judgement X and others v. Austria,[143] the Austrian Parliament passed an amendment to the Civil Code allowing the adoption for unmarried same-sex couples. The Court's ruling affirmed the prohibition of discrimination on the grounds of sexual orientation and its reasoning was based on the

[141] Idem.

[142] Idem.

[143] See X. and others v. Austria, application 19010/07.

fact that, while Austria allowed unwed heterosexual couples the right to adopt, it prohibited adoption by unmarried same-sex couples.[144] In 2015, the Austrian Constitutional Court declared the adoption ban on same-sex couples in registered civil partnerships unconstitutional[145] and "found that the general exclusion by law of registered partners from jointly adopting a child as contracting parties to an adoption contract, while allowing the joint parenthood of registered partners in other constellations, was inconsistent and could not be justified on the grounds of protecting the child's best interests."[146] A few months after this decision, it was declared that no further legal amendments were necessary and by virtue of new interpretation joint adoption by same-sex couples was officially allowed in Janurary 2016.[147]

4.3.1.2 Gender Identity

Currently there exists no specific legislation on changing sex/gender in Austria but the legal grounds for a change of name can be found in the Personal Status Act (Personenstandsgesetzand)[148] and the Change of Name Act (Namensrechtsänderun gsgesetz).[149] In 1996, the Ministry of the Interior issued an internal order, the so-called Transsexual Order (Transsexuellen-Erlass),[150] stating that after a change of gender a name can only be changed if the person provides a medical opinion on several physical and medical prerequisites and has changed the notification of his/her sex in the Register of Births (Geburtenregister).[151] The change of notification in the Register of Births could only be affected if the person was not married.[152] The Constitutional Court annulled this order due to formal publication deficiencies and it ruled that there is no legally valid reason to restrict the correction of incorrect data to unmarried persons.[153]

According to the Change of Name Act, changing name does not necessarily require a change of civil status,[154] however, a first name matching the corresponding gender identity may only be adopted after having changed civil status in accordance with the Personal Status Act.[155] Gender neutral names may be adopted without such

---

[144] International Justice Resource Center, "In X. and Others v. Austria, ECtHR Finds Discriminatory Restriction on Same-Sex Couple Adoption Violates Convention".

[145] See Constitutional Court Freyung 8, A-1010 Vienna G 119-120/2014-12 11 December 2014.

[146] Austria Constitutional Court, Important decisions, Identification: AUT-2015-1-001.

[147] ILGA-Europe, Rainbow Map, "Austria".

[148] Austria/BGBl 1983/60, last amended by BGBl I 2005/100.

[149] Austria/BGBl 1988/195, last amended by BGBl 1995/25.

[150] BMI Zahl: 36.250/66-IV/4/9, (27.11.1996).

[151] Nowak (2010), p. 27.

[152] Idem.

[153] See Verfassungsgerichtshof/B947/05, from 21.06.2006.

[154] See para. 3 of Namensänderungsgesetz where entry in civil registry is merely defined as of declaratory nature,

[155] ILGA-Europe, Rainbow Map, "Austria".

a change.[156] In 2009, the Administrative Supreme Court ruled that severe surgeries are not a condition for the correction of the sex/gender and therefore no gender reassignment surgeries are required for trans individuals.[157] Later, in another case on a transgender woman the Administrative Court decided for the second time that gender reassignment surgeries are not necessary.[158] The Constitutional Court has also pronounced on gender assignment surgeries and has concluded that it should not be a prerequisite for name changes.[159]

In 2010, a letter from the Ministry of Interiors emphasised the relevance of all other criteria, which were applied since 1983.[160] It has been reported that currently "usually 1 or 2 letters from psychological experts are required, which confirm (a) the gender identity (not it's disorder), (b) its irreversibility and (c)that actions have been taken to bring the appearance into line with that of the desired gender".[161]

4.3.1.3 Intersex

As stated by ILGA Europe, although there have been efforts to study the percentage of surgeons who operate on intersex children, most of the doctors didn't reply to the call for information.[162] In 2016, the Minister of Health issued a press release expressing that new guidelines on the treatments of intersex infants will be issued.[163] To date, there are no binding guidelines for the treatment of intersex children and no plan on banning non-consensual treatments legally.[164]

In 2018, an intersex individual reached the Constitutional Court aiming to change the male gender entry in the central civil status register to "inter," "other," "X," "undefined," or a similar term, or to strike the gender entry in its entirety.[165] The Court examined the constitutionality of the provision of the Personal Status Act ex officio and based its reasoning on Article 8 of the ECHR stating that the right to respect for the individual's gender identity includes the right to a gender description that conforms to their gender identity or be free to not declare a gender at all[166]: "Article 8 of the ECHR therefore grants individuals with variations in sex characteristics other than male or female the constitutionally guaranteed right to have their gender variation recognised as a separate gender identity in gender-

[156] Idem.

[157] See VwGH Zl. 2008/17/0054-8 from 27. 2. 2009.

[158] See Verwaltungsgerichtshof/2008/06/0032 from 15.09.2009.

[159] See Verfassungsgerichtshof/B1973/08 from 03.12.2009.

[160] ILGA-Europe, Rainbow Map, "Austria".

[161] Idem.

[162] Idem.

[163] Idem.

[164] Idem.

[165] See VfGH G 77/2018 and Library of Congress, "Austria: Court Allows Intersex Individuals to Register Third Gender Other Than Male or Female".

[166] VfGH G 77/2018, paras. 18 and 23.

related provisions; in particular, it protects individuals with alternative gender identities against having their gender assigned by others."[167] In addition, the Court interpreted the law under a non-binary lens elaborating on the fact that "The term used in sect.2 para.2 point 3 of the 2013 Civil Register Act is so general that it can, without any difficulty, be interpreted to include alternative gender identities."[168] The Court after having examined all potential gender idenfitication terms, stated that public authorities are allowed to examine whether a chosen term expresses what it intends to convey since article 8 of the ECHR does not require an arbitrary choice of terms to describe one's gender.[169] The reasoning of the Court was influenced by a previous German decision on the same issue and referenced the German jurisprudence as well.[170]

With this decision, the justices aim to end harmful "normalising" surgeries and grant the right to intersex to register as a third gender which could be named "inter", "other", "X" or "undefined". The decision of the Court is deeply influenced by the reasoning of the German Constitutional Court on intersex and the third gender. In both cases, the term "gender identity" is predominantly used rather the term "sex characteristics" which is more relevant in the case of intersex. Therefore, by reading the case, a confusion may be created as to whether the issue at stake is about intersex or trans. Recognising a third gender creates also implications for other fields of law, for instance, Austria will be soon passing legislation on same-sex marriages allowing same-sex couples to marry exactly as heterosexuals. If the wording of the new law is as the Court has suggested and it is similar to German legislation on the matter, then it would be possible to grant the right to marry to intersex individuals through interpretation.

4.3.2 Germany

4.3.2.1 Sexual Orientation

Registered life partnerships (a form of civil partnerships) were first instituted in Germany in 2001 with the Act on Registered Life Partnerships (Gesetz über die Eingetragene Lebenspartnerschaft). Section 1 on the form and requirements of life partnership states that: "A life partnership shall be entered into by two persons of the same sex who, being present at the same time, declare in person to a registrar that they wish to maintain a partnership for life (life partners)."[171] The Act on Registered

[167] Verwaltungsgerichtshof Österreich, "Intersex persons have the right to adequate entry into civil register".

[168] Idem.

[169] Idem, para. 39.

[170] See Sect. 4.3.2.3.

[171] Act on Registered Life Partnerships of 16 February 2001 (Federal Law Gazette I p. 266), Section 1 (1), (official English version).

Life Partnerships also granted several rights and obligations to same-sex couples in numerous areas including inheritance, alimony, health insurance, immigration, hospital and jail visitations and name change.[172] In 2017, same-sex marriage was legalised and the new provision of the Civil Code (Bürgerliches Gesetzbuch) stipulates that "The marriage is made by two persons of different or the same sex for life".[173] The main change between registered life partnerships and marriage equality under German law is that same-sex couples now have the right to jointly adopt children[174] as according to the German civil code "a married couple may adopt a child only jointly".[175] Prior to that, same-sex couples had limited adoption rights allowing only stepchild adoption.[176]

In 2006, Germany implemented the European Directives on non-discrimination and passed the Equal Treatment Act (Allgemeines Gleichbehandlungsgesetz) that banned discrimination based on sexual orientation and gender identity in employment, education, health services and the provision of goods and services[177]: "The purpose of this Act is to prevent or to stop discrimination on the grounds of race or ethnic origin, gender, religion or belief, disability, age or sexual orientation."[178] However, anti-discrimination provisions in the rest of areas vary across Germany as there are state laws that specifically include anti-discrimination provisions on sexual orientation and gender identity. For instance, Bremen has included anti-discrimination provisions on sexual orientation and gender identity in its state Constitution since 2001.[179]

4.3.2.2 Gender Identity

Trans legal recognition is guaranteed under the Act on the change of first name and determination of gender identity in special cases (Transsexual Act-TSG) (Gesetz über die Änderung der Vornamen und die Feststellung der Geschlechtszugehörigkeit in besonderen Fällen (Transsexuellengesetz—TSG)). The Act included two options for transsexuals: the "Minor Solution" which provides regulations on the change of the first name without altrering the person's gender status and the "Major Solution"

[172] See Act on Registered Life Partnerships of 16 February 2001 (Federal Law Gazette I p. 266), last amended by Article 2 of the Act of 20 July 2017 (official English version).

[173] Bürgerliches Gesetzbuch (BGB) § 1353 Eheliche Lebensgemeinschaft, (1) Die Ehe wird von zwei Personen verschiedenen oder gleichen Geschlechts auf Lebenszeit geschlossen (translated by the author).

[174] Deutsche Welle, "German president signs gay marriage bill into law".

[175] Civil Code (BGB), Section 1741 Admissibility of the adoption (official English version).

[176] See Act on Registered Life Partnerships, Section 9 Stipulations in respect of children of a life partner (official English version).

[177] See Act Implementing European Directives Putting into Effect the Principle of Equal Treatment, Section 2 (official English version).

[178] Act Implementing European Directives Putting into Effect the Principle of Equal Treatment, Section 1 (official English version).

[179] Landesverfassung der Freien Hansestadt Bremen, Artikel 2.

on the change of gender status; in both cases, a judge decides.[180] For both the name and gender status change there are several requirements: the applicant must "not identify with the birth assigned sex/gender, but with the other one", should feel "a compulsion to live according to his/her ideas for at least three years" and it needs to be assumed that "the feeling of belonging to the other sex/gender is not going to change".[181] For the change of gender status, the applicant may not be married, and it is required to be "permanently infertile" and to have undergone a gender reassignment surgery.[182] It has to be noted that when the Act was enacted in 1980, it was described as "the most progressive law in the world" and the "most human and comprehensive of all solutions…so far in any state under the rule of law".[183]

In 2008, Germany's Federal Constitutional Court found the Act constitutional except for its marriage provision[184] because it forced individuals to choose between protected fundamental rights and the Constitution guarantees that marriage is protected as a basic right as well as the individual integrity.[185] The Court held that "the legislation could not force divorce on a person who, but for his or her marriage, fulfilled all the other criteria for recognition but should create a mechanism by which the union could continue in a different "but equally provided for" form".[186] Moreover, the Court concluded that "Section 8(1)(2) limited unacceptably the ability of a married transsexual person to fully enjoy the constitutional right to realise his or her self-determined sexual identity and suggested that, because only a small number of transsexuals were confronted by this situation, it was open to the legislature, in lieu of some other reform, to allow married transsexuals to obtain legal recognition of their identity while maintaining their marriage relationship".[187] The same year, a report issued by the Aktion Transsexualität und Menschenrecht e.V. / ATME (Campaign Transsexuality and Human Rights) shed light on the implications that the Act was imposing on transsexual people in Germany. It specified that "on the grounds of lack of a juridical recognition in their gender, transsexuals are at the mercy of the psychiatrists".[188]

---

[180] International Models Project on Women's Rights, "Current Legal Framework: Transgender Issues in Germany".

[181] Gesetz über die Änderung der Vornamen und die Feststellung der Geschlechtszugehörigkeit in besonderen Fällen(Transsexuellengesetz – TSG, Erster Abschnitt, §1 Voraussetzungen.

[182] Idem, Zweiter Abschnitt, § 8 Voraussetzungen.

[183] Translated quotations from the German Bundestag debate on the bill (164th session of the 8th electoral term): Member of the Bundestag Dr. Rolf Meinecke (SPD), Plenarprotokoll 8/164, p. 13174, and Member of the Bundestag Torsten Wolfgramm (FDP), Plenarprotokoll 8/164, p. 13175. See Federal Ministry for Family Affairs, Senior Citizens, Women and Youth, "Report on Reform of the Transsexuals Act (Transsexuellengesetz),2016, p. 5.

[184] Entscheidungen des Bundesverfassungsgerichts [BVerfGE] [Federal Constitutional Court] May 27, 2008, 1 Bundesverfassungsgericht BvL 10/05.

[185] International Commission of Jurists, BvL 10/05, Federal Constitutional Court of Germany (27 May 2008) (Case summary).

[186] Idem.

[187] Idem.

[188] Alternative Report Follow-up Germany 2011 submitted by German Women's Rights Organisations in Response to the Written Information of Germany on the steps undertaken to

In 2011, a trans woman challenged her general rights of personality before the Federal Constitutional Court and the component of the right to sexual self-determination.[189] The complainant was born male, but she perceived herself as belonging to the female gender. She had only changed her name to a female one based on the "Minor solution" provided by the Act since she had not undergone a gender reassignment surgery and it was impossible to change her gender status. When she applied to register a civil partnership together with her female partner, she was refused by the registrar on the grounds that a civil partnership was exclusively reserved for parties of the same gender.[190] The complainant argued that she could not enter into a marriage because marriages were only for opposite-sex couples and therefore she would legally be considered as a man making it impossible for her to live a life free of discrimination.[191] The Court held that forcing the complainant to enter a marriage would cause severe consequences since her intimate sphere would not be protected against unwanted disclosure, which is constitutionally guaranteed by the Basic Law.[192] In addition, the requirements imposed by the Act on forced sterilisation and gender reassignment surgery were not compatible with the right to sexual self-determination and physical integrity.[193] As a result, the Court found that Section 8 of the Act was unconstitutional.

Despite the Court's decisions, the Act has not yet been reformed. German experts have demanded urgent action for the protection of trans rights with Richard Köhler stating that "There is urgent need for reforms. Trans people in Germany are still left alone with a substantive amount of discrimination. Germany lags behind in Europe. Changes for an explicit protection against discrimination and a human rights compatible legal gender recognition procedure are overdue. The German Government should urgently show political leadership and implement the recommendations of the expert commission."[194] Apart from the provisions that have been declared unconstitutional, trans individuals have to face numerous barriers posed by the rest of the regulations as well. For instance, the fact that the procedure takes place before the court is "an access barrier in itself" as because of this provision, proceedings under the Act are given lower priority.[195] The Act is also applied only to German nationals

implement the recommendations contained in paragraphs 40 and 62 and as requested as a follow up report in paragraph 67 of the Concluding Observations of the CEDAW Committee, 12 February 2009 [CEDAW/C/DEU/CO/6], p. 17.

[189] International Commission of Jurists, 1 BvR 3295-07, Federal Constitutional Court, Germany (11 January 2011) (Case summary).

[190] Idem.

[191] Idem.

[192] Idem.

[193] Idem.

[194] Transgender Europe, "German Experts demand urgent Action for Trans Rights".

[195] Federal Ministry for Family Affairs, Senior Citizens, Women and Youth, "Report on Reform of the Transsexuals Act (Transsexuellengesetz),2016, p. 10.

posing a severe restriction on the ability of non-German nationals to exercise their basic rights.[196]

The Transsexuals Act violates basic rights and international human rights conventions such as the ECHR. The German Federal Ministry for Family Affairs, Senior Citizens, Women and Youth recommends that the legislature replaces it with a new act that reflects the current needs of trans individuals.[197] It proposes the repeal of the Transsexuals Act and the adoption of an "Act Concerning the Recognition of Gender Identity and for the Protection of Self-Determination in Gender Assignment" (Gesetz zur Anerkennung der Geschlechtsidentität und zum Schutz der Selbstbestimmung bei der Geschlechtszuordnung).[198]

4.3.2.3 Intersex

It is estimated that approximately 80,000–120,000 people in Germany are intersex.[199] In 2008, the Association of Intersexual People/XY-Women (Verein Intersexuelle Menschen e.V. / XY-Frauen) submitted a Shadow Report to the United Nations Committee on the Elimination of All Forms of Discrimination Against Women which revealed human rights violations that intersex people face in Germany.[200] The Report highlighted that "in Germany as well as in numerous other countries, intersexual persons are target of irreversible medication and surgery from early childhood on".[201] Medical interferences on intersex individuals result in lifelong obligatory medical treatments and most of the times, intersex children will be medically treated in order to adjust to what is perceived as being "female" or "male".[202] In 2012, the German Ethics Council on Intersexuality introduced Ethical Guidelines and Recommendations on the Medical Treatment of intersex after it was instructed to review the situation of intersex people by the Committee on the Elimination of All Forms of Discrimination Against Women (CEDAW). The Ethical Guidelines of the Council included the minimisation of the physical and psychological risks of the intersex child, the sustainment of fertility and of physical conditions for a fulfilled sex life, the introduction of further treatments and the respect of parental wishes and beliefs.[203] With regards to the medical treatment of intersex, the Council recommended that irreversible treatments should be considered thoroughly,

[196] Idem.

[197] Idem, p. 16.

[198] Idem.

[199] Idem, p. 5.

[200] Association of Intersexual People/XY-Women (Verein Intersexuelle Menschen e.V. / XY-Frauen), Shadow Report to the 6th National Report of the Federal Republic of Germany on the United Nations Convention on the Elimination of All Forms of Discrimination Against Women (CEDAW), 2008.

[201] Idem.

[202] Idem.

[203] Statement of the German Ethics Council on Intersexuality, 2012, p. 4.

should not be performed without the consent of the patient and/or parents and should be postponed until the patient is able to voice an opinion.[204] Between 2005 and 2014, there was no decrease on the statistics regarding intersex surgeries performed on infants in Germany.[205]

In 2017, the Committee on the Elimination of Discrimination Against Women considered the combined seventh and eighth periodic reports of Germany on its implementation of the provisions of the Convention on the Elimination of Discrimination against Women and Germany was asked to explain measures that have been taken to prohibit the practice of intersex genital mutilation on and postpone this irreversible surgery until the child was old enough to give consent.[206] At that time, the German delegation stated that Germany "was still discussing whether to establish a fund for the compensation of victims of intersex genital mutilation" and that irreversible intersex surgeries were performed when they were considered life-saving and considering the best interest of the child.[207]

Even though the situation on intersex surgeries in Germany can be considered as "alarming", Amnesty International reported that current German legislation does not ban non-emergency, invasive and irreversible surgeries on intersex and legal experts disagree on whether existing provisions of Civil law on the prohibition of the sterilisation[208] of children cover gonadectomies of intersex children.[209]

4.3.2.3.1 Reparations

The decision of the Regional Court of Cologne on In re Völling made Christiane Völling[210] the first intersex to have successfully sued for damages due to the performance of a non-consensual intersex surgery. Christiane Völling, was born with genitalia outside of the typical male/female binary and was assigned a male gender at birth. At the age of fourteen, during a medical examination, the existence of female reproductive organs was diagnosed.[211] The plaintiff was informed that although she was still identifying as male, she was 60% female. In 1976, after an analysis of Völling's chromosome, a normal female chromosomal pattern was discovered.

---

[204] Idem, p. 5.

[205] See Klöppel (2016).

[206] CEDAW/C/DEU/7-8, Consideration of reports submitted by States parties under article 18 of the Convention, Seventh and eighth periodic reports of States parties due in 2014, Germany.

[207] The United Nations Office at Geneva, "Committee on the Elimination of Discrimination Against Women Considers the Reports of Germany" CEDAW17/009E.

[208] Section 1631c of the Civil Code: Prohibition of sterilization: "The parents may not consent to a sterilization of the child. Nor can the child itself consent to the sterilization. [...]."(official English version).

[209] Amnesty International (2017), p. 51.

[210] Christiane Völling is now identifying as female. Therefore, the words "she" and "her" will be used in this text.

[211] International Commission of Jurists, In re Völliing, Regional Court Cologne, 6 February 2008 (Case summary).

However, the plaintiff was then given the diagnosis "suspicion of female pseudohermaphroditism with an over-functioning cortex of the suprarenal gland" and "no discussion was held with the plaintiff about her normal female chromosomal constitution, which was disclosed in the letter from August 2, 1977, as [it was assumed] this only limitedly interpretable result could have possibly confused her".[212] The sex reassignment surgery was performed in 1977 and according to the anesthesia report it was mentioned as "testovarectomy".[213] The plaintiff reached the Court claiming that the physician failed to provide accurate information on the nature and extent of the non-consensual surgical procedure in which the female sexual organs were removed.[214] In detail, the plaintiff stated "that the organs were normally developed and fully functional and that this fact was apparent during the surgery".[215] Furthermore, "with appropriate therapeutic treatment for Androgenital Syndrom she could have led the life of a woman, including experiencing a fulfilled female sexuality, as well as procreated".[216]

The Court held that the plaintiff had not been appropriately informed about the "nature, content and extent" of the sex reassignment surgery she was subjected to. In the Court's opinion "the defendant had failed to demonstrate that she had a sound reason for not fully disclosing to the plaintiff the details of her condition and the defendant's assertion that information was withheld in order not to "confuse" the plaintiff was unsustainable".[217] The justices also concluded that the defendant had an obligation to inform the patient on the change of her medical diagnosis and obtain her fully informed consent before the operation.[218] Last, the Court noted that, "although the defendant was not directly responsible for the general medical treatment plan (…), as a surgeon he ought to have understood and fundamentally reviewed the information available to him and his responsibility to disclose it".[219]

In 2015, Michaela "Michaa" Raab won damages and compensation after suing the University of Erlangen-Nuremberg Clinic who failed to properly advise her and performed an intersex genital mutilation.[220] The Nuremberg State Court issued a first decision and ruled the Erlangen University Clinic to pay damages and compensation to Michaela "Micha" Raab for non-consensual intersex treatments, including partial clitoris amputation, castration and imposition of hormones.[221] The Court dismissed the case against the surgeon based on the fact that the lack of disclosure of

[212] In re Völliing, Regional Court Cologne, 6 February 2008, (English version), para. 7.

[213] Idem, para. 8.

[214] In re Völliing, Regional Court Cologne, 6 February 2008, (English version).

[215] Idem, para. 11.

[216] Idem.

[217] International Commission of Jurists, In re Völliing, Regional Court Cologne, 6 February 2008 (Case summary).

[218] Idem.

[219] Idem.

[220] Zwischengeschlecht, "Nuremberg Hermaphrodite Lawsuit: Michaela "Micha" Raab Wins Damages and Compensation for Intersex Genital Mutilations".

[221] Idem.

the diagnosis, karyotype and treatment options was not his fault, but the responsibility of other doctors, and held the clinic liable.[222] Zwischengeschlecht also reported that there is another civil suit ongoing in Munich against a Bavarian clinic where intersex surgeries were performed.[223] The fact that German jurisprudence has recognised the right to reparations for intersex individuals who have been victims of involuntary intersex surgeries, means that the invasive and harmful nature of those surgeries is recognsied but still, their performance is not outlawed.

4.3.2.3.2 Identification Documents

In 2012, the German Ethics Council submitted its opinion on the situation of intersex rights in Germany and recommended that a provision should be made for persons whose sex cannot be determined to register as "other".[224] Accordingly, in 2013, the German Civil Status Law (Personenstandsgesetz (PStG)) was modified to cover cases where it was not possible to assign the child a sex.[225] In those cases, the sex marker in the birth registry would be left blank: "if the child can be assigned to neither the female nor the male sex, then the child is to be entered into the register of births without such a specification".[226] This development was criticised by intersex civil society organisations. For instance, Organisation Intersex International (OII) Europe mentioned that "the new provisions could encourage the (potential) parents and doctors even more to avoid an "ambiguous" child at any cost (through abortion, prenatal "treatment" or so-called disambiguating surgical and / or hormonal interventions)" and that "instead of leaving sex registration open for all, and not just intersex children, once again special rules are created, which produce exclusions."[227] The Council of Europe also criticised the German legal framework stating that "Human rights practitioners fear that the lack of freedom of choice regarding the entry in the gender marker field may now lead to an increase in stigmatisation and to "forced outings" of those children whose sex remains undetermined. This has raised the concern that the law may also lead to an increase in pressure on parents of intersex children to decide in favour of one sex."[228]

In 2016, Germany's Hight Court ruled that the German law could not allow the entry of a third option of "inter" or "diverse" in the birth registry as it found no violation since intersex people have been able to leave the gender entry in birth

---

[222] Idem.

[223] Idem.

[224] Bundestag document, Bundestagsdrucksache – BTDrucks 17/9088, p. 59 (translation by the German Ethics Council).

[225] The Bundestag on 31 January 2013 unanimously adopted recommendation 17/12192, see Deutscher Bundestag Drucksache 17/12192.

[226] Section 22(3) of the German Civil Status Law as translated by OII Europe.

[227] OII Europe, "Sham package for Intersex: Leaving sex entry open is not an option".

[228] Council of Europe (2015), p. 38.

registries blank since 2013.[229] Nonetheless, a year later, the German Constitutional Court held that Civil Status Law must allow a third gender option because the current civil law violated the right to personality and the ban on discrimination.[230] In detail, although by reading the decision of the Court and the terminology used on sex and gender, it is not clear if intersex violations are perceived as violations based on sex characteristics or gender or gender identity, the justices moved towards the "right direction" by holding that the right of personality also protects gender identity as the assignment of gender plays a crucial role for a person's self-conception and the way the person is perceived by others.[231] Current Civil Status Law allows for a "no entry"/blank option that does not reflect that individuals such as the complainant do not see themselves as genderless persons but as having a gender beyond male or female. In addition, the Basic Law does not require that civil status must be exclusively binary[232] and gender may not serve as a basis for unequal legal treatment. Therefore, persons concerned could be able to choose another positive designation of a gender that is not male nor female, such as "inter/diverse" or "diverse" as the complainant indicated in that case.

The decision of the German Constitutional Court aims to end harmful and involuntary surgeries on intersex infants by allowing them to choose a third option on birth certificates. In addition, in Germany, health insurance cards depend on the personal code and gender on birth certificates and intersex people whose sex/gender does not match their documentation have been facing challenges and discrimination.[233] The Court provided the legislature with two solutions, first it could either completely abolish the requirement of registering a gender at birth or second it could allow intersex people the option of registering a third gender. It also pointed out that the legislature is not restricted to the terms "inter" or "diverse" suggested by the complainant.[234] The decision of the Court has interpreted as introducing a "third gender" in Germany which will be accessible only to intersex. Even though this solution could decrease human rights violations against intersex, it could be argued that it introduces further discriminations within non-binary individuals as it creates a gender that is only accessible to intersex leaving behind other minorities such as trans or agender individuals. Moreover, it has been already stated that intersex civil society organisations have highlighted that sex/gender classifications which attempt to classify intersex as a third sex/gender do not respect intersex individual's diversity and right to self-determination.

In December 2018, the German Parliament introduced "diverse" (divers) as gender marker entry in addition to "male" and "female" and received a lot of criticism by both trans and intersex rights organisations.[235] Transgender Europe criticised the

---

[229] Reuters, "German high court rejects 'intersex' as third gender category".

[230] BVerfG, Order of the First Senate of 10 October 2017- 1 BvR 2019/16- paras. (1-69).

[231] Idem, Section 1. "The general right of personality protects the complainant's gender identity".

[232] Idem, para. 50.

[233] Amnesty International (2017), p. 52.

[234] BVerfG, Order of the First Senate of 10 October 2017- 1 BvR 2019/16, para. 65.

[235] Transgender Europe, "Germany introduces Third Gender – fails Trans People".

new law mentioning that "Any change of gender marker needs to be based on self-determination. Trans and intersex communities have been suffering for too long from the hands of doctors. This needs to stop. The law needs to protect against human rights violations and not invite new abuse."[236] OII Europe published its statement on social media stating that "A lot of intersex people do not have access to their medical records and are in significant danger of re-traumatisation if they need to obtain a medical certificate. The law offers an exception to the medical statement and replaces it with an oath under "special circumstances". There is no clarity yet about how these circumstances will be determined. German lawyers of the strategic litigation group #DritteOption have already confirmed that this oath will have to refer to medical diagnoses and medical treatments and that this will exclude any intersex person who has no precise knowledge of the facts to be explained."[237]

4.3.2.3.3 Marriage

The previous provision of the Civil Status Law on birth registration was criticised as problematic not only because intersex people were considered as genderless -since their gender option was left blank- but also because it was not clear whom the child would be able to marry when they grow up. With the new decision of the Constitutional Court and the recognition of a third gender/sex in Germany, the wording of the law on same-sex marriage covers intersex since it stipulates that "the marriage is made by two persons of different or the same sex for life".[238] Indeed, the German Ethics Council has stated that persons whose sex is recorded as "other" should be able to enter into registered civil partnership[239] and some Members were of the view that intersex persons should be permitted to marry any other person.

It could be argued that intersex people who are married could also adopt children under the German civil code which states that "a married couple may adopt a child only jointly".[240]

[236] Idem.

[237] OII Europe, "Really Germany? Germany misses the chance for basing its third gender marker law on human rights".

[238] Bürgerliches Gesetzbuch (BGB) § 1353 Eheliche Lebensgemeinschaft, (1) Die Ehe wird von zwei Personen verschiedenen oder gleichen Geschlechts auf Lebenszeit geschlossen.

[239] See Deutscher Ethikrat, 2012.

[240] Civil Code (BGB), Section 1741 Admissibility of the adoption (official English version).

4.3.3 *Greece*

4.3.3.1 Sexual Orientation

The Greek Constitution (Ελληνικό Σύνταγμα) does not provide any definition of marriage, but it stipulates that "the family, being the cornerstone of the preservation and advancement of the Nation, as well as marriage, (…) shall be under the protection of the State".[241] This provision suggests that the Constitution protects family and marriage and the latter is not a necessary condition of the former.[242] It also suggests that the common legislator cannot abolish the institution of marriage nor amend it, constituting the expansion of the scope of marriage to same-sex couples unconstitutional.[243] However, there is a minority legal opinion according to which, the relevant articles on marriage of the Civil Code (Αστικός Κώδικας) should be interpreted in the light of Article 4 paragraph 2 on sex equality and thus allow -de lege lata- for same-sex marriage.[244] Obviously, this could not apply to non-binary individuals as extending the scope of marriage to individuals such as trans and intersex would be unconstitutional due to the binary understanding of Article 4 paragraph 2 which grants sex equality only to men and women: "Greek men and women have equal rights and equal obligations" excluding Greek citizens who fall outside the binary.

The Greek Civil Code (Αστικός Κώδικας) does not mention explicitly the sex difference as a prerequisite for marriage,[245] and therefore, in 2008, the Mayor of Tilos performed marriages between two same-sex couples. The marriages were declared as "invalid" by the Supreme Court (Δικαστήριο του Αρείου Πάγου).[246] The justices held that "under the Civil Code the difference of sex of the prospective spouses is considered as self-evident. (…) This view is reinforced by the explicit reference under the Law 3719/2008 that establishes civil unions and Article 1 uses explicitly the term "heterosexuals"".[247]

The Law 3719/2008 Reforms on the family, the child, the society and other provisions (Νόμος υπ'αριθ. 3719/2008 Μεταρρυθμίσεις για την οικογένεια, το παιδί, την κοινωνία και άλλες διατάξεις) which was excluding same-sex couples from its scope,[248] was challenged at the ECtHR in Vallianatos and Others v. Greece.[249] The applicants argued that the Law infringed their right to respect for their private and

[241] The Constitution of Greece, Article 21 (1).

[242] See Dagtoglou Prodromos (2005).

[243] Fessas (2011), p. 192.

[244] See Papadopoulou (2008), Vidalis (19960, Papazisi (2007) and Vangelis Mallios, "A right to marry: Constitutional privilege of Heterosexuals or Right of Homosexuals as well?".

[245] See Civil Code, Chapter Two: Marriage.

[246] Supreme Court, Decision 1428/2017.

[247] Idem, para. 2.

[248] See Mallios (2010) and Karavokyris (2015).

[249] See Pervou (2014).

family life and discriminated them on the grounds of sexual orientation.[250] On the other hand, the government argued that same-sex couples could regulate their rights and obligations on a contractual basis, thus their inclusion in the Law was not necessary.[251] In addition, the objective of the civil-unions law was to protect children born outside marriage and strengthen the institution of the family "in the traditional sense" even without the precondition of marriage.[252] The Court was not convinced by the government's arguments and after examining the trends within Europe on civil-unions, it highlighted that the "Council of Europe member States, when they opt to enact legislation introducing a new system of registered partnership as an alternative to marriage for unmarried couples, include same-sex couples in its scope".[253] Greece implemented the decisions of the Court 2 years later and Law 3719/2008 was amended by the provisions of Law 4356/2015 Civil union, exercise of rights, criminal and other provisions (Νόμος Υπ'αριθ. 4356/2015, Σύμφωνο συμβίωσης, άσκηση δικαιωμάτων, ποινικές και άλλες διατάξεις). According to Article 1 of the current Greek Law regulating the Civil Unions "A contract between two adults, regardless of their gender/sex, governing their life as a couple, shall be entered into means of a notarised instrument in the presence of the parties".[254]

In 2018, the Council of State (Συμβούλιο της Επικρατείας) pronounced on the validity of Law 4356/2015. In detail, the Court elaborated on the question as to which extend the above Law affects the institution of marriage and the moral perceptions (morals). In its reasoning it clarified that: "The adoption and regulation of this alternative form of registered partnership does not affect the institution of marriage which is protected by the Constitution, from which it differs significantly, since it aims to cover different social needs and in particular, to recognise and protect de facto partnership relations, which while they constitute part of the modern reality, they remain outside the legal order either because the parties do not wish (to do so), or because they do not have the legal capacity (same sex couples) to subject their relationship under the protection of marriage".[255] The reasoning of the Court was based on modern prevailing trends in Europe with regards to the institution of "family" and it referenced case law of the ECtHR, the EU and European States.[256]

Law 4538/2018 Measures for the promotion of the institutions of fostering and adoption and other provisions (Νόμος 4538/2018 Μέτρα για την προώθηση των Θεσμών της Αναδοχής και Υιοθεσίας και άλλες διατάξεις) granted same-sex couples the right to foster children. Article 8 stipulates that "appropriate to be foster parents, in accordance with the provisions, are families consisting of spouses or in

---

[250] Vallianatos and Others v. Greece, Applications nos. 29381/09 and 32684/09, judgment of 7 November 2013, para. 3.

[251] Idem.

[252] Idem, para. 80.

[253] Idem, para. 91.

[254] Greek Law regulating the Civil Union, (English version on constitutionalism.gr).

[255] Council of State, Decision 2003/2018, para. 14.

[256] See Council of State, Decision 2003/2018 and on the evolution of the notion of "family" in Europe and Greece see Papadopoulou (2015).

civil union, with or without children, or single persons, unmarried or divorced, or widowed, with or without children (…) the choice is always based on the best interest of the minor, in the light of the International Convention on the Rights of the Child (…)”.[257]

Discrimination in employment is prohibited on the grounds of sexual orientation and gender identity under the Law 3304/2005 Application of the principle of equal treatment regardless of racial or ethnic origin, religion or belief, disability, age or sexual orientation (Νόμος υπ'αριθ. 3304/2005 Εφαρμογή της αρχής της ίσης μεταχείρισης ανεξαρτήτως φυλετικής ή εθνοτικής καταγωγής, θρησκευτικών ή άλλων πεποιθήσεων, αναπηρίας, ηλικίας ή γενετήσιου προσανατολισμού) that implemented the European Union Directives. Law 4285/2014 on combating certain forms and manifestations of racism and xenophobia by means of criminal law and other provisions (Νόμος υπ'αριθ. 4285 για την καταπολέμηση ορισμένων μορφών και εκδηλώσεων ρατσισμού και ξενοφοβίας μέσω του ποινικού δικαίου και άλλες διατάξεις) criminalises hate speech and violence based on sexual orientation and gender identity.[258] Law 4356/2015 Civil union, exercise of rights, criminal and other provisions (Νόμος Υπ'αριθ. 4356, Σύμφωνο συμβίωσης, άσκηση δικαιωμάτων, ποινικές και άλλες διατάξεις) amended the provisions of the Criminal Code to include sexual orientation, gender identity and sex characteristics.[259] In 2016, further anti-discrimination protections on the grounds of sexual orientation, gender identity and sex characteristics were introduced to implement European Union Directives on non-discrimination.[260]

4.3.3.2 Gender Identity

In 2017, Law 4491/2017 on the Legal recognition of gender identity (Νόμος υπ'αριθ. 4491/2017 Νομική αναγνώριση της ταυτότητας φύλου) was an important step towards accessible legal gender recognition.[261] In the past, the procedure of legal gender recognition presupposed a gender reassignment surgery[262] but in 2016 a decision of the County Court of Athens (Ειρηνοδικείο Αθηνών) ruled that a person who wants to change their legal gender is not obliged to have undergone a gender reassignment surgery: “forced sterilisation, gender reassignment surgery from female to male and vice versa, as a prerequisite for the legal gender recognition of trans individuals, (…) is considered as an extreme demand and practice and violates Article 8 of the ECHR (…). Also, the above requirements impinge on the right to equality and non-discrimination of Articles 2 and 26 of the ICCPR”.[263]

---

[257] Law 4538/2018.

[258] Law 4285/2014, Article 1.

[259] Law 4356/2015, Article 81A and Article 29.

[260] Law 4443/2016.

[261] See Fountedaki (2017) and Papadopoulou (2017).

[262] See Law 4144/2013.

[263] Aristotle University of Thessaloniki, “Historical Court decision on gender recognition without surgery”.

The Legal Gender Recognition Law granted trans people the right to change their legal gender freely and abolished former prerequisites including medical interventions and gender reassignment surgeries that led to sterilisation. This right is granted to individuals from age 17 and even underaged children between the age of 15 and 17 have access to the process but under certain conditions including obtaining a certificate from a medical council.[264] The law has been criticised as certain limitations are considered as opposed to human rights principles, for instance individuals who wish to recognise their gender legally, have to appear before a judge and need to be single[265] and both requirements violate the right to self-determination and protection of families.[266] It needs to be noted that, the Draft Law of the Legislative Committee of the Ministry of Justice as of 18 November 2016 (Σχέδιο Νόμου της Νομοπαρασκευαστικής Επιτροπής του Υπουργείου Δικαιοσύνης για την αναγνώριση της ταυτότητας φύλου (18.11.2016)), did not include any provision on the marital status of trans individuals.[267] Paragraph 3 on the marital status of trans individuals first appears in the Bill of Ministry of Justice, Transparency and Human Rights ((Κατατεθέν) Σχέδιο Νόμου του Υπουργείου Δικαιοσύνης, Διαφάνειας και Ανθρωπίνων Δικαιωμάτων) and is added in Article 3 between the prerequisites for the legal recognition of gender.[268]

In 2018, the County Court of Marousi (Ειρηνοδικείο Αμαρουσίου) approved a non-binary person's request to have its[269] male birth name changed to a gender-neutral one by adding a female name next to it. In its reasoning on the name change, the Court held that the applicant's name "is an indispensable and permanent feature of its personality (…) and goes hand in hand with the free development of its personality under Article 5 (1) of the Constitution which guarantees the right of everyone to the free development of personality and the rejection of such request would generate undesirable consequences for the applicant in respect of its personal and social status and image".[270] The applicant also aimed for the change of its gender on identification documents and it requested the Court to change the current male gender marker to "blank" ("-") since it identifies as a non-binary individual. The Court rejected its request based on Law 4491/2017 which "did not include the case of the registration of a third gender for those who wish, i.e. non-binary individuals who do not identify themselves with the gender binary. (…) the freedom of self-determination and self-development does not necessarily imply the positive obligation of the legislator for legal recognition (of gender)".[271] The applicant had also referred to the

[264] Law 4491/2017, Article 3.

[265] Idem, Article 3 (3) and Article 4.

[266] Transgender Europe, "New Greek Gender Recognition law fails human rights".

[267] Draft Law of the Legislative Committee of the Ministry of Justice as of 18 November 2016.

[268] See Bill of Ministry of Justice, Transparency and Human Rights, "Legal Recognition of Gender Identity- National Mechanism for the preparation, monitoring and evaluation of action plans for children's rights".

[269] The applicant identifies with "it".

[270] County Court of Marousi, Decision 67/2018.

[271] Idem.

U.S. case law and specifically in two State Court decisions on non-binary individuals, but the Court stressed that the facts of this case are different since in the U.S. decisions, those individuals were allowed to identify as non-binary for medical purposes. The Court explained that in the first case, the person was born as intersex and in the second case there was medical proof that acknowledged that the individual should be considered as non-binary.[272]

The decision of the County Court of Marousi indicates that the Legal Gender Recognition Law does not introduce a "third gender" in Greece but seeks to safeguard trans rights by allowing them to change their gender without undergoing harmful and irreversible gender reassignment surgeries. The County Court also referred to the U.S. case law on intersex and clarified that in this case there were no "medical purposes" and therefore the applicant could not identify with a third, blank gender. The above reasoning of the Court leads to two main conclusions: first, the medicalisation of intersex is perceived as an "advantage" by the Greek judge because it implies that nature made an "error" and it has to be "fixed" by recognising legally intersex individuals and second, it opens the way for intersex individuals to be recognised as "third/non-binary gender" in Greece in the future.

4.3.3.3 Intersex

There is no data available on the exact percentage of intersex in Greece and it remains unclear whether intersex surgeries are performed on infants or adults. It appears that according to the Fundamental Rights Agency, Greece is among the 18 EU Member States that allow a certain delay in the registration of a new birth.[273] It has been reported that intersex people are usually confused with trans "health care practitioners in our country (Greece) often treat in the same way trans and intersex people, and there are medical records diagnosing trans individuals as "hermaphrodites" that should not be accepted".[274] This situation is also reflected on Greek law. Article 7 of the Draft Law of the Legislative Committee of the Ministry of Justice prohibited explicitly non-therapeutic surgeries on intersex infants in its first paragraph: "any medical treatment, such as surgery or hormonal treatment, for the total or partial alteration of sex characteristics of a minor is prohibited, unless if it is required under the interest of the minor's health". Accordingly, such procedures would be allowed only to save a minor's life and under the approval of a team of experts including doctors, psychologists and social workers.[275] Then, paragraph 2 guaranteed the right to operated intersex infants to legally recognise their acquired sex before the Court. However, Article 7 was disappeared in the Bill and even though Law 4491/2017 now includes the definition of "sex characteristics" under

[272] Idem.

[273] European Union Fundamental Rights Agency, 2015, p. 4.

[274] Galanou (2014), p. 94.

[275] Draft Law of the Legislative Committee of the Ministry of Justice as of 18 November 2016, Article 7, para. 1.

Article 2 para. 2, this definition seems pointless as Article 7 on intersex infants has been deleted. The same confusion can be observed in Greek case law. In 2013, the One-member First-Instance Court of Heraklion (Μονομελές Πρωτοδικείο Ηρακλείου) accepted the application of an individual who was claiming to be born as "hermaphrodite" but was registered as "female" and wished to change his gender from female to male after having undergone a gender reassignment surgery.[276] It is vague whether this case was about a trans individual who was described as "hermaphrodite" or about an intersex individual. It can be observed that, first, the medical proof submitted to the Court uses the term "hermaphrodite" which is outdated and degrading and second, as in the previous case of the County Court of Marousi, probably the diagnosis of "hermaphroditism" is used to "convince" the justices. In either case, according to Greek jurisprudence, intersex individuals can change their gender on identification documents following the same procedure as trans which under the new law does not require harmful medical interventions.

4.3.3.3.1 Non-discrimination and Violence

Since 2015, the ground "sex characteristics" is explicitly included in Greek law. Law 4356/2015 introduced three provisions concerning intersex. Article 17 enumerates the responsibilities of the National Council against Racism and Intolerance including the protection of individuals and groups targeted because of their sex characteristics.[277] Article 21 amends the Article 81 A of the Penal Code on racist crimes and amends the penalty framework to include the case that a crime is committed against a person on the grounds of sex characteristics[278] and Article 29 amends Article 361 B of the Penal Code to read as "anyone who supplies or offers services (…) excluding individuals on the grounds of sex characteristics is punished (…)".[279] The above amendments on intersex result from the efforts of the Trans Association to add provisions on the Criminal Code to protect sexual minorities and non-binary individuals in particular against hate speech and violence.[280] Afterwards, Law 4443/2016 which aims to implement European Union Directives, aims to combat discrimination against sexual minorities. Part A of the Law includes numerous Articles on the prohibition of discrimination based on sex characteristics in employment.[281]

All the above developments demonstrate that Greek legal frameworks have significantly evolved since the decision of the ECtHR on same sex couples and civil unions. Greece is gradually introducing laws and case-law that protect non-binary individuals including intersex. By the same token, these advances impact also the

[276] One-member First-Instance Court of Heraklion, 255/2013.

[277] Law 4356/2015, Article 17.

[278] Idem, Article 21.

[279] Idem, Article 29.

[280] Efsyn.gr, "First time, equal before the law".

[281] Law 4443/2016, Part A.

current understanding and interpretation of the Greek Constitution. As it was already mentioned, Article 4 paragraph 2 of the Constitution grants equal rights and obligations only to Greek women and men reinforcing the binary of sex and gender. When the Greek Constitution was drafted non-binary individuals were not visible and at the time, the main goal was to protect women who in the past used to be discriminated against men. The introduction of non-binary legislation reiterates the need for a reform of Article 4 (2) which could be read as "Greeks regardless of their sex and gender have equal rights and equal obligations". Until then, the Constitution should be seen as a living instrument that follows the evolution of the Greek and European society and therefore Article 4 (2) should be read in conjunction with Article 2 (1) "respect and protection of the value of the human being constitute the primary obligations of the State", Article 5 (1) "all persons shall have the right to develop freely their personality (…)" and Article 25 "the rights of the human being as an individual and as a member of the society and the principle of the welfare state rule of law are guaranteed by the State". This interpretation will allow for a comprehensive protection of non-binary individuals and their recognition as equal citizens who are subjects to equal rights and obligations.

4.3.3.3.2 Civil Unions

The wording of the new Greek law on civil unions that provides for a contract between two adults, regardless of their gender/sex[282] includes individuals from all the spectrum of sex and gender and therefore intersex individuals are entitled to enter in civil unions. In addition, a decision of the Minister of Interior amended the previous binary form of civil status certificates and replaced the terms "man" and "woman" with the terms "first party" and "second party" with the aim to amplify the registration of same sex couples' partnerships.[283] Even though the Minister's goal was to implement the new Law on civil unions, it is clear that Greece is moving towards "gender neutral" legal terminology. In addition, the reasoning of the Council of State in its decision 2003/2018, shows that the Court is in line with modern societal and legal developments opening the way for broader and more inclusive future interpretations of the Law.

[282] Greek Law regulating the Civil Union, (English version on constitutionalism. gr).

[283] Decision 39/22-1-2016 of the Minister of Interior that amends the previous decision 131360/12476/8-5-2013.

4.3.4 *Malta*

4.3.4.1 Sexual Orientation

The Civil Unions Act allowed civil unions for same-sex couples and produced similar rights to marriage including the right to adopt children jointly.[284] Later, the Cohabitation Act recognised cohabiting couples who have been living together for at least 2 years and granted them more rights including in the field of parental decision-making.[285] The Act describes cohabitation as "a cohabitation between two persons" covering all individuals regardless of sex and gender.[286] In 2017, the Marriage Act granted the right to marry to all individuals as well and replaced all gender-specific references in Maltese law with gender-neutral terminology.[287] For instance, it substituted the words "husband or wife" with the word "spouse".[288] In 2018, the Embryo Protection Act was amended and the previous definition of "prospective parent" was substituted to read as "any person regardless of gender or sexual orientation, who has attained the age of majority and is a receiver or user of the medically assisted procreation techniques regulated under this Act;".[289]

4.3.4.2 Gender Identity

In 2013, the new government reached an out-of-court settlement with Joanne Cassar who was a transgender woman and was denied the right to marry her partner. Joanne had reached the ECtHR claiming the recognition of the respect of her right to marry.[290] Subsequently, the Civil Code was amended to allow trans people to be fully recognised in the acquired gender and be able to marry their opposite sex partner.[291] In 2014, the Maltese Constitution was amended to include "gender identity": "Whereas every person in Malta is entitled to the fundamental rights and freedoms of the individual, that is to say, the right, whatever his (…) sex, sexual orientation or gender identity, but subject to respect for the rights and freedoms of others and for the public interest (…)"[292] and this development made Malta the first European country to name "gender identity" in its Constitution.[293] The same year, the Equal

[284] Civil Unions Act 2014, Chapter 530.

[285] Cohabitation Act 2017.

[286] Idem.

[287] Marriage Act and other Laws (Amendment) of 2017, Act No. XXIII of 2017.

[288] Idem.

[289] Act No. XXIV of 2018, An Act to amend the Embryo Protection Act, Cap. 524, para. 2 (d).

[290] See Joanne Cassar against Malta, Application no. 36982/11.

[291] See Civil Code (Amendment) Act, 2013.

[292] Constitution of Malta, para. 32.

[293] Dalli, "Transgender Europe applauds Malta for naming gender identity".

Treatment in Employment (Amendment) Regulations included the ground of "gender reassignment".[294]

In 2015, Gender Identity, Gender Expression and Sex Characteristics (GIGESC) Act was introduced to cover all individuals who do not belong to the sex/gender binary. In detail, the law's aim was to meet current standards set out by local and international institutions and protect trans, genderqueer and intersex people against discrimination.[295] Paragraph 13 (2) of the Act explicitly eliminated unlawful discrimination based on sexual orientation, gender identity, gender expression and sex characteristics. The Act included the grounds of "gender identity", "gender expression" and "sex characteristics" in line with international developments on sex and gender terminology and it also contained the term "lived gender" which is defined as "each person's gender identity and its public expression over a sustained period of time".[296] Furthermore, under the GIGESC Act, trans individuals can change their gender and name through a simple administrative procedure that does not require compulsory medical and surgical interventions.[297] Moreover, the change of gender should not affect rights, relationships and obligations arising out of parenthood or marriage and succession.[298]

Among the greatest achievements of the Act, is that it does not only cover "gender identity" but "gender expression" as well, expanding its scope to the gender spectrum as a whole. In addition, it has succeeded to depathologise fully sexual orientation, gender identity and gender expression: "the pathologisation of any form of sexual orientation, gender identity and, or gender expression as may be classified under the International Classification of Diseases or any other similar internationally recognised classification, shall be null and void in Malta."[299] In 2016, the depathologisation of sexual orientation, gender identity and sex characteristics was further strengthened with the Affirmation of Sexual Orientation, Gender Identity and Gender Expression Act which was introduced to ensure "that all persons have a sexual orientation, a gender identity and a gender expression, and that no particular combination of these three characteristics constitutes a disorder, disease, illness, deficiency, disability and, or shortcoming; and to prohibit conversion practices as a deceptive and harmful act or interventions against a person's sexual orientation, gender identity and, or gender expression".[300] Furthermore, the Affirmation Act banned the performance of unlawful conversion practices.[301]

---

[294] See Employment and Industrial Relations Act (Cap. 452), Equal Treatment in Employment (Amendment) Regulations, 2014.

[295] Ministry for Social Dialogue, Consumer Affairs and Civil Liberties, Gender Identity, Gender Expression & Sex Characteristics Act.

[296] Gender Identity, Gender Expression & Sex Characteristics Act, Chapter 540, para. 2.

[297] Idem, para. 4.

[298] Idem, para. 3 (2) (a) and (b).

[299] Idem, para. 15 (2).

[300] Affirmation of Sexual Orientation, Gender Identity and Gender Expression Act, Chapter 567.

[301] Idem, para. 3.

4.3.4.3 Intersex

4.3.4.3.1 Physical Integrity and Bodily Autonomy

The GIGESC Act banned harmful and involuntary surgeries performed on intersex infants and protected explicitly their right to bodily integrity and physical autonomy: "shall be unlawful for medical practitioners or other professionals to conduct any sex assignment treatment and/or surgical intervention on the sex characteristics of a minor which treatment and/or intervention can be deferred until the person to be treated can provide informed consent: Provided that such sex assignment treatment and/or surgical intervention on the sex characteristics of the minor shall be conducted if the minor gives informed consent through the person exercising parental authority or the tutor of the minor".[302] The Act states that only in exceptional circumstances the treatment shall be affected by an agreement reached between an interdisciplinary team and the persons exercising parental authority for the intersex person who is unable to provide consent.[303] Still, any medical intervention driven by social factors without the consent of the minor is outlawed.[304] In the case that the interdisciplinary team and the persons exercising parental authority decide on the treatment of the intersex child, it should be ensured that the best interests of the child, as guaranteed under the Convention on the Rights of the Child, are considered.[305] In 2018, a legal notice[306] introduced "gender identity and sex characteristics related conditions" in the entitlement schedule relative to the National Health Service (NHS) and a consultation to ensure the best healthcare services on these grounds was subsequently launched.[307]

The GIGESC Act did not only ban intersex treatments and surgeries but most importantly it acknowledged social factors that lie behind the performance of those interventions. Developments in Malta on intersex have been characterised as "a landmark case for intersex rights within European law reform"[308] by intersex organisations. At the same time, the Act is considered to set the conditions for the creation of an equal society as it recognises and protects intersex -and trans- persons in all spheres of life.[309]

[302] Gender Identity, Gender Expression & Sex Characteristics Act, para. 14 (1).

[303] Idem, para. 14 (2).

[304] Idem.

[305] Idem, para. 14 (5) (a).

[306] See LN 44 of 2018.

[307] LGBTIQ Equality Strategy & Action Plan 2018-2022, P. 8.

[308] OII Europe, "Press Release: OII-Europe applauds Malta's Gender Identity, Gender Expression and Sex Characteristics Act".

[309] Transgender Europe, "Malta Adopts Ground-breaking Trans and Intersex Law".

4.3.4.3.2 Identification Documents

Intersex persons in Malta can change their gender on identification documents through the “Change of gender identity” procedure under the GIGESC Act. Similar to trans individuals, a simple declaration based on the person’s self-determination is required which enables individuals to pursue their lives without further interference.[310] As it has been already mentioned in this research, the issues that intersex individuals face are based primarily on “sex characteristics” and not on “gender identity”. It could be argued that the Act could explicitly mention that the provisions on the change of gender markers on identification documents do not apply only to people who want to recognise their gender identity but to intersex people as well. This way, confusions between the needs of trans and intersex individuals can be avoided.

In 2015, the Maltese government also amended its own public policy and introduced a third “X” option on identification documents.[311] According to Silvan Agius, human rights policy coordinator at the Ministry for Social Dialogue, the Maltese laws regulating identification documents were not specifying that sex has to be limited to male or female[312] and therefore the government was able to reform its policy.

4.3.4.3.3 The Right to Found a Family

Intersex can cohabitate, marry and adopt in Malta under the Cohabitation Act and the Marriage Act respectively.[313] They can also access Assisted Reproductive Technologies under the Embryo Protection Act that redefined “prospective parent” in 2018 to remove discriminatory exclusions on the basis of sexual orientation, gender identity, gender expression and sex characteristics.[314]

---

[310] See Gender Identity, Gender Expression & Sex Characteristics Act, Chapter 540 and Transgender Europe, “Malta Adopts Ground-breaking Trans and Intersex Law”.

[311] Dalli, “Male, Female or X: the new gender options on identification documents”.

[312] Idem.

[313] See Sect. 4.3.4.1.

[314] LGBTIQ Equality Strategy & Action Plan 2018–2022, p. 8.

4.3.5 *Portugal*

4.3.5.1 Sexual Orientation

Portugal amended its Constitution (Constituçao) in 2004 to include sexual orientation as a protected ground.[315] Article 13 of the Constitution prohibits discrimination: "no one shall be privileged, favoured, prejudiced, deprived of any right or exempted from any duty on the basis of ancestry, sex, (...) or sexual orientation".[316] Law No. 23/2010 (Lei n. 23/2010) aimed to recognise de facto unions between same-sex couples. However, de facto unions are defined under the law as: "de facto union is the legal situation of two persons that regardless of their sex, live in conditions similar to those of spouses for more than two years"[317] and this wording covers intersex individuals as well. Law No. 9/2010 (Lei n. 9/2010 Casamento Civil Entre Pessoas do Mesmo Sexo) legalised civil marriage between persons of the same sex.[318] Law No. 2/2016 (Lei n. 2/2016) guaranteed same sex couple's right to adoption and Article 5 stipulated that "all legal provisions relating to marriage, adoption, civil custody and other similar legal relations shall be interpreted in light of this law, regardless of the sex of the spouses".[319] By reading the Law No. 2/2016, it seems that the legislator was aiming to allow access to adoption for same sex couples, but the wording of Article 5 allows for a broader interpretation and grants the right to marry and to adopt to intersex individuals.

4.3.5.2 Gender Identity

Law No. 7/2011 (Lei n. 7/2011) allowed trans persons to change their legal gender on birth certificates. The applicant had to apply for a change of gender and submit a "report prepared by a multidisciplinary team of clinical sexology clinic at the health facility public or private, domestic or foreign that proves the diagnosis of gender identity disorder, also designated by transsexuality."[320] In April 2018, a new law was approved that did not require the applicant to be diagnosed as mentally ill to change gender on birth certificates.[321] A month later, Portugal's President Marcelo Rebelo de Sousa vetoed the law and considered the need of a medical test for trans individuals under the age of 18.[322] Finally, Law No. 38/2018 (Lei No. 38/2018) was passed to protect the right of self-determination of trans individuals. Article 2 para. 1 of the

[315] See Law No. 1/2004, of 24th of July Sixth Constitutional Revision (Lei n. 1/2004, de 24 de Julho, Sexta Revisão Constitucional).

[316] Constitute, Portugal's Constitution of 1976 with Amendments through 2005.

[317] Law No. 23/2010, Article 1 (2).

[318] See Law No. 9/2010, Article 1.

[319] Law No. 2/2016, Article 5.

[320] Law No. 7/2011, Article 3 (b).

[321] Reuters, "Portugal approves law to boost transgender rights, protect intersex infants".

[322] BBC, "Portugal's president vetoes new gender-change law".

Law outlaws discrimination on the grounds of gender identity, gender expression and sex characteristics. Furthermore, Article 3 guarantees the right to self-determination of gender identity and gender expression covering all non-binary individuals and therefore, the procedure of name and gender change on identification documents is now based on the right to self-determination of the individual and not on a "disorder".[323] Nonetheless, after the President's veto, the law was amended to include a provision according to which minors between the ages of 16 and 18 are able to change their name and gender with parental consent and a report that is based on a psychological opinion affirming the applicant's decision-making capacity and informed will.[324]

4.3.5.3 Intersex

Law No. 38/2018 (Lei No. 38/2018) establishes the right to self-determination for intersex people[325] and prohibits discrimination based on sex characteristics.[326] Most significantly, the Law recognises that "everyone has the right to maintain the primary and secondary sex characteristics"[327] which implies that any intervention on intersex bodily integrity and autonomy would be illegal. However, the subsequent Article, does not ban harmful and involuntary surgeries performed on intersex infants but asserts that: "except in situations of a proven health risk, surgical, pharmacological or other treatments and interventions involving modifications on the body and sex characteristics of the minor intersex person shall not be performed until the moment that the person's gender identity is manifested".[328] Then, the Law stipulates that "the intersex person can request the procedure of change of sex in the civil registry and the consequent alteration of first name, once the person's gender identity is manifested".[329]

OII Europe found the law insufficient for the protection of intersex infants as it does not "state how the knowledge of this "manifestation" of a minor's gender identity is to be established. Nor does it require a prove of whether the child has the capacity to consent to these medical interventions. At the same time, the law seems to imply that medical treatment is unlawful even in situations of proven health risks, before the minor's gender identity has manifested."[330] In addition, StopIGM stated that "the law seems grossly insufficient, as it doesn't explicitly prohibit Intersex Genital Mutlilation (IGM) by criminalising or adequately sanctioning the practice, nor address obstacles to access to justice and redress for IGM survivors, namely the

[323] Law No. 38/2018, Articles 1, 3, 6.

[324] Idem, Article 2.

[325] Idem, Article 1.

[326] Idem, Article 2.

[327] Idem, Article 4.

[328] Idem, Article 5.

[329] Idem, Article 7 (3).

[330] OII Europe, "Portugal adopts law protecting intersex people".

statutes of limitations, nor include extraterritorial protections from IGM – all of which would be essential requirements stipulated by international law".[331] Together with all the above comments, it could also be argued that the Portuguese law even though it protects self-determination and sex characteristics, by mentioning that an intersex individual has to manifest a gender identity, it implies that it does not accept intersex infants the way they are born but it is expected that at some point in their lives a gender identity will be manifested. This provision also creates confusion with regards to the preferred terminology since it does not draw clear limits on the differences between sex characteristics and gender identity.

4.3.6 Regional Protections

The United Kingdom (UK)[332] and Spain have not legislated on intersex at a State level but there are some developments at regional levels. Scotland and Jersey have introduced some legal provisions on intersex but since only Scotland is a member of the European Union, Jersey's legislation will not be examined.[333] In Spain, the Basque Country has legislated on intersex. Considering that those developments are only limited to regional levels, they will be briefly presented and analysed.

4.3.6.1 The Basque Country, Spain

4.3.6.1.1 Intersex

Law 14/2012 on non-discrimination based on gender identity (Ley 14/2012, de no discriminación por motivos de identidad de género y de reconocimiento de los derechos de las personas transexuales) includes references to "intersex persons": "This law intends, therefore, to address the specificities of this group (meaning trans persons), giving response, from that singularity, to the sense of equality concerning transsexual persons when it comes to securing their medical and social rights, as well as rights of those diagnosed with different degrees of intersexuality."[334] Moreover, Article 5 on the means to combat transphobia, is also applied to intersex persons.

---

[331] StopIGM, "Portugal: New Law Fails to Protect Intersex Children from IGM".

[332] This thesis was conducted before March 2018 when it is scheduled that the UK will leave the European Union.

[333] For the situation of intersex on Jersey, see "Discrimination (Sex and Related Characterisics) (Jersey) Regulations 2015".

[334] Exposition of motives III.

4.3.6.2 Scotland, United Kingdom

4.3.6.2.1 Intersex

The Scottish Offences (Aggravation by Prejudice) Act 2009 refers to the aggravation of offences by prejudice relating to sexual orientation or transgender identity. Although it mentions intersex, it seems that it equates intersex with a form of gender identity: "In this section, reference to transgender identity is reference to transvestism, transsexualism, intersexuality or having, by virtue of the Gender Recognition Act 2004 (c. 7), changed gender, or any other gender identity that is not standard male or female gender identity."[335] In 2016, the First Minister announced that the Gender Recognition Act will be amended to recognise legally people who are identified as "non-binary gender",[336] probably this will also include intersex.

4.4 EU Countries That Implicitly Protect Intersex Rights

As it was already mentioned, the EU has published two reports on the situation of intersex rights. In both reports it is stated that there are jurisdictions that cover intersex implicitly and those countries are Denmark, Finland, the Netherlands, Romania, Slovenia and Sweden.[337] In those cases, intersex rights are covered under the grounds of "gender", "gender identity" or "both gender and gender identity".[338] Since the above reports were published in 2015 and more significant developments have taken place, Belgium, Ireland and Luxembourg that introduced legislation based on self-determination recently, will be examined. Subsequently, implicit legal frameworks will be compared to frameworks that cover intersex explicitly with the aim to answer the question regarding which legal frameworks protect intersex efficiently and at the same time promote the values of the EU.

---

[335] Scottish Offences (Aggravation by Prejudice) Act 2009, Article 8 (a) (b).

[336] Gardham, "Scotland to give legal recognition to people who are neither male nor female".

[337] European Union Agency for Fundamental Rights, 2015, p. 4 and ILGA Europe, OII Europe, 2015, p. 15 (the report published by ILGA and OII Europe uses the FRA report as a reference). The reports also include Austria but the situation in the country has changed recently to cover intersex explicitly.

[338] European Union Agency for Fundamental Rights, 2015, p. 4.

4.4.1 *Belgium*

In 2017, the Belgian Parliament approved a reform bill to the Belgian gender recognition law.[339] The Law to reform transgender-related regimes with respect to the reference to a change in the registration of sex in civil status records and its effects (Loi réformant des régimes relatifs aux personnes transgenres en ce qui concerne la mention d'une modification de l'enregistrement du sexe dans les actes de l'état civil et ses effets/ Wet tot hervorming van regelingen inzake transgenders wat de vermelding van een aanpassing van de registratie van het geslacht in de akten van de burgerlijke stand en de gevolgen hiervan betreft) enabled the change of gender marker and name in a simple administrative procedure before the civil registry.[340] After a waiting period of 3 months, the applicant has to confirm their intention to change their officially registered gender marker.[341] The procedure is open for people from age 16 and minors have to also submit a medical expert statement.[342] Intersex people who wish to change their gender and name on identification documents will have to follow the same procedure as trans. Moreover, according to ILGA Europe, even though Anti-discrimination Law (Loi tendant à lutter contre certaines formes de discrimination) includes only "sex" and not sex characteristics as a discrimination ground, jurisprudence and introductory texts to legislation seem to indicate that "sex" is understood as to include intersex.[343]

4.4.2 *Denmark*

In 2017, the UN Child Rights Committee condemned involuntary genital surgeries performed on intersex infants in Denmark as "a harmful practice" and dismissed government claims based on the argument of "helping intersex children".[344] The Committee called Denmark to "ensure that no one is subjected to unnecessary medical or surgical treatment during infancy or childhood, guarantee bodily integrity, autonomy and self-determination for the children concerned and provide families with intersex children with adequate counselling and support; develop and implement a child rights-based health-care protocol for intersex children, setting out the procedures and steps to be followed by health teams and undertake investigation of incidents of surgical and other medical treatment of intersex children without

[339] Transgender Europe, "Belgium-New Gender Recognition Law with obstacles".

[340] Transgender Europe, "Belgium: Legal Gender Recognition Law (2017)".

[341] Idem.

[342] Idem.

[343] ILGA Europe, Rainbow Map, "Belgium".

[344] See StopIGM.org, "Denamrk: UN slams intersex genital mutilation-again!" and CRC/C/DNK/CO/5 "Concluding observations on the fifth periodic report of Denmark*".

informed consent and adopt legal provisions in order to provide redress to the child victims of such treatment, including adequate compensation".[345]

Despite all the above developments, a 2018 report to the UN Committee Against Torture by StopIGM.org stated that genital mutilation of intersex children persists in Danish university clinics as those interventions are misrepresented as "health care".[346] In addition, according to Amnesty International, "if an individual with a variation of sex characteristics is assigned the "wrong" gender via surgery or other treatment, they would have to go through the existing system on trans to be able to affirm their gender and this has implications not only for legal gender recognition of gender but also for access to appropriate healthcare".[347] "Individuals who seek, for example, hormone treatment appropriate to their identified gender, not their assigned gender, must seek recognition through the process designed for trans people".[348]

In relation with the legal recognition of gender, before 2014, the Act on Sterilisation and Castration was the basis for approving legal gender change.[349] In 2014, the Danish gender recognition law[350] was the first in Europe based on the self-determination of the individual.[351] The law abolished requirements for medical interventions including psychiatric diagnosis, sterilisation or hormonal treatment.[352] It introduced a simple administrative procedure that allows applicants to receive a new gendered social security number and matching personal documents such as a passport, driving license and birth certificate in accordance with the new gender.[353] Alongside the gender recognition reforms that took place in 2014, Denmark's previous practice of enabling trans people to apply for an "X" in international passports became official law.[354] Intersex individuals will have to follow the same procedure as trans in order to be legally recognised and it is unclear whether an intersex individual could also use the "X" option with regards to international passports or if it is reserved only to trans. Moreover, even though Demark was the first European country to protect trans rights and recognise that there are individuals who do not fit in the binary, legislation on intersex is still absent.

---

[345] CRC/C/DNK/CO/5, 2017, para. 24.

[346] StopIGM.org/Zwischengeschlecht.org, 2018, pp. 7–10.

[347] Amnesty International (2017), p. 51.

[348] Idem.

[349] ILGA Europe, Rainbow Map, "Denmark".

[350] See Gender Identity Law (Lov om ændring af lov om Det Centrale Personregister).

[351] Transgender Europe, "Historic Danish Gender Recognition Law comes into Force".

[352] Idem.

[353] Idem.

[354] Transgender Europe, "Denmark: X in Passports and New Trans Law Works".

4.4.3 *Finland*

The Finnish National Advisory Board on Social Welfare and Health Care Ethics ETENE issued a position statement in 2016 on the care and treatment of intersex children. According to the statement, intersex infants are operated in Finland: "a child's gender is determined fairly soon after the birth, and external genitals of intersex children are surgically modified during childhood and adolescence."[355] It is also stated that in the case of intersex children, the child's gender can be left undetermined in the beginning but later "the Finnish population register system requires that the gender of the child be determined because the national identification number includes data about the gender of the person".[356] "The national identification number can be altered under some special and strictly defined conditions, for example when a person changes gender"[357] as in the case of trans individuals.

Consistent with the Act on Legal Recognition of the Gender of Transsexuals (the Trans Act) (Lakitransseksuaalin sukupuolen vahvistamisesta annetun lain muuttamisesta), the gender registered in the Population Information System can be changed only if the applicant presents a medical statement certifying that they permanently feel to belong to the "opposite" gender, live in that gender role, and that they have been sterilised or are for some other reason infertile.[358] Trans Decree issued by the Ministry of Social Affairs and Health states that in order to obtain the medical statement necessary for legal gender recognition, trans people have to undergo a psychiatric monitoring process and receive a psychiatric diagnosis.[359] Civil society organisations have heavily questioned the legal gender recognition system in Finland and have characterised he process as based "on outdated gender stereotypes of "woman" and "man" against which the gender identity of the person in question is tested".[360] It is clear that, intersex people will have to go through the same harmful procedure that involves irreversible consequences to modify their identification documents.

According to Transgender Europe, in 2015, the Gender Equality Act was revised, and gender identity and gender expression are embedded in the concept of gender: "This is done by stating that the prohibition to discriminate on the basis of gender covers also discrimination of the basis of gender identity or gender expression. People with intersex conditions are also covered".[361] ILGA and OII Europe also mention that the Act includes "gender features of the body", which is meant to

[355] National Advisory Board on Social Welfare and Health Care Ethics ETENE, 2016, p. 2.

[356] Idem.

[357] Idem.

[358] See Trasek ry and Seta ry, 2016, p. 5 and Act on Legal Recognition of the Gender of Transsexuals (the Trans Act) Article 1 para. 1.

[359] See Idem and A decree of the Ministry of Social Affairs and Health on the organisation of the examination and treatment aiming at the change of gender as well as on the medical statement for the confirmation of gender of a transsexual.

[360] Trasek ry and Seta ry, 2016, p. 5.

[361] Transgender Europe, "More equality for trans persons in Finland".

protect intersex people against discrimination.[362] The term "gender features of the body" can be considered as absurd, since gender is a social construct and is not linked with sex characteristics which are exclusively biological. Finland could update its legal terminology by following international and EU guidelines.

4.4.4 Ireland

StopIGM.org has reported that in Ireland, "doctors in public, university and private clinics are regularly performing intersex genital mutilation practices, i.e. non-consensual, medically unnecessary, irreversible cosmetic genital surgeries, sterilising procedures, and other harmful treatments on intersex children, which have been described by survivors as genital mutilation and torture, which are known to cause severe, lifelong physical and psychological pain and suffering, and which have been repeatedly recognised by this Committee and other UN bodies as constituting harmful practices, violence and torture or ill-treatment.[363] Indeed, in 2016, the Committee on the Rights of the Child expressed its concern "about cases of medically unnecessary surgeries and other procedures on intersex children before they are able to provide their informed consent, which often entail irreversible consequences and can cause severe physical and psychological suffering, and the lack of redress and compensation in such cases".[364] The Committee urged Ireland to "ensure that no-one is subjected to unnecessary medical or surgical treatment during infancy or childhood, guarantee bodily integrity, autonomy and self-determination to children concerned, and undertake investigation of incidents of surgical and other medical treatment of intersex children without informed consent and adopt legal provisions in order to provide redress to the victims of such treatment, including adequate compensation".[365]

Since 2015, there was no legal avenue for trans people who wanted to recognise their gender legally.[366] The Gender Recognition Act recognised the change of gender and provided for gender recognition certificates.[367] Moreover, it does not require any compulsory medical and surgical interventions or a gender identity disorder diagnosis.[368] The law has been criticised concerning the restrictions imposed to trans people aged 16–18 as they require medical observation, parental consent and a court order.[369] There are no provisions for trans individuals under 16 years old.[370]

---

[362] ILGA Europe and OII Europe, 2015, p. 15.

[363] StopIGM.org/ Zwischengeschlecht.org (2015), p. 6.

[364] CRC/C/IRL/CO/3-4, 2016, para. 39.

[365] Idem, para. 40 (a) (b).

[366] McDonald (2015).

[367] Gender Recognition Act 2015, Number 25 of 2015.

[368] Idem, Section 10 "Requirements on application for a gender recognition certificate".

[369] The Guardian, "Ireland passes law allowing trans people to choose their legal gender".

[370] Idem.

In the absence of explicit intersex frameworks, ntersex people who wish to change their legal gender, they will have to follow the same procedure as trans applicants.

4.4.5 Luxembourg

In 2017, the National Ethics Commission (Commission Nationale d'Éthique) published Opinion 27 on gender diversity. In this opinion, it presented the situation on trans and intersex people in the country and elaborated on the fact that due to the binary legal system, trans and intersex people's rights are at stake.[371] Even though the Opinion clarifies that "a binary conception risks putting the so-called intersex or transgender people in particularly vulnerable situations and contributes to the violation of their fundamental rights", some elaborations on trans and intersex are not clear. For instance, it is mentioned that "Just as " the " woman or " the " man does not exist, no person is completely transgender or intersex"[372] which can be considered as confusing. After all, the Commission recommends the promotion of "research on transgender and intersex issues with an interdisciplinary approach in various fields such as medicine, law, economics, statistics, health, education, philosophy, equal opportunities, human rights".[373] A year later, Luxembourg received its first reprimand by the Committee on the Elimination of Discrimination against Women (CEDAW) which referred also to the situation of intersex. The Committee recommended Luxembourg to "prohibit non-consensual sex reassignment surgery on intersex persons, develop and implement a rights-based health-care protocol for intersex children (...)" and "adopt legal provisions to provide redress to intersex persons who are victims of surgical or other medical interventions without their free, prior and informed consent or that of their parents".[374]

In 2017, a bill was presented by the Ministry of Justice of Luxembourg and as stated by Rosa Lëtzebuerg Centre of Information Gay and Lesbian Luxembourg (CIGALE Centre d' Information Gay et Lesbien Luxembourg), its aim was to improve the rights and the lives of trans and intersex people through the establishment of a simple procedure for the change of gender marker and name on the civil status certificates.[375] In detail, the Bill to amend the mention of sex and of the first names in civil status and to modify the Civil Code (Projet de loi relative à la

[371] National Ethics Commission (Commission Nationale d'Éthique), "Opinion 27 Opinion regarding gender diversity", July 2017 and for information on the situation of intersex infants and children in Luxembourg see Intersex & Transgender Luxembourg, "Complément Commun au Rapport supplémentaire au 3e et 4e rapport national (2001-2009) sur les droits de l'enfant au Luxembourg, Les droits des enfants trans' et des enfants intersexes, L'exemple de leur situation au Luxembourg", November 2012.

[372] National Ethics Commission, 2017, p. 1.

[373] Idem, p. 15.

[374] CEDAW/C/LUX/CO/6-7, 2018, para. 28.

[375] Rosa Lëtzebuerg Centre of Information Gay and Lesbian Luxembourg, 2018, p. 7.

modification de la mention du sexe et du ou des prénoms à l'état civil et portant modification du Code civil) concerns all Luxembourgish adults who have the intimate and constant conviction of not belonging to the sex indicated in the birth certificate.[376] In the explanatory text, it is stated that the Bill covers transgender or intersex people, and, in both cases, the persons concerned may feel the need to change sex, if the sex initially listed in the birth certificate is not the one to which they aspire.[377] The Bill which is in line with the recommendations and resolutions of the Council of Ministers and the Parliamentary Assembly of the Council of Europe also bans medical treatments and gender reassignment surgeries which lead to sterilisation and grant the right to trans and intersex individuals to modify their identification documents based on self-determination.[378] The Bill was approved on 25 July 2018.[379]

As can be seen, the Law does not refer explicitly to "intersex persons" but uses a broader wording to cover "all Luxembourgish" adults. On the one hand, a broad wording grants all non-binary individuals the right to change their gender and names on identification documents but on the other hand, the Law has failed to address the specific needs of persons who identify as non-binary. One has to consult the explanatory text of the Bill in order to realise who is covered and who is not under the Law. At the same time, although the Bill clarifies that intersex and trans are not the same and should not be confused, Article 1 refers to all persons who "feel" the need to change sex. This mostly applies to trans individuals since intersex people were born intersex but their right to identify as such was violated by medical practitioners who assigned them a sex at birth based on the binary. Overall, the Law can be considered as a major effort of Luxembourg to follow European and international developments but by grouping all non-binary individuals, it fails to recognise and protect their specific needs.

4.4.6 Netherlands

The Equal Rights Act 1994 (Algemene Wet Gelijke Behandeling) bans discrimination on the grounds of sexual orientation in employment, housing and public and private accommodations.[380] The Ministry of the Interior and Kingdom Relations published a report highlighting the need to amend the Act and include gender identity and gender expression as explicit protected grounds.[381] The report also

[376] Bill to amend the mention of sex and of the first names in civil status and to modify the Civil Code (Projet de loi relative à la modification de la mention du sexe et du ou des prénoms à l'état civil et portant modification du Code civil), Article 1.

[377] Idem, p. 11, Article 1.

[378] Idem, Article 2.

[379] Luxembourg Times, "New law facilitates transgender, intersex name and gender change".

[380] See Equal Rights Act 1994 as translated to English by Equal Rights Trust.

[381] See Explanatory report to make explicit the prohibition of discrimination on grounds of gender identity and gender expression in the Equal Treatment Act (Verkenning expliciteren verbod van

mentioned the case of intersex people and recommended to ban explicitly discrimination against them.[382] Afterwards, a Bill was approved by the House which is currently under consideration.[383]

On 11 February 2016, the Netherlands Network Intersex/DSD (NNID) announced the victory of Dutch adoption parents over the binary system.[384] The parents discrovered that their Chinese adopted baby, who had been identified as male by the Chinese authorities, was a girl with an intersex condition.[385] They decided to leave the sex undecided for a while, and therefore wished to obtain a passport for the baby who had to travel from China to the Netherlands with an X.[386] Even though there is a legal "gap" for these situations, the parents managed to convince the registrar to permit this.[387] A similar legislative "gap" had come into the light also in 2004, where the registrar had originally denied the request of the parents but in the end a Court decision ruled that the child's best interests were at stake and ordered the registrar to issue a new passport to an intersex infant.[388]

In 2013, the Law for changing the registered sex on the birth certificate (Wet wijziging van de vermelding van het geslacht in de akte van geboorte) allowed transgender people to legally change their gender on their birth certificates and other official documents without undergoing sterilisation and sex-reassignment surgery.[389] The new Law abolished the previous outdated legal framework which was first introduced in 1985.[390] At that time, the Netherlands was among the first European nations to adopt legislation enabling transgender people to change their registered gender but years later, that legislation became inconsistent with the current understanding of the Netherlands' obligations under international human rights law.[391] Prior to that, in 1970, the legislator introduced the option to postpone decisions on

---

discriminatie op grond van genderidentiteit en genderexpressie in de Algemene wet gelijke behandeling (Awgb), 2016.

[382] Idem, pp. 6–7.

[383] Winq., "Eindelijk: officieel verbod op transgenderdiscriminatie".

[384] Netherlands Network Intersex/DSD, "Eerste Nederlandse paspoort zonder geslachtsregistratie" (in Dutch).

[385] Scherpe et al. (2018), p. 298.

[386] Idem.

[387] Idem.

[388] See Rechtbank's-Gravenhage, 12.07.2004, ECLI:NL:RBSGR:2004:AQ7020 and Scherpe et al. (2018), p. 298.

[389] Human Rights Watch, "The Netherlands: Victory for Transgender Rights" and Act of 18 December 2013 amending Book 1 of the Civil Code and the Municipal Personal Records Database Act in connection with changing the conditions for the authority to change the indication of sex in the birth certificate (Wet van 18 december 2013 tot wijziging van Boek 1 van het Burgerlijk Wetboek en de Wet gemeentelijke basisadministratie persoonsgegevens in verband met het wijzigen van de voorwaarden voor en de bevoegdheid ter zake van wijziging van de vermelding van het geslacht in de akte van geboorte).

[390] Idem.

[391] Idem.

a baby's sex.[392] The public prosecutor could order the registrar to note on a birth certificate that the baby's sex was unknown and once the sex was clear, the entry could be changed.[393] "In practice, this often meant that parents, with the consent of the public prosecutor, would postpone the child's registration until its sex could be established, after which the birth of the child would be registered with special authorisation from the public prosecutor".[394] The above practice was abandoned when in 1995 Article 1:17(2) was replaced by Article 1:19(d) BW.[395] This article is still in force and provides the option of a provisional birth certificate which, after 3 months must be replaced by a final document indicating the child's sex as male or female.[396] If after 3 months it still is impossible to determine the child's sex, there is the option to state that impossibility on the final certificate.[397]

On 28 May 2018, the District Court of Limburg ruled in favour of a Dutch citizen who wished to be recognised as a "third gender" despite the fact that current Dutch legal frameworks do not provide for the possibility to be registered as such.[398] The Court applied Article 1:19d BW which is used in the case of infants with non-conforming sex characteristics to an adult who had already been attributed a gender marker.[399] Previously, in an interim decision of November 2017, the Court in Limburg had ordered the Academic Hospital in Maastricht to examine the person concerned to establish whether they had an intersex condition, as claimed by the public prosecutor.[400] "The Court argued that a decision on the request could only be taken if an intersex condition was established and stated that if that turned out to be the case, the decision might not be "at the free disposal of the parties to the case".[401] The medical experts reported to the Court that an examination of the applicant's chromosomes could not verify whether they were born with an intersex condition.[402] Despite the findings of the interim decision, the Court concluded that the attribution of gender should be based on "gender experience" than sex characteristics and according to Marjolein van den Brink "even though the Court began with an intersex perspective it ended by treating it as a transgender issue but still the legal solution applied relates to intersex conditions, rather than (trans)gender identity".[403] The

[392] Then Article 1:17(2) Burgerlijk Wetboek (BW), the Dutch Civil Code, as referred by Marjolein van den Brink, See Scherpe et al. (2018), p. 296.

[393] Then Article 1:29 BW, as referred by Marjolein van den Brink, See Scherpe et al. (2018), p. 296.

[394] Scherpe et al. (2018), p. 296.

[395] Idem.

[396] Article 1:19(d) BW read in conjunction with Article 45(1) Besluit Burgerlijke Stand (BBS) 1994 as referred by Marjolein van den Brink, See Scherpe et al. (2018), p. 296.

[397] Scherpe et al. (2018), p. 296.

[398] See Rechtbank Limburg, 28-05-2018, C/03/232248 / FA RK 17-687.

[399] Scherpe et al. (2018), p. 300.

[400] Idem and Rechtbank Limburg, 06.11.2017, C/03/232248 / FA RK 17-687, ECLI:NL:RBLIM:2017:10713.

[401] Scherpe et al. (2018), p. 300.

[402] Idem.

[403] Idem, p. 301.

ruling referenced precedent from India and Nepal[404] and drew extensively on domestic and international documents, including the Yogyakarta Principles, relevant to gender neutral options in its reasoning.[405] The Court stated that self-identification prevails over bodily appearance or medical status and suggested the Dutch legislature initiate legislation to ensure that gender-neutral self-identification is provided for under Dutch law.[406] Last, the Court ordered the registrar to draw up a new birth certificate, rather than correct the existing certificate, thus effectively dealing with the case as if the applicant was an infant without an attributed gender.[407]

It has to be noted that in 2016, at the 65th Session of the UN Committee on the Elimination of Discrimination against Women the Netherlands were questioned over surgeries performed on intersex infants after the submission of a report that was co-authored by the Netherlands Network Intersex/DSD Foundation (NNID).[408] The report stated that the Law for changing the registered sex on the birth certificate does not allow access to legal gender recognition for trans and intersex persons under the age of 16[409] and recommended that access to legal gender recognition should be guaranteed for both intersex and trans children and adults without obstacles that infringe the individual's right to self-determination.[410] Moreover, it is indicated that "Health care for intersex children in the Netherlands is based on 'predict and control': when an intersex child is born, health professionals try to predict the future gender of the child and control the outcome of this prediction by means of medically unnecessary and irreversible surgery, treatment with hormones, other normalizing treatments and psychological support, without the free and fully informed consent of the child".[411] In 2018, the Committee Against Torture and expressed its concern about the situation of intersex persons in the country: "unnecessary and irreversible surgery and other medical treatment are performed on intersex children without informed consent and impartial counselling. It is concerned that these procedures, which cause long-term physical and psychological suffering, have not been the object of any inquiry, sanction or reparation and that there is no specific legal provisions providing redress and rehabilitation to the victims."[412] Despite all the calls for intersex rights protection, the country has not still outlawed intersex surgeries and there is no explicit intersex legal framework on intersex

[404] See Sects. 3.5.1.2 and 3.5.1.3.

[405] Dittrich Boris, "Dutch Court Signals Need for Gender Neutral Option".

[406] Idem.

[407] Scherpe et al. (2018), p. 301.

[408] StopIGM.org, "The Netherlands questioned over Intersex Genital Mutilations- Gov promises "discussions"- Reprimands expected today".

[409] Federatie van Nederlandse Verenigingen tot Integratie van Homoseksualiteit – COC Nederland Nederlands Netwerk voor Intersekse/DSD - NNID Transgender Netwerk Nederland – TNN, 2016, para. 9.

[410] Idem, para. 12 (a).

[411] Idem, para. 34.

[412] CAT/C/NLD/7, 2018, para. 52.

rights. Existing case-law is seems "promising" as the justices have ruled in favour of intersex individuals even though there are no legal provisions on intersex.

4.4.7 Romania

Romanian legislation does not mention the term "transgender" or equivalent terms.[413] "Transgender persons are theoretically protected by provisions in anti-discrimination legislation, but there are no clear guidelines for changing registration status or undergoing sex reassignment surgery".[414] Legal gender recognition for trans individuals is available in Romania and usually the applicant has to undergo sex reassignment surgery.[415] Trans persons can change their name and gender identity through the combination of different Laws[416] but there is no explicit procedure on the matter. Consequently, the above legal procedure has been characterised as "vague and incomplete, resulting in inconsistency in judicial practice concerning legal recognition of gender identity".[417] The judges that apply the law give their own interpretation and, in several cases, they have asked for medical/surgical interventions.[418] In addition, due to the non-explicit legal procedure for gender recognition, "it is often impossible for transgender persons to get documents reflecting their gender identity, which leads to difficulties in obtaining all services requiring identity documents (e.g., health care, transportation passes, and banking services)".[419] Currently, two Romanian trans men have reached the ECtHR[420] claiming that their right to privacy and right to found a family have been violated as the legal framework on gender recognition is uncertain and subjects trans people to lengthy judicial procedures and pathologising and invasive medical requirements.[421]

This "vague" legal procedure applied to trans individuals in Romania allows also for intersex individuals to apply for legal gender recognition, but they may also have to be subjected to invasive surgeries. ILGA-Europe has already called Romania to

---

[413] Danish Institute for Human Rights, 2009, p. 10.

[414] Idem.

[415] See Accept and ECPI, "Persoane trans în România: Recunoaşterea juridică a identităţii de gen" 2014.

[416] See Civil Code (Codul Civil actualizat 2015), Law no. 119/1996 regarding civil status acts and documents, republished (LEGE nr. 119 din 16 octombrie 1996 (**republicată**)(*actualizată*) cu privire la actele de stare civilă*), Government Ordinance no 41/2003 regarding the administrative procedures for the acquisition and modification of names (Ordonanţa nr. 41/2003 privind dobândirea şi schimbarea pe cale administrativă a numelor persoanelor fizice) and ILGA Europe, Rainbow Map, "Romania".

[417] U.S. Department of State, 2016, p. 42.

[418] ILGA Europe, Rainbow Map, "Romania".

[419] Idem.

[420] X. against Romania and Y. against Romania (Applications no. 2145/16 and 20607/16).

[421] Transgender Europe, "Third Party Intervention X v Romania and Y v Romania".

develop a fair, transparent legal framework for legal gender recognition, based on a process of self-determination, free from abusive requirements.[422]

4.4.8 *Slovenia*

Discrimination against trans and intersex persons in Slovenia is encompassed in the Constitution (Ustava) under Article 14 which prohibits discrimination on the basis of "any other personal circumstance".[423] There are no laws explicitly addressing the status of trans persons and legal gender recognition is not specifically regulated.[424] According to ILGA Europe, the Laws that are applied for the name and gender change are the Rules on the implementation of the Births, Deaths and Marriages Registry Act (Pravilnik o izvrševanju zakona o matičnem registru) and the Personal Name Act (Zakon o osebnem imenu (ZOI-1)). In the absence of explicit regulation, "it is up to individual doctors to decide whether to refer transsexual clients to specialists who then decide on the appropriate sex reassignment process".[425]

ILGA Europe has reported that "on 31st January 2017 the Ministry of Internal Affairs sent a circular to all Administrative Units in Slovenia informing them that all persons seeking legal gender recognition must present a certified statement that they have had genital operation and that the certified statement issued by a psychiatrist stating that a person "changed their gender" is no longer enough. However, no negative decision based on this circular has been issued. The circular is in breach of Article 37 of the Rules on the implementation of the Births, Deaths and Marriages Registry Act."[426] Considering the situation on legal gender recognition, ILGA Europe has concluded that there is "a possible deterioration of respect for human rights of transgender persons in Slovenia that is not directly based in laws but rather arbitrary and illegal interpretations of laws and rules."[427] Like in Romania, intersex people may be covered as the legal framework on legal gender recognition is non-specific but all the above developments impact negatively all non-binary persons who wish to recognise their gender including intersex.

---

422 ILGA Europe, 2018, p. 109.

423 Constitution, Official Gazette of the Republic of Slovenia Nos. 33/91-I, 42/97, 66/2000, 24/03, 69/04, 68/06, and 47/13 (Ustava, Uradni list RS, št. 33/91-I, 42/97, 66/2000, 24/03, 69/04, 68/06, 47/13).

424 See Mavcic and Avbelj (2008).

425 Danish Institute for Human Rights, 2009, p. 11.

426 ILGA Europe, Rainbow Map, "Slovenia".

427 Idem.

4.4.9 Sweden

Sweden introduced the Gender Recognition Act in 1972 (Lag (1972:119) om fastställande av könstillhörighet i vissa fall) which was considered as groundbreaking and made Sweden the first country in the world to allow trans people to legally correct their gender.[428] The Gender Recognition Act stipulates that a person's gender can be legally recognised "if he or she has perceived that belongs to the other gender over a long period of time, has presented in accordance with this gender identity for a while and must be expected to live in accordance with this gender identity also in the future".[429] Next, it states that a person can also legally recognise his/her gender if "he or she has a congenital deviation in the sex development and a change of the gender is consistent with the development of the gender identity and the most consistent with the applicant's physical condition".[430] The wording of the Act seems to cover both intersex and trans persons and this can be explained based on the background of the Act as at the time, persons who were born with bodies deemed typical for their assigned gender were named non-somatic intersexuals ("transsexual"), and the term somatic intersexuals used to describe persons with variant sex development.[431] Moreover, "both categories of 'intersexuals' targeted by the Gender Classification Act were presumed to want or need surgery of some kind to support their gender, such that some form of physical conformity, rather than gender identity alone, shaped the resulting rules of law".[432] Accordingly, para. 4 of the Gender Recognition Act, specifies that "In connection with the application of recognition of gender in accordance with § 1 or 2, permission may be given for genital surgical procedures in order to make them more like the genitalia of the other gender. Permission may be granted only if the requirements for recognition of gender are met". In 2012, the Administrative Court of Appeals of Stockholm argued that the requirement to undergo sterilisation violates the Swedish Constitution and the ECHR.[433] Consequently, surgical interventions and sterilisation[434] are not

[428] Scherpe et al. (2018), p. 255.

[429] Sweden's Gender Recognition Act (1972:119) as reformed in 2012, para. 1 (English version).

[430] Idem, para. 2.

[431] For the historical background of the Gender Recognition Act see Scherpe et al. (2018), p. 262, and Chapter "The Legal Status of Intersex Persons in Sweden", 1.2. Legal background and evolution in particular by Jameson Garland.

[432] Idem.

[433] See International Commission of Jurists, "No. 1968-12, Administrative Court of Appeals of Stockholm, Sweden (19 December 2012)". In 2017, the Administrative Court of Appeals of Stockholm found that a woman who was born male had the right to change her legal identity back to that of a man, even though she had female genitalia after a gender reassignment surgery. The Court concluded that the person had displayed male gender identification for a sufficiently long time and for a sufficiently stable period, so that ambivalence could not be weighed as a factor in the case. (See Global Legal Monitor, "Sweden: Court Says Previous Sex Change Not a Bar to Second Change of Legal Gender Identity").

[434] In an effort to move away from previous abusive provisions, a government compensation scheme was announced for trans people who had been sterilised in 2013 and was adopted by the Parliament in 2018 (ILGA Europe, Rainbow Map, "Sweden").

compulsory but are not explicitly banned either. The current Act does not depathologise non-binary individuals and fails to align with current international standards.

In 2014, the final report of an inquiry issued by the Swedish government proposed to repeal the Act and replace it with two new laws, one concerning legal gender and one on surgical alteration of sex organs and removal of sex glands.[435] The report was criticised by Erika Alm as not having "addressed thoroughly intersex people's needs and conditions, and that has been the case every time the Act has been reviewed since it was adopted".[436] It has to be added that, intersex infants in Sweden are often subjected to "normalising" surgical procedures soon after birth and those interventions are unregulated.[437] The replacement laws are expected to be brought to the Riksdag by the spring of 2018 and could therefore enter force in the second half of 2019.[438] Nevertheless, as stated by Jameson Garland, "even with a new law replacing the Gender Classification Act, registered gender in Sweden will remain binary as long as the Population Registration Act is not amended. For intersex persons and children born with intersex conditions, the Population Registration Act remains a critical barrier to self-determination because it reinforces a legal presumption that medical personnel will determine which gender is appropriate for children and what medical procedures should be imposed on them to reinforce that gender".[439] In detail, the Population Registration Act (Folkbokföringslag (1991:481)) holds the medical personnel as primarily responsible for reporting births to the Tax Agency "as soon as possible", though in cases where this is not possible, the custodian of the child may do so.[440]

It is remarkable that even though Sweden has eliminated nearly all of the gender-based distinctions in Swedish law,[441] registration as male or female remains a reality and current legal frameworks on legal gender recognition are outdated. Possibly, it is a matter of time for the country to introduce explicit laws on gender identity and sex characteristics that are in line with current international human rights standards.

[435] See Swedish government report SOU 2014:91 and Swedish Secretariat for Gender Research, "Government inquiry leaves out intersex people".

[436] Swedish Secretariat for Gender Research, "Government inquiry leaves out intersex people".

[437] See Garland (2016).

[438] The Local, "Sweden to modernize law on changing gender".

[439] Scherpe et al. (2018), p. 257, mentioned on the Chapter "The Legal Status of Intersex Persons in Sweden" by Jameson Garland.

[440] See Folkbokföringslag (1991:481) para. 24 and Scherpe et al. (2018), p. 266.

[441] Scherpe et al. (2018), p. 274.

4.5 Intersex Rights in Progress

This section will not be used for the comparative study, but it aims to provide the reader with a complete picture on the situation of intersex rights in the EU. First, the case of France will be presented as significant developments on intersex have taken place in the country. Then, the question of the accommodation of intersex under non-discrimination law will be examined as it has concerned both the EU and its Member States during the last years.

4.5.1 France

In 2016, the Committee on the Rights of the Child issued the Concluding observations on the fifth periodic report of France and expressed its concern "on medically unnecessary and irreversible surgery and other treatment which is routinely performed on intersex children".[442] The Committee urged France to "develop and implement a rights-based health care protocol for intersex children, ensuring that children and their parents are appropriately informed of all options, that children are involved, to the largest extent, in decision-making about their treatment and care, and no child is subjected to unnecessary surgery or treatment".[443] A year later, the French Senate published a parliamentary inquiry on the rights of intersex people.[444] Vincent Guillot from Organisation Intersex International (OII) commented that with this report, the French state has recognised the existence of intersex people, but the systematic use of medical and pejorative vocabulary does not lead to the depathologisation of intersex.[445]

There is no provision under the French Civil Code that states that male and female are the only sexes that can be registered, therefore the answer to how many sexes there should be, depends on interpretation. According to Benjamin Moron-Puech, "To answer this question, one can look at other legal texts. Some provisions (including Article 1 and 3 of the French Constitution) use expressions such as 'both

[442] CRC/C/FRA/CO/5, 2016, para. 47. France has been reprimanded three times in total for this issue by the UN: In January 2016 by the Committee on the Rights of the Child, in May 2016 by the Committee against Torture, and in July 2016 by the Committee on the Elimination of Discrimination against Women (See StopIGM.org., "There we go (2): France condemns "mutilation of intersex children", proposes "prohibition").

[443] Idem, para. 48 (b).

[444] See Information Report compiled on behalf of the delegation to women's rights and equal opportunities between men and women on variations of sexual development: lift a taboo, fight stigma and exclusions by Maryvonne Blondin and Corinne Bouchoux, Senators, 2017 (Rapport d'information fait au nom de la délégation aux droits des femmes et à l'égalité des chances entre les hommes et les femmes sur les variations du développement sexuel : lever un tabou, lutter contre la stigmatisation et les exclusions, Par Mmes Maryvonne Blondin et Corinne Bouchoux, Sénatrices).

[445] Société, "Vincent Guillot: Il faut cesser les mutilations des enfants intersexes en France".

sexes', 'two sexes' or 'man and woman', all of which seems to exclude intersex".[446] In 2017, the Court of Cassation (Court de Cassation) pronounced on the matter and decided that the French law does not allow for a gender marker other than male or female.[447] The Court ruled that "the acknowledgment by the judge of a neutral sex would have a profound impact on French legal rules, that were built upon the duality of sexes and it therefore would require many coordination changes of statutory provisions".[448] In addition, it found that this is not contrary to Article 8 of the ECHR since "the duality of the sex markers in civil status pursues a legitimate aim because it is needed for the social and legal organization of which it constitutes a founding element".[449] With this decision, the Court does not focus on the interests of the plaintiff and fails to follow international and European developments. The justices do not seem to consider the difficulties that the plaintiff will have to encounter because of this non-recognition of sex.[450] In other words, it prefers to sacrifice the interests and rights of the minority for the sake of the majority which is founded on the sex dichotomy.

4.5.2 The Non-discrimination "Trap"

The findings of the report issued by the European Union Agency for Fundamental Rights (FRA) on intersex, show that there are European countries with open lists of grounds of discrimination, offering the ground of "other", which could be used to protect intersex people.[451] Those countries are Bulgaria, Estonia, Hungary, Italy, Luxembourg, Poland, Portugal, Romania, Spain and Slovakia.[452] However, it is added that "given the social and legal invisibility of intersex issues in society and in the legal system, considering such an approach can perpetuate this invisibility. It could also result in acts of discrimination against intersex people remaining unchallenged. Using this ground of protection remains largely untested and unclear in practice, given the scarcity of case law".[453]

From the countries analysed in the previous sections on explicit and implicit intersex frameworks, this research has already examined Luxembourg, Portugal, Romania and Spain. Since the publication of the FRA report, Portugal has already introduced explicit non-discrimination legislation together with Greece. Spain

---

[446] Scherpe et al. (2018), p. 311.

[447] See Decision n. 531 of 4 Mai 2017 (16-17.189), Court of Cassation, First Civil Chamber, (Arrêt n° 531 du 4 mai 2017 (16-17.189) - Cour de cassation - Première chambre civile -ECLI:FR:CCASS:2017:C100531) (in French).

[448] Idem, para. 8, as translated by Benjamin Moron-Puech.

[449] Idem.

[450] Scherpe et al. (2018), p. 316.

[451] European Union Agency for Fundamental Rights (2015), p. 4.

[452] Idem.

[453] Idem.

protects discrimination against intersex explicitly at regional levels and therefore it is highly possible that the ground "other" could be interpreted in a way to cover intersex. Luxembourg and Romania protect intersex implicitly and an open list of grounds of discrimination could possibly include intersex through interpretation as well. In contrast, the situation in the rest of the countries differs significantly. ILGA Europe in its 2018 Annual Review of the Human Rights Situation of Lesbian, Gay, Bisexual, Trans and Intersex People in Europe has placed Bulgaria,[454] Italy,[455] Poland[456] and Slovakia[457] very low in the list of European countries that protect LGBT and Intersex rights.[458] Estonia[459] and Hungary[460] have performed slightly better but there are still significant problems in LGBT and Intersex legislation.[461]

The issue of non-discrimination and intersex has also concerned the European Union since 2015 when the European Union Agency for Fundamental Rights published a comparative legal analysis on the "Protection against discrimination on grounds of sexual orientation, gender identity and sex characteristics in the EU". The report states that "regardless of their sexual orientation or gender identity, intersex people should benefit from protection from discrimination on the ground of sex under Article 21 of the EU Charter of Fundamental Rights"[462] and it adds that intersex persons are covered under "sex" in Directive 2006/54/EC.[463] The Agency highlights that "given that intersex discrimination concerns physical characteristics it is better covered under sex discrimination than under discrimination on the basis of

[454] In Bulgaria, a highly controversial judgment of the Supreme Court of Cassation stated that gender reassignment surgeries were not necessary to modify one's legal gender but people requesting a legal change of gender do have to undergo hormone therapy. See ILGA Europe (2018), pp. 50–51.

[455] In Italy, the Law on Transsexualism is not based on self-determination, but some restrictions are imposed to individuals who wish to modify their gender on identification documents. See ILGA Europe, 2018, pp. 78–79 and Rainbow Europe, "Italy".

[456] In Poland, the absence of any clear protocol or training for medical professionals was highlighted in a comparative study and the recommendations of that report included the introduction of a legal gender recognition process based on self-determination, underlining the glaring legal gap. See ILGA Europe (2018), pp. 104–105.

[457] In Slovakia, there is no fair, transparent legal framework for legal gender recognition, based on a process of self-determination, free from abusive requirements. See ILGA Europe (2018), pp. 116–117.

[458] See ILGA Europe, "Annual Review of the Human Rights Situation of Lesbian, Gay, Bisexual, Trans and Intersex People in Europe", 2018.

[459] In Estonia, there is no fair, transparent legal framework for legal gender recognition, based on a process of self-determination, free from abusive requirements. See ILGA Europe (2018), pp. 60–61.

[460] In Hungary, towards the end of 2017, a new decree was added to the national birth registry regulations and now legal gender recognition has a legal basis for the first time. However, the procedure still needs to be improved by introducing a clear framework, free from abusive requirements. See ILGA Europe (2018), pp. 72–73.

[461] See ILGA Europe, "Annual Review of the Human Rights Situation of Lesbian, Gay, Bisexual, Trans and Intersex People in Europe", 2018.

[462] European Union Agency for Fundamental Rights, Update 2015, p. 71.

[463] See Sect. 4.1.3.

sexual orientation and/or gender identity".[464] Moreover, Mitchell Travis has stressed that recognising intersex under EU anti-discrimination law can "boost" intersex rights in three ways: "a) it offers legal protection to marginalised and vulnerable group b) it manages this in a manner that does not rely upon further medicalisation of the intersex individual and c) it retains the autonomy of the individual by allowing them to choose their sex and gender identities as they deem appropriate for the situation".[465] Nonetheless, the reality on EU non-discrimination legislation on intersex differs as according to the Agency's findings, "so far it appears that the directive has not been implemented in this manner; FRA's research did not find legislation or case law clarifying whether intersex people are protected from discrimination on the ground of sex in Member States".[466] It has to be noted that still, the above Directive would cover intersex only in the area of employment.[467]

ILGA-Europe has highlighted that the situation on LGBT and Intersex anti-discrimination legislation in general in Europe is "fragmented" as many countries have introduced some sort of anti-discrimination legislation, but others have no legal framework which prohibits discrimination of LGBT and Intersex.[468] Accordingly, if Member States fail to clarify whether intersex people are covered under the ground of "sex" despite the EU's efforts, how could one be certain that an open list of discrimination based on the ground "other" could cover intersex and their needs especially in Member States where intersex rights are completely invisible?

---

[464] European Union Agency for Fundamental Rights, Update 2015, p. 70.

[465] Travis (2015), p. 199.

[466] European Union Agency for Fundamental Rights, Update 2015, p. 71.

[467] "In 2008, the European Commission proposed a directive that would ban discrimination on the grounds of age, disability, religion or belief and sexual orientation in all areas of EU competence, but the proposed directive is yet to be adopted." See ILGA Europe, "Employment". "The proposed Directive, if adopted, will extend the protection from discrimination on the grounds of religion or belief, disability, age, or sexual orientation to the areas of social protection, education and access to goods and services. This Directive would eliminate the hierarchy of rights that currently exists in the EU by giving the listed grounds the same protections guaranteed under the Race Directive." See ILGA Europe, "Equality for All".

[468] ILGA-Europe, "Anti-discrimination law".

4.6 Remarks: Intersex and the EU Fundamentals

4.6.1 Explicit Frameworks and "Limited" Intersex Expectations

4.6.1.1 The Emergence of the "Third Gender" in the EU

In 2013, in an effort to protect intersex rights and end harmful and invasive surgeries on intersex infants, the German Civil Status Law (Personenstandsgesetz (PStG)) was amended to cover intersex by introducing a blank sex marker in the birth registry. This development was criticised by intersex civil society organisations and the Council of Europe who feared that this could lead to more "normalising" intersex surgeries as parents would prefer to avoid stigmatisation and forced outings. At the same time, intersex would be considered as "genderless" and would not be able to identify with their own sex. On the other hand, this option seemed "convenient" in cases where the child's intersex sex, would reveal as it grew up, and this is not rare within intersex.[469] Later, in 2017, the German Federal Constitutional Court ruled that the German Civil Status Law must allow a "positive" third-gender option which could be called "intersex/diverse" and go beyond the blank option that was introduced in 2013. The Court elaborated on the fact that the previous blank option was not in line with the general right of personality in conjunction with the constitutional requirement of non-discrimination and equal treatment. In the reasoning of the decision, the justices used numerous times the term "gender identity" to elaborate on the specific needs of intersex. This could be explained, as the decision of the Court was impacted by previous national jurisprudence on the legal recognition of trans even though trans and intersex are different cases with different needs. The Constitutional Court's previous decisions on trans aimed to "acknowledge and strengthen the transgender person's sense of belonging to the respective social group by enabling their full legal transition to their self-perceived gender".[470] On the contrary, this cannot be applied on intersex since, the primary problem faced by intersex individuals is that "the acceptance of a self-attribution" to an "intersex/diverse" sex/gender is hardly going to make a difference in helping to solve the issues that arise from having to live in a binary social gender society".[471]

Given that German legal frameworks are also binary, the introduction of a third gender for intersex impacts the rule of law significantly. First and foremost, same-sex marriage was recently legalised in Germany and the Civil Code (Bürgerliches Gesetzbuch) now stipulates that "The marriage is made by two persons of different or the same sex for life".[472] In addition, married same-sex couples can adopt a child.

---

[469] See Sect. 1.6.2.

[470] Scherpe et al. (2018), p. 379.

[471] Idem.

[472] Bürgerliches Gesetzbuch (BGB) § 1353 Eheliche Lebensgemeinschaft, (1) Die Ehe wird von zwei Personen verschiedenen oder gleichen Geschlechts auf Lebenszeit geschlossen (translated by the author).

Considering that now in Germany there are three sexes, do intersex people have the right to marry and adopt under the law as well? Probably the answer to this question would be positive through interpretation but until an intersex person challenges the law before the Court, it remains uncertain. To date, the German Ethics Council does not have a common position on the matter as some Members are in favour and others are not.[473] According to Tobias Helms, "it would have been easy and much better if the wording of the new law (on same-sex marriage) had defined marriage as an institution entered into "two persons""[474] but during the drafting of the law, intersex people were not taken into consideration. Instead, "the main thrust of the new law was to clarify that the institution of marriage is no longer restricted to two persons of a different sex".[475]

The issue of the integration of a "third gender" into existing binary legal systems was exactly what the French justices feared when they rejected the application of an intersex individual for legal recognition and "sacrificed" the rights of intersex who constitute a minority for the sake of the binary majority, when ruling that the introduction of a neutral sex would have a profound impact on the French rule of law. That being the case, the German decision is definitely a courageous step towards intersex recognition but is the German rule of law "ready enough" to accommodate a third gender?

Another issue that arises by the establishment of a "third gender" is that instead of pursuing equality, further discrimination can occur within minorities. In the case of the German decision, only intersex people can access the third option whereas the legal procedure for the legal recognition under the Transsexuals Act keeps on violating basic rights of trans people and international human rights conventions. Moreover, other individuals that fall outside the binary such as agender, genderqueer etc. remain completely invisible. Therefore, although the intentions of the justices were to grant the basic right of legal recognition to intersex persons, it could be argued that the fundamental principle of equality is at stake.

Austria followed German jurisprudence when an intersex individual reached the Austrian Constitutional Court. The Court interpreted the law under a non-binary lens and granted the right to intersex to register as a third gender which could be defined as "inter", "other", "X" or "undefined". Currently, Austria is in the process of passing new legislation on the recognition of marriages between same-sex couples and hopefully the legislator will consider the implications that follow the recognition of a third gender and adopt the adequate wording. As in the case of Germany, another issue that emerges is the jeopardy of the fundamental principle of equality. In Austria trans people are unprotected under the law as there is no explicit legislation on the matter of legal recognition of gender.

The cases of Austria and Germany lead us to another issue which is whether gender should be abolished under the law. The German Constitutional Court hinted

---

[473] See Deutscher Ethikrat, 'Intersexualität", 2012.

[474] Scherpe et al. (2018), p. 375. See Chap. 4 and the cases of Australia and New Zealand where marriage is an institution between "two persons".

[475] Idem.

this possibility in its decision and in addition, in 2014, the German Ethics Council asked the legislator to consider whether entering a person's gender in the civil status register is still necessary.[476] Scholars in Germany have been also debating the emergence of a gender-neutral family law under the term "sexless family law".[477] Tobias Helms has underlined that in such case, the fact that must not be overlooked is that civil status issues are of international character.[478] He explains that "even if German (family) law were framed in gender-neutral terms, the German authorities and courts would still have to apply foreign law under which legal sex will continue to come into play for the foreseeable future; for this reason alone, it seems sensible to continue to include a gender entry in the civil status register".[479] It is obvious that if we consider that civil status issues are of international character, the introduction of a third gender does not seem an adequate solution either. In the previous Chapter, it was already examined how the third gender operates in Asia,[480] Oceania[481] and the Americas.[482,483] Australia, New Zealand and the U.S. have introduced a third gender option to safeguard intersex people's rights but in South Asia the third gender remains an abstract concept of historical, cultural and religious character and linked with "casts". Consequently, since the "third gender" is legally recognised only in few countries and even in those cases, there is no common understanding of its concept, how could this solution function in the international legal sphere?

Given these points and despite all the questions that may rise, the introduction of a "third gender" may be a courageous effort towards the protection of intersex rights but it is moving in the wrong direction as it does not lead to sex/gender equality but rather creates further discrimination within non-binary groups. The paradox is that in both Austria and Germany the law has still not challenged the "source" of intersex rights violations which is the performance of involuntary, harmful and invasive surgeries on intersex infants. Hence, the decisions of the Courts should be seen as the beginning of a new era and the recognition of intersex as a legal gender as only an effort towards equality.

4.6.1.2 The Need for Comprehensive Intersex Laws

Greece, Portugal and Malta are the only EU Member States that have passed explicit legislation on intersex. Among the three countries, Malta is the only one who has managed to introduce a human right centered and comprehensive legal framework on intersex. The 2015 GIGESC Act incorporates a "beyond the binary" approach

[476] BT-Drucks 17/9088, p. 59 (Empfehlung No. 4 zum Personenstandsrecht).
[477] See Büchler and Cottier (2005).
[478] Scherpe et al. (2018), p. 380.
[479] Idem.
[480] See Table 3.4. Legislation, case law, practices on intersex people's rights in Asia.
[481] See Table 3.3. Legislation, case law, practices on intersex people's rights in Oceania.
[482] See Table 3.2. Legislation, case law, practices on intersex people's rights in Americas.
[483] See Sect. 3.6.2.

that enables individuals to move between genders without significant restrictions.[484] Even though the Maltese legislation does not abandon the need for gender markers in identification documents, it acknowledges that "such markers are not absolutely essential in navigating legal existence"[485] and allows intersex -and non-binary individuals- to enjoy their human rights and individual freedoms. The Act is probably the first law worldwide that explicitly depathologises and destigmatises intersex through its wording and its emphasis on the fact that intersex surgeries are socially motivated. Consequently, "it facilitates intersex people to change their gender by which they are legally recognised while simultaneously offering comprehensive protection from unwanted medical interventions".[486] More importantly, the introduction of a comprehensive legal framework for intersex is not only limited to the GIGESC Act but Malta has also amended family law provisions to include gender neutral terminology. This way, intersex people can live in their sex/gender and exercise freely their basic right to found a family.

In contrast, Greece and Portugal may have introduced explicit provisions on intersex but it is doubtful whether intersex rights are sufficiently protected. In the case of Greece, even though discrimination is banned on the ground of sex characteristics, Greek case law continues applying a binary legal approach and intersex are pathologised and medicalised. The Greek judge, influenced by the binary society he/she lives in, seems more willing to grant legal recognition to an intersex individual as he/she perceives the applicant as an "error" of nature that needs to be integrated in the binary legal system. As a result, even though provisions on non-discrimination on intersex exist, the Greek judges tend to discriminate against intersex by not perceiving them as "normal". Moreover, Greece, in an effort to modernise its legal framework on same sex couples and follow European developments it has opened the door to "gender neutral" legal terminology but it is unclear whether the legislator was aiming for this at the first place. Under the same token, Portugal, while it banned discrimination based on sex characteristics, it did not ban intersex surgeries and did not depathologise intersex as an intersex individual can enjoy his/her human rights only if his/her "gender identity is manifested". The Portuguese law on intersex has failed to cover the specific needs of intersex and the approach of the legislator seems "confusing" and not intersex rights centered. Last, Spain and the UK have introduced some minor legal frameworks on intersex but only at regional levels.

Obviously, existing explicit laws on intersex highlight the need for comprehensive intersex legal frameworks. European jurisdictions seem to "hesitate" to introduce frameworks that go beyond the binary legal understanding of sex as it is highly connected to ethics, societal foundations, history and tradition. Accordingly, even though the legislator may aim to protect intersex rights, still has to face the binary reality and all the legal implications that a non-binary understanding could "produce" to fundamental principles such as the principle of gender equality which is

[484] Scherpe et al. (2018), p. 364.

[485] Idem, as referred by Tanya Ni Mhuirthile.

[486] Idem.

still limited between two sexes. The Maltese example shows that it is possible to introduce comprehensive non-binary legal frameworks and stop sacrificing the rights of the minority to protect the majority.

4.6.2 *Turning a Blind Eye on Human Rights: Implicit Frameworks on Intersex*

4.6.2.1 The Impact of "Sex" and "Gender" on Statutory Interpretation

Implicit legal frameworks require adequate interpretation in order to be applied in the case of intersex and protect their rights. Different approaches exist in legal interpretation and different schools of thought have emerged over the years. Two main approaches are literal and purposive interpretation. Literal interpretation (or the plain meaning rule), that flourished in the second half of the twentieth century, aims to ensure precise word-for-word meaning of the text.[487] Purposive interpretation, which is often preferred in our days, expresses the legislative purpose of the text[488] with some theorists defining purposive interpretation more narrowly and others more broadly.[489] The common goal of statutory interpretation is to realise and understand the intentions of the author although there is no "true" interpretation but rather "proper" interpretation[490]; meaning that it may transform or evolve since it is constantly impacted by several external factors. In other words, prevailing interpretative and legislative systems directly impact interpretation i.e. "the interpretative system that is proper in democratic regime is not necessarily the proper system of interpretation in a totalitarian regime".[491] With this in mind, how the evolving perception of sex and gender can impact statutory interpretation?

Sex and gender have a strong socio-political character and they have been drastically evolving over the years. As stated by Rozina Rudevska, in legal discourse there are three principal stages of the meaning of the concept "gender". In the first stage, the concept "gender" was understood as polite form of the word "sex" and it was used as a synonym for women, especially within gender mainstreaming policies of the United Nations.[492] The second phase implied that there are only two genders, masculine and feminine, and they correspond to male and female sex.[493] This concept was used primarily by feminist legal theory and allowed to study all inequalities between men and women.[494] The third phase is related to the latest trends in

[487] Rudevska (2018), p. 104.

[488] Idem.

[489] Barak (2007), p. 4.

[490] Idem, p. 11.

[491] Idem.

[492] Rudevska (2018), p. 109.

[493] Idem, p. 110.

[494] Idem.

social sciences which argue that gender is independent from biology[495] and constitutes a social construct. The evolution of the understanding of sex and gender is obvious on legal texts and it can be primarily observed with the emergence of new legal terminology such as the terms "gender identity", "gender expression" and "sex characteristics".[496] This can be justified as legislative systems tend to "create the words in their new meanings that result from new socio-political frameworks, unique normative regulations and legal standards that respond to new tendencies in legislative discoursal practices".[497] Thus, it can be observed that legal texts and case-law during the past years have been advancing to accommodate the whole spectrum of sex and gender.

Under those circumstances, the law cannot turn a blind eye on current social and political developments with regards to sex and gender. Its interpretation should be adapted to modern developments, protect non-binary groups including intersex who remain socially excluded and vulnerable and play a "progressive pedagogical role" of integration.[498]

4.6.2.2 All Roads Do Not Lead to Intersex

As stated by the European Union Fundamental Rights Agency, in certain Member States, laws are considered to cover intersex implicitly under the grounds of "gender" and "gender identity". In other words, countries that have introduced laws on the legal recognition of trans may allow intersex to access legal recognition through interpretation. In that case, to cover intersex, purposive interpretation should be applied as it permits for a broader understanding of the law which is based on the "purpose" of the legislator. If it is assumed that the legislator introduced a legal framework on legal gender recognition for people who do not identify with the binary female/male with the purpose to be recognisable under the law and avail the full rights contained in law, then intersex people could be covered as well. Still, declaring that intersex people are implicitly protected under the ground of "gender identity" can raise numerous issues: (a) consequences of legal gender recognition frameworks that are non-human rights centered nor transparent will negatively impact intersex (b) intersex individuals will still have to fit in the binary and choose between the options of female and male and (c) the lack of fair and transparent legal frameworks for intersex will persist.

Among the countries that were analysed in this Chapter, Finland, Romania and Slovenia require gender reassignment surgeries for legal gender recognition. In Romania and Slovenia in particular, there is no clear procedure, but a combination of different laws is applied, and the judge usually decides in favour of gender reassignment surgeries as a prerequisite for legal recognition. As a result, an intersex

[495] Idem, p. 111.

[496] See Sect. 1.5.2.

[497] Rudevska (2018), p. 104.

[498] Papadopoulou (2015), p. 55.

individual who wishes to modify his/her identification documents will have to go through the same harmful procedure. In Belgium, Denmark, Ireland and the Netherlands, legal gender recognition procedure is based on the self-determination of the individual, but it is limited to trans individuals. In that case, intersex access to legal recognition is primarily based on the discretion of the judge. In the Netherlands, the judges have been applying purposive interpretation so far to cover intersex. For instance, recently, the District Court of Limburg ruled in favour of a Dutch citizen who wished to be recognised as a "third gender" even though the Dutch law does not provide for this possibility. It has to be added that legal gender recognition based on self-determination may also include restrictions that impact intersex such as the requirement of age, or of being divorced in order to access it. Among all the countries examined only Luxembourg's implicit law on intersex can be considered as adequate; the wording "all Luxembourgish individuals" allows for all individuals to access legal gender recognition. In addition, intersex persons are mentioned in the explanatory text of the law on gender recognition.

In most of the above countries, the UN and National Agencies have issued reports on the alarming situation around intersex people and the performance of invasive intersex surgeries that grossly violate their rights. Nevertheless, none of those countries have introduced explicit legal frameworks that will end surgeries performed on intersex infants and safeguard their rights. Instead, intersex will have to follow legal paths that are constructed for the needs of trans people and fit into the binary in order to be recognised under the law. Belgium and Finland have introduced anti-discrimination laws on intersex but in practice, intersex individuals are discriminated as they are subjected to surgeries and remain invisible under the law.

Provided that implicit frameworks cannot cover the needs of intersex and guarantee their rights sufficiently as they are flawed, and their application is based on interpretation, the question would be, do explicit laws deliver more solid frameworks for intersex? The analysis of explicit laws on intersex has proven that every legal text requires interpretation. Intersex issues have become visible only recently and jurisdictions are still adjusting to this novel sex/gender era. As a result, even explicit frameworks need to be adjusted to modern developments concerning sex and gender and this can be achieved through adequate interpretation which at the same time depends majorly on the legal tradition of each jurisdiction. Above all, the existence of both explicit and implicit frameworks on intersex highlight a common need for comprehensive, fair and transparent frameworks on intersex rights.

4.6.3 Securing Intersex Rights in Line with the EU Values

The main question of this comparative study is whether existing legal frameworks on intersex promote and are in line with the EU values which are: human dignity, freedom, democracy, equality, rule of law and respect for human rights. Those values are of great meaning as they signify the end of the EU as a solely value-based community and the genesis of a collective entity founded upon fundamental principles[499] that protect the individual. The Council of Europe and the European Union share the same fundamental values: human rights as enshrined in the ECHR, democracy and the rule of law.[500] All the above-mentioned values must be seen as interrelated and interconnected to allow for just societies and laws to flourish. The present state on intersex rights within the EU and its Member States and the rapid growth of non-binary individuals' visibility and rights' movements in general have been challenging those values and "testing" the foundations of the EU.

To date, only Malta protects the right to bodily autonomy of intersex and acknowledges that intersex surgeries are a "product" of social motives and attitudes on "sex" and "gender". In the rest of EU Member States, intersex infants are legally unprotected and exposed to human rights violations emanating from the performance of involuntary, harmful and invasive sex "normalising" surgeries. Austria, Germany, Malta and Portugal guarantee access to identification documents for intersex people and other countries including Greece condemn discrimination against intersex. Even though the TFEU explicitly states in its Article 2 that among the EU's values are the "respect of human rights, including the rights of persons belonging to minorities", in the vast majority of EU countries, the lack of explicit and comprehensive legal frameworks on intersex leads to the emergence of an invisible minority that is repeatedly discriminated against the binary majority and when minority rights are unprotected, the majority's rights lose their significance as well.

It can be concluded that neither explicit nor implicit laws on intersex may promote EU values to the fullest, but a tendency could be observed among Member States to move beyond the binary and recognise intersex and non-binary individuals who fall outside of it, and this is also highlighted by laws and case-law on gender identity that has been developing significantly during the past decade. This trend is also apparent in the ECtHR's precedence, as the Court has been aiming to protect sexual minorities especially through the repeated explicit condemn of medical surgeries or treatments that lead to sterilisation. This growing tendency which targets to embrace non-binary rights, emphasises the need for EU law to follow developments among EU societies and expand the understanding of "sex" and "gender". The EU may have "made some impact on the project of gender equality because of its binding legal Directives on equal treatment in employment but there is potential for further reductions in gender inequality"[501] and this can be achieved by departing from the traditional concept of "dichotomous sex/gender equality" and move to a "non-dichotomous sex/gender equality" which will be adapted to current societal developments and legal needs.

The need of law and EU law in particular to follow societal developments on gender was already highlighted by Advocate General Tesauro in his opinion on P. v. S. and Cornwall County Council which was delivered on 14 December 1995 and stated that: "the law is faced with that reality (referring to transsexuality) and is destined to come up against it to an increasing degree. This is inevitable. In society

[499] Mos (2013), p. 81.

[500] Council of Europe, "Values: Human rights, Democracy, Rule of Law".

[501] Wallby (2004), p. 6.

as it is today, in which customs and morals are changing rapidly, citizens are guaranteed ever wider and deeper protection of their freedoms (…) To my mind, the law cannot cut itself off from society as it actually is, and must not fail to adjust to it as quickly as possible. Otherwise it risks imposing outdated views and taking on a static role. In so far as the law seeks to regulate relations in society, it must on the contrary keep up with social change and must therefore be capable of regulating new situations brought to light by social change and advances in science".[502]

In a period of time where EU values are claimed to be "in crisis",[503] the exclusion of non-binary individuals under EU law conflicts with the principles of liberal democracy which is primarily promoted by the EU and its key feature is to prioritise the protection of basic rights and liberties of citizens.[504] In that case, EU law, instead of "erasing" intersex bodies through the "silent" acceptance and "legitimisation" of invasive surgeries that aim to fit individuals in the sex/gender binary, should recognise and protect intersex bodies, benefit from them to promote diversity, safeguard the values that it is built upon and sustain liberal democracy. As John Stuart Mill has underscored, "The only freedom which deserves the name is that of pursuing our own good in our own way, so long as we do not attempt to deprive others of theirs or impede their efforts to obtain it. Each is the proper guardian of his own health, whether bodily, or mental or spiritual".[505]

---

[502] P. v S. AND Cornwall County Council Opinion of Advocate General Tesauro delivered on 14 December 1995, para. 8.

[503] See Pachmann (2017), Chopin and Macek (2018) and Kanellopoulou-Malouhou (2012).

[504] Chung (2018), p. 2.

[505] Mill (1859), p. 16.

Chapter 5
The Future: Intersex Shaping Inclusive Laws

5.1 Intersex Rights: Expectations and Realities

After having examined the situation of intersex rights in both regional and international levels, it can be observed that jurisdictions are still "struggling" to accommodate intersex. Intersex rights are explicitly protected only in few countries while there is a global trend for implicit protection of intersex. According to the findings of this research, this tendency can be justified if we consider the legal evolution of "sex" and "gender". Intersex movements have been advocating for intersex rights only since the 1990s and therefore the legislator, confronted with a relatively new reality, seems "hesitant" to challenge the male/female binary as it is well-founded in both societies and the law. "Sexual orientation" and "gender identity" issues were addressed first as they became visible prior to issues surrounding "intersex" and/or "sex characteristics" and in the absence of explicit and comprehensive intersex rights' frameworks, intersex people benefit from frameworks on SOGI rights even though they do not address their specific needs. A typical example is legal recognition where the developments on the field of "gender identity" have been major during the previous years and many jurisdictions around the globe tend to apply existing "gender identity" frameworks on intersex to protect their rights while intersex do not identify with the binary as trans individuals do. Under the same token, legal frameworks on "sexual orientation" have impacted intersex as well and especially their right to marry and found a family.

This Chapter will elaborate on two main questions that rise from the current intersex rights situation: to which extend the above developments cover sufficiently intersex people's rights and needs? And how can intersex be accommodated in legal frameworks and achieve sex/gender equality beyond binaries? The aim of this concluding Chapter is to first, based on the outcomes of the previous chapters, provide a commentary on the intersex rights situation that prevails around the globe in the moment. This way, the reader will be able to realise the exact progress that has been made -or not- with regards to intersex rights. Second, the need for a broad

N. Pikramenou, *Intersex Rights*, https://doi.org/10.1007/978-3-030-27554-9_5

interpretation of "sex" in legal texts will be presented as a "transitional" solution to the problem of accommodation of intersex under current legal frameworks until sex/gender equality beyond binaries is established. In other words, the emerging concept of sexless/genderless equality will be presented as the key to inclusive, diverse, equal and just societies (Table 5.1).

Table 5.1 Intersex rights protected explicitly and/or implicitly by country

Jurisdictions	Bodily integrity	Legal recognition	Marriage/Family	Anti-discrimination
Argentina		X		
Australia		X	X	X
Austria		X	X	
Bangladesh		X		
Belgium		X		X
Chile	(X)	X	X	X
Colombia	X	X		
Denmark		X		
Finland		X		X
Germany		X	X	
Greece		X	X	X
India		X		
Ireland		X		
Kenya		X		
Luxembourg	X	X		
Malta	X	X	X	X
Nepal		X		
Netherlands		X		
New Zealand		X	X	
Pakistan		X		X
Philippines		X		
Portugal		X	X	X
Romania		X		
Slovenia		X		X
South Africa		X	X	X
Basque Country (Spain)				X
Sweden		X		
Uganda		X		
Scotland (UK)				X
United States	(X)	(X)		
Viet Nam		X		

5.1.1 *Intersex Surgeries: The Source of Gross and Unchallenged Violations*

The ban of intersex surgeries has always been a top priority of intersex rights organisations due to its social motives, invasive nature and the violation of fundamental human rights including the rights to bodily integrity, physical autonomy, self-determination and health. The first demand of the Malta Declaration is "to put an end to mutilating and "normalising" practices such as genital surgeries, psychological and other medical treatments through legislative and other means. Intersex people must be empowered to make their own decisions affecting own bodily integrity, physical autonomy and self-determination".[1] The Statement of Riga, the Vienna Statement, the Darlington Statement, the Statement of Intersex Asia and of the African Intersex Movement, all call for the immediate prohibition of medical interventions on intersex, including surgical and hormonal interventions, that alter the sex characteristics of infants and children without personal consent. The demands of the above statements are also reflected on Yogyakarta Principles, the reports issued by the UN Special Rapporteur on Torture who has characterised intersex surgeries as a "torture", the Council of Europe, the World Health Organization and the European Union. In 2016, UN experts including the Committee against Torture, the Committee on the Rights of the Child and the Committee on the Rights of Persons with Disabilities, along with the Council of Europe Commissioner for Human Rights, the Inter-American Commission on Human Rights and United Nations Special Rapporteurs called for an urgent end to human rights violations against intersex persons committed in medical settings and urged States to prohibit medically unnecessary surgery and procedures on intersex children.[2] In addition to the above demands with regards to intersex surgeries, the Malta Declaration also called to "put an end to preimplantation genetic diagnosis, pre-natal screening and treatment, and selective abortion of intersex fetuses"[3] but PGD has not yet been addressed by the examined jurisdictions.

Despite all the above demands and calls, intersex surgeries that constitute the most severe "source" of human rights violations against intersex remain unchallenged under the vast majority of legal frameworks. To date, the only jurisdiction worldwide that has explicitly outlawed the performance of intersex surgeries due to its social motives and protects bodily integrity of intersex is Malta. Luxembourg follows, with the implicit ban of intersex surgeries as the law does not mention intersex, but it is included in the preparatory text. The Colombian Constitutional Court has also adopted a human rights' approach in a series of decisions with regards to intersex surgeries and, based on the principles of human dignity and equality, has

[1] OII Europe, Malta Declaration, (1 December 2013).

[2] United Nations Human Rights Office of the High Commissioner, Intersex Awareness Day, "End violence and harmful medical practices on intersex children and adults, UN and regional experts urge", 2016.

[3] OII Europe, Malta Declaration (1 December 2013).

prohibited the performance of those treatments on intersex infants. On human dignity in particular, which has been used broadly by the Colombian Court in the case of sexual minorities, Jürgen Habermas has underlined that "lawmakers and judges often arrive at different results in different cultural contexts; today this is apparent, for example, in the regulation of controversial ethical issues (…) Thus appealing to the concept of human dignity undoubtedly made it easier to reach an overlapping consensus".[4] However, even though the performance of intersex surgeries clearly violates the right to human dignity, only the Colombian Constitutional Court has relied on it to such extent to outlaw sex "normalising" surgeries performed on intersex infants. The lack of legal protection of intersex persons' bodily integrity and self-determination demonstrates that behind the performance of those surgeries lies a highly social background founded on the binary of female and male. Physicians driven by their social perception on sex/gender keep on performing those surgeries despite all the efforts made by the international human rights community. Foucault has criticised the medical field with regards to its attitude towards intersex and has stated that the field is "made up of evasions since, given its inability or refusal to speak of sex itself, it concerned itself primarily with aberrations, perversions, exceptional oddities, pathological abatements, and morbid aggravations".[5] Paternalism within the medical field and social stereotypes on sex/gender prevent the legislators and justices from banning explicitly intersex surgeries as well, and therefore the performance of those surgeries is implicitly "legitimised". The highly ethical and social background of intersex surgeries has also led to controversies as in the case of Chile where Circular 18 which aimed to ban sex "normalising" surgeries and depathologise intersex was overturned a year later by Circular 7 that pathologised again intersex. In the United States, the Court of Appeals for the Fourth Circuit followed a paternalistic approach when it ruled that the physician "did not mean to" violate the applicant's rights. Even though intersex surgeries are performed widely in the U.S., only the California State Legislature has denounced intersex surgeries through the introduction of a resolution. In Germany, several Court decisions have provided for reparations for intersex people who were victims of sex non-consensual "normalising" surgeries but remarkably intersex surgeries are yet to be outlawed.

Other rights that are violated due to the performance of intersex surgeries but remain unchallenged are the right to informed consent, the access to decision-making, medical records and justice. Informed consent and access to decision-making is properly addressed by the Maltese law which grants the right to informed consent to the minor. The Colombian justices also applied a child's rights' approach when ruled that the permission of the parents in the case of such surgeries should be "qualified and persistent"[6] and in the failure to do so, no surgery could be performed until the child could reach an independent decision. There are also jurisdictions which may have attempted to follow a child's rights approach, but they have "gotten

[4] Habermas (2010), p. 467.

[5] Foucault (2012a), p. 53.

[6] T-551/99, para. 29.

it wrong", i.e. in the case of Portugal, where the law grants the right to bodily integrity to intersex individuals, but it also prescribes that surgeries on intersex infants should not be performed until the moment that the person's gender identity is manifested.

The overall legal situation highlights the need for the explicit ban of intersex surgeries which constitute a torture and cause irreversible harm to intersex individuals. Intersex children, and teenagers/adults in some cases i.e. as in Christiane Völling's case, are striped of the rights granted to the binary majority as their ability to construct their self is taken away by physicians and parents who still maintain the authority to decide for their sex and gender and impose their sense and ideas of "normalcy". It is remarkable that though current trends differ from the Middle Age's highly religious drive for binary certainty in sex and gender, intersex individuals remain pathologised and traces of the past heteronormative era are still present in the influx of surgery performed on intersex individuals.[7] As Butler indicates "although we struggle for rights over our own bodies, the very bodies for which we struggle are not quite ever only our own".[8] In the case of intersex, the State and the legislator, by remaining silent in front of this gross injustice and not outlawing intersex surgeries seem to "own" intersex people's bodies as they intrude into their integrity and that, constitutes them accomplices to all human rights violations that intersex persons are subjected to. The explicit ban of intersex surgeries is mandatory to administer justice, but it will not be "enough" if it is not coupled with the adoption of a non-paternalistic approach that safeguards intersex rights and respects the best interests of the child.

5.1.2 Legal Recognition or When the State Decides for Intersex Bodies

Another reason why intersex surgeries are being performed over the years is the legal recognition of intersex including sex/gender markers on birth certificates, identification documents and passports. The Malta Statement recommends "to register intersex children as females or males, with the awareness that, they may grow up to identify with a different sex or gender" and "to ensure that sex or gender classifications are amendable through a simple administrative procedure after the request of the individuals concerned. All adults and capable minors should be able to choose between female (F), male (M), non-binary or multiple options. In the future, as with race or religion, sex or gender should not be a category on birth certificates or identification documents for anybody".[9] The Statements by the African Intersex Movement and the Asian Intersex Movement reaffirmed the Malta

[7] Andrew (2009), p. 47.

[8] Butler (2004), p. 21.

[9] Idem.

Statement's demands on intersex legal recognition. The Vienna Statement proposes to "install an easy administrative process to facilitate gender/sex marker change on the basis of self-determination and self-declaration. A neutral marker should be made available".[10] The Darlington Statement added also the problematic of the introduction of a "third gender" and intersex: "(a) as with race or religion, sex/gender should not be a legal category on birth certificates or identification documents for anybody. While sex/gender classifications remain legally required, sex/gender assignments must be regarded as provisional (b) given existing social conditions, we do not support the imposition of a third sex classification when births are initially registered (c) recognising that any child may grow up to identify with a different sex/gender, and that the decision about the sex of rearing of an intersex child may have been incorrect, sex/gender classifications must be legally correctable through a simple administrative procedure at the request of the individual concerned (d) individuals able to consent should be able to choose between female (F), male (M), non-binary, alternative gender markers, or multiple options".[11] At international levels, only the Council of Europe has called for non-binary gender classifications to be available on a voluntary, opt-in basis and for greater consideration of the implications of new sex classifications on intersex people.[12] Probably this is due to the fact that legal recognition relies heavily on the scrutiny of the State.

Among 31 jurisdictions that were examined in this research, 16 have legislated explicitly on the legal recognition of intersex people. Those jurisdictions have approached intersex legal recognition in different ways and nine of them have introduced the option of a "third gender". In 15 jurisdictions, intersex people who wish to be legally recognised will have to follow the same procedure as trans even though their needs and demands are completely different.

With regards to case law on the legal recognition of intersex, it is noteworthy to examine how justices have approached it among jurisdictions. In Kenya, when an intersex individual reached the Court in 2010, the justices rejected the intersex petitioner's assertion that "sex" in the Constitution should be interpreted to include a third category of gender. The Court based its reasoning on the fact that the petition was contrary to the traditional Kenyan society and its social, moral and religious values. Three years later, the Court recognised the right of an intersex individual to be legally recognised and it stated that the Kenyan society was at that time ready for it. In both cases, the Kenyan justices did not rely on credible legal sources including international human rights documents on intersex rights but rather on their personal judgment with regards to societal developments in the country. In Philippines, the Court used Wikipedia as a source to analyse intersex and reasoned that in such cases, nature should take its course and granted the plaintiff the right to be legally recognised. However, previously, the justices had rejected a trans individual's case on legal recognition as according to them, transgenderism did not fall within the sphere of "natural". In Greece, even though the Court rejected the legal recognition

[10] OII Europe, Statement of the 1st European Intersex Community Event, Vienna, 2017.

[11] Idem.

[12] Council of Europe (2015), pp. 37–40.

of a non-binary individual, in its reasoning it mentioned intersex and opened the way for a future legal recognition as intersex is perceived by the justices as a "natural error". In all these decisions, the justices have been functioning as "moral reasoners" using primarily morals in order to pronounce on the legal recognition of intersex. It can be argued that intersex rights do have a highly moral and ethical content and do raise ethical and moral questions, and this brings us to the question of whether justices own superior skills when addressing moral issues about rights[13] which enable them to deliver a "common sense of justice". In the above-examined cases, the justices have used morals to establish their reasoning which is based on a subjective perception on the matter, functioning as common citizens rather than examining global trends through precedence in other countries, consulting reports on intersex published by national NGOs or international human rights sources which could lead to the establishment of an objective perception on the matter.[14] The justices in the case of intersex legal recognition are attempting to voice society's pulse on the matter, expressing the "common sense of justice", a concept which could be characterised as extremely ambiguous. In the modern era, it is impossible to identify what is "common" as we live in open, pluralistic and multicultural societies, founded upon complex communicative structures.[15] Therefore, what is usually perceived as "common sense of justice" is a heterogeneous amalgam comprised by diverse beliefs on social ethics, spontaneous representations and prejudices of the common mind.[16] Justices may seem best placed to settle moral and ethical issues embedded in law but those issues should be adjudicated in line with national as well as international developments. Highly ethical issues need to be addressed not as one would make a personal moral decision but in the name of the whole society,[17] including sexual minorities such as intersex. Colombian justices seem to be the only who interpreted the Constitution in the light of modern trends and with the aim to safeguard individual rights in diverse and evolving societies, as they reasoned that "considering the principle of human dignity and the right to equality, there is no reason to justify that infants and children whose sex cannot be identified at birth, are not registered and remain "invisible" for the State and society".[18]

When it comes to legal frameworks, the countries that have introduced explicit laws on intersex legal recognition are Malta, Portugal, South Africa and Uganda. In Malta, intersex individuals can change their gender on identification documents through the "change of gender identity" procedure which requires a simple declaration based on self-determination. The Maltese government has also amended its public policy to introduce an "X" option on identification documents. In Portugal, the law is quite ambiguous as an intersex individual can alter his/her identification

[13] Waldron (2009), p. 2.

[14] See Papantoniou (1983).

[15] Stamatis (2005), p. 822.

[16] Idem, p. 824.

[17] Waldron (2009), p. 2.

[18] T-450A/13, para. 6.2.

documents once "the person's gender identity is manifested".[19] In South Africa, intersex people can change their sex on official documents but this change is limited within the female/male binary and requires a report by a psychologist or social worker corroborating that the applicant has been living for 2 years in the gender role corresponding to the sex description. In Uganda, intersex people are called "hermaphrodites" under the law and they need to be operated in order to become "fully male" or "fully female" and identify as such. Then, in 15 jurisdictions intersex people follow the laws on gender identity recognition which are designed for trans in order to change sex on identification documents, even though their needs are different. The fundamental difference between trans and intersex is that "transsex individuals often desire the future body that they should have, while intersex individuals often mourn the body they had before an unwanted normalizing surgery interfered with it".[20] At the same time, both intersex and trans movements "challenge the principle that a natural dimorphism should be established or maintained at all costs"[21] and this seems to confuse the legislator who instead of introducing explicit and comprehensive frameworks for each case, prefers to group trans and intersex under the umbrella of "gender identity". Intersex people in that case, will have to first, identify with the binary and second, go through harmful gender reassignment surgeries exactly as trans in jurisdictions where the legal recognition of trans is not based on the right to self-determination.

Some jurisdictions, in an effort to protect intersex rights, have introduced "third gender" classifications. Australia, New Zealand and some states in the U.S. have adopted the third option "X" to safeguard non-binary people's rights. Austria and Germany have introduced a third option for intersex individuals in identification documents. In South Asian countries including Bangladesh, India, Nepal and Pakistan, a "third gender" is introduced for both trans and intersex as according to tradition they constitute a distinct "cast". As it has been already analysed, again, "third gender" options fail to protect intersex people's rights including their right to self-determination and free development of personality and lead to further discriminations within the already discriminated and marginalised sexual minorities.

All the above developments rise questions with regards to state interference and the exercise of individual freedoms. Traditional constitutional theory distinguishes the relation between the state and the individual in "negative" (status negativus) and "positive" (status positivus).[22] The state has the negative obligation to not interfere with the right to self-determination and free development of personality and the positive obligation to create the social circumstances and provide the individual with the means to exercise these rights.[23] This functional connection between the state and the individual constitutes the foundations of democracy.[24] The International

[19] Law No. 38/2018, Article 7 (3).

[20] Ben-Asher (2006), p. 51.

[21] Butler (2004), p. 6.

[22] Kasimatis (1980), p. 154. See also Jellinek (2011).

[23] See Kasimatis (1980), Manesis (1982), Tsatsos (1988) and Peters (2016).

[24] Idem, p. 156.

Covenant on Civil and Political Rights (ICCPR) in its Article 17 prescribes the right of every person to be protected against "arbitrary or unlawful interference with his privacy, family, home or correspondence, nor to unlawful attacks on his honour and reputation.". The Human Rights Committee in General Comment No. 16 indicates that in the view of the Committee, the right of Article 17 of the ICCPR is guaranteed against all interferences whether they emanate from the state or natural or legal persons.[25] The General Comment adds in paragraph 7 that "as all persons live in society, the protection of privacy is necessarily relative". The European Court of Human Rights (ECtHR) has developed jurisprudence based on Article 8 ECHR, elaborating on the objective of this article which is that in democratic societies, the individual is entitled to live without the state controlling his/her activities.[26] Moreover, the ECtHR has held that there is no state interference as long as the state does not interfere with the de facto existence of the right to privacy.[27] The Court also discussed the justified interference with the right to privacy in Pretty v. the United Kingdom and ruled that the prohibition of assisted suicide in the UK constituted an unjustified interference with the right to privacy as the right to self-determination encompasses the right to decide about one's body.[28]

In the case of intersex individuals, states interfere with their right to self-determination as the vast majority of jurisdictions have not introduced fair and comprehensive legal frameworks that respect their rights. As a result, intersex persons remain "invisible" under societies and laws and they are stripped of the adequate social circumstances that would allow them to enjoy their rights. In jurisdictions where intersex people have to go through involuntary and harmful surgeries that lead to sterilisation, the states subject intersex persons to torture, interfere with the most intimate aspects of a person's private life and deny them the ability to live in dignity.

Intersex rights organisations have issued several recommendations on how legal recognition issues surrounding intersex could be resolved. Nonetheless, even though they have pronounced on the matter, they seem to not have reached a common ground to the problem of legal recognition. In the meantime, demands for sexless/genderless identification documents are growing. Principle 31 of Yogyakarta Principles +10 urges states to "ensure that official identity documents only include personal information that is relevant, reasonable and necessary as required by the law for a legitimate purpose, and thereby end the registration of the sex and gender of the person in identity documents such as birth certificates, identification cards, passports and driver licenses, and as part of their legal personality". Transgender

[25] Human Rights Committee (HRC), CCPR General Comment No. 16, para. 1.

[26] See Airey v. Ireland, Application No. 6289/73, judgement of 9 October 1979 and Marckx v. Belgium, Application No. 6833/74, judgment of 13 June 1979.

[27] See Johnston et al. v. Ireland, Application No. 9697/82, judgment of 18 December 1986.

[28] Pretty v. The United Kingdom, Application No. 2346/02, judgment of 29 April 2002, paras. 70-78.

Europe has fully endorsed the above principle and called for the full abolition of gender markers on official identity documents.[29]

Given these points and considering the above-examined legal frameworks on intersex legal recognition, jurisdictions seem to be in front of a major defy; they are called to follow rapid societal developments and challenge the legal binary to accommodate intersex. There are jurisdictions that have made some efforts to protect intersex rights but in the vast majority of countries, the legislator seems "reluctant" in front of this new legal era and chooses to violate intersex people's rights to preserve the binary foundations of both law and society. The legislator has to face the past which is founded upon the male/female binary, the challenging present where more and more individuals are "coming out" and revealing their identities and the upcoming sexless/genderless legal future. Hence, at the moment, the law is called to "transition" from binary to non-binary and in the future, to sexless/genderless. This transition will have to happen gradually as the binary has been prevailing for many decades and is enshrined deeply in the foundations of law and society. With this in mind, a possible solution to the current legal problems arising from intersex legal recognition would be to introduce a third blank box which will not introduce a "third gender" but it will operate as an alternative option for individuals who do not fit in the binary. Then, the applicants, based on their right to self-determination, they will be able to fill this option with the identity they desire i.e. intersex, queer, agender, trans. This could be a "transitional solution" that will guarantee sexual minorities' rights while both the laws and societies are preparing for the sexless/genderless future.

5.1.3 The Genderless Right to Found a Family

The Darlington Statement has called "for all adults to have the right to marry and form a family irrespective of their sex characteristics"[30] and the Public Statement by the Asian Intersex Movement has demanded to "ensure equal and non-discriminatory legal protection for intersex people in marriage and adoption laws".[31] The Council of Europe has also stressed that harmful surgeries performed on intersex individuals violate -among other rights- the right to found a family.[32] As it was already noted, the right to family for intersex does not only include civil unions, marriage and family-planning but the access to the wide range of Assisted Reproductive Technologies (ART) and adoption as well.

Malta is the only jurisdiction where intersex people can cohabitate, marry, adopt and access ART as all gender-specific references in Maltese law have been replaced with gender-neutral terminology. Then, there are several countries that passed leg-

[29] TGEU Position Paper on Gender Markers, 2018, p. 1.

[30] Darlington Statement, 2017, para. 12.

[31] Public Statement by the Asian Intersex Movement, 2018, para. 19.

[32] Council of Europe (2015), p. 25.

islation with the aim to recognise same-sex civil unions and marriage but as their wording is gender-neutral they also cover sexual minorities including intersex. In Chile, the Civil Code was amended to describe marriage as "the union between two people".[33] In Australia, the union of "a man and a woman" was amended to "two people".[34] In New Zealand, marriage was amended to be defined as "the union of two people, regardless of their sex, sexual orientation or gender identity".[35] In Greece, the law on civil unions provides for a contract between two adults, regardless of their gender/sex.[36] In Portugal, similar wording has been introduced enabling intersex to access civil unions, marriage and adoption. There are also cases where "sex" is not limited to binary categorisation under the law and therefore intersex persons are covered. In South Africa, "intersex" was included under the legal definition of "sex" and therefore the Civil Union Act applies to intersex as well, granting them the right to marry. In Austria and Germany, the introduction of the "third gender" has significantly impacted family law even though there is still no consensus on how the law must be interpreted after this evolution.

Bearing in mind all the above, a shift can be observed in family law where "families" are no longer limited between "men and women", departing from its previous "nuclear" sense to a broader or even sexless/genderless concept. It was mentioned earlier that in Germany, scholars have been already debating the emergence of a gender-neutral family law under the term "sexless family law".[37] Existing literature has challenged the traditional definitions of family and proposed alternative definitions for alternative forms of families. Herring, Probert and Gilmore, considered that "family" is a term of limited legal significance comparing to others such as "marriage", "parent" and "parenthood" and reflected on different approaches in defining "family". They introduced the "formalistic definition" which is certain under the law through i.e. marriage or civil partnership; the "function-based definition" that concerns the person caring for the child who needs the rights, duties and support of the law; "the normal meaning of the word" which is a social construct as there is no objective truth on what constitutes a family; the "self-definition approach" which relies on groups or pairs who identify as "families"; the "care-centred family law" which may also be called "sexless family law" and is not based on sexual relationships but on care and dependency, and the "no definition" where the law could rely on terms such as marriage, civil partnership and avoid defining the term "family".[38] They concluded that "the search for one perfect definition is likely to be doomed, but what we can strive for is the definition of "family" best suited to the

---

[33] Legislatura 365, Modifica diversos cuerpos legales para regular, en igualdad de condiciones, el matrimonio de parejas del mismo sexo.

[34] The Parliament of the Commonwealth of Australia, House of Representatives, Marriage Amendment Bill 2017.

[35] Marriage (Definition of Marriage) Amendment Act 2013, Section 2 amended.

[36] Greek Law regulating the Civil Union.

[37] See Büchler and Cottier (2015), pp. 115, 127 and 131–132.

[38] Herring et al. (2015), Debate 1 "What is a family?".

particular circumstances".[39] With this in mind, and considering the current circumstances and trends in law,[40] could a genderless family law guarantee intersex people's right to found a family?

Okin had elaborated on genderless families and how they could lead to justice between genders from a feminist perspective in her book "Justice, Gender, and the Family": "I claim that the genderless family is more just, in three important respects (…): it is more just to women; it is more conducive to equal opportunity both for women and for children of both sexes; and it creates a more favorable environment for the rearing of citizens of a just society. Thus, while protecting those whom gender now makes vulnerable, we must also put our best efforts into promoting the elimination of gender".[41] She also highlighted the benefits of a genderless society to children as "they would not suffer in the ways that they do now because of the injustices done to women".[42] When Okin wrote the book back in the 1990s, she was aiming to end injustices that occur within the binary; nowadays it is undeniable that the binary itself is also a source of injustice for whoever does not identify as male/female. From the above-examined jurisdictions, it is obvious that we are heading towards a genderless family law and considering that traditional family law "is unjust, excluding those who want to create family relationships but are denied the legal capacity to do so; perpetuating an unfair sex/gender system; educating children in injustice",[43] probably genderless/sexless family law would eliminate gender inequalities for both those who identify with the binary and those who fall outside of it.

5.1.4 *Discriminated Repeatedly*

The Malta Declaration has urged states "to build intersex anti-discrimination legislation in addition to other grounds, and to ensure protection against intersectional discrimination"[44] and that was also reaffirmed by the Public Statement by the African Intersex Movement.[45] The Statement of Riga and the Darlington Statement[46] have recommended "the adoption of anti-discrimination legislation on the ground of sex characteristics – regardless of the specific appearance or configuration of these characteristics".[47] The Vienna Statement has suggested that "if adding a new ground ("sex characteristics") is not an option "sex characteristics" should be

[39] Idem, p. 11.

[40] See also Eekelaar and Nhlap (1998).

[41] Okin Moller (1989), pp. 183–184.

[42] Idem, p. 184.

[43] Morgan and Douglas (1994), p. 52.

[44] OII Europe, Malta Declaration (2013), "Demands".

[45] Public Statement by the African Intersex Movement, 2017, "Demands".

[46] Darlington Statement, 2017, para. 9.

[47] OII Europe, Statement of Riga, 2014, para. 2.

included explicitly in the ground of "sex". Intersex people must benefit from the same rights and protections given to other citizens."[48] The Darlington Statement has addressed discrimination in employment in particular, and called for the ban of "genetic discrimination, including in insurance and employment".[49] Last, the Malta Statement, the Darlington Statement, the Public Statement by the African Intersex Movement and the Asian Intersex Movement have all called for equal participation and access in sports.

At international levels, significant steps have been taken to protect intersex people against discrimination. The UN Committee on Economic Social and Cultural Rights (CESCR), has stated that "other status" as recognised in Art. 2(2) of the ICESCR can be interpreted to include "intersex".[50] The Committee on the Elimination of All Forms of Discrimination Against Women (CEDAW) has issued recommendations and developed jurisprudence[51] on intersectional discrimination and has explicitly mentioned "intersex". The United Nations has urged governments to "ban discrimination on the basis of sex characteristics"[52] and the Council of Europe, in its report on the human rights of intersex people, has underlined the lack of anti-discrimination legislation on intersex which leads to impunity.[53]

At regional levels and with regards to the already examined jurisdictions, several steps have been taken as well to eliminate non-discrimination even though discrimination in sports and employment, which is among the primary demands of intersex organisations has not been tackled adequately. In Australia, the Sex Discrimination Act prohibits discrimination in employment, education, provision of services and accommodation under the ground of "intersex status". The Act contains two exemptions, the first applies to the internal appointment, training or practices with religious bodies and the second concerns sports but it is not applicable to children under 12 years old or persons participating in coaching, refereeing or administering sporting activities.[54] In Chile, the Act on System of Guarantees of Rights of the Childhood (Ley de Garantías y Derechos de la Niñez) protects intersex children from discrimination.[55] In South Africa, the Promotion of Equality and Prevention of Unfair Discrimination Act, 2000 was amended to include intersex in its definition of "sex". The Transgender Persons (Protection of Rights) Act in Pakistan bans discrimination against intersex people in employment. The ground "sex characteristics" is explicitly included in Greek, Portuguese and Maltese anti-discrimination law. Spain and

[48] OII Europe, Statement of the 1st European Intersex Community Event, 2017.

[49] Darlington Statement, 2017, para. 11.

[50] E/C.12/GC/20, 2009, para. 32.

[51] See Jallow v. Bulgaria, 2012; S.V.P. v. Bulgaria, 2012; Kell v. Canada, 2012; A.S. v. Hungary, 2006; R. P. B. v. the Philippines, 2014; M.W. v. Denmark, 2016, among others and inquiries (in particular, concerning Mexico (2005) and Canada (2015)).

[52] United NatIons Free & Equal, Fact Sheet "Intersex".

[53] Council of Europe (2015), p. 43.

[54] See Sex Discrimination Act 1984.

[55] MOVILH, "Camara de Diputados aprueba incorporar a niños y niñas LGBTI en proyecto de ley sobre derechos de la infancia".

the UK ban discrimination against intersex but only at regional levels. In Belgium, "sex" has been interpreted to include "intersex", in Finland intersex people are protected against discrimination under the ground "gender features of the body"[56] and in Slovenia, intersex persons are protected under the ground "any other personal circumstance".[57]

The situation on discrimination laws on intersex at regional levels can be portrayed as vague and confusing for several reasons. First, intersex people's legal demands to ensure protection against "intersectional discrimination" and discrimination on the ground of "sex characteristics" are unheard since Australia uses the term "intersex status" which has been heavily criticised by intersex organisations, Finland uses the wording "gender features of the body" which is irrelevant to intersex and unclear and Slovenia uses "any other personal circumstance" which is ambiguous as well. Moreover, there are several countries in the European Union (EU), as indicated above, which claim that intersex is protected under the ground "other". This term due to its broad understanding leaves intersex rights protection up to interpretation and this has been proved extremely risky since as it was already elaborated, justices tend to adopt a subjective perception rather than an objective perception on the matter of intersex due to its highly ethical nature.

Second, intersex people's discrimination in sports and employment as stressed by intersex organisations has not been addressed. Australia has passed anti-discrimination legislation regarding intersex participation in sports and employment, but the two included exemptions constitute the source of new discriminations for intersex. The first exemption prohibits the internal appointment, training or practices of intersex in religious bodies demonstrating the role that religion has played in the binary understanding of sex and gender roles and the pathologisation of intersex.[58] The second exemption limits access in sports for intersex in certain fields and at the same time promotes ageism.

Third and foremost, it is essential to realise that intersex people are discriminated repeatedly in all aspects of their lifetime: they are discriminated at birth by physicians, parents and the state as invasive and harmful surgeries are being performed to alter their bodies, fit them in the binary and recognise them legally. Then, they are discriminated when binary legal frameworks do not grant them the right to found a family and access equally employment and sports as the binary female/male majority. Hence, several questions may arise when examining current anti-discrimination legal frameworks on intersex. For instance, how effective is Chile's anti-discrimination laws on intersex children while at the same time, they are pathologised and subjected to surgeries? How effective are Greece's and Portugal's anti-discrimination laws while there is a lack of fair and comprehensive frameworks on intersex legal recognition? How certain is that in South Africa, justices will interpret discrimination based on "sex" as including intersex when intersex infanticide is

[56] ILGA Europe and OII Europe, 2015, p. 15.

[57] Constitution, Official Gazette of the Republic of Slovenia Nos. 33/91-I, 42/97, 66/2000, 24/03, 69/04, 68/06, and 47/13.

[58] See Sect. 1.4.1.

yet to be challenged in the country? Under the same token, Belgium may include "intersex" in the definition of "sex" but there is no legal framework on the legal recognition of intersex. Those issues highlight the need for effective anti-discrimination frameworks which must be coupled with comprehensive intersex legal frameworks in all spheres in order to protect intersex rights adequately. Legislative developments on intersex must be holistic and involve changes in all areas so that intersex individuals are granted the same rights as the binary majority and be able to live in equal and just societies. This may entail a reorientation of jurisdiction but Malta's comprehensive and fair legal framework on intersex shows that this is certainly "not outside the realms of possibility".[59]

5.2 Concluding Thoughts: Towards Equality for All

During the last 20 years, intersex persons have been addressing injustices and gross human rights violations that have been subjected to since birth and advocating for human rights and equality. Most of their legal demands remain unheard and they are yet to be adequately incorporated in the law. The vast majority of jurisdictions remains silent in front of repeated injustices and keeps on sacrificing intersex rights to preserve the rights of the majority despite all the efforts and calls of international human rights organisations and institutions. Nonetheless, there are numerous jurisdictions that have gradually started shifting from a binary to a non-binary legal understanding of "sex" and "gender". Some interpret "sex" to include intersex and others have reformed their legal frameworks to cover intersex rights. Moreover, there are jurisdictions that have started adopting gender-neutral terminology moving towards sexless/genderless laws that protect all individuals including those who fall both within and outside the binary. Hence, the findings of this research reveal that non-binary legal frameworks form part of a transitional era which is showing the way to a genderless/sexless legal future. The law is now called not only to accommodate non-binary individuals including intersex, but it has to confront the emerging sexless/genderless legal trend.

This is not the first time that legal frameworks are called to evolve to include those who are susceptible to violations because of their sex/gender. Women were completely invisible under the law for many decades and a typical example is the wording of the Universal Declaration of Human Rights where at first, references to "men" constituted a synonym for humanity; from 1947 to 1962 the Commission on the Status of Women succeeded to introduce more inclusive language in an effort to change discriminatory legislation and foster global awareness of women's rights.[60] Despite all the efforts made by women to be included in legal frameworks, gender inequality within the binary is still a reality. The United Nations has stressed that "gender equality is not only a fundamental human right, but a necessary foundation

[59] Garland and Mitchell (2018), p. 21.

[60] UN Women, "A brief history of the Commission on the Status of Women".

for a peaceful, prosperous and sustainable world" though it added that "while the world has achieved progress towards gender equality and women's empowerment (...), women and girls continue to suffer discrimination and violence".[61] The Council of Europe has highlighted that achieving gender equality "is central to the protection of human rights, the functioning of democracy, respect for the rule of law, and economic growth and competitiveness" and then has mentioned that "despite the improvement of women's legal status in Europe, effective equality is far from being a reality".[62]

Considering that the male/female binary constitutes a source of inequalities for both those who identify with it and those who do not, sexless/genderless equality may be the key to achieve equality for all. Okin has argued that the elimination of gender will lead to increased justice to women and the "standards of justice would become humanist, as they have never been before".[63] In the same fashion, the elimination of gender could also lead to increased justice to all individuals who do not identify with the binary and this democratic lawmaking could give rise to a political order founded upon human rights.[64] Future laws will be about "persons" or "persons regardless of gender" as in the examples of several countries such as Malta, Greece, Australia, New Zealand. At the moment, sexless/genderless law has started appearing mostly in family law, but discussions have been growing for its expansion in other fields such as legal recognition which constitutes a cornerstone for non-binary individuals. The Malta Declaration explicitly states that "in the future, as with race or religion, sex or gender should not be a category on birth certificates or identification documents for anybody".[65]

The transformation from binary frameworks to sexless/genderless frameworks has started happening already as jurisdictions are experiencing a transitional era during which they are moving from the binary past, to the non-binary present and probably later to the genderless/sexless future. Currently, jurisdictions are facing a new reality where individuals are "coming out" as non-binary and demand justice and equal rights. Some jurisdictions are reforming their laws to accommodate emerging needs but probably the key for this transitional period lies in interpretation. It is now evident that genders are not two and the case of intersex people shows that sexes are not two either. In addition, there are several human rights documents issued by international human rights organisations calling for the recognition of intersex. Consequently, sex cannot be anymore interpreted as binary but rather as a "spectrum" or a "continuum". The European Union set the example when Advocate General Tesauro in his opinion on the P. v. S. case in 1995, stated that "it is necessary to go beyond the traditional classification and recognize that, in addition to the man/woman dichotomy, there is a range of characteristics, behaviour and roles

[61] UN Sustainable Development Goals, "Goal 5: Achieve gender equality and empower all women and girls".

[62] Council of Europe (2015), p. 2.

[63] Okin Moller (1989), p. 184.

[64] Habermas (2010), p. 469.

[65] OII Europe, Malta Declaration (2013), "Demands".

shared by men and women, so that sex itself ought rather to be thought of as a continuum".[66] Intersex rights organisations have been also calling for a broader interpretation of sex, and the Statement of Riga has urged for the challenge of "the definition of sex as consisting of only male and female and promote the knowledge that sex is a continuum, as is gender".[67] Interpretation may be a daunting task, as it may entail sharp decisions as far as ethics and human rights are concerned and in this regard, the justices, following modern societal and legal developments on sex and gender, should use intersex as a means to interpret "sex" in a broad way and administer justice. Then, "conceiving of intersex as an aspect of sex would also allow for additional, specific legislative action".[68]

To sum up, the findings of this research have demonstrated that legal frameworks despite their flaws, have started slowly embracing the sex/gender non-binary but above all, it is confirmed that sexless/genderless law is not an idea, nor a theoretical concept, it is a reality that is gradually growing and is paving the way to the formulation of a new concept of equality beyond binaries. In the sexless/genderless future, equality will not be about sexes and genders but about humans; till then, intersex should be used as a means to introduce inclusive laws and eliminate inequalities.

[66] P. v S. AND Cornwall County Council Opinion of Advocate General Tesauro delivered on 14 December 1995, para. 17.

[67] OII Europe, Statement of Riga, 2014, objective 1.

[68] Tobler (2014), p. 541. See also Palk and Grunsted (2018).

Bibliography

Books

Akchurin W, Kartzke R (2007) The ethics of gender selection. In: McIntosh D, Drabic R, Huber K, Vinogradov I, Bassick M (eds) The ethical imperative in the context of evolving technologies. University of Colorado Leeds School of Business, pp 21–33
Anderson SP (2009) Feminism and patriarchy. In: Hass A, Jasper D, Jay E (eds) The Oxford handbook of English literature and theology. Oxford Handbooks Online
Barak A (2007) Purposive interpretation in law. Princeton University Press
Bourdieu P (1998) Masculine domination. Stanford University Press
Büchler A, Cottier M (2015) Intersexualität, Transsexualität und das Recht" Geschlechtsfreiheit und körperliche Integrität als Eckpfeiler einer neuen Konzeption. Freiburger FrauenStudien 17, (in German only). https://www.ius.uzh.ch/dam/jcr:54618db1-62b2-43b8-9b2f-4e77e77d40d2/BuechlerCottierIntersexualitaetTranssexualitaetRecht.pdf
Butler J (1990) Gender trouble, feminism and the subversion of identity. Routledge
Butler J (2004) Undoing gender. Routledge, New York
Cawadias AP (1943) Hermaphroditus the human intersex. Heinemann Medical Books, London
Colapinto J (2000) As nature made him. Harper Collins
Dagtoglou Prodromos D (2005) Human Rights, Sakoulas, (in Greek)
Davis G (2011) DSD is a perfectly fine term: reasserting medical authority through a shift in intersex terminology. In: PJ MG, Hutson DJ (eds) Sociology of diagnosis (advances in medical sociology), vol 12. Emerald Group Publishing Limited, pp 155–182
De Beauvoir S (1949) Le Deuxième Sexe, Première partie: formation. Gallimard, Paris. (in French)
Dreger AD (1999) A history of intersexuality. In: Dreger AD (ed) Intersex in the age of ethics. University Publishing Group, Hagerstown
Eekelaar J, Nhlap T (eds) (1998) The changing family, international perspectives on the family and family law private bodies. Hart
Fausto-Sterling A (2000a) Sexing the body. Basic Books
Feder KE (2014) Making sense of intersex: changing ethical perspectives in biomedicine. Indiana University Press
Fekete B (2011) Cultural comparative law? In: Cserne P, Könczöl M (eds) . Legal and political theory in the post-national age, Peter Lang, pp 40–51
Fenton-Glynn C (2018) Australia. In: Scherpe MJ, Dutta A, Helms T (eds) . The legal status of intersex persons, Intersentia, pp 243–254
Foucault M (1977) Discipline and punish. Pantheon Books

N. Pikramenou, *Intersex Rights*, https://doi.org/10.1007/978-3-030-27554-9

Foucault M (1980) Herculine Barbin: being the recently discovered memoirs of a nineteenth century French hermaphrodite (trans: McDougall R). Pantheon Books, New York
Foucault M (1990) Objective. In: The history of sexuality. Vintage, New York
Foucault M (1996) The social extension of the norm in foucault live: collected interviews, 1961–1984. In: Lotringer S (ed) (trans: Honchroth L, Johnston J), 2nd edn. Semiotext (e), New York
Foucault M (2012a) The history of sexuality: an introduction, vol 1, initially published in 1990. Knopf Doubleday Publishing Group
Foucault M (2012b) The history of sexuality: the use of pleasure, initially published in 1984, vol 2. Knopf Doubleday Publishing Group
Foucault M (2012) The history of sexuality: the care of the self, initially published in 1984, vol 3. Knopf Doubleday Publishing Group
Fountedaki K (2004) Civil medical liability (in Greek). Sakkoulas
Fountedaki K (2017) The draft law of the legislative committee of the Ministry of Justice on the recognition of gender identity (in Greek). In: The recognition of gender identity in view of the draft law of the legislative committee of the Ministry of Justice. Sakkoulas, pp 59–80
Galanou M (2014) Gender identity and expression: terminology, distinctions, stereotypes and myths. Transgender Association. (in Greek)
Garland J (2016) On science, law, and medicine: the case of gender- "normalizing" interventions on children who are diagnosed as different in sex development. Uppsala University
Ghattas C (2013) Human Rights between sexes: a preliminary study on the life situations of inter∗ individuals. Heinrich Böll Foundation
Glenn HP (2010) Legal traditions of the world. Oxford University Press
Greenberg J (2018) United States. In: Scherpe MJ, Dutta A, Helms T (eds) The legal status of intersex persons, Intersentia, pp 339–356
Greer S, Gerards J, Slowe R (2018) Human rights in the Council of Europe and the European Union. Cambridge University Press
Hall K, Bucholtz M (eds) (1995) Gender articulated: language and the socially constructed self. Routledge, London
Harding R (2011) Regulating sexuality: legal consciousness in lesbian and gay lives, Winner of the Hart-SLSA Socio-Legal Book Prize 2011, and the Hart-SLSA Early Career Prize 2011. Routledge
Herring J, Probert R, Gilmore S (2015) Great debates in family law, 2nd edn. Palgrave
Higgins R (2012) Themes and theories. Oxford Scholarship Online
Holmes M (2007) What is gender? Sociological approaches. SAGE Publications
Huffer L (2009) Rethinking the foundations of queer theory. Columbia University Press
Husa J (2015) A new introduction to comparative law. Hart
Jellinek G (2011) System of subjective public rights (in German), 2nd Revised edn. Siebeck Mohr
Johnson LJ, Repta R (2012) Sex and gender. Beyond the binaries. In: Oliffe JL, Greaves L (eds) Designing and conducting gender, sex, and health research. Sage, pp 17–39
Jones M (2018) Intersex genital mutilation- a western version of fgm. In: Freeman M (ed) Children's rights: new issues, new themes, new perspectives, Brill
Kanellopoulou-Malouhou N (2012) "The emancipation of Europe" (in Greek). Papazisi Publishing
Kangaude G, Afulukwe O, Ntwari G et al (2017) Legal grounds: reproductive and sexual rights in Sub-Saharan African Courts, vol III. Pretoria University Law Press
Karkazis K (2008) Fixing sex: intersex, medical authority, and lived experience. Duke University Press
Kasimatis G (1980) "Constitutional Law II" (in Greek). Sakkoulas
Kessler JS (1998) Lessons from the intersexed. Rutgers University Press
Klöppel U (2016) Zur Aktualität kosmetischer Operationen "uneindeutiger Genitalien im Kindesalter(in German), Volume 42 of Zentrum für Transdisziplinäre Geschlechterstudien: Texte, Bulletin, Humboldt-Universität zu Berlin, Zentrum für Transdisziplinäre Geschlechterstudien
Korff D (2006) The right to life: a guide to the implementation of Article 2 of the European Convention on Human Rights. In: Human rights handbooks No. 8, Council of Europe, pp 6–8

Kosta V, Skoutaris N, Tzevelekos V (2014) The EU accession to the ECHR, modern studies in European law. Hart

Kuhnle S, Sander A (2010) The emergence of the welfare state. In: Castles FC, Leibfried S, Lewis J, Obinger H, Pierson C (eds) The Oxford handbook of the welfare state. Oxford University Press, Oxford

Koyama E, Lisa Weasel (2001) Teaching intersex issues: a guide for teachers in women's, gender & queer studies. Intersex Society of North America, June 3 http://isna.org/pdf/teaching-intersex-web.pdf

Lind AS (2011) The Right to Health from a Constitutional Perspective – the Example of the Nordic Countries, in Nordic Health Law in a European Context Welfare State Perspectives on Patients' Rights and Biomedicine. International Law E-books online, pp 67–76

Linda LL (2014) Gender roles: a sociological perspective, the sociology of gender theoretical perspectives and feminist frameworks. Routledge

Lindsey LL (2014) Chapter 1, The sociology of gender theoretical perspectives and feminist frameworks. In: Gender roles: a sociological perspective. Routledge, London

Manesis A (1982) Constitutional rights (in Greek). Sakkoulas

Michaels R (2011) Comparative law, section of the book Oxford handbook of European private law. In: Basedow J, Hopt K, Zimmermann R (eds) Oxford University Press, the section consulted in this thesis is available here https://scholarship.law.duke.edu/cgi/viewcontent.cgi?article=3014&context=faculty_scholarship

Mill SJ (1859) On liberty. Batoche Books, Kitchener, p 2001

Monateri PG (ed) (2012) Methods of comparative law. Research handbooks in comparative law, Edward Elgar Publishing Limited

Morgan A, Douglas J (1994) Constituting families: a study in governance: United Kingdom association for legal and social philosophy. Franz Steiner Verlag

Morland I (2006) Postmodern intersex in ethics and intersex. Springer, Netherlands

Namwase S, Jjuuko A (2017) Protecting the human rights of sexual minorities in contemporary Africa. In: Scheepers E, Lakhani I (eds) Somewhere over the rainbow: the continued struggle for the realisation of Lesbian and Gay Rights in South Africa. Pretoria University Law Press

Nanda S (1999) "Neither Man nor Woman" The Hijras of India. Wadsworth Publishing Company

Ní Mhuirthile T (2015) Building bodies: a legal history of intersex in ireland in sexual politics in modern Ireland. Irish Academic Press

Okin Moller S (1989) Justice, gender and the family. Basic Books, Inc., Publishers, New York

Papadopoulou L (2015) The legal notion of "family" and same sex couples: lessons from the ECtHR (in Greek). In: The book in honour of Efi Kounougeri-Manoledaki. Sakkoulas, pp 1–56

Papadopoulou L (2017) The constitutional foundation of the right to harmonise psycho-social and legal gender (in Greek) in the draft law of the legislative committee of the Ministry of Justice on the recognition of gender identity. Sakkoulas, pp 37–59

Papadopoulou L (2019) Sexual orientation and gender identity law in the European Union and its Court of Justice. In: Ziegler AR (ed) Oxford handbook of international LGBTI law-sexual orientation, gender identity, gender expression and sex characteristics (SOGIESC) law from an international-comparative perspective. Oxford University Press

Papantoniou N (1983) General principles of civil law (in Greek). Sakkoulas

Papazisi T (2007) Same-sex family. In: Chatzitryfon N, Papazisi T (eds) Same-sex families (in Greek). Epikentro

Peters A (2016) Beyond human rights, the legal status of the individual in international law. Cambridge University Press

Pierceson J, Piatti-Crocker A, Schulenberg S (2013) Same-sex marriage in Latin America: promise and resistance. Rowman & Littlefield

Plant Raymond (2010) The Neo-liberal State. University Press Scholarship Online, Oxford Scholarship Online

Plato, Symposium, Written 360 B.C.E. E-book

Prerna R (2013) Foucault's ethics: living as a middle sex or intersex subject. A project for American University

Preves ES (2008) Intersex and identity: the contested self. Rutgers University Press
Reimann M, Zimmermann R (eds) (2006) The Oxford Handbook of Comparative Law, Oxford, Chapter 10 by Ralf Michael is consulted in this thesis, available here https://scholarship.law.duke.edu/cgi/viewcontent.cgi?article=2033&context=faculty_scholarship
Rubio-Marín R (2018) Colombia. In: Scherpe MJ, Dutta A, Helms T (eds) The legal status of intersex persons. Intersentia, pp 319–338
Scherpe MJ (ed) (2015) The legal status of transsexual and transgender persons. Intersentia
Scherpe MJ, Dutta A, Helms T (eds) (2018) The legal status of intersex persons. Intersentia
Schiek D, Waddington L, Bell M (2007) Cases, materials and text on national, supranational and international non-discrimination law: Ius Commune casebooks for the common law of Europe. Hart, Oxford
Siculus D (1935) Library of history, Book IV, Loeb Classical Library Volumes 303 and 340, C.H. Oldfather. Harvard University Press, Cambridge
Spargo T (1999) Foucault and queer theory, Icon Books UK. Totem Books USA
Speer AS (2004) Gender talk: feminism, discourse and conversation analysis. Routledge
Sytsma ES (2006) Ethics and intersex. Springer
The Netherlands Institute for Social Research (2014) Living with intersex/DSD. Netherlands Institute for Social Research
Tsatsos D (1988) Constitutional law (in Greek). Sakkoulas
Van den Brink M (2018) The Netherlands. In: Scherpe MJ, Dutta A, Helms T (eds) The legal status of intersex persons. Intersentia, pp 293–304
Van Kersbergen K, Vis B (2014) Comparative welfare state politics. development, opportunities, and reform. Cambridge University Press, Cambridge
Vidalis T (1996) The constitutional dimension in marriage and family (in Greek). Sakkoulas
Waaldijk C, Bonini-Baraldi MT (2006) Sexual orientation discrimination in the European Union: national laws and the employment equality directive. Leiden University
Ward MRM (2016) The importance of gender reflexivity in the research process, gender identity and research relationships, studies in qualitative methodology, vol 14. Emerald Group Publishing Limited
Weatherill S (2016) Law and values in the European Union. Oxford University Press
Zweigert K, Koetz H (1998) An introduction to comparative law, 3rd edn. Oxford University Press

Journals

Alderson P (2007) Competent children? Minors consent to health care treatment and research. Soc Sci Med 65:2272–2283
Andorno R (2014) Human dignity and human rights. ResearchGate, 45–57
Araceli G-V (2009) Michel Foucault, Judith Butler and Intersexuality's critical, subversive and deconstructive bodies and identities. ResearchGate, 235–244
Arora P (2017) Right to access reproductive technologies – a right or a wrong? J For Med Leg Aff 2(1):114
Arribas VG, Carrasco L (2003) Gender equality and the EU, an assessment of the current issues. Eipascope 1:22–30
Baratz BA (2016) Re: "Surgery in disorders of sex development (DSD) with a gender issue: If (why), when, and how?". J Pediatr Urol 12(6):442–443
Bauer GR, Hammond R, Travers R, Kaay M, Hohenadel K, Boyce M (2009) I don't think this is theoretical; this is our lives: how erasure impacts health care for transgender people. J Assoc Nurs AIDS Care 20(5):348–361
Bayefsky JM (2016) Comparative preimplantation genetic diagnosis policy in Europe and the USA and its implications for reproductive tourism. Reprod Biomed Soc Online 3:41–47
Becker M (1999) Patriarchy and inequality: towards a substantive feminism. Univ Chicago Legal Forum 1999(1):21–88

Behrmann J, Ravitsky V (2013) Queer liberation, not elimination: why selecting against intersex is not "straight" forward. Am J Bioethics 13(10):39–59

Ben-Asher N (2006) The necessity of sex change: a struggle for intersex and transsex liberties. Harv J Law Gender 29:51–98

Blackless M, Charuvastra AD, Fausto-Sterling A, Lauzanne K, Lee E (2000) How sexually dimorphic are we? Review and synthesis. Am J Human Biol 12:151–166

Blackstone MA (2003) Gender roles and society In: Julia RM, Richard ML, Lawrence BS (eds) Human ecology: an encyclopedia of children, families, communities, and environments. Santa Barbara, pp 335–338

Bonilla D (2016) Parejas Del Mismo Sexo En Colombia: Tres Modelos Para Su Reconocimiento Jurídico Y Político (Same-Sex Couples in Colombia: three models for their Legal and Political Recognition) SSRN: https://ssrn.com/abstract=2772232 or https://doi.org/10.2139/ssrn.2772232

Butler J (1988) Performative acts and gender constitution: an essay in phenomenology and feminist theory. Theatre J 40(4):519–531

Campbell M (2015) CEDAW and women's intersecting identities: a pioneering new approach to intersectional discrimination. Revista Direito GV, São Paulo 11(2):479–504

Carpenter M (2016) The human rights of intersex people: addressing harmful practices and rhetoric of change. Reprod Health Matters 46(47):74–84

Chan RW, Raboy B, Patterson CJ (1998) Psychosocial adjustment among children conceived via donor insemination by lesbian and heterosexual mothers. Child Dev 69:443–457

Chase C (1998) Hermaphrodites with attitude: mapping the emergence of intersex political activism. GLQ A J Lesbian Gay Stud 4(2):189–211

Chase C (2002) "Cultural practice" or "reconstructive surgery"? U.S. genital cutting, the intersex movement, and medical double standards. In: Stanlie MJ, Robertson CC (eds) Genital cutting and transnational sisterhood: disputing US polemics. University of Illinois Press, Urbana, pp 126–152

Chopin T, Macek L (2018) In the face of the European Union's political crisis: the vital cultural struggle over values. Fondation Robert Shuman The Research and Studies Centre on Europe. European Issue no 479

Chung H (2018) The impossibility of liberal rights in a diverse word. Economics and philosophy. Cambridge University Press, pp 1–27

Cornwall S (2009) Theologies of resistance: intersex/DSD, disability and queering the real world. In: Holmes M (ed) Critical intersex. Ashgate, Farnham

Cornwall S (2013) Asking about what is better: intersex, disability, and inaugurated eschatology. J Religion Disability Health 17(4):369–392

Cornwall S (2014) Sex otherwise: intersex, christology, and the maleness of jesus. J Feminist Stud Religion 30(2):23–39

Cornwall S (2015) Intersex and the rhetorics of disability and disorder: multiple and provisional significance in sexed, gender, and disabled bodies. J Disability Religion 19(2):106–118

Corrales J (2015) The politics of LGBT rights in Latin America and the Carribean: research Agenda. Eur Rev Latin Am Caribb Stud 100:53–62

Creighton MS, Michala L, Mushtaq I, Yaron M (2014) Childhood surgery for ambiguous genitalia: glimpses of practice changes or more of the same. Psychol Sex 5(1):34–43

Creighton S (2001) Surgery for intersex. J Royal Soc Med 94(5):218–220

Creighton S, Minto C (2001) Managing intersex: most vaginal surgery in childhood should be deferred. BMJ 323(7324):1264–1265

Crissman HP, Warner L, Gardner M, Carr M, Schast A, Quittner AL, Kogan B, Sandberg DE (2011) Children with disorders of sex development: a qualitative study of early parental experience. Int J Pediart Endocrinol 1(10). https://doi.org/10.1186/1687-9856-2011-10

Cruz BD (2016) Transgender rights after obergefell. UMKC Law Rev 84(3):692–705

Daaboul J, Frader J (2001) Ethics and the management of the patient with intersex: a middle way. J Pediatr Endocrinol Metab 14(9):1575–1583

Damiano L (2011) When parents can choose to have the "Perfect" child: why fertility clinics should be required to report preimplantation genetic diagnosis data. Family Court Rev 49(4):846–859
Daukšiené I, Grigonis S (2015) Accession of the EU to the ECHR: issues of the co-respondent mechanism. Int Comp Jurisp 1(2):98–105
Davis G (2013) The social costs of preempting intersex traits. Am J Bioethics 13(10):51–53
Dayner EJ, Lee AP, Hook PC (2004) Medical treatment of intersex: parental perspectives. J Urol 172(4):1762–1765
De Suttler P (2001) Gender reassignment and assisted reproduction, present and future reproductive options for transsexual people. Human Reprod 16(4):612–614
Defeis FE (1999) The treaty of Amsterdam: the next step towards gender equality? Boston Coll Int Comp Law Rev 23(1)
DeLaet LD (2012) Genital autonomy, children's rights, and competing rights claims in international human rights law. Int J Children's Rights 20:554–583
Devine WJ (2018) Gender, steroids, and fairness in sport. Ethics Philos 13(2):161–169. https://doi.org/10.1080/17511321.2017.1404627
Diamond M, Garland J (2014) Evidence regarding cosmetic and medically unnecessary surgery on infants. J Pediatr Urol 10(1):2–6
Dorumat-Dreger A (1998) Ambiguous sex or ambivalent medicine? Hast Center Rep 28(3):24–35
Ehrenreich N, Mark B (2005) Intersex surgery, female genital cutting, and the selective condemnation of "cultural practices". Harv Civil Rights Civil Liber Law Rev 40:72–140
Ehrhardt AA (2007) John Money, Ph.D. J Sex Res 44(3):223–224
Engstrom P (2017) Human rights: effectiveness of international and regional mechanisms. International Studies Association and Oxford University Press, http://internationalstudies.oxfordre.com/view/10.1093/acrefore/9780190846626.001.0001/acrefore-9780190846626-e-214. Accessed 10 July 2018
Fausto-Sterling A (1993) The five sexes: why male and female are not enough. Sciences, 20–24. https://www.researchgate.net/profile/Anne_Fausto-Sterling/publication/239657377_The_Five_Sexes_Why_Male_and_Female_are_not_Enough/links/00b7d525802a725b6b000000/The-Five-Sexes-Why-Male-and-Female-are-not-Enough.pdf. Accessed 8 Sept 2018
Fausto-Sterling A (2000b) The five sexes, revisited. Sciences 40(4). https://pdfs.semanticscholar.org/21a4/4d10b40354a974c8d1d3a9a0e66fef731e75.pdf. Accessed 10 Dec 2018
Feder EK, Dreger A (2016) Still ignoring human rights in intersex care. J Pediatr Urol 12(6):436–437
Fessas GA (2011) National Report: Greece. J Gender Soc Policy Law 19(1):187–209
Ford K (2001) "First, do no harm": the fiction of legal parental consent to genital-normalizing surgery on intersexed infants. Yale Law Policy Rev 19(2):469–488
Fujimura M (2000) The welfare state, the middle class, and the welfare society. Rev Popul Soc Policy 9:1–23
Garland F, Mitchell T (2018) Legislating intersex equality: building the resilience of intersex people through law. Legal Stud 38(4):587–606
Garland J (2006) Sex as a form of gender and expression after lawrence v Texas. Columbia J Gender Law 15:297–324
Glenn HP (2007) "The National Tradition". Electronic J Comp Law 11(3). https://www.ejcl.org/113/article113-1.pdf
Goodliffe J, Hawkins GD (2006) Explaining commitment: states and the convention against torture. J Polit 68(2):358–371
Gough B, Weyman N, Alderson J, Butler G, Stoner M (2008) They did not have a word': the parental quest to locate a 'true sex' for their intersex children. Psychol Health 23(4):493–507
Greenberg J, Herald M, Strasser M (2010) Beyond the Binary: what can feminists learn from intersex transgender jurisprudence. Michigan J Gender Law 17(1):13–37
Habermas J (2010) The concept of human dignity and the realistic Utopia of human rights. Metaphilosophy 41(4):464–480
Haig D (2004) The inexorable rise of gender and the decline of sex: social change in academic titles, 1945–2001. Arch Sex Behav 33(2):87–96

Hathaway O (2002) Do human rights treaties make a difference?. Yale Law J 111(8):1935–2042
Henkin L (1989) The universality of the concept of human rights. The annals of the American Academy of political and social science. Sage Publications, Inc. in association with the American Academy of political and social science. Human Rights Around World 506(1):10–16
Herek GM (2000) The psychology of sexual prejudice. Curr Dir Psycol Sci 9:19–22
Hermer L (2002) Paradigms revised: intersex children, bioethics & the law. Ann Health Law 11(1):195
Hester JD (2004a) Intersex (es) and informed consent: how physicians' rhetoric constraints choice. Theoretical Medicine, Kluwer Academic Publishers 25:21–49
Hester JD (2004b) Intersexes and the end of gender: corporeal ethics and postgender bodies. J Gender Stud 13(3):215–225
Hoecke VM (2015) Methodology of comparative legal research. Law Method, 1–35. https://doi.org/10.5553/rem/.000010
Holmes M (2011) The intersex enchiridion: naming and knowledge in the clinic. Somatechnics 1(2):87–114
Hunter DN (2001) The sex discrimination argument in gay rights. J Law Policy, 397–416
Ilyayambwa M (2012) Homosexual rights and the law: a South African constitutional metamorphosis. Int J Humanit Soc Sci 2(4):50–58
Ireland-Piper D, Weinert K (2014) Is there a "Right" to Sport?. Bond University. Sports Law e-journal, https://works.bepress.com/danielle_irelandpiper/. Accessed 10 Feb 2018
Ittelson A, Tamar-Mattis A (2016) Avoiding liability in the treatment of intersex patients. J Pediatr Urol 16(6):439–440
Jobson AG, Theron BL, Kaggwa KJ, Kim H-J (2012) Transgender in Africa: Invisible, inaccessible, or ignored? SAHARA-J: J Soc Aspects HIV/AIDS 9(3):160–163
Jones G (2001) Proper judicial activism. Regent Univ Law Rev 14:141–179
Jones L (2009) The third sex: gender identity development of intersex persons. Grad J Couns Psychol 1(2):10–16
Kahn JA (2002) Explaining the Welfare State. The University of Chicago Press. Soc Serv Rev 76(75th Anniversary):189–195
Karavokyris G (2015) Family life and personal autonomy. Marangopoulos Foundation for Human Rights, Civil partnership of same sex couples. The adaptation of the greek legislation. Andy's Publisher, pp 87–97
Kazyak E, Burke K, Stange M (2018) Logics of freedom: debating religious freedom laws and gay and lesbian rights. Socius Sociol Res Dynamic World 4(18). https://doi.org/10.1177/2378023118760413
Kennedy A (2016) Fixed at birth: medical and legal erasures of intersex variations. UNSW Law J 39(2):813–842
Kerry S (2009) Are you a boy or a girl? Foucault and the intersex. ResearchGate. https://www.researchgate.net/publication/228791097_Are_you_a_boy_or_a_girl_Foucault_and_the_intersex_movement. Accessed 1 Sept 2018
Kessler JS (1990) The medical construction of gender: case management of intersex infants. Signs J Women Cult Soc 16(1):3–21
Kim SK, Kim J (2012) Disorders of sex development. Korean J Urol 53:1–8
Kishka-Kamari F (2001) "First, do no harm": the fiction of legal parental consent to genital-normalizing surgery on intersexed infants. Yale Law Policy Rev 19(2):469–488
Koh HH (1997) Why do nations obey international law? Yale Law J 106(8):2599–2659
Koppelman A (1995) Why discrimination against lesbians and gay men is sex discrimination. N Y Univ Law Rev 69(2)
Lane J-E, Mæland R (1998) Welfare states or welfare societies? Statsvetenskaplig Tidskrift 2:1–20
Lauri S (2011) Gender identity discrimination in European judicial discourse. Equal Rights Rev 7:11–26
Lee AP, Nordenström A, Houk PC, Ahmed SF, Auchus R, Baratz A, Baratz DK, Liao L-M, Lin-Su K, Looijenga 3rd LH, Mazur T, Meyer-Bahlburg HF, Mouriquand P, Quigley AC, Sandberg

ED, Vilain E, Witchel S and the Global DSD Update Consortium (2016) Global disorders of sex development update since 2006: perceptions, approach and care. Hormone Res Pediatr 85:158–180
Logie HC, James L, Tharao W, Loutfy RM (2012) We don't exist: a qualitative study of marginalization experienced by HIV-positive lesbian, bisexual, queer and transgender women in Toronto, Canada. J Int AIDS Soc 15(2). https://doi.org/10.7448/IAS.15.2.17392
Lundberg T, Hegarty P, Roen K (2018) Making sense of 'Intersex' and 'DSD': how laypeople understand and use terminology. Psychol Sex 9(2). https://doi.org/10.1080/19419899.2018.1453862
Macioce F (2011) Individual liberty and self-determination. Libertarian Pap 3(3):1–18
Magritte E (2012) Working together in placing the long term interests of the child at the heart of the DSD evaluation. J Pediatr Urol 8(6):571–575
Mallios V (2010) Ensuring civil-unions for same sex couples: Greek reality and European dimension (ECHR). https://www.constitutionalism.gr/1583-katohyrwsi-symbiwsis-omofylwn-elliniki-pragmatikot/ Accessed 10 July 2018
Mallios V. A right to marry: Constitutional privilege of Heterosexuals or Right of Homosexuals as well? www.manesis.blogspot.com Accessed 5 Jul 2018
Mather L (2013) Law and society, The Oxford Handbook of Political Science, Oxford Handbooks Online. http://www.oxfordhandbooks.com/view/10.1093/oxfordhb/9780199604456.001.0001/oxfordhb-9780199604456-e-015?print=pdf. Accessed 30 May 2019
McKayl T, Angotti N (2016) Ready rhetorics: political homophobia and activist discourses in Malawi, Nigeria, and Uganda. Springer Science+Business Media, New York. https://doi.org/10.1007/s11133-016-9342-7
Meier SC, Labuski MC (2013) The demographics of the transgender population", international handbook on the demography of sexuality. Springer Science+Business, pp 289–327. https://doi.org/10.1007/978-94-007-5512-3_16
Money J (1955) Hermaphroditism, gender and precocity in hyperadrenocorticism: psychologic findings. Bull Johns Hopkins Hosp 96(6):253–264
Moravscik A, Nicolaïdis K (1999) Explaining the treaty of Amsterdam: interests, influence, institutions. J Common Mark Stud 37(1):59–85
Morland I (2009) What can queer theory do for intersex?. J Lesbian Gay Stud, Duke University Press, 15(2):285–312
Morton-Brown M (1999) Queer linguistics vs. compulsory heterosexuality. Text Perform Q 19(3):248–256
Mos M (2013) Conflicted normative power Europe: the European Union and sexual minority rights. J Contemp Eur Res 9(1):78–93
Mos M (2014) Of Gay rights and christmas ornaments: the political history of sexual orientation non-discrimination in the treaty of Amsterdam. J Common Mark Stud 52(3):632–649
Mouriquand PDE, Brindusa GD, Gay C-L, Meyer-Bahlburg HFL, Baker L, Baskin LS, Bouvattier C, Braga LH, Caldamone AC, Duranteau L, Ghoneimim AEL, Hensle TW, Hoebeke P, Kaefer M, Kalfa N, Kolon TF, Manzoni G, Mure P-Y, Lee P (2016) Surgery in disorders of sex development (DSD) with a gender issue: If (why), when, and how? J Pedriatr Urol 12(93):139–149
Nagle-Ortiz EL (1995) Evolution of the Colombian judiciary and the constitutional court. Indiana Int Comp Law Rev 6:78–93
Newbould MJ (2016) What do we do about women athletes with testes? Med Ethics 42:256–259
Nisker J (2013) Informed choice and PGD to prevent "intersex conditions". Am J Bioeth 13(10):47–49
Ocampo BM (2011) "Sex" in the workplace: approaches to sexual orientation and gender identity discrimination in the workplace absent anti-discrimination law. Philipp Law J 86:190–232
Oshri O, Sheafer T, Shenhav RS (2016) A community of values: democratic identity formation in the European Union. Eur Union Polit Sage J 17(1):114–137
Pachmann A (2017) Crisis of values in the European Union. Reg Form Dev Stud 22(2):133–142
Palk L, Grunsted S (2018) Born free: toward an expansive definition of sex. Michigan J Gender Law 25(1). https://repository.law.umich.edu/mjgl/vol25/iss1/2. Accessed 15 Dec 2018

Papadopoulou L (2001–2002) In(di)Visible Citizens(hip): same-sex partners in European Union immigration law. Yearb Eur Law 21:229–262
Papadopoulou L (2008) Same-sex marriage. Dikaiomata tou Anhtropou (Journal) 38/2008, 405 (in Greek)
Parker GR (2007) Sexuality, health and human rights. Am J Public Health 97(6):972–973
Pervou I (2014) Commentary on the ECHR case "Vallianatos and Others v. Greece". https://www.constitutionalism.gr/vallianatos-comment-pervou/. Accessed 5 July 2018
Pitsiladis Y, Harper J, Betancurt OJ, Matrinez-Patino M-J, Parisi A, Wang G, Pigozzi F (2016) Beyond fairness: the biology of inclusion for transgender and intersex athletes. Curr Sports Med Rep 15(6):386–388
Puppinck G (2012) Prohibition of pre-implantation genetic diagnosis: the ECHR censors the Italian law. Eur Centre Law Just, 386–388. https://eclj.org/eugenics/echr/prohibition-of-pre-implantation-genetic-diagnosis-the-echr-censors-the-italian-law. Accessed 2 Dec 2017
Reis E (2007) Divergence or disorder: the politics of naming intersex. Perspect Biol Med 50(4):535–543
Reis E, Kessler S (2010) Why history matters: fetal sex and intersex. Am J Bioeth 10(9):58–59
Robertson AJ (2003) Procreative liberty in the era of genomics. Am J Law Med 29:439–487
Rodriguez Rust P (2000) Bisexuality: a contemporary paradox for women. J Soc Issues 56(2):205–221
Rosenbloom A (2014) LGBT discrimination in Africa. Kaleidoscope J 5(2):54–70
Rudevska B (2018) Interpretation of the concept *Gender* in legal discourse. Baltic J English Lang Liter Cult 8:101–119
Salako SE (2011) Informed consent under the European Convention on biomedicine and the UNESCO declaration on bioethics. Med Law 30(1):101–113
Sax L (2002) How common is intersex? A response to Anne Fausto-Sterling. J Sex Res 39(3):174–178
Shanner L (1995) The right to procreate: when rights claims have gone wrong. McGill Law J 40:823–874
Shelby Deeney M (2013) Bioethical considerations of preimplantation genetic diagnosis for sex selection. Wash Univ Jurisp Rev 5(2):333–360
Siems MM (2009) The taxonomy of interdisciplinary legal research: finding the way out of the desert. J Commonw Law Legal Edu 7(1):5–17
Skillen A (1985) Welfare State versus welfare society? J Appl Philos 2(1):3–17
Skopalová J (2010) Social deviations, labelling and normality. Human Aff 20:327–337
Smith C (2000) The Sovereign State v Foucault: law and disciplinary power. Sociol Rev Found 48(2):283–306
Sonksen P, Ferguson-Smith AM, Bavington LD, Holt IGR, Cowan AD, Catlin HD, Kidd B, Davis G, Davis P, Edwards L, Tamar-Mattis A (2015) Medical and ethical concerns regarding women with hyperandrogenism and elite sport. J Clin Endocrinol Metab 100(3):825–827
Sparrow R (2013) Gender eugenics? The ethics of PGD for intersex conditions. Am J Bioeth 13(10):29–38
Stamatis K (2005) The "common sense of justice" as a misleading criterion of correctness. (in Greek), Nomiko vima, Issue 5
Stanley AE (2014) Gender Self-Determination. University of Melbourne, pp 89–91. https://ericastanleydotnet.files.wordpress.com/2014/06/gender-self-determination-stanley-tsq.pdf. Accessed 5 Mar 2019
Steuli CJ, Vayena E, Cavicchia-Balmer Y Huber J (2013) Shaping parents: impact of contrasting professional counseling on parents' decision making for children with disorders of sex development. J Sex Med 10:1953–1960
Taekema S, Van der Burg W (2015) Introduction: the incorporation problem in interdisciplinary legal research. Erasmus Law Rev 2:55–64
Teetzel S (2006) On transgendered athletes, fairness and doping: an international challenge. Sport Soc 9(2):227–251

Thorn DE (2014) Drop the Knife! Instituting policies of nonsurgical intervention for intersex infants. Family Court Rev 52(3):610–621
Tiilikka P (2013) Access to information as a human right in the case law of the European Court of human rights. J Media Law 5:79–103
Tobler C (2014) Equality and non-discrimination under the ECHR and EU law a comparison focusing on discrimination against LGBTI persons. ZaöRV 74:521–561. https://edoc.unibas.ch/34809/1/74_2014_3_a_521_562.pdf. Accessed 20 July 2018
Travis M (2015) Accommodating intersexuality in European Union anti-discrimination law. Eur Law J 21(2):180–199
UNFPA (2005) Human Rights Principles. https://www.unfpa.org/resources/human-rights-principles#. Accessed 25 Mar 2019
Voeten E (2017) Competition and complementarity between global and regional human rights institutions. Global Policy 8(1):119–123
Vreeland JR (2007) Political institutions and human rights: why dictatorships enter into the United Nations Convention against Torture. Int Organ 62(1):65–101
Waldron J (2009) Judges as moral reasoners. Oxford University Press, New York. University School of Law 7(1):2–24
Wallby S (2004) The European Union and gender equality: emergent varieties of gender regime. Soc Polit Int Stud Gender State Soc 11(1):4–29
Walters M (2007) Sexual orientation discrimination in the European Union: the framework directive and the continuing influence of the European Parliament. Int J Discrim Law 8(4):263–293
Weber S (2011) Language and gender research from a queer linguistic perspective: a critical evaluation by Michaela Koch (2008), Reviewed by Shannon Weber. Gender Lang 5(1):153–157
Wellman M (1958) The concept of normal in medicine. Can Med Assoc J 79:43–45
White LR (2014) Preferred private parts: importing intersex autonomy for M.C. v. Aaronson. Fordham Int Law J 37(3). https://ir.lawnet.fordham.edu/ilj/vol37/iss3/2 Accessed 10 Apr 2018
Wilms G (2017) Protecting fundamental values in the European Union through the rule of law: article 2 and 7 TEU from a legal, historical and comparative angle. Florence: European University Institute, Robert Schuman Centre for Advanced Studies. https://doi.org/10.2870/083300
Woodward K, Woodward S (2015) Gender studies and interdisciplinarity. Palgrave Commun. https://doi.org/10.1057/palcomms.2015.18
Yamin EA (2005) The right to health under international law and its relevance to the United States. Am J Public Health 95(7):1156–1161
Zavaletta Schoch A (2005) Undoing gender (review). The Comparatist 29:152–153
Zhou C, Zhou X, Lei Wang X, Hesketh T (2011) Son preference and sex-selective abortion in China: informing policy options. Int J Public Health 57(3):459–465

International Law and Documents

Annual report of the United Nations High Commissioner for Human Rights and reports of the Office of the High Commissioner and the Secretary-General, A/HRC/19/41, "Discriminatory laws and practices and acts of violence against individuals based on their sexual orientation and gender identity" https://www.ohchr.org/documents/issues/discrimination/a.hrc.19.41_english.pdf
Committee on the Rights of the Child, CRC/C/DNK/CO/5 "Concluding observations on the fifth periodic report of Denmark*", 2017, http://www.refworld.org/docid/5a0ebb974.html
Convention on the Rights of the Child, CRC/C/GC/12 General Comment No. 12 The right of the child to be heard, 2009 http://www2.ohchr.org/english/bodies/crc/docs/AdvanceVersions/CRC-C-GC-12.pdf
Convention on the Rights of the Child, CRC/C/GC/15 General comment No. 15 (2013) on the right of the child to the enjoyment of the highest attainable standard of health (art. 24), 2013 http://www.refworld.org/docid/51ef9e134.html

Convention on the Rights of Persons with Disabilities, 6 December 2006 http://www.un.org/disabilities/documents/convention/convention_accessible_pdf.pdf
CESCR General Comment No. 14: The Right to the Highest Attainable Standard of Health (Art. 12) Adopted at the Twenty-second Session of the Committee on Economic, Social and Cultural Rights, on 11 August 2000 (Contained in Document E/C.12/2000/4) http://www.refworld.org/pdfid/4538838d0.pdf
Constitution of the World Health Organization, Basic Documents, Forty-fifth edition, Supplement, October 2006 http://www.who.int/governance/eb/who_constitution_en.pdf
Convention against Torture and Other Cruel, Inhuman or Degrading Treatment or Punishment (UNCAT) Adopted and opened for signature, ratification and accession by General Assembly resolution 39/46 of 10 December 1984 entry into force 26 June 1987, in accordance with article 27 (1) http://www.ohchr.org/EN/ProfessionalInterest/Pages/CAT.aspx
Committee on the Rights of the Child, CRC/C/CHE/CO/2-4, Concluding observations on the combined second to fourth periodic reports of Switzerland, 26 February 2015 file:///C:/Users/nicole/Downloads/G1503613.pdf
Committee on the Rights of the Child, CRC/C/CHL/CO/4-5, Concluding observations on the combined fourth and fifth periodic reports of Chile, 30 October 2015
Committee on the Rights of the Child, CRC/C/IRL/CO/3-4, Concluding observations on the combined third and fourth periodic reports of Ireland, 29 January 2016
Committee on the Rights of the Child, CRC/C/FRA/CO/5, Concluding observations on the fifth periodic report of France, 29 January 2016
Committee on the Elimination of All Forms of Discrimination against Women CEDAW/C/DEU/7-8, Consideration of reports submitted by States parties under article 18 of the Convention, Seventh and eighth periodic reports of States parties due in 2014, Germany
Committee on the Elimination of Discrimination against Women CEDAW/C/LUX/CO/6-7, Concluding observations on the combined sixth and seventh periodic reports of Luxembourg*, 9 March 2018
Committee on the Elimination of Discrimination against Women (CEDAW) Case of Jallow v. Bulgaria, 2012
Committee on the Elimination of Discrimination against Women (CEDAW) S.V.P. v. Bulgaria, 2012
Committee on the Elimination of Discrimination against Women (CEDAW) Kell v. Canada, 2012
Committee on the Elimination of Discrimination against Women (CEDAW) A.S. v. Hungary, 2006
Committee on the Elimination of Discrimination against Women (CEDAW) R. P. B. v. the Philippines, 2014
Committee on the Elimination of Discrimination against Women (CEDAW) M.W. v. Denmark, 2016, among others and inquiries
Committee on Economic, Social and Cultural Rights, General Comment No. 20, E/C.12/GC/20 http://www.refworld.org/docid/4a60961f2.html
Committee on the Elimination of Discrimination against Women, General Recommendation No. 28 on the Core Obligations of States Parties under Article 2 of the Convention on the Elimination of All Forms of Discrimination against Women, 19 October 2010 available on http://www2.ohchr.org/english/bodies/cedaw/docs/CEDAW-C-2010-47-GC2.pdf
Committee on the Elimination of Discrimination against Women, General Recommendation No. 35 on gender-based violence against women, updating general recommendation No. 19, 14 July 2017 http://tbinternet.ohchr.org/Treaties/CEDAW/Shared%20Documents/1_Global/CEDAW_C_GC_35_8267_E.pdf
Convention on the Elimination of All Forms of Discrimination against Women, adopted by the United Nations Geneal Assembly on 18 December 1979 and entered into force as an international treaty on 3 September 1981 http://www.un.org/womenwatch/daw/cedaw/text/econvention.htm#intro
Convention on the Rights of the Child, Adopted and opened for signature, ratification and accession by General Assembly resolution 44/25 of 20 November 1989 entry into force 2 September 1990, in accordance with article 49 http://www.ohchr.org/en/professionalinterest/pages/crc.aspx

Committee on Economic, Social and Cultural, General comment No. 4, CESCR General Comment No. 4: The Right to Adequate Housing (Art. 11 (1) of the Covenant) Adopted at the Sixth Session of the Committee on Economic, Social and Cultural Rights, on 13 December 1991 (Contained in Document E/1992/23) http://www.refworld.org/pdfid/47a7079a1.pdf
Declaration on the Elimination of Violence against Women, 20 December 1993 http://www.un.org/ga/search/view_doc.asp?symbol=A/RES/48/104
General Comment No. 4 on the African Charter on Human and Peoples' Rights: The Right to Redress for Victims of Torture and Other Cruel, Inhuman or Degrading Punishment or Treatment (Article 5), Adopted at the 21st Extra-Ordinary Session of the African Commission on Human and Peoples' Rights, held from 23 February to 4 March 2017 in Banjul, The Gambia
General recommendations made by the Committee on the Elimination of Discrimination against Women: General Recommendation No. 19 (llth session, 1992) http://www.un.org/womenwatch/daw/cedaw/recommendations/recomm.htm
General recommendation No. 35 on gender-based violence against women, updating general recommendation No. 19, Committee on the Elimination of Discrimination against Women, CEDAW/C/GC/35 https://tbinternet.ohchr.org/Treaties/CEDAW/Shared%20Documents/1_Global/CEDAW_C_GC_35_8267_E.pdf
General recommendation No. 33, General recommendation on women's access to justice, CEDAW/C/GC/33 https://tbinternet.ohchr.org/Treaties/CEDAW/Shared%20Documents/1_Global/CEDAW_C_GC_33_7767_E.pdf
General recommendation No. 15 on women and AIDS, A/45/38 https://www.refworld.org/docid/453882a311.html
General recommendation No. 18 on women with disabilities, A/46/38 https://www.legal-tools.org/doc/ba95ff/pdf/
General recommendation No. 21 on equality in marriage and family relations, A/49/38 https://www.refworld.org/docid/48abd52c0.html
General recommendation No. 24 on women and health, A/54/38/Rev.1, chap. I https://www.refworld.org/docid/453882a73.html
General recommendation No. 26 on women migrant workers, CEDAW/C/2009/WP.1/R https://www2.ohchr.org/english/bodies/cedaw/docs/gr_26_on_women_migrant_workers_en.pdf
General recommendation No. 27 on older women and protection of their human rights, CEDAW/C/GC/27 https://www.refworld.org/docid/4ed3528b2.html
General recommendation No. 30 on women in conflict prevention, conflict and post-conflict situations, CEDAW/C/GC/30 https://www.refworld.org/docid/5268d2064.html
General recommendation No. 31 on harmful practices, CEDAW/C/2014/III/CRP https://tbinternet.ohchr.org/Treaties/CEDAW/Shared%20Documents/1_Global/INT_CEDAW_SED_59_22653_E.pdf
General recommendation No. 32 on the gender-related dimensions of refugee status, asylum, nationality and statelessness of women, CEDAW/C/GC/32 https://www.refworld.org/docid/54620fb54.html
General recommendation No. 34 on the rights of rural women, CEDAW/C/GC/34 https://tbinternet.ohchr.org/Treaties/CEDAW/Shared%20Documents/1_Global/INT_CEDAW_GEC_7933_E.pdf
Human Rights Committee, CCPR General Comment No. 16: Article 17 (Right to Privacy), the Right to Respect of Privacy, Family, Home and Correspondence, and Protection of Honour and Reputation, 8 April 1988
Human Rights Committee, General Comment 22, "Article 18: Compilation of General Comments and General Recommendations Adopted by Human Rights Treaty Bodies," UN Doc. HRI/GEN/1/Rev.1, 1994
Human Rights Council, A/HRC/19/41, Discriminatory laws and practices and acts of violence against individuals based on their sexual orientation and gender identity, 17 November 2011 http://www.ohchr.org/Documents/Issues/Discrimination/A.HRC.19.41_English.pdf

Human Rights Council, A/HRC/29/23, Discriminatory laws and practices and acts of violence against individuals based on their sexual orientation and gender identity, 4 May 2015 http://www.un.org/en/ga/search/view_doc.asp?symbol=A/HRC/29/23&referer=/english/&Lang=E

Human Rights Council A/HRC/22/53, "Report of the Special Rapporteur on torture and other cruel, inhuman or degrading treatment or punishment, Juan E. Méndez", 2013, available on http://www.ohchr.org/Documents/HRBodies/HRCouncil/RegularSession/Session22/A.HRC.22.53_English.pdf

Human Rights Council A/HRC/31/57, "Report of the Special Rapporteur on torture and other cruel, inhuman or degrading treatment or punishment", 2016 available on https://documents-dds-ny.un.org/doc/UNDOC/GEN/G16/000/97/PDF/G1600097.pdf?OpenElement

Human Rights Council A/HRC/31/37 "Protection of the family: contribution of the family to the realization of the right to an adequate standard of living for its members, particularly through its role in poverty eradication and achieving sustainable development", 2016

Human Rights Council A/HRC/32/33, "Report of the Special Rapporteur on the right of everyone to the enjoyment of the highest attainable standard of physical and mental health", 4 April 2016 http://undocs.org/A/HRC/32/33

Human Rights Council, A/HRC/WG.6/26/UGA/2 "Compilation prepared by the Office of the United Nations High Commissioner for Human Rights in accordance with paragraph 15 (b) of the annex to Human Rights Council resolution 5/1 and paragraph 5 of the annex to Council resolution 16/2: Uganda, 29 August 2016

Human Rights Council, A/HRC/RES/17/19, 17/19 Human rights, sexual orientation and gender identity, 14 July 2011 https://documents-dds-ny.un.org/doc/UNDOC/GEN/G11/148/76/PDF/G1114876.pdf?OpenElement

Human Rights Council, A/HRC/RES/27/32, 27/32 Human rights, sexual orientation and gender identity, 2 October 2014 https://documents-dds-ny.un.org/doc/UNDOC/GEN/G14/177/32/PDF/G1417732.pdf?OpenElement

Human Rights Council, A/HRC/RES/32/2, Protection against violence and discrimination based on sexual orientation and gender identity, 30 June 2016 http://www.un.org/en/ga/search/view_doc.asp?symbol=A/HRC/RES/32/2

Istanbul Convention on preventing and combating violence against women and domestic violence, Council of Europe Treaty Series- No. 210 https://rm.coe.int/CoERMPublicCommonSearchServices/DisplayDCTMContent?documentId=090000168008482e

International Covenant on Economic, Social and Cultural Rights, Adopted and opened for signature, ratification and accession by General Assembly resolution 2200A (XXI) of 16 December 1966 entry into force 3 January 1976, in accordance with article 27 http://www.ohchr.org/EN/ProfessionalInterest/Pages/CESCR.aspx

International Covenant on Civil and Political Rights, Adopted and opened for signature, ratification and accession by General Assembly resolution 2200A (XXI) of 16 December 1966 entry into force 23 March 1976, in accordance with Article 49 http://www.ohchr.org/en/professionalinterest/pages/ccpr.aspx

The Yogyakarta Principles on the Application of International Human Rights Law in relation to Sexual Orientation and Gender Identity, 2006 http://www.yogyakartaprinciples.org/principles_en.htm

The Yogyakarta Principles plus 10, Additional Principles And State Obligations On the Application of International Human Rights Law in Relation to Sexual Orientation, Gender Identity, Gender Expression And Sex Characteristics to Complement the Yogyakarta Principles, adopted on 10 November 2017, Geneva http://yogyakartaprinciples.org/wp-content/uploads/2017/11/A5_yogyakartaWEB-2.pdf

Universal Declaration of Human Rights, Adopted by the General Assembly of the United Nations on 10 December 1948 http://www.ohchr.org/EN/UDHR/Documents/UDHR_Translations/eng.pdf

United Nations A/RES/70/1, Resolution adopted by the General Assembly on 25 September 2015, 2015, available on http://www.un.org/ga/search/view_doc.asp?symbol=A/RES/70/1&Lang=E
United Nations CCPR/C/107/R.3 "Draft General comment No. 35, Article 9: Liberty and security of person", 2 September 2015
United Nations Charter. http://www.un.org/en/sections/un-charter/un-charter-full-text/
United Nations Human Rights Commission, Campaign Dossier, Resolution on Sexual Orientation and Human Rights http://www.iglhrc.org/sites/default/files/213-1.pdf
United Nations Human Rights Office of the High Commissioner, Intersex Awareness Day, "End violence and harmful medical practices on intersex children and adults, UN and regional experts urge", 2016. https://www.ohchr.org/EN/NewsEvents/Pages/DisplayNews.aspx?NewsID=20739&LangID=E
275: Resolution on Protection against Violence and other Human Rights Violations against Persons on the basis of their real or imputed Sexual Orientation or Gender Identity, Adopted at the 55th Ordinary Session of the African Commission on Human and Peoples' Rights in Luanda, Angola, 28 April to 12 May 2014
2006 Joint Statement, 3rd Session of the Human Rights Council, Joint Statement, Ambassador & Permanent Representative of Norway to the United Nations Office in Geneva http://arc-international.net/global-advocacy/sogi-statements/2006-joint-statement/
EqualRightsTrust, Case Summary: P v. S and Cornwall County Council, Case C-13/94, [1996] IRLR 347 http://www.equalrightstrust.org/ertdocumentbank/Microsoft%20Word%20-%20P%20v%20S.pdf
Joined Cases C-148/13 to C-150/13, requests for a preliminary ruling under article 267 TFEU, from the Raad van State (Netherlands), made by decision of 20 March 2013, received at the Court on 25 March 2013, in the proceedings, A (C-148/13), B (C-149/13), C (C-150/13) v Staatssecretaris van Veiligheid en Justitie, Judgment of the Court (Grand Chamber), 2 December 2014 http://curia.europa.eu/juris/document/document.jsf?docid=160244&doclang=EN
EqualRightsTrust, Joined cases A (C-148/13), B (C-149/13), C (C-150/13) v Staatssecretaris van Veiligheid en Justitie Preliminary ruling under article 267 TFEU, from the Raad van State (Netherlands), Case Summary http://www.equalrightstrust.org/ertdocumentbank/Case%20summary%20-%20CJEU%20Preliminary%20ruling%20'Homosexuality%20test'.pdf
Case C-117/01, K.B. v National Health Service Pensions Agency and Secretary of State for Health. Reference for a preliminary ruling: Court of Appeal (England & Wales) (Civil Division) - United Kingdom. Judgment of the Court of 7 January 2004 http://curia.europa.eu/juris/liste.jsf?language=en&jur=C,T,F&num=C-117/01&td=ALL
Opinion of Advocate General Ruiz-Jarabo Colomer delivered on 10 June 2003 K.Bv National Health Service Pensions Agency and Secretary of State for Health Reference for a preliminary ruling: Court of Appeal (England & Wales) (Civil Division) - United Kingdom https://eur-lex.europa.eu/legal-content/EN/TXT/HTML/?uri=CELEX:62001CJ0117&from=EN
Case C-423/04, Sarah Margaret Richards v Secretary of State for Work and Pensions. Reference for a preliminary ruling: Social Security Commissioner - United Kingdom, Judgment of the Court (First Chamber) of 27 April 2006 http://curia.europa.eu/juris/liste.jsf?language=en&num=C-423/04

European and EU Law and Documents

Burri S, Prechal S, (European Network of Legal Experts in the field of Gender Equality) (2010) EU gender equality law – update 2010. Office for Official Publications of the European Communities, Luxembourg
Charter of Fundamental Rights of the European Union, 2000/C 364/01, 18. 12. 2000 http://www.europarl.europa.eu/charter/pdf/text_en.pdf

Committee of Ministers, Recommendation CM/REC (2010)5 of the Committee of Ministers to member states on measures to combat discrimination on grounds of sexual orientation or gender identity, Adopted by the Committee of Ministers on 31 March 2010 https://search.coe.int/cm/Pages/result_details.aspx?ObjectID=09000016805cf40a

Consolidated version of the treaty on the functioning of the European Union, 26/10/2012, C 326/47 http://eur-lex.europa.eu/legal-content/EN/TXT/PDF/?uri=CELEX:12012E/TXT&from=EN

Council of the European Union, "Guidelines to promote and protect the enjoyment of all human rights by lesbian, gay, bisexual, transgender and intersex (LGBT) persons", Foreign Affairs Council Meeting, Luxembourg, 24 June 2013 https://eeas.europa.eu/sites/eeas/files/137584.pdf

Council of Europe, "Equality between women and men", 2015 https://rm.coe.int/168064f51b

Council of Europe, Committee of Ministers, Recommendation No. R (97) 5 on the Protection of Medical Data (Feb. 13, 1997) http://hrlibrary.umn.edu/instree/coerecr97-5.html

Consolidated versions of the Treaty on European Union and the Treaty on the Functioning of the European Union 2012/C 326/01. https://eur-lex.europa.eu/legal-content/EN/TXT/?uri=CELEX:12012M/TXT

Convention for the Protection of Human Rights and Dignity of the Human Being with regard to the Application of Biology and Medicine: Convention on Human Rights and Biomedicine, 1997 https://rm.coe.int/168007cf98

Explanatory Report to the Convention for the protection of Human Rights and Dignity of the Human Being with regard to the Application of Biology and Medicine: Convention on Human Rights and Biomedicine, Oviedo, 4.IV.1997 https://rm.coe.int/16800ccde5

Council of the European Union, "Guidelines to promote and protect the enjoyment of all human rights by lesbian, gay, bisexual, transgender and intersex (LGBTI) persons", 24/6/2013 https://eeas.europa.eu/sites/eeas/files/137584.pdf

Details of Treaty No.126, European Convention for the Prevention of Torture and Inhuman or Degrading Treatment or Punishment, 1987 https://www.coe.int/en/web/conventions/full-list/-/conventions/treaty/126

Directive 2004/58/EC of the European Parliament and of the Council of 29 April 2004 on the right of citizens of the Union and their family members to move and reside freely within the territory of the Member States amending Regulation (EEC) No 1612/68 and repealing Directives 64/221/EEC, 68/360/EEC, 72/194/EEC, 73/148/EEC, 75/34/EEC, 75/35/EEC, 90/364/EEC, 90/365/EEC and 93/96/EEC https://eur-lex.europa.eu/LexUriServ/LexUriServ.do?uri=OJ:L:2004:229:0035:0048:en:PDF

Directive 75/117/EEC of 10 February 1975 on the approximation of the laws of the Member States relating to the application of the principle of equal pay for men and women, date of end of validity 14/08/2009. https://eur-lex.europa.eu/legal-content/en/ALL/?uri=CELEX%3A31975L0117

Directive 2000/78/EC of 27 November 2000 establishing a general framework for equal treatment in employment and occupation, 2.12.2000 http://hrlibrary.umn.edu/instree/EUframeworkdirective2000.pdf

Directive 2006/54/EC of the European Parliament and of the Council of 5 July 2006 on the implementation of the principle of equal opportunities and equal treatment of men and women in matters of employment and occupation (recast). https://eur-lex.europa.eu/legal-content/EN/TXT/?uri=CELEX%3A32006L0054

Directive 2010/41/EU of the European Parliament and of the Council of 7 July 2010 on the application of the principle of equal treatment between men and women engaged in an activity in a self-employed capacity and repealing Council Directive 86/613/EEC. https://eur-lex.europa.eu/legal-content/EN/TXT/?uri=celex%3A32010L0041

Doc. 14404 of the Parliamentary Assembly, "Promoting the human rights of and eliminating discrimination against intersex people", 25 September 2017 http://semantic-pace.net/tools/pdf.aspx?doc=aHR0cDovL2Fzc2VtYmx5LmNvZS5pbnQvbncveG1sL1hSZWYvWDJILURXLWV4dHIuYXNwP2ZpbGVpZD0yNDAyNyZsYW5nPUVO&xsl=aHR0cDovL3NlbWFudGlj

cGFjZS5uZXQvWHNsdC9QZGYvWFJlZi1XRC1BVC1YTUwyUERGLnhzbA==&xsltparams=ZmlsZWlkPTI0MDI3
Doc. 13297 of the Parliamentary Assembly, "Children's right to physical integrity", 06 September 2013 http://www.assembly.coe.int/nw/xml/XRef/Xref-XML2HTML-en.asp?fileid=20057&lang=en
European Commission, Summary report "Legislation and policies on gender identity and sex characteristics", 27 October 2016 file:///Users/nikolettapikramenou/Downloads/ReportGPEgenderidentity%20(3).pdf
European Convention on Human Rights as amended by Protocols Nos, 11 and 14, supplemented by Protocols Nos, 1,4,6,7,12 and 13 http://www.echr.coe.int/Documents/Convention_ENG.pdf
European Parliament, Committee on Civil Liberties, Justice and Home Affairs, "On the EU Roadmap against homophobia and discrimination on grounds of sexual orientation and gender identity" (2013/2183 (INI)), Rapporteur: Ulrike Lunacek, 8 January 2014 http://www.europarl.europa.eu/sides/getDoc.do?pubRef=-//EP//TEXT+REPORT+A7-2014-0009+0+DOC+XML+V0//EN
European Social Charter, European Treaty Series - No. 163, Strasbourg 3V. 1993 https://rm.coe.int/168007cf93
European Union Agency for Fundamental Rights, "The fundamental rights situation of intersex people", 04/2015
European Union Agency for Fundamental Rights, "Protection against discrimination on grounds of sexual orientation, gender identity and sex characteristics in the EU, Comparative legal analysis", Update 2015
Explanatory report to Protocol No. 12 to the 1950 Convention for the Protection of Human Rights and Fundamental Freedoms, entered into force on 1 April 2005, ETS No. 177 https://rm.coe.int/16800cce48
Official Journal of the European Union C 303/17 – 14.12.2007. https://eur-lex.europa.eu/legal-content/EN/TXT/?uri=CELEX%3A32007X1214%2801%29
Recommendation 2021 of the Parliamentary Assembly, "Tackling discrimination on the grounds of sexual orientation and gender identity", 2013 http://assembly.coe.int/nw/xml/XRef/Xref-XML2HTML-en.asp?fileid=20011&lang=en
Recommendation of the Committee of Ministers to member states on the protection of women against violence, Rec (2002) https://rm.coe.int/16805e2612
Resolution 2048 of the Parliamentary Assembly, "Discrimination against transgender people in Europe", 2015 http://assembly.coe.int/nw/xml/XRef/Xref-XML2HTML-en.asp?fileid=21736&lang=en
Resolution 1728 of the Parliamentary Assembly, "Discrimination on the basis of sexual orientation and gender identity", 2010 http://semantic-pace.net/tools/pdf.aspx?doc=aHR0cDovL2Fzc2VtYmx5LmNvZS5pbnQvbncveG1sL1hSZWYvWDJILURXLWV4dHIuYXNwP2ZpbGVpZD0xNzg1MyZsYW5nPUVO&xsl=aHR0cDovL3NlbWFudGljcGFjZS5uZXQvWHNsdC9QZGYvWFJlZi1XRC1BVC1YTUwyUERGLnhzbA==&xsltparams=ZmlsZWlkPTE3ODUz
Resolution 1952 of the Parliamentary Assembly, "Children's right to physical integrity", 2013 http://assembly.coe.int/nw/xml/xref/xref-xml2html-en.asp?fileid=20174&lang=en
Resolution 2191 of the Parliamentary Assembly "Promoting the human rights and eliminating discrimination against intersex people", 2017 http://semantic-pace.net/tools/pdf.aspx?doc=aHR0cDovL2Fzc2VtYmx5LmNvZS5pbnQvbncveG1sL1hSZWYvWDJILURXLWV4dHIuYXNwP2ZpbGVpZD0yNDIzMiZsYW5nPUVO&xsl=aHR0cDovL3NlbWFudGljcGFjZS5uZXQvWHNsdC9QZGYvWFJlZi1XRC1BVC1YTUwyUERGLnhzbA==&xsltparams=ZmlsZWlkPTI0MjMy
Resolution 1829 of the Parliamentary Assembly, "Prenatal sex selection", 2011 http://assembly.coe.int/nw/xml/XRef/Xref-XML2HTML-EN.asp?fileid=18020&lang=en
Recommendation 1635 (2003) of the Parliamentary Assembly on Lesbians and gays in sport

Recommendation 1474 (2000) of the Parliamentary Assembly on situation of lesbians and gays in Council of Europe member states
Recommendation 1470 (2000) of the Parliamentary Assembly on Situation of gays and lesbians and their partners in respect of asylum and immigration in the member states of the Council of Europe
Recommendation 1117 (1989) of the Parliamentary Assembly on the condition of transsexuals
Recommendation 924 (1981) of the Parliamentary Assembly on Discrimination against homosexuals
Resolution 756 (1981) of the Parliamentary Assembly on discrimination against homosexuals
The Treaty of Amsterdam amending the Treaty of the European Union, the Treaties establishing the European Communities and certain related acts, Signed on 2 October 1997, and entered into force on 1 May 1999
The Treaty of Rome, 25 March 1957 https://ec.europa.eu/romania/sites/romania/files/tratatul_de_la_roma.pdf

European and EU Jurisprudence

European Court of Human Rights

Airey v. Ireland, Application No. 6289/73, judgement of 9 October 1979 http://ww3.lawschool.cornell.edu/AvonResources/Airey.PDF
A.P., Garçon and Nicot v. France, Applications nos. 79885/12, 52471/13 and 52596/13, 6 April 2017 https://jurisprudencia.mpd.gov.ar/Jurisprudencia/A.P.,%20Gar%C3%A7on%20and%20Nicot%20v.%20Francia.pdf
B. v. France, Application no. 13343/87 25 March 1992 http://hudoc.echr.coe.int/eng?i=001-57770#{"itemid":["001-57770"]}
Bensaid v. the United Kingdom, Application no. 44599/98, 6 February 2001 https://hudoc.echr.coe.int/eng#{"dmdocnumber":["697083"],"itemid":["001-59206"]}
Chapin and Charpentier v. France, Application no. 40183/07, final judgment 09 September 2016 https://hudoc.echr.coe.int/eng#{%22itemid%22:[%22001-163436%22]}
Christine Goodwin v. the United Kingdom application no. 28957/95, 11.7.2002 http://hudoc.echr.coe.int/eng-press?i=003-585597-589247#{"itemid":["003-585597-589247"]}
Costa and Pavan v. Italy, application no. 54270/10, final judgment 11 February 2013 https://hudoc.echr.coe.int/eng#{%22itemid%22:[%22001-112992%22]}
Dudgeon v UK, Series A, No. 45, 23 September 1981, http://www.hrcr.org/safrica/dignity/Dudgeon%20_UK.htm
Identoba and Others v. Georgia application no. 73235/12, 12 May 2015 http://hudoc.echr.coe.int/eng?i=001-154400#{"itemid":["001-154400"]}
Johnston et al. v. Ireland, Application No. 9697/82, judgment of 18 December 1986
Joanne Cassar against Malta, Application no. 36982/11 https://hudoc.echr.coe.int/eng?i=001-111018#{%22itemid%22:[%22001-111018%22]}
K.H. and Others v. Slovakia, Application no. 32881/04, 28 April 2009, https://hudoc.echr.coe.int/eng-press#{"itemid":["003-2718812-2971322"]}
Laskey, Jaggard and Brown v UK, application no. 21627/93; 21628/93; 21974/93, 19 February 1997. https://hudoc.echr.coe.int/eng#{"dmdocnumber":["695898"],"itemid":["001-58021"]}
M.A.K. and R.K. v. the United Kingdom, applications nos. 45901/05 and 40146/06, 23 March 2010
Marckx v. Belgium, Application No. 6833/74, judgment of 13 June 1979 https://hudoc.echr.coe.int/eng#{%22dmdocnumber%22:[%22695411%22],%22itemid%22:[%22001-57534%22]}

Modinos v Cyprus, application no. 15070/89, 22 April 1993. https://hudoc.echr.coe.int/eng#{"dmdocnumber":["695711"],"itemid":["001-57834"]}
Mouta v. Portugal, Application No. 33290/96, judgment of 21 December 1999
Oliari and Others v. Italy, Applications nos. 18766/11 and 36030/11, final judgment 21/10/2015 https://hudoc.echr.coe.int/eng#{%22itemid%22:[%22001-156265%22]}
Pretty v UK, Application no. 2346/02, 29 April 2002. https://hudoc.echr.coe.int/eng#{"itemid":["001-60448"]}
Requêtes nos 2145/16 et 20607/16 X. contre la Roumanie et Y. contre la Roumanie introduites respectivement le 19 décembre 2015 et le 4 avril 2016 https://hudoc.echr.coe.int/eng#{%22itemid%22:[%22001-180607%22]}
Schalk and Kopf v. Austria, application no. 30141/04, final judgment 22/11/2010 https://hudoc.echr.coe.int/eng#{%22dmdocnumber%22:[%22870457%22],%22itemid%22:[%22001-99605%22]}
S.H. and Others v. Austria, application no. 57813/00, 1 April 2010. https://www.ieb-eib.org/en/pdf/cedh-shothers-c-austria-20100401.pdf
Storck v. Germany, Application no. 54270/10, 16 June 2005, 28 August 2012
Y.F. v. Turkey, Application no. 24209/94, 22/10/2003 https://www.coe.int/t/dg2/equality/domesticviolencecampaign/resources/Y.F.%20v.%20TURKEY_en.asp
Y.Y. v. Turkey, Application no. 14793/08, final judgment 10 June 2015 https://hudoc.echr.coe.int/eng#{%22itemid%22:[%22001-153134%22]}
Vallianatos and Others v. Greece, Applications nos. 29381/09 and 32684/09, judgment of 7 November 2013 https://hudoc.echr.coe.int/eng#{%22itemid%22:[%22001-128294%22]}
Van Kuck v. Germany, application no. 35968/97, 12 June 2003. https://hudoc.echr.coe.int/eng#{"itemid":["001-61142"]}
Vo v. France, application no. 53924/00, judgment of 8 July 2004 https://hudoc.echr.coe.int/eng#{"dmdocnumber":["776914"],"itemid":["001-69374"]}
X. and others v. Austria, application 19010/07, 19 February 2013 https://fidh.org/IMG/pdf/xvaustria_ecthrjudgment_19feb2013_en_.pdf

European Court of Justice

Case C-267/06, Tadao Maruko v. Versorgungsanstalt der deutschen Bühnen, Judgment of the Court (Grand Chamber) of 1 April 2008, http://curia.europa.eu/juris/liste.jsf?num=C-267/06
Opinion of Advocate General Ruiz-Jarabo Colomer delivered on 6 September 2007, Case C-267/06, Tadao Maruko v. Versorgungsanstalt der deutschen Bühnen http://curia.europa.eu/juris/document/document.jsf?text=&docid=62433&pageIndex=0&doclang=EN&mode=lst&dir=&occ=first&part=1&cid=664117
Case C-147/08, Jürgen Römer v Freie und Hansestadt Hamburg, Judgment of the Court (Grand Chamber) of 10 May 2011 http://curia.europa.eu/juris/document/document.jsf?text=&docid=80921&pageIndex=0&doclang=EN&mode=lst&dir=&occ=first&part=1&cid=666259
Case C-377/98, Netherlands v European Parliament and Council, of 9 October 2001 http://eur-lex.europa.eu/legal-content/EN/TXT/?uri=CELEX%3A61998CJ0377
Case C-13/94, P v S and Cornwall County Council. - Reference for a preliminary ruling: Industrial Tribunal, Truro - United Kingdom. - Equal treatment for men and women - Dismissal of a transsexual, Judgment of the Court of 30 April 1996 http://eur-lex.europa.eu/legal-content/EN/TXT/?uri=CELEX%3A61994CJ0013
Case C- 673/16, Coman and others v. Romania, Judgment of the Court (Grand Chamber) 5 June 2018, https://eur-lex.europa.eu/legal-content/EN/TXT/HTML/?uri=CELEX:62016CJ0673&from=EN

Case C-528/13, Geoffrey Léger v Ministre des Affaires sociales, de la Santé et des Droits des femmes and Établissement français du sang, Judgment of the Court (Fourth Chamber) 29 April 2015, https://eur-lex.europa.eu/legal-content/EN/TXT/HTML/?uri=CELEX:62013CJ0528&from=FR

Court of Justice of the European Union, Press Release No. 46/15, "The permanent deferral from blood donation for men who have had sexual relations with another man may be justified, having regard to the situation prevailing in the Member State concerned" https://curia.europa.eu/jcms/upload/docs/application/pdf/2015-04/cp150046en.pdf

P. v S. and Cornwall County Council, Opinion of Advocate General Tesauro delivered on 14 December 1995

European Union Member States Law and Documents

Austria

Austria/BGBl 1988/195, last amended by BGBl 1995/25

Austria/BGBl 1983/60, last amended by BGBl I 2005/100

BMI Zahl: 36.250/66-IV/4/9, (27.11.1996)

Nowak M (2010) "Legal Study on Homophobia and Discrimination on Grounds of Sexual Orientation and Gender Identity"

Registered Partnership Act (Eingetragene Partnerschaft-Gesetz – EPG) (in German). https://www.jusline.at/gesetz/epg

Verfassungsgerichtshof Österreich, "Distinction between marriage and registered partnership violates ban on discrimination" https://www.vfgh.gv.at/medien/Ehe_fuer_gleichgeschlechtliche_Paare.en.php

Belgium

Anti-discrimination Law (Loi tendant à lutter contre certaines formes de discrimination). https://www.unia.be/files/Z_ARCHIEF/10_mai_2007.pdf

The Law to reform transgender-related regimes with respect to the reference to a change in the registration of sex in civil status records and its effects (Loi réformant des régimes relatifs aux personnes transgenres en ce qui concerne la mention d'une modification de l'enregistrement du sexe dans les actes de l'état civil et ses effets/ Wet tot hervorming van regelingen inzake transgenders wat de vermelding van een aanpassing van de registratie van het geslacht in de akten van de burgerlijke stand en de gevolgen hiervan betreft) http://www.ejustice.just.fgov.be/cgi_loi/change_lg.pl?language=fr&la=F&cn=2017062503&table_name=loi

Denmark

Act on Sterilisation and Castration (originally Act no. 130 of 1-Jun-1929)

Gender Identity Law (Lov om ændring af lov om Det Centrale Personregister) (in Danish only) https://www.ft.dk/RIpdf/samling/20131/lovforslag/L182/20131_L182_som_fremsat.pdf

Finland

Act on Legal Recognition of the Gender of Transsexuals (the Trans Act) (unofficial English version) http://trasek.fi/wp-content/uploads/2011/03/TransAct2003.pdf
Lakitransseksuaalin sukupuolen vahvistamisesta annetun lain muuttamisesta (Finnish version) https://www.finlex.fi/fi/laki/alkup/2016/20160252?fbclid=IwAR0aRVMfdO1pMyd4qZubRzj7qNDn2Dpa22SHgiO4Gmb531O9nXAUXld3zKQ
A decree of the Ministry of Social Affairs and Health on the organisation of the examination and treatment aiming at the change of gender as well as on the medical statement for the confirmation of gender of a transsexual (unofficial English version) http://trasek.fi/wp-content/uploads/2011/03/TransDecree2003.pdf

France

Défenseur des droits, Opinion No. 17-04, 20 February 2017
Information Report compiled on behalf of the delegation to women's rights and equal opportunities between men and women on variations of sexual development: lift a taboo, fight stigma and exclusions by Maryvonne Blondin and Corinne Bouchoux, Senators, 2017 (Rapport d'information fait au nom de la délégation aux droits des femmes et à l'égalité des chances entre les hommes et les femmes sur les variations du développement sexuel: lever un tabou, lutter contre la stigmatisation et les exclusions, Par Mmes Maryvonne BLONDIN et Corinne BOUCHOUX, Sénatrices) https://www.senat.fr/rap/r16-441/r16-4411.pdf

Germany

Act Implementing European Directives Putting into Effect the Principle of Equal Treatment (official English version) http://www.antidiskriminierungsstelle.de/SharedDocs/Downloads/DE/publikationen/AGG/agg_in_englischer_Sprache.pdf;jsessionid=95D39C8FCA95BF9119AD888CF37B945B.1_cid340?__blob=publicationFile&v=6
Alternative Report Follow-up Germany 2011 submitted by German Women's Rights Organisations in Response to the Written Information of Germany on the steps undertaken to implement the recommendations contained in paragraphs 40 and 62 and as requested as a follow up report in paragraph 67 of the Concluding Observations of the CEDAW Committee, 12 February 2009 [CEDAW/C/DEU/CO/6] https://www.institut-fuer-menschenrechte.de/fileadmin/user_upload/PDF-Dateien/Pakte_Konventionen/CEDAW/cedaw_state_report_germany_6_2007_Zwischenbericht_2011_parallel_en.pdf
Association of Intersexual People/XY-Women (Verein Intersexuelle Menschen e.V. / XY-Frauen), Shadow Report to the 6th National Report of the Federal Republic of Germany on the United Nations Convention on the Elimination of All Forms of Discrimination Against Women (CEDAW), 2008 http://www2.ohchr.org/english/bodies/cedaw/docs/ngos/AIP_Germany43_en.pdf
Bundestag document, Bundestagsdrucksache – BTDrucks 17/9088
Bürgerliches Gesetzbuch (BGB) "Bürgerliches Gesetzbuch in der Fassung der Bekanntmachung vom 2. Januar 2002 (BGBl. I S. 42, 2909; 2003 I S. 738), das zuletzt durch Artikel 6 des Gesetzes vom 12. Juli 2018 (BGBl. I S. 1151) geändert worden ist" German Civil Code (BGB) Civil Code in the version promulgated on 2 January 2002 (Federal Law Gazette [Bundesgesetzblatt] I page 42, 2909; 2003 I page 738), last amended by Article 4 para. 5 of the Act of 1 October

2013 (Federal Law Gazette I page 3719) (official English version) https://www.gesetze-im-internet.de/englisch_bgb/englisch_bgb.pdf
Das Allgemeine Gleichbehandlungsgesetz vom 18. August 2006 in der am 5. Februar 2009 in Kraft getretenen Fassung. General Act on Equal Treatment of 14th August 2006 (Federal Law Gazette I, page 1897), last amended by Article 15, para 66 of the Act of the Act of 5 February 2009 (Federal Law Gazette 1, page 160) (official English version) http://www.gesetze-im-internet.de/englisch_agg/index.html
Deutscher Bundestag Drucksache 17/12192, http://dip21.bundestag.de/dip21/btd/17/121/1712192.pdf
Deutscher Ethikrat, « Intersexualität", 2012 https://www.ethikrat.org/fileadmin/Publikationen/Stellungnahmen/deutsch/DER_StnIntersex_Deu_Online.pdf
Entscheidungen des Bundesverfassungsgerichts [BVerfGE] [Federal Constitutional Court] May 27, 2008, 1 Bundesverfassungsgericht [BVL] 10/05
Federal Ministry for Family Affairs, Senior Citizens, Women and Youth, "Report on Reform of the Transsexuals Act (Transsexuellengesetz), 2016 https://www.bmfsfj.de/blob/119714/868b768ed3bf80b514219b9a2aeb3a8c/report-on-reform-of-the-transsexuals-act-data.pdf
German Civil Code BGB Civil Code in the version promulgated on 2 January 2002 (Federal Law Gazette [Bundesgesetzblatt] I page 42, 2909; 2003 I page 738), last amended by Article 4 para. 5 of the Act of 1 October 2013 (Federal Law Gazette I page 3719) https://www.gesetze-im-internet.de/englisch_bgb/englisch_bgb.pdf
German Ethics Council on Intersexuality, "Ethical Guidelines and Recommendations on the Medical Treatment", 2012 https://grapsia.files.wordpress.com/2012/10/2012friederike2012maassen.pdf
Gesetz über die Änderung der Vornamen und die Feststellung der Geschlechtszugehörigkeit in besonderen Fällen(Transsexuellengesetz - TSG) http://www.gesetze-im-internet.de/tsg/BJNR016540980.html
Gesetz über die Eingetragene Lebenspartnerschaft, "Lebenspartnerschaftsgesetz vom 16. Februar 2001 (BGBl. I S. 266), das zuletzt durch Artikel 2 Absatz 1 des Gesetzes vom 20. Juli 2017 (BGBl. I S. 2787) geändert worden ist". Act on Registered Life Partnerships Act on Registered Life Partnerships of 16 February 2001 (Federal Law Gazette I p. 266), last amended by Article 2 of the Act of 20 July 2017 (official English version). http://www.gesetze-im-internet.de/englisch_lpartg/englisch_lpartg.pdf
International Commission of Jurists, 1 BvL 10/05, Federal Constitutional Court of Germany (27 May 2008). https://www.icj.org/sogicasebook/1-bvl-1005-federal-constitutional-court-of-germany-27-may-2008/
International Commission of Jurists, 1 BvR 3295-07, Federal Constitutional Court, Germany (11 January 2011) (Case summary). https://www.icj.org/sogicasebook/1-bvr-3295-07-federal-constitutional-court-germany-11-january-2011/ Official decision in German https://www.icj.org/wp-content/uploads/2012/07/1-BvR-3295-07-Federal-Constitutional-Court-Germany-German.pdf
Landesverfassung der Freien Hansestadt Bremen, Artikel 2 https://www.transparenz.bremen.de/sixcms/detail.php?gsid=bremen2014_tp.c.75088.de&asl=bremen203_tpgesetz.c.55340.de&template=20_gp_ifg_meta_detail_d#jlr-VerfBRV18Art2
Personenstandsgesetz (PStG) PStG Ausfertigungsdatum: 19.02.2007 Vollzitat: "Personenstandsgesetz vom 19. Februar 2007 (BGBl. I S. 122), das zuletzt durch Artikel 2 Absatz 2 des Gesetzes vom 20. Juli 2017 (BGBl. I S. 2787) geändert worden ist" (in German only) http://www.gesetze-im-internet.de/pstg/PStG.pdf
The United Nations Office at Geneva, "Committee on the Elimination of Discrimination Against Women Considers the Reports of Germany" CEDAW17/009E https://www.unog.ch/unog/website/news_media.nsf/(httpNewsByYear_en)/9F8ED815BA5A5E23C12580CE005BBD79?OpenDocument

Greece

Civil Code (in Greek)

Decision 39/22-1-2016 of the Minister of Interior that amends the previous decision 131360/12476/8-5-2013 (in Greek)

Law 3304/2005 (Νόμος υπ'αριθ. 3304/2005 Εφαρμογή της αρχής της ίσης μεταχείρισης ανεξαρτήτως φυλετικής ή εθνοτικής καταγωγής, θρησκευτικών ή άλλων πεποιθήσεων, αναπηρίας, ηλικίας ή γενετήσιου προσανατολισμού) (in Greek) http://www.ypakp.gr/uploads/files/2538.pdf

Law 3719/2008 (Νόμος υπ'αριθ. 3719/2008 Μεταρρυθμίσεις για την οικογένεια, το παιδί, την κοινωνία και άλλες διατάξεις) (in Greek) http://users.uoa.gr/~ggeorgiades/3719-2008.pdf

Law 4144/2013 (Νόμος 4144/2013 προβλέπει τη διόρθωση της ληξιαρχικής πράξης γέννησης σε περίπτωση αλλαγής φύλου) (in Greek)

Law 4285/2014 (Νόμος υπ'αριθ. 4285 για την καταπολέμηση ορισμένων μορφών και εκδηλώσεων ρατσισμού και ξενοφοβίας μέσω του ποινικού δικαίου και άλλες διατάξεις) (in Greek) http://www.ministryofjustice.gr/site/LinkClick.aspx?fileticket=Ik2xQr3jIkg%3D&tabid=132

Law 4356/2015 (Νόμος Υπ'αριθ. 4356, Σύμφωνο συμβίωσης, άσκηση δικαιωμάτων, ποινικές και άλλες διατάξεις) (in Greek) Greek Law regulating the Civil Union (σύμφωνο συμβίωσης) (in English) https://www.constitutionalism.gr/wp-content/uploads/2016/01/Law-3718-Law-4356_-Articles-1-14_.pdf

Law 4443/2016 (Νόμος Υπ. Αριθ. 4443/2016: Ι) Ενσωμάτωση της Οδηγίας 2000/43/ΕΚ περί εφαρμογής της αρχής της ίσης μεταχείρισης προσώπων ασχέτως φυλετικής ή εθνοτικής τους καταγωγής, της Οδηγίας 2000/78/ΕΚ για τη διαμόρφωση γενικού πλαισίου για την ίση μεταχείριση στην απασχόληση) (in Greek) https://www.e-nomothesia.gr/kat-anthropina-dikaiomata/nomos-4443-2016-fek-232a-9-12-2016.html

Draft Law of the Legislative Committee of the Ministry of Justice as of 18 November 2016 (in Greek)

Bill of Ministry of Justice, Transparency and Human Rights, "Legal Recognition of Gender Identity- National Mechanism for the preparation, monitoring and evaluation of action plans for children's rights"(in Greek)

Law 4491/2017 on the Legal Gender Recognition passed (Νόμος υπ'αριθ. 4491/2017 Νομική αναγνώριση της ταυτότητας φύλου) (in Greek) https://www.e-nomothesia.gr/kat-nomothesia-genikou-endiapherontos/nomos-4491-2017-fek-152a-13-10-2017.html

Law 4538/2018 or the Child Adoption Law (Νόμος Υπ'αριθ. 4538/2018 Μέτρα για την προώθηση των Θεσμών της Αναδοχής και Υιοθεσίας και άλλες διατάξεις) (in English) https://www.e-nomothesia.gr/oikogeneia/nomos-4538-2018-phek-85a-16-5-2018.html

The Constitution of Greece (in English) http://www.hri.org/docs/syntagma/artcl25.html#A21

Ireland

Gender Recognition Act 2015, Number 25 of 2015 http://www.irishstatutebook.ie/eli/2015/act/25/enacted/en/pdf

Luxembourg

Bill to amend the mention of sex and of the first names in civil status and to modify the Civil Code (Projet de loi relative à la modification de la mention du sexe et du ou des prénoms à l'état civil et portant modification du Code civil) http://mj.public.lu/actualites/2017/05/Conference-de-presse-du-17-mai-2017/Projet-de-loi-relative-a-la-modification-de-la-mention-du-sexe.pdf

Intersex & Transgender Luxembourg, "Complément Commun au Rapport supplémentaire au 3e et 4e rapport national (2001-2009) sur les droits de l'enfant au Luxembourg, Les droits des enfants trans' et des enfants intersexes, L'exemple de leur situation au Luxembourg", (in French only) November 2012 https://itgl.lu/wp-content/uploads/2015/04/RADELUX_enfants-trans-et-intersexes.pdf

National Ethics Commission (Commission Nationale d'Éthique), "Opinion 27 Opinion regarding gender diversity", July 2017 https://cne.public.lu/dam-assets/fr/publications/avis/avis-27-en.pdf

Rosa Lëtzebuerg Centre of Information Gay and Lesbian Luxembourg (CIGALE Centre d' Information Gay et Lesbien Luxembourg), "Luxembourg: Overview on the situation of lesbian, bisexual and queer women and recommendations to end violence, discrimination and invisibility, A parallel report submitted for the 69th Session of the Committee on the Elimination of Discrimination against Women (review of the combined 6th and 7th periodic reports of Luxembourg)", January 2018 https://tbinternet.ohchr.org/Treaties/CEDAW/Shared%20Documents/LUX/INT_CEDAW_NGO_LUX_29967_E.pdf

Malta

Act No. XXIV of 2018, An Act to amend the Embryo Protection Act, Cap. 524 http://justiceservices.gov.mt/DownloadDocument.aspx?app=lp&itemid=29136&l=1

Affirmation of Sexual Orientation, Gender Identity and Gender Expression Act, Chapter 567 http://www.justiceservices.gov.mt/DownloadDocument.aspx?app=lom&itemid=12610&l=1

Civil Code (Amendment) Act, 2013 http://www.justiceservices.gov.mt/DownloadDocument.aspx?app=lp&itemid=25178&l=1

Civil Unions Act 2014, Chapter 530 http://www.justiceservices.gov.mt/DownloadDocument.aspx?app=lom&itemid=12172&l=1

Cohabitation Act 2017 http://justiceservices.gov.mt/DownloadDocument.aspx?app=lp&itemid=28146&l=1

Constitution of Malta http://justiceservices.gov.mt/DownloadDocument.aspx?app=lom&itemid=8566

Gender Identity Gender Expression and Sex Characteristics Act (Malta, 2015), https://tgeu.org/gender-identity-gender-expression-sex-characteristics-act-malta-2015/

Employment and Industrial Relations Act (Cap. 452), Equal Treatment in Employment (Amendment) Regulations, 2014 http://www.justiceservices.gov.mt/DownloadDocument.aspx?app=lp&itemid=26271&l=1

LGBTIQ Equality Strategy & Action Plan 2018-2022 https://meae.gov.mt/en/Documents/LGBTIQ%20Action%20Plan/LGBTIQActionPlan_20182022.pdf

LN 44 of 2018 http://justiceservices.gov.mt/LegalPublications.aspx?pageid=32&type=4

Marriage Act and other Laws (Amendment) of 2017, Act No. XXIII of 2017 http://www.justiceservices.gov.mt/DownloadDocument.aspx?app=lp&itemid=28609&l=1

Ministry for Social Dialogue, Consumer Affairs and Civil Liberties, Gender Identity, Gender Expression & Sex Characteristics Act https://meae.gov.mt/en/Public_Consultations/MSDC/Pages/Consultations/GIGESC.aspx

Netherlands

Act of 18 December 2013 amending Book 1 of the Civil Code and the Municipal Personal Records Database Act in connection with changing the conditions for the authority to change the indication of sex in the birth certificate (Wet van 18 december 2013 tot wijziging van Boek 1 van het Burgerlijk Wetboek en de Wet gemeentelijke basisadministratie persoonsgegevens in verband met het wijzigen van de voorwaarden voor en de bevoegdheid ter zake van wijziging van de vermelding van het geslacht in de akte van geboorte) https://zoek.officielebekendmakingen.nl/stb-2014-1.html

Committee against Torture, Concluding observations on the seventh periodic report of the Netherlands, CAT/C/NLD/7, 2018 https://tbinternet.ohchr.org/Treaties/CAT/Shared%20Documents/NLD/CAT_C_NLD_CO_7_33166_E.pdf

Equal Rights Act 1994 (Algemene Wet Gelijke Behandeling) (translated to English by Equal Rights Trust) http://www.equalrightstrust.org/ertdocumentbank//Microsoft%20Word%20-%20Equal_Treatment_Act_1994.pdf

Federatie van Nederlandse Verenigingen tot Integratie van Homoseksualiteit – COC Nederland Nederlands Netwerk voor Intersekse/DSD - NNID Transgender Netwerk Nederland – TNN, "Shadow Report for the 65th Session of the Committee on the Elimination of All Forms of Discrimination Against Women (CEDAW), 6th Periodic Review of the Kingdom of the Netherlands, Discrimination of Lesbian, Bisexual, Transgender and Intersex persons in the Netherlands", Amsterdam/Geneva September 2016 http://intersex.shadowreport.org/public/2016-CEDAW-Netherlands-NNID-etc.pdf

Law for changing the registrered sex on the birth certificate (Wet wijziging van de vermelding van het geslacht in de akte van geboorte) https://www.eerstekamer.nl/behandeling/20140110/publicatie_wet_8/document3/f=/vjgafjzdpczd.pdf

The Ministry of the Interior and Kingdom Relations, "Explanatory report to make explicit the prohibition of discrimination on grounds of gender identity and gender expression in the Equal Treatment Act (Verkenning expliciteren verbod van discriminatie op grond van genderidentiteit en genderexpressie in de Algemene wet gelijke behandeling (Awgb)", 2016 (in Dutch) https://www.tweedekamer.nl/kamerstukken/brieven_regering/detail?id=2016Z13019&did=2016D26770

Portugal

Constitute, Portugal's Constitution of 1976 with Amendments through 2005 https://www.constituteproject.org/constitution/Portugal_2005.pdf

Law 1/2004, of 24th of July, Sixth Constitutional Revision (Lei n. 1/2004, de 24 de Julho, Sexta Revisão Constitucional) (in Portuguese only) http://www.pgdlisboa.pt/leis/lei_mostra_articulado.php?nid=79&tabela=leis&ficha=1&pagina=1&so_miolo=

Law n. 23/2010, Article 1 (2) (Lei n. 23/2010) (in Portuguese only) https://dre.pt/pesquisa/-/search/343919/details/maximized

Law 9/2010 on Same-Sex Marriage (Lei n. 9/2010 Casamento Civil Entre Pessoas do Mesmo Sexo) (in Portuguese only) http://www.pgdlisboa.pt/leis/lei_mostra_articulado.php?nid=1249&tabela=leis&ficha=1&pagina=1&so_miolo=

Law No. 7/2011 (Lei n. 7/2011) https://tgeu.org/portugal-gender-identity-law/

Law 2/2016 (Lei n. 2/2016) (in Portuguese only) https://dre.pt/application/conteudo/73740375

Law No. 38/2018 (Lei No. 38/2018) (in Portuguese only) https://dre.pt/web/guest/home/-/dre/115933863/details/maximized?serie=I&day=2018-08-07&date=2018-08-01

Romania

Accept and ECPI, "Persoane trans în România: Recunoaşterea juridică a identităţii de gen" 2014 (in Romanian only) http://www.ecpi.ro/persoane-trans-in-romania-recunoasterea-juridica-a-identitatii-de-gen/

Civil Code (Codul Civil actualizat 2015) http://www.euroavocatura.ro/print2.php?print2=lege&idItem=1182 (in Romanian only)

Danish Institute for Human Rights, "The social situation concerning homophobia and discrimination on grounds of sexual orientation in Romania", March 2009

Law no. 119/1996 regarding civil status acts and documents, republished (LEGE nr. 119 din 16 octombrie 1996 (**republicată**)(*actualizată*) cu privire la actele de stare civilă*) https://www.primariatm.ro/evpers/legislatie/legi.actualizate/lege.119.1996.pdf (in Romanian only)

Government Ordinance no 41/2003 regarding the administrative procedures for the acquisition and modification of names (Ordonanţa nr. 41/2003 privind dobândirea şi schimbarea pe cale administrativă a numelor persoanelor fizice) https://lege5.ro/Gratuit/gq3dgnrs/ordonanta-nr-41-2003-privind-dobandirea-si-schimbarea-pe-cale-administrativa-a-numelor-persoanelor-fizice (in Romanian only)

U.S. Department of State, "Romania 2016 Human Rights Report", 2016 https://www.state.gov/documents/organization/265676.pdf

Slovenia

Constitution, Official Gazette of the Republic of Slovenia Nos. 33/91-I, 42/97, 66/2000, 24/03, 69/04, 68/06, and 47/13 (Ustava, Uradni list RS, št. 33/91-I, 42/97, 66/2000, 24/03, 69/04, 68/06, 47/13)

https://www.us-rs.si/media/constitution.pdf (in English)

https://www.us-rs.si/o-sodiscu/pravna-podlaga/ustava/ (in Slovenian)

Danish Institute for Human Rights, "The social situation concerning homophobia and discrimination on grounds of sexual orientation in Slovenia", March 2009

Mavcic and Avbelj (2008) "Legal Study on Homophobia and Discrimination on Grounds of Sexual Orientation in Slovenia", FRALEX

Personal Name Act (Zakon o osebnem imenu (ZOI-1)) http://www.pisrs.si/Pis.web/pregledPredpisa?id=ZAKO3890 (in Slovenian)

Rules on the implementation of the Births, Deaths and Marriages Registry Act (Pravilnik o izvrševanju zakona o matičnem registru) http://www.pisrs.si/Pis.web/pregledPredpisa?id=PRAV5572 (in Slovenian)

Spain

Law 14/2012 on non-discrimination based on gender identity (Ley 14/2012, de no discriminación por motivos de identidad de género y de reconocimiento de los derechos de las personas transexuales) (in Spanish only) https://www.boe.es/boe/dias/2012/07/19/pdfs/BOE-A-2012-9664.pdf

Sweden

Gender Recognition Act in 1972 (Lag (1972:119) om fastställande av könstillhörighet i vissa fall) https://www.riksdagen.se/sv/dokument-lagar/dokument/svensk-forfattningssamling/lag-1972119-om-faststallande-av_sfs-1972-119 (Swedish version)
https://tgeu.org/sweden-gender-recognition-act-reformed-2012/ (English version)
Swedish government report SOU 2014:91 (in Swedish) https://tgeu.org/wp-content/uploads/2015/07/Sweden_Report_Age-Requirement-LGR.pdf (in Swedish)
The Population Registration Act (Folkbokföringslag (1991:481)) (in Swedish)

United Kingdom

Discrimination (Sex and Related Characterisics) (Jersey) Regulations 2015 https://www.jerseylaw.je/laws/enacted/pages/RO-061-2015.aspx
Scottish Offences (Aggravation by Prejudice) Act 2009 http://www.legislation.gov.uk/asp/2009/8

European Union Member States Jurisprudence

Austria

Austria Constitutional Court, Important decisions, Identification: AUT-2015-1-001 https://www.vfgh.gv.at/downloads/Bulletin_2015-1_G_119-120-2014_11.12.2014.pdf
Constitutional Court Freyung 8, A-1010 Vienna G 119-120/2014-12 11 December 2014 https://www.vfgh.gv.at/downloads/VfGH_G_119-120-2014_AdoptionsV_EN_korr_4.4.17.pdf
Verfassungsgerichtshof/B947/05, from 21.06.2006
VwGH Zl. 2008/17/0054-8 from 27. 2. 2009
Verwaltungsgerichtshof/2008/06/0032 from 15.09.2009
Verfassungsgerichtshof/B1973/08 from 03.12.2009
VfGH G 77/2018 (in German) https://www.vfgh.gv.at/downloads/VfGH_Entscheidung_G_77-2018_unbestimmtes_Geschlecht_anonym.pdf
Verwaltungsgerichtshof Österreich, "Intersex persons have the right to adequate entry into civil register" https://www.vfgh.gv.at/medien/Civil_register_-_Intersex_persons.en.php

France

Decision n. 531 of 4 Mai 2017 (16-17.189), Court of Cassation, First Civil Chamber, (Arrêt n° 531 du 4 mai 2017 (16-17.189) - Cour de cassation - Première chambre civile -ECLI:FR:CCASS:2017:C100531) (in French) https://www.courdecassation.fr/jurisprudence_2/premiere_chambre_civile_568/531_4_36665.html

Germany

In re Völling, Regional Court Cologne, 6 February 2008
English version: https://www.icj.org/wp-content/uploads/2008/02/In-re-Volling-Regional-Court-Cologne-Germany-English.pdf
German version: https://www.icj.org/wp-content/uploads/2008/02/In-re-Volling-Regional-Court-Cologne-Germany-German.pdf
Case Summary: https://www.icj.org/sogicasebook/in-re-volling-regional-court-cologne-germany-6-february-2008/
Landgericht Köln, 151 Ns 169/11, 07.05.2012 http://www.justiz.nrw.de/nrwe/lgs/koeln/lg_koeln/j2012/151_Ns_169_11_Urteil_20120507.html

Greece

Aristotle University of Thessaloniki, "Historical Court decision on gender recognition without surgery", (in Greek) http://medlawlab.web.auth.gr/%CE%B9%CF%83%CF%84%CE%BF%CF%81%CE%B9%CE%BA%CE%B7-%CE%B4%CE%B9%CE%BA%CE%B1%CF%83%CF%84%CE%B9%CE%BA%CE%B7-%CE%B1%CF%80%CE%BF%CF%86%CE%B1%CF%83%CE%B7-%CE%B3%CE%B9%CE%B1-%CE%B1%CE%BB%CE%BB%CE%B1%CE%B3/ (consulted on 29 August 2018)
Council of State, Decision 2003/2018 (in Greek)
County Court of Marousi, Decision 67/2018 (in Greek) https://www.constitutionalism.gr/wp-content/uploads/2018/02/2018-67_Eirinodikeio-Amarousiou_Jason-Antigone.pdf
One-member First-Instance Court of Heraklion, 255/2013 (in Greek)
Supreme Court, Decision 1428/2017 (in Greek)

Netherlands

Rechtbank's-Gravenhage, 12.07.2004, ECLI:NL:RBSGR:2004:AQ7020 (in Dutch)
Rechtbank Limburg, 28-05-2018, C/03/232248 / FA RK 17-687 (in Dutch) https://uitspraken.rechtspraak.nl/inziendocument?id=ECLI:NL:RBLIM:2018:4931
Rechtbank Limburg, 06.11.2017, C/03/232248 / FA RK 17-687,ECLI:NL:RBLIM:2017:10713 (in Dutch)

Sweden

International Commission of Jurists, "No. 1968-12, Administrative Court of Appeals of Stockholm, Sweden (19 December 2012)" https://www.icj.org/sogicasebook/no-1968-12-administrative-court-of-appeals-of-stockholm-sweden-19-december-2012/

Regional Law and Documents

Africa

African (Banjul) Charter on Human and Peoples' Rights Adopted 27 June 1981, OAU Doc. CAB/LEG/67/3 rev. 5, 21 I.L.M. 58 (1982), entered into force 21 October 1986 http://www.achpr.org/files/instruments/achpr/banjul_charter.pdf
Astraea Lesbian Foundation for Justice, "Public Statement by the African Intersex Movement" https://www.astraeafoundation.org/stories/public-statement-african-intersex-movement/

Kenya

Constitution of Kenya, 2010 http://www.kenyalaw.org/lex/actview.xql?actid=Const2010
International Commission of Jurists, "Richard Muasya v. the Hon. Attorney General, Hight Court of Kenya (2 December 2010) https://www.icj.org/sogicasebook/richard-muasya-v-the-hon-attorney-general-high-court-of-kenya-2-december-2010/ (consulted on 10 April 2018)
Kenya National Commission on Human Rights, "Reading Sexual and Reproductive Health Rights in Kenya: A Myth or a Reality?", A Report of the Public Inquiry into Violations of Sexual and Reproductive Health Rights in Kenya, April 2012 http://www.knchr.org/portals/0/reports/reproductive_health_report.pdf
National Gay and Lesbian Human Rights Commission, Network for Adolescent and Youth of Africa, Gay and Lesbian Coalition of Kenya, East Africa Trans & Advocacy Network, "The Human Rights Situation, Case Law, and Research on Protections on Grounds of Sexual Orientation, Gender Identity, and Expression in the Republic of Kenya", June 5 2017 https://static1.squarespace.com/static/581a19852994ca08211faca4/t/593945a41b10e322cb15ac71/1496925610274/KENYA+IE-SOGI+SUBMISSION.pdf
Republic of Kenya in the High Court of Kenya at Nairobi Petition No 705 of 2007 https://www.icj.org/wp-content/uploads/2012/07/Richard-Muasya-v.-the-Hon.-Attorney-General-High-Court-of-Kenya.pdf
The Kenya Gazette, Vol. CXIX—No. 67, May 26 2017
The Republic of Kenya, Laws of Kenya, Penal Code Chapter 63 https://srhr.org/abortion-policies/documents/countries/02-Kenya-Penal-Code-2014.pdf
The Republic of Kenya, Laws of Kenya, Persons Deprived of Liberty Act, 2014 http://www.ilo.org/dyn/natlex/docs/ELECTRONIC/101067/121601/F-1842141901/KEN101067.pdf
The Kenya Human Rights Commission, "A Study of the LGBTI Community's Search for Equality and Non-discrimination in Kenya", 2011 available on http://www.khrc.or.ke/mobile-publications/equality-and-anti-discrimination/70-the-outlawed-amongst-us/file.html

South Africa

Alteration of Sex Description and Sex Status Act, 2003 https://upload.wikimedia.org/wikipedia/commons/d/d3/Alteration_of_Sex_Description_and_Sex_Status_Act_2003.pdf
Children's Act 38 of 2005, amended by Children's Amendment Act 41 of 2007, Child Justice Act 75 of 2008 http://www.justice.gov.za/legislation/acts/2005-038%20childrensact.pdf
Civil Union Act, 2006 https://www.gov.za/sites/www.gov.za/files/a17-06_1.pdf

Prevention and Combating of Hate Crimes and Hate Speech Bill, (As introduced in the National Assembly (proposed section 75); explanatory summary of Bill published in Government Gazette No. 41543 of 29 March 2018 https://www.parliament.gov.za/storage/app/media/Docs/bill/9febb155-8582-4a15-bf12-5961db2828c2.pdf

The Constitution of the Republic of South Africa 1996, as adopted on 8 May 1996 and amended on 11 October 1996 by the Constitutional Assembly http://www.wipo.int/edocs/lexdocs/laws/en/za/za107en.pdf

Judicial Matters Amendment Act, 2005 http://www.justice.gov.za/legislation/acts/2005-022.pdf

Uganda

Bill No. 18, The Anti Homosexuality Act, 2009 http://www.lgbt-ep.eu/wp-content/uploads/2013/12/UGANDA-Anti-Homosexuality-Bill.pdf

Bill No. 35, Sexual Offences Bill, 2015 http://parliamentwatch.ug/bills/the-sexual-offenses-bill-2016/#.WuiTJ9NubUp

Government of Uganda, Constitution of Uganda, 2005 https://assets.publishing.service.gov.uk/government/uploads/system/uploads/attachment_data/file/582248/Uganda_-_SOGI_-_CPIN_-_v3_0e__January_2017_.pdf

Government of Uganda, Penal Code Act 1950, http://www.wipo.int/wipolex/en/text.jsp?file_id=170005

Registration of Persons Act 2015 https://www.ulii.org/ug/legislation/act/2015/4-6

Americas

American Convention on Human Rights, Adopted at the Inter-American Specialized Conference on Human Rights, San José, Costa Rica, 22 November 1969 https://www.cidh.oas.org/basicos/english/basic3.american%20convention.htm

Atravia Murillo et al (In Vitro Fertilization) v. Costa Rica, Preliminary objections, merits, reparations and costs, Judgment, Inter-Am. Ct. H.R., (ser C) No. 257, 2012 http://www.corteidh.or.cr/docs/casos/articulos/seriec_257_ing.pdf

I/A Court H.R. Gender identity, and equality and non-discrimination with regard to same-sex couples. State obligations in relation to change of name, gender identity, and rights deriving from a relationship between same-sex couples (interpretation and scope of Articles 1(1), 3, 7, 11(2), 13, 17, 18 and 24, in relation to Article 1, of the American Convention on Human Rights). Advisory Opinion OC-24/17 of November 24, 2017. Series A No. 24

Gelman v. Uruguay, Merits and Reparations, Judgment, Inter-Am. Ct. H. R. (ser C) No. 221, 2011 http://corteidh.or.cr/docs/casos/articulos/seriec_221_ing.pdf

Argentina

Código Civil y Comercial de la Nación, entró en vigencia el 1o de Agosto de 2015 http://servicios.infoleg.gob.ar/infolegInternet/anexos/235000-239999/235975/norma.htm#11

Ley 20.968 Tipifica Delitos de Tortura y de Tratos Crueles, Inhumanos y Degradantes https://www.leychile.cl/Navegar?idNorma=1096847

Ley 23.592 Actos Discriminatorios, Adóptanse medidas para quienes arbitrariamente impidan el pleno ejercicio de los derechos y garantías fundamentals reconocidos en la Constitución Nacional, Sancionada: Agosto 3 de 1988, Promulgada: Agosto 23 de 1988 http://servicios.infoleg.gob.ar/infolegInternet/anexos/20000-24999/20465/texact.htm

Ley 26.394 Justicia Militar, Derógase el Código de Justicia Militar y todas las normas, resoluciones y disposiciones de carácter interno que lo reglamentan. Modifícanse el Código Penal y el Código Procesal Penal de la Nación http://www.ara.mil.ar/archivos/Docs/Codigo%20de%20Disciplina%20de%20las%20FFAA.pdf

Ley 26.743 Identidad de Género, Establécese el derecho a la identidad de género de las personas, Sancionada: Mayo 9 de 2012, Promulgada: Mayo 23 de 2012 https://www.tgeu.org/sites/default/files/ley_26743.pdf

TGEU, English Translation of Argentina's Gender Identity Law as approved by the Senate of Argentina on May 8, 2012

Ley 26.791 Modificaciones, Sancionada: Noviembre 14 de 2012, Promulgada: Diciembre 11 de 2012 http://servicios.infoleg.gob.ar/infolegInternet/anexos/205000-209999/206018/norma.htm

Ley 28. 862: Reproducción Médicamente Asistida, Acceso integral a los procedimientos y técnicas medico-asistenciales de reproducción médicamente asistida, Sancionada: Junio 5 de 2013, Promulgada de Hecho: Junio 25 de 2013 http://www.psi.uba.ar/academica/carrerasdegrado/psicologia/sitios_catedras/obligatorias/723_etica2/material/normativas/ley_26862_y_reglamentacion.pdf

Matrimonio Civil, Ley 26.618, Código Civil. Modificación, Sancionada: Julio 15 de 2010, Promulgada: Julio 21 de 2010

OPINIÓN CONSULTIVA OC-24/17 DE 24 DE NOVIEMBRE DE 2017 SOLICITADA POR LA REPÚBLICA DE COSTA RICA IDENTIDAD DE GÉNERO, E IGUALDAD Y NO DISCRIMINACIÓN A PAREJAS DEL MISMO SEXO OBLIGACIONES ESTATALES EN RELACIÓN CON EL CAMBIO DE NOMBRE, LA IDENTIDAD DE GÉNERO, Y LOS DERECHOS DERIVADOS DE UN VÍNCULO ENTRE PAREJAS DEL MISMO SEXO (INTERPRETACIÓN Y ALCANCE DE LOS ARTÍCULOS 1.1, 3, 7, 11.2, 13, 17, 18 Y 24, EN RELACIÓN CON EL ARTÍCULO 1 DE LA CONVENCIÓN AMERICANA SOBRE DERECHOS HUMANOS http://www.corteidh.or.cr/docs/opiniones/seriea_24_esp.pdf

Chile

Acuerdo de Solución Amistosa, Caso P-946-12 http://www.movilh.cl/documentacion/2016/Acuerdo-MOVILH-Estado.pdf

Circular No 07, Complementa circular no 18 que instruye sobre ciertos aspectos de la atención de salud a niños y niñas intersex, 23 Ago. 2016 http://normativas.minsal.cl/CIRCULARES/CIRCULAR_7_16_SP.pdf

Circular No 18, Instruye sobre ciertos aspectos de la atención de salud a niños y niñas intersex, 22 Dic. 2015 http://normativas.minsal.cl/CIRCULARES/circular_18_15_sp.pdf

Ciruclar No 21, Reitera instrucción sobre la atención de personas trans en la red asistencial, 14 Jun. 2012 http://www.indh.cl/wp-content/uploads/2012/08/Circular-21.pdf

Circular No 34, Instruye sobre la atención de personas trans y fortalecimiento de la estrategia de hospital amigo a personas de la diversidad sexual en establecimientos de la red asistencial, Ministerio de Salud Subsecretaría de Salud Pública Subsecretaría de redes asistenciales http://www.movilh.cl/documentacion/trans/Circular-Salud-Trans.pdf

Ley Número 20.609, Establece Medidas Contra La Discriminación https://www.leychile.cl/Navegar?idNorma=1042092

Ley Número 20.940, Moderniza El Sistema de Relaciones Laborales https://www.leychile.cl/Navegar?idNorma=1094436

Ley 20.845, De Inclusión Escolar que regula la admission de los y las estudiantes, elimina el financiamento compartido y prohíbe el lucro en establecimientos educacionales que reciben aportes del estado, Fecha Publicación 08-06-2015, Fecha Promulgación 29-05-2015 http://www.movilh.cl/documentacion/2016/leydeinclusion.pdf

Legislatura 365, Modifica diversos cuerpos legales para regular, en igualdad de condiciones, el matrimonio de parejas del mismo sexo https://www.camara.cl/pley/pley_detalle.aspx?prmID=11934&prmBoletin=11422-07

Ordinario Circular No 1297/2012, Guía Técnica, "Peritaje de Sexología Forense para Personas Trans e Intersex", 9 Nov. 2012 http://otdchile.org/wp-content/uploads/2017/04/Ord-Circular-1297-de-2012-Adj-Guia-Tecnica-1.pdf

Registro Civil e Identificación, Programa Equidad de Género 2017, "Datos Registrales con Enfoque de Género", Fecha corte: 30 de junio de 2017, Publicación: Julio 2017 http://www.registrocivil.cl/transparencia/DatoInteresCiudadano/Datos_Registrales_por_Genero_2017_1.pdf

Sistema de Garantías de Derechos de la Niñez: Proyecto informado por la Comisión de Familia y Adulto Mayor https://www.bcn.cl/obtienearchivo?id=repositorio/10221/23993/2/BCN_Proyecto%20Garantias%20Infancia%20Familia.pdf

Colombia

Constitución Política de Colombia, Actulizada con los Actos Legislativos a 2016 http://www.corteconstitucional.gov.co/inicio/Constitucion%20politica%20de%20Colombia.pdf and translation in English by Marcia W. Coward, Peter B. Heller, Anna I. Vellve Torras, and Max Planck Institute https://www.constituteproject.org/constitution/Colombia_2005.pdf

Ley No. 1482 de 2011, "Por medio de la cual se modifica el Código Penal y se establecen otras disposiciones" http://wsp.presidencia.gov.co/Normativa/Leyes/Documents/ley148230112011.pdf

United States

American Psychological Association & National Association of School Psychologists, "Resolution on gender and sexual orientation diversity in children and adolescents in schools. Retrieved from http://www.apa.org/about/policy/orientation-diversity.aspx

Elders M. Joycelyn, M.D., M.S. 15th Surgeon General of the United States, Satcher David, M.D., Ph.D., FAAFP, FACPM, FACP 16th Surgeon General of the United States, Carmona Richard, M.D., M.P.H., FACS 17th Surgeon General of the United States, "Re-Thinking Genital Surgeries on Intersex Infants", Palm Center, p. 1-4, 2017

Section 1557: Protecting Individuals Against Sex Discrimination https://www.hhs.gov/sites/default/files/1557-fs-sex-discrimination-508-7-28-17rev.pdf

Senate Concurrent Resolution No. 110, Introduced by Senator Wiener https://openstates.org/ca/bills/20172018/SCR110/

SB-179 Gender identity: female, male or nonbinary, Senate Bill No. 179, Chapter 853 https://leginfo.legislature.ca.gov/faces/billNavClient.xhtml?bill_id=201720180SB179

Tennessee Senate Bill 1556, 2016 https://legiscan.com/TN/text/SB1556/id/1319613

Oceania

Darlington Statement, Intersex Human Rights Australia, 10 March 2017 https://ihra.org.au/darlington-statement/

Australia

Australian Human Rights Commission, "Sex Files: the legal recognition of sex in documents and government records", 2009 https://www.humanrights.gov.au/our-work/sexual-orientation-sex-gender-identity/publications/sex-files-legal-recognition-sex#Heading353
Commonwealth of Australia Constitution Act (The Constitution), This compilation was prepared on 4 September 2013 taking into account alterations up to Act No. 84 of 1977
Intersex Human Rights Australia, "Submission on the ethics of genetic selection against intersex traits", 2014. https://ihra.org.au/25621/submission-ethics-genetic-selection-intersex-traits/
Sex Discrimination Amendment (Sexual Orientation, Gender Identity and Intersex Status) Act 2013, No. 98, 213, An Act to amend the Sex Discrimination Act 1984, and for related purposes https://www.legislation.gov.au/Details/C2013A00098
The Parliament of the Commonwealth of Australia, House of Representatives, Sex Discrimination Amendment (Sexual Orientation, Gender Identity and Intersex Status) Bill 2013, Explanatory Memorandum http://parlinfo.aph.gov.au/parlInfo/search/display/display.w3p;query=Id%3A%22legislation%2Fems%2Fr5026_ems_1fcd9245-33ff-4b3a-81b9-7fdc7eb91b9b%22
The Parliament of the Commonwealth of Australia, House of Representatives, Marriage Amendment (Definition and Religious Freedoms) Bill 2017, Explanatory Memorandum https://theaustralianatnewscorpau.files.wordpress.com/2017/09/marriage-dean-smith-bill-2017-em-05-0-1.pdf
The Parliament of Australia, Second Report "Involuntary or coerced sterilisation of intersex people in Australia", Chapter 3 "Surgery and the assignment of gender" https://www.aph.gov.au/Parliamentary_Business/Committees/Senate/Community_Affairs/Involuntary_Sterilisation/Sec_Report/index

New Zealand

Attorney-General, "Crown Law opinion on transgender discrimination", 2006 https://www.beehive.govt.nz/release/crown-law-opinion-transgender-discrimination
Births, Deaths, Marriages, and Relationships Registration Act 1995 http://www.legislation.govt.nz/act/public/1995/0016/73.0/DLM364150.html
Human Rights Act 1993 http://www.legislation.govt.nz/act/public/1993/0082/latest/DLM304475.html
Human Rights Commission, "To Be Who I am", Report of the Inquiry into Discrimination Experienced by Transgender People, 2007 https://www.hrc.co.nz/files/5714/2378/7661/15-Jan-2008_14-56-48_HRC_Transgender_FINAL.pdf
Human Rights Commission, Human Rights in New Zealand 2010, Section Four-Rights of Specific Groups "19. Rights of Sexual and Gender Minorities" https://www.hrc.co.nz/files/1914/2388/0525/HRNZ_10_rights_of_sexual_and_gender_minorities.pdf
Human Rights Commission, Intersex Roundtable Report 2016 "The practice of genital normalization on intersex children in Aotearoa New Zealand" https://www.hrc.co.nz/files/5914/8124/9497/HRC_Intersex_Roundtable.pdf

Internal Affairs, "General information regarding Declarations of Family Court as to sex to be shown on birth certificates" https://www.dia.govt.nz/diawebsite.nsf/Files/GeninfoDeclarationsofFamilyCourt/$file/GeninfoDeclarationsofFamilyCourt.pdf

Intersex Trust Aotearoa New Zealand, Alternate NGO Submission on the sixth periodic report to the United Nations on the Convention against Torture and Other Cruel, Inhuman or Degrading Treatment or Punishment from New Zealand, January 2015

Marriage (Definition of Marriage) Amendment Act 2013 http://www.legislation.govt.nz/act/public/2013/0020/latest/DLM4505010.html

New Zealand Parliament, Human Rights (Gender Identity) Amendment Bill https://www.parliament.nz/en/pb/bills-and-laws/bills-proposed-laws/document/00DBHOH_BILL6476_1/human-rights-gender-identity-amendment-bill

New Zealand Parliament, Wall, Louisa, 2014 https://www.parliament.nz/en/pb/hansard-debates/rhr/document/50HansS_20140416_00000973/wall-louisa-statutes-amendment-bill-no-4-first-reading

New Zealand Crimes Act 1961, s. 204A; Attorney General's Department, Review of Australia's Female Genital Mutilation Legal Framework – Final Report, 2013

OII Australia, Submission to the Australian Human Rights Commission: Sexual Orientation, Gender Identity and Intersex Rights Snapshot Report, February 2015

Asia

ASEAN Human Rights Declaration and the Phnom Penh Statement on the Adoption of the ASEAN Human Rights Declaration (AHRD) http://www.asean.org/storage/images/ASEAN_RTK_2014/6_AHRD_Booklet.pdf

Asia Pacific Forum, "Promoting and Protecting Human Rights in relation to Sexual Orientation, Gender Identity and Sex Characteristics", A Manual for National Human Rights Institutions, 2016 http://www.asiapacificforum.net/media/resource_file/SOGI_and_Sex_Characteristics_Manual_86Y1pVM.pdf

Charter of the Association of Southeast Asian Nations, The ASEAN Charter http://asean.org/storage/images/archive/publications/ASEAN-Charter.pdf

Intersex Day, Statement of Intersex Asia and Asia intersex forum, 17 February 2018 https://intersexday.org/en/intersex-asia-2018/

Bangladesh

The Penal Code, 1860 (Act. No. XLV of 1860) http://www.wipo.int/edocs/lexdocs/laws/en/bd/bd020en.pdf

Home Office, "Country Policy and Information Note Bangladesh: Sexual orientation and gender identity", November 2017 https://assets.publishing.service.gov.uk/government/uploads/system/uploads/attachment_data/file/660538/Bangladesh_-_SOGI_-_CPIN_-_v3.0__Nov_2017_.pdf

Nepal

The Constitution of Nepal, Date of Publication in Nepal Gazette, 20 September 2015 (2072.6.3) http://www.wipo.int/edocs/lexdocs/laws/en/np/np029en.pdf

Pakistan

Pakistan Penal Code (XLV of 1860) 6th October, 1860 https://www.oecd.org/site/adboecdanti-corruptioninitiative/46816797.pdf
Transgender Persons (Protection of Rights) Act, 2018, 10th May 2018 http://paklawyer.com/blog/transgender-persons-protection-rights-act-2018/
U.S. State government report, Pakistan 2017 Human Rights Report https://www.state.gov/documents/organization/277535.pdf

Philippines

Republic Act (RA) 9262, Anti-Violence Against Women and Their Children Act of 2004, National Commission on the Role of Filipino Women (NCRFW) http://www.pcw.gov.ph/sites/default/files/documents/resources/ra_9262_and_irr.pdf
REPUBLIC ACT NO. 9048 March 22, 2001
Republic Act No. 9048 March 22, 2001, An Act Authorizing the City or Municipal Civil Registrar or the Consul General to Correct a Clerical or Typographical Error in an Entry and/or Change of First Name of Nickname in the Civil Register without Need of a Judicial Order, Amending for this Purpose Articles 376 and 412 of the Civil Code of the Philippines https://www.lawphil.net/statutes/repacts/ra2001/ra_9048_2001.html
The Family Code of the Philippines: Executive Order No. 209, July 6, 1987 http://www.chanrobles.com/executiveorderno209.htm#.W1MEMNgzZ-U
The Revised Penal Code of the Philippines, An Act Revising the Penal Code and Other Penal Laws http://www.chanrobles.com/revisedpenalcodeofthephilippines.htm#.W1LzctgzZ-U
UNDP-USAID, "Being LGBT in Asia: The Philippines Country Report", A Participatory Review and Analysis of the Legal and Social Environment for Lesbian, Gay, Bisexual and Transgender (LGBT) Individuals and Civil Society, 2014 https://www.usaid.gov/sites/default/files/documents/1861/2014%20UNDP-USAID%20Philippines%20LGBT%20Country%20Report%20-%20FINAL.pdf

Viet Nam

Decree no. 87/2001/ND-CP of November 21, 2001 on sanctions against administrative violations in the field of marriage and family https://vanbanphapluat.co/decree-no-87-2001-nd-cp-of-november-21-2001-on-sanctions-against-administrative-violations-in-the-field-of-marriage-and-family
Decree No. 110/2013/ND-CP on regulating sanction of administrative violation in the field of judicial assistance, judicial administration, marriage and family, civil judgment enforcement, enterprise and cooperative bankruptcy https://luatminhkhue.vn/en/circular/decree-no-

110-2013-nd-cp-on-regulating-sanction-of-administrative-violation-in-the-field-of-judicial-assistance%2D%2Djudicial-administration%2D%2Dmarriage-and-family%2D%2Dcivil-judgment-enforcement%2D%2Denterprise-and-cooperative-bankruptcy.aspx
The Marriage and Family Law, No. 22/2000/QH10 of June, 2000 http://www.moj.gov.vn/vbpq/en/lists/vn%20bn%20php%20lut/view_detail.aspx?itemid=373
Viet Nam Civil Code No. 91/2015/QH13 of November 24, 2015 http://www.wipo.int/wipolex/en/text.jsp?file_id=445413
Vietnam Marriage and Family Law 2014 http://vietnamlawenglish.blogspot.com/2014/06/viet-nam-marriage-and-family-law-2014.html

Regional Jurisprudence

Africa

Kenya

Baby 'A' (suing through the Mother E.A.) & another v. Attorney General & 6 others [2014] eKLR, petition no. 266 of 2013 https://www.crin.org/en/library/legal-database/baby-suing-through-mother-ea-and-cradle-children-foundation-v-attorney
Richard Muasya v. the Hon. Attorney General, Hight Court of Kenya Petition No. 705 of 2007 https://www.icj.org/wp-content/uploads/2012/07/Richard-Muasya-v.-the-Hon.-Attorney-General-High-Court-of-Kenya.pdf

South Africa

Du Toit and Another v Minister of Welfare and Population Development and Others (CCT40/01) [2002] ZACC 20; 2002 (10) BCLR 1006; 2003 (2) SA 198 (CC) 10 September 2002 http://www.saflii.org.za/za/cases/ZACC/2002/20.html
Minister of Home Affairs and Another v Fourie and Another (CCT 60/04) [2005] ZACC 19; 2006 (3) BCLR 355 (CC); 2006 (1) SA 524 (CC) 1 December 2005
National Coalition for Gay and Lesbian Equality and Another v. Minister of Justice and Others, Case CCT 11/98, South Africa: Constitutional Court, 9 October 1998, http://www.refworld.org/cases,ZAF_CC,48246cf72.html

Uganda

Prof J. Oloka Onyango & 9 Others v Attorney Gerneral (Constitutional Petition No. 08 of 2014) [2014[UGCC 14 (1 August 2014) https://www.ulii.org/ug/judgment/constitutional-court/2014/14/

Americas

Colombia

C-075 de 2007, Regimen Patrimonial de Compañeros Permanentes-Pareja homosexuals/Parejas Homosexuales y Union Marital de Hecho-Protección patrimonial/Parejas Homosexuales-Vulneración de la dignidad humana y libre desarrollo de la personalidad al excluirlos de regimen de protección patrimonial http://www.corteconstitucional.gov.co/relatoria/2007/c-075-07.htm

C-811/2007, Régimen de Seguridad Social en Salud de Pareja Homosexual

C-336/2008, Norma demanda por la cual se definen las unines maritales de hecho y regimen patrimonial entre compañeros permanentes Por la cual se crea el Sistema de seguridad social integral y se dictan otras disposiciones

C-798/2008, Acción Penal por Insasistencia Alimentaria entre Miembros de Paraja Homosexual

International Commission of Jurists, "Sentencia SU 337/99, Constitutional Court of Colombia (12 May 1999)" https://www.icj.org/sogicasebook/sentencia-su-33799-constitutional-court-of-colombia-12-may-1999/

T-856/2007, Derecho a la Intimidad de Enfermo de Sida, Obligación de afiliar como beneficiarios a los compañeros permanentes de los cotizantes sin importar cuál sea su sexo, a partir de la adopción de la Sentencia C-521 de 2007

T-1241/2008, Pension de Sobrevivientes en Parejas del Mismo Sexo

C-029/2009, Pretension de Exequibilidad Condicionada en Demanda de Inconstitucionalidad

T-392/17, Acción de tutela presentada por Charlotte Schenider Callejas contra la Secretaría Distrital de Salud de Bogotá, Asunto: Presupuestos de efectividad del derecho fundamental de petición; las personas transgénero como sujetos de especial protección constitucional; la protección constitucional especial de personas portadoras de VIH/SIDA y su derecho a la estabilidad laboral reforzada; la naturaleza de los contratos de prestación de servicios y sus diferencias con una relación laboral; el principio de primacía de la realidad sobre las formas

T-063/15, Acción de Tutela Contra la Registraduria Nacional del Estado Civil-Procedencia para modificar el sex en el registro civil de une persona transgénero via notarial

T-804/14, Orientación Sexual e Identidad de Género-Caso de persona con orientación sexual e identidad de género distinta que le niegan cupo en institución educativa para cursar grado once

T-918/12, Derecho a la identidad sexual

T-231/13, Acción de Tutela contra la Registraduria Nacional-Caso en que no se expide cédula de ciudadanía por cuanto figura en el Registro Civil de Nacimiento como sexo femenino cuando corresponde a masculino

T-876/12, Tratamiento Medico- Caso en que Secretaría de Salud y EPSS niegan cirugía de cambio de sexo

C-683/15, Demanda de inconstitutionalidad contra los articulos 64,66 y 68 (parciales) de la Ley 1098 de 2006, "por la cual se expide el Código de la Infancia y la Adolescencia", y contra el artículo 1o (parcial) de la Ley 54 de 1990 "por la cual se definen las unions maritales de hecho y regimen patrimonial entre compañeros permanentes"

C-071/15, Parejas del mismo sexo- Sólo pueden adopter cuando la solicitud recaiga en el hijo biológico de su compañero o compañera permanente

T-276/12, Garantias Constitucioanles en el Marco de los Procesos de Restablecimiento de Derechos de los Niños

T-477/95, Readecuación de Sexo del Menor/Consentimento del Paciente-Cambio de sexo/Teoria de la Información-Cambio de sexo

SU-337/99, Principio de Publicidad del Proceso- Armonización con la intimidad del menor y su familia/Sentencia de Revisión de Tutela-Publicidad parcial para el caso

T-912/08, Línea jurisprudencial sobre los requisitos del consentimiento sustituto informado de los padres para la cirugías de asignación de sexo y remodelación genital

T-450A/13, Derecho a la Personalidad Juridica del Niño-Desconocimiento por no inscripción en el registro civil por ambiguëdad genital

United States

Bowers v. Hardwick, 478 U.S. 186, 1986 https://supreme.justia.com/cases/federal/us/478/186/case.html

Lawrence v. Texas, 539 U.S. 558, 2003 https://supreme.justia.com/cases/federal/us/539/558/case.html

M.C. v. Aaronson, No. 13-2178, United States Court of Appeals for the Fourth Circuit http://www.ca4.uscourts.gov/Opinions/Unpublished/132178.U.pdf

Obergefell v. Hodges, No. 14-556. Argued April 28, 2015, Decided June 26, 2015 https://www.supremecourt.gov/opinions/14pdf/14-556_3204.pdf

Windsor v. United States, No. 12-307, Argued March 27, 2013, Decided June 26, 2013 https://www.supremecourt.gov/opinions/12pdf/12-307_6j37.pdf

Zzyym v. Pompeo (formerly Zzyym v. Tillerson & Zzyym v. Kerry), In the United States District Court for the District of Colorado, Judge R. Brooke Jackson, Civil Action No. 15-cv-02362-RBJ

Oceania

Australia

High Court of Australia, NSW Registrar of Births, Deaths and Marriages v Norrie [2014] HCA 11, Judgment Summary http://www.hcourt.gov.au/assets/publications/judgment-summaries/2014/hca-11-2014-04-02.pdf

NSW Registrar of Births, Deaths and Marriages v Norrie [2014] HCA 11 2 April 2014 S273/2013 http://ww3.lawschool.cornell.edu/AvonResources/NSW%20Registrar%20of%20Births,%20Deaths%20and%20Marriages%20v%20Norrie%20[2014]%20HCA%2011%20(2%20April%202014).pdf

Re: Carla (Medical procedure) [2016] FamCA 7 (20 January 2016), Family Court of Australia http://www.austlii.edu.au/cgi-bin/sinodisp/au/cases/cth/FamCA/2016/7.html

Asia

India

M/S. Kusum Ingots & Alloys Ltd vs Union Of India And Anr on 28 April, 2004 https://indiankanoon.org/doc/1876565/

National Legal Services Authority v Union of India and Others (Writ Petition No. 400 of 2012 with Writ Petition No. 604 of 2013) Case summary http://www.equalrightstrust.org/ertdocumentbank/NLSA%20v%20Union%20of%20India.pdf

National Legal Services Authority v Union of India and Others (Writ Petition No. 400 of 2012 with Writ Petition No. 604 of 2013) Decision http://www.refworld.org/cases,IND_SC,5356279d4.html

Naz Foundation v. Government of NCT of Delhi and Others WP (C) No. 7455/2001 http://www.equalrightstrust.org/ertdocumentbank//Naz%20Foundn%20v%20%20Govt%20of%20NCT%20of%20Delhi%20_2_%20_3_.pdf

Shivani Bhat v. State of NCT of Delhi and Ors., Delhi High Court on 5 October, 2015 https://indiankanoon.org/doc/10525112/

Nepal

International Commission of Jurists, Sunil Babu Pant and Others/ v. Nepal Government and Others, Supreme Court of Nepal (21 December 2007) https://www.icj.org/sogicasebook/sunil-babu-pant-and-others-v-nepal-government-and-others-supreme-court-of-nepal-21-december-2007/

Rajani Shah v. National Women Commission et al., Supreme Court of Nepal, April 11, 2013

Sunil Babu Pant and Others/ v. Nepal Government and Others, Supreme Court of Nepal (21 December 2007) https://www.gaylawnet.com/laws/cases/PantvNepal.pdf

Pakistan

International Commission of Jurists, Khaki v. Rawalpindi, Supreme Court of Pakistan (12 December 2009), Case summary https://www.icj.org/sogicasebook/khaki-v-rawalpindi-supreme-court-of-pakistan-12-december-2009/

Khaki v. Rawalpindi, Supreme Court of Pakistan, Constitution Petition No. 43 of 2009 https://www.icj.org/wp-content/uploads/2012/07/Khaki-v.-Rawalpindi-Supreme-Court-of-Pakistan.pdf

Philippines

International Commission of Jurists, Republic of the Philippines v. Jennifer Cagandahan, Supreme Court of the Philippines, Second Division, 12 September 2008, Case summary https://www.icj.org/sogicasebook/republic-of-the-philippines-v-jennifer-cagandahan-supreme-court-of-the-philippines-second-division-12-september-2008/

Republic of the Philippines v. Jennifer Cagandahan, G.R. No. 166676, Supreme Court of the Philippines, Second Division, 12 September 2008 https://www.icj.org/wp-content/uploads/2012/07/Republic-of-the-Philippines-v.-Jennifer-Cagandahan-Supreme-Court-of-the-Philippines-Second-Division.pdf

Rommel Jacinto Dantes Silverio v. Republic of the Philippines, G.R. No. 174689: October 22, 2007 http://www.chanrobles.com/scdecisions/jurisprudence2007/oct2007/gr_174689_2007.php

Reports

Agius S (2015) "Human Rights and Intersex People", Issue Paper, https://s3cdn-observadoron-time.netdna-ssl.com/wp-content/uploads/2015/05/issuepaper-on-intersex2015_en.pdf

American Psychiatric Publishing, APA, "Gender Dysphoria", 2013

Amnesty International (2017) "First, Do No Harm: Ensuring the Rights of Children with Variations of Sex Characteristics in Denmark and Germany", https://www.ilga-europe.org/sites/default/files/eur0160862017english.pdf

Australian Human Rights Commission (2009) "Sex Files: the legal recognition of sex in documents and government records"

Australian Human Rights Commission (2009) "Surgery on intersex infants and human rights"

Australian Human Rights Commission, "Resilient Individuals: Sexual Orientation, Gender Identity and Intersex Rights", National Consultation Report 2015

Biblioteca del Congreso Nacional de Chile Informe, "Cambio de sexo registral en Chile: procedimiento legal y jurisprudencia"

Center for Reproductive Rights (2012) "Whose Right to Life? Women's Rights and Prenatal Protections under Human Rights and Comparative Law", available on https://www.reproductiverights.org/sites/crr.civicactions.net/files/documents/RTL_3%2014%2012.pdf

Centro de Derechos Humanos, Facultad de Derecho, Universidad Diego Portales; Tomás Vial Solar (editor general) (2016) "Informe anual sobre Derechos Humanos en Chile 2016", http://www.derechoshumanos.udp.cl/derechoshumanos/images/InformeAnual/2016/Godoy_ddhh-personasintersex.pdf

Civil Society Coalition on Human Rights and Constitutional Law (CSCHRCL), Human Rights Awareness and Promotion Forum (HRAPF), Rainbow Health Foundation (RHF), Sexual Minorities Uganda (SMUG), Support Initiative for Persons with Congenital Disorders (SIPD) (October 2014) "Uganda Report of Violations Based on Sex Determination, Gender Identity, and Sexual Orientation",

Council of Europe, Human Rights and Gender Identity (2009) available on https://wcd.coe.int/ViewDoc.jsp?p=&id=1476365&direct=true#P61_8834

Council of Europe, Human Rights and Intersex people (2015) available on https://rm.coe.int/16806da5d4

Darlington Statement: Joint consensus statement from the intersex community retreat in Darlington (March 2017) available on https://oii.org.au/wp-content/uploads/key/Darlington-Statement.pdf

EqualJus, "The Equal Jus Legal Handbook to LGBT Rights in Europe", https://www.ilga-europe.org/sites/default/files/Attachments/equal_jus_legal_handbook_to_lgbt_rights_in_europe_0.pdf

European Union Agency for Fundamental Rights (FRA) (2009) "Homophobia and Discrimination on the grounds of sexual orientation in the EU Member States, Part I Legal Analysis", http://fra.europa.eu/sites/default/files/fra_uploads/192-FRA_hdgso_report_Part%201_en.pdf

European Union Agency for Fundamental Rights (FRA) (2015) "The fundamental rights situation of intersex people", http://fra.europa.eu/en/publication/2015/fundamental-rights-situation-intersex-people

European Commission (2012) "Trans and Intersex people, Discrimination on the grounds of sex, gender identity and gender expression", http://www.teni.ie/attachments/35bf473d-1459-4baa-8f55-56f80cfe858a.PDF

European Court of Human Rights (2016) Research Report "Bioethics and the case-law of the Court", https://www.echr.coe.int/Documents/Research_report_bioethics_ENG.pdf

European Court of Human Rights (2015) Thematic Report "Health-related issues in the case-law of the European Court of Human Rights", https://www.echr.coe.int/Documents/Research_report_health.pdf

Explanatory Report to the Convention for the protection of Human Rights and Dignity of the Human Being with regard to the Application of Biology and Medicine: Convention on Human Rights and Biomedicine, 1997 https://rm.coe.int/16800ccde5

Finnish Immigration Service (December 2015) “Status of LGBT people in Cameroon, Gambia, Ghana and Uganda”

Flores AR, Andrew P (March 2018) “Polarized Progress, Social Acceptance of LGBT People in 141 Countries, 1981 to 2014”, The Williams Institute UCLA School of Law

Flores AR, Andrew P (March 2018) “Examining the Relationship between Social Acceptance of LGBT people and Legal Inclusion of Sexual Minorities”, The Williams Institute UCLA School of Law

Free&Equal United Nations for LGBT Equality, “Factsheet on International Human Rights Law and Sexual Orientation & Gender Identity”, available on https://www.unfe.org/system/unfe-6-UN_Fact_Sheets_v6_-_International_Human_Rights_Law__and_Sexual_Orientation___Gender_Identity.pdf

Ghattas CD (December 2015) “Standing up for the Human Rights of Intersex People-How Can you Help?”, ILGA Europe, Oii Europe, https://www.ilga-europe.org/sites/default/files/how_to_be_a_great_intersex_ally_a_toolkit_for_ngos_and_decision_makers_december_2015_updated.pdf

Global Citizenship Commission, “The Universal Declaration of Human Rights in the 21st Century: A Living document in a Changing World” Article 5: The Anti-Torture Provision Appendix E to the Report of the Global Citizenship Commission, 2016 available on https://www.openbook-publishers.com/shopimages/The-UDHR-21st-C-AppendixE2.pdf

Holmes A. Henry, “Glossary of Terms Relating to Sexuality and Gender”, available on http://www.nationalmecha.org/documents/GS_Terms.pdf

Human Rights Watch (2018) “All We Want is Equality” Religious Exemptions and Discrimination against LGBT People in the United States

Human Rights Watch and Interact (July 2017) “I Want to Be Like Nature Made Me” Medically Unnecessary Surgeries on Intersex Children in the US, available on https://interactadvo-cates.org/wp-content/uploads/2017/07/Human-Rights-Watch-interACT-Report-Medically-Unnecessary-Surgeri-on-Intersex-Children-in-the-US.pdf

Human Rights Watch (2016) “I Want to Live With My Head Held High” Abuses in Bangladesh’s Legal Recognition of Hijras, https://www.hrw.org/sites/default/files/report_pdf/bangla-desh1216_web.pdf

Human Genetics Alert (December 2002) “The case against sex selection”, Human Genetics Alert Campaign Briefing

Human Rights first, “Communities Under Siege: LGBTI Rights Abuses in Uganda” https://www.humanrightsfirst.org/wp-content/uploads/Discrimination-against-LGBTI-Ugandans-FINAL.pdf

Icelandic Human Rights Centre, “An overview of the case law on the prohibition of discrimination of the ECJ and the ECtHR” http://www.humanrights.is/static/files/Itarefni/an-overview-of-the-case-law-on-the-prohibition-of-discrimination-of-the-ecj-and-the-ecthr-emilie.pdf

ILGA-Europe, “Annual Review of the Human Rights Situation of Lesbian, Gay, Bisexual, Trans and Intersex People in Europe”, 2018 https://www.ilga-europe.org/sites/default/files/2018/full_annual_review.pdf

ILGA, “State-Sponsored Homophobia, A World Survey of Sexual Orientation Laws: Criminalisation, Protection and Recognition”, 11th Edition, Updated to October 2016 https://ilga.org/downloads/02_ILGA_State_Sponsored_Homophobia_2016_ENG_WEB_150516.pdf

ILGA: Carroll Aengus and Mendos Lucas Ramón “State Sponsored Homophobia 2017: A world survey of sexual orientation laws: criminalisation, protection and recognition”, 2017, http://ilga.org/downloads/2017/ILGA_State_Sponsored_Homophobia_2017_WEB.pdf

Independent Advisory Group on Country Information, “Country Policy and Information Note Uganda: Sexual orientation and gender identity”, Version 3.0e, January 2017 https://assets.publishing.service.gov.uk/government/uploads/system/uploads/attachment_data/file/582248/Uganda_-_SOGI_-_CPIN_-_v3_0e__January_2017_.pdf

Instituto Nacional contra la Discriminación, la Xenofobia y el Racismo, Intersexualidad; dirigido por Javier Alejandro Bujan. - 1a ed. - Ciudad Autónoma de Buenos Aires http://201.216.243.171/biblioteca/wp-content/uploads/2016/03/intersexualidad.pdf

Inter-American Commission on Human Rights, "Violence against LGBTI Persons", OAS/Ser.L/V/II.rev.1 Doc. 36 12 November 2015 http://www.oas.org/en/iachr/reports/pdfs/violencelgbtipersons.pdf

International Association of Athletics Federations, IAAF Regulations Governing Eligibility of Females With Hyperandrogenism to Compete in Women's Competitions. effective May 1, 2011. Updated December 11, 2012 www.iaaf.org/about-iaaf/documents/medical

International Commission of Jurists, SOGI Casebook: "Chapter six: Intersex" https://www.icj.org/sogi-casebook-introduction/chapter-six-intersex/

International Conference on Population and Development (ICPD), Program of Action available on http://www.unfpa.org/sites/default/files/pub-pdf/programme_of_action_Web%20ENGLISH.pdf

Inter Laura and Aoi Hana (2017) Circular 7, 2016: A Step Back in the Fight for the Human Rights of Intersex People in Chile, https://brujulaintersexual.files.wordpress.com/2017/07/circular-7-english.pdf

International Olympic Committee. IOC Regulations on Female Hyperandrogenism. www.olympic.org/Documents/Commissions_PDFfiles/Medical_commission/IOC-Regulations-on-Female-Hyperandrogenism.pdf

Justicia Intersex and StopIGM.org / Zwischengeschlecht.org (March 2017) "NGO Report To the 6th and 7th Periodic Report of Argentina on the Convention Against Torture (CAT)", http://intersex.shadowreport.org/public/2017-CAT-Justicia-Intersex-Zwischengeschlecht-IGM.pdf

Koyama Emi, Dr. Weasel Lisa, Intersex Society of North America, "Teaching Intersex Issues A Guide for Teachers in Women's, Gender & Queer Studies", June 2001 http://isna.org/pdf/teaching-intersex-web.pdf

Kilkelly U, Donnelly M (2006) "The Child's Right to be heard in the Healthcare Setting: Perspectives of children, parents and health professionals", https://www.dcya.gov.ie/documents/research/The_Childs_Right_to_be_Heard_in_the_Healthcare_Setting.pdf

Koffemena NR (June 2010) "(The right to) personal autonomy in the case law of the European Court of Human Rights". Thesis, University of Leiden, https://openaccess.leidenuniv.nl/bitstream/handle/1887/15890/N.R.+Koffeman+-+(The+right)+to+personal+autonomy+in+the+case+law+of+the+ECtHR+(2010).pdf;jsessionid=CCE1BCA991B6F07C20983D3CBCA63C81?sequence=3

Lee AP, Houk PC, Ahmed F, Hughes A (2006) Ieuan in collaboration with the participants in the International Consensus Conference on Intersex organized by the Lawson Wilkins Pediatric Endocrine Society and the European Society for Paediatric Endocrinology, "Consensus Statement on Management of Intersex Disorders", available on http://pediatrics.aappublications.org/content/118/2/e488?sso=1&sso_redirect_count=1&nfstatus=401&nftoken=00000000-0000-0000-0000-000000000000&nfstatusdescription=ERROR%3a+No+local+token

Living Free & Equal (2016) "What States Are Doing to Tackle Violence and Discrimination Against Lesbian, Gay, Bisexual, Transgender and Intersex People", United Nations, https://www.ohchr.org/Documents/Publications/LivingFreeAndEqual.pdf

MOVILH (2017) Historia anual de las personas LGBTI, XVI. Informe Anual de Derechos Humanos, Diversidad sexual y de género en Chile, Hechos http://www.movilh.cl/documentacion/2018/Informe-DDHH-2017-Movilh.pdf

National Intersex Meeting Report 2018, "National Dialogue on the Protection and Promotion of the Human Rights of Intersex People" http://www.justice.gov.za/vg/lgbti/2018-NationalIntersexMeetingReport.pdf

Observatorio de Derechos Humanos –Chile (Andrés Rivera Duarte) International Gay and Lesbian Human Rights Commission (IGLHRC) (January 2015) "The Situation of Trans and Intersex Children in Chile", Submitted to the United Nations Committee on the Rights of the

Child on the Occasion of its Pre-sessional Working Group Meeting to Consider Chile's Joint Fourth and Fifth Periodic Report, https://www.outrightinternational.org/sites/default/files/ChileTransIntersexLR.pdf

OHCHR (2016) "Living Free and Equal", http://www.ohchr.org/Documents/Publications/LivingFreeAndEqual.pdf

OHCHR (2002) Factsheet: "No one shall be subjected to torture or to cruel, inhuman or degrading treatment or punishment", available on http://www.ohchr.org/Documents/Publications/FactSheet4rev.1en.pdf

OHCHR (May 2014) UN Women, UNAIDS, UNDP, UNFPA, UNICEF and WHO, "Eliminating forced, coercive and otherwise involuntary sterilization, An interagency statement", available on http://www.who.int/reproductivehealth/publications/gender_rights/eliminating-forced-sterilization/en/

OII Europe, Malta Declaration (1 December 2013) available on https://oiieurope.org/malta-declaration/

OII Europe, Statement of Riga, 8th of October 2014 https://oiieurope.org/statement-of-riga/

OII Europe, STATEMENT of the 1st European Intersex Community Event (Vienna, 30st – 31st of March 2017) https://oiieurope.org/statement-1st-european-intersex-community-event-vienna-30st-31st-march-2017/

Pinde R, Malhotra A (2006) "Son Preference and Daughter Neglect in India, What happens to Living Girls?", International Center for Research on Women, https://www.unfpa.org/sites/default/files/resource-pdf/UNFPA_Publication-39764.pdf

Parliamentary Assembly of the Council of Europe (PACE), Doc. 14404, "Promoting the human rights of and eliminating discrimination against intersex people", 25-09-2017 available on http://semantic-pace.net/tools/pdf.aspx?doc=aHR0cDovL2Fzc2VtYmx5LmNvZS5pbnQvbncveG1sL1hSZWYvWDJlLURXLWV4dHIuYXNwP2ZpbGVpZD0yNDAyNyZsYW5nPUVO&xsl=aHR0cDovL3NlbWFudGljcGFjZS5uZXQvWHNsdC9QZGYvWFJlZi1XRC1BVC1YTUwyUERGLnhzbA==&xsltparams=ZmlsZWlkPTI0MDI3

Setting: Perspectives of children, parents and health professionals", The National Children's Strategy Research Series, 2006 https://www.dcya.gov.ie/documents/research/The_Childs_Right_to_be_Heard_in_the_Healthcare_Setting.pdf

Silvis J (2014) "Human Rights as a Living Concept: Case-law overview", http://www.ejtn.eu/Documents/About%20EJTN/Independent%20Seminars/Human%20Rights%20BCN%2028-29%20April%202014/Case_Law_Digest_Human_Rights_as_a_Living_Concept_SILVIS.pdf

StopIGM.org/ Zwischengeschlecht.org (2018) "Intersex Genital Mutilations: Human Rights Violations of Persons with Variations of Sex Anatomy, NGO Report for LoIPR to the 8th Report of Denmark on the Convention against Torutre (CAT)", http://intersex.shadowreport.org/public/2018-CAT-LoIPR-Denmark-NGO-Zwischengeschlecht-Intersex-IGM.pdf

StopIGM.org/ Zwischengeschlecht.org (2015) ""Intersex Genital Mutilations: Human Rights Violations of Persons with Variations of Sex Anatomy, NGO Report to the 3rd and 4th Periodic Report of Ireland on the Convention on the Rights of the Child (CRC)", http://intersex.shadow-report.org/public/2015-CRC-Ireland-NGO-Zwischengeschlecht-Intersex-IGM.pdf

Support Initiative for Persons with Congenital Disorders, Baseline Survey on Intersex Realities in East Africa, 2015-2016 – specific focus on Uganda, Kenya and Rwanda http://www.hirschfeld-eddy-stiftung.de/fileadmin/images/laenderberichte/Uganda/2017-01-23_Baseline_Survey_on_Intersex_Realities_in_East_Africa.pdf

Swiss National Advisory Commission on Biomedical Ethics (2012) On the management of differences of sex development: Ethical issues relating to "intersexuality", Opinion No. 20/2012, Berne, November 2012

Tamar-Mattis A (2012) "Medical Treatment of People with Intersex Conditions as Torture and Cruel, Inhuman or Degrading Treatment or Punishment", Report to the UN Special Rapporteur on Torture, available on https://interactadvocates.org/wp-content/uploads/2017/03/interACT-Report-for-UNSRT-on-Intersex.pdf

The Global Forum on MSM & HIV & OutRight Action International (2017) "Agenda 2030 for LGBTI health and well-being", available on https://www.outrightinternational.org/sites/default/files/sdg2030_05052017_0.pdf
Thapa JS (September 2015) "LGBT Uganda Today: Continuing Danger Despite Nullification of Anti-Homosexuality Act", Human Rights Campaign, https://assets2.hrc.org/files/assets/resources/Global_Spotlight_Uganda__designed_version__September_25__2015.pdf
Transgender Europe Position Paper on Gender Markers, 13 June 2018 https://tgeu.org/wp-content/uploads/2018/07/Gender-Marker-Position-Approved-13-June-2018-formatted.pdf
Transgender Europe, Trans Network Balkan, ILGA Europe, Subversive Front, "X. v. the former Yugoslav Republic of Macedonia (Application no 29683/16)", Written Comments https://tgeu.org/wp-content/uploads/2017/10/2017-07-28_X-v.-Macedonia_TPI_FINAL.pdf
Trasek ry and Seta ry, "The Cruel, Inhuman and Degrading Treatment of Trans and Intersex people in Finland" Submission to the UN Committee Against Torture 59th Session November 2016 https://tbinternet.ohchr.org/Treaties/CAT/Shared%20Documents/FIN/INT_CAT_CSS_FIN_25540_E.pdf
United Nations Free & Equal (2016) "Factsheet Intersex", available on https://unfe.org/system/unfe-65-Intersex_Factsheet_ENGLISH.pdf
United Nations Human Rights Office of the High Commissioner (2017) "Tackling Discrimination against Lesbian, Gay, Bi, Trans, & Intersex People, Standards of Conduct for Business", available on https://www.unfe.org/wp-content/uploads/2017/09/UN-Standards-of-Conduct.pdf
UNDP, USAID (2014) "Being LGBT in Asia: Nepal Country Report" Bangkok, http://www.asia-pacific.undp.org/content/dam/rbap/docs/Research%20&%20Publications/hiv_aids/rbap-hhd-2014-blia-nepal-country-report.pdf
UNFPA and The Danish Institute for Human Rights (2014) "Reproductive Rights are Human Rights", available on http://www.ohchr.org/Documents/Publications/NHRIHandbook.pdf
U.S. Department of State, "Kenya 2016 Human Rights Report", available on https://www.state.gov/documents/organization/265478.pdf
Valleala A (2014) Legal recognition of same-sex family life in the jurisprudence of the European Court of Human Rights Master's thesis published by the University of Helsinki
WHO (June 2015) "Sexual health, human rights and the law", available on http://www.who.int/reproductivehealth/publications/sexual_health/sexual-health-human-rights-law/en/
WHO (2011) "Preventing gender-biased sex selection", An interagency statement OHCHR, UNFPA, UNICEF, UN Women and WHO, available on http://apps.who.int/iris/bitstream/10665/44577/1/9789241501460_eng.pdf
Women's Sports Foundation, "Participation of Intersex Athletes in Women's Sports" available on https://www.womenssportsfoundation.org/wp-content/uploads/2016/08/participation-of-intersex-athletes-in-womens-sports.pdf
Zillén K, Garland J, Slokenberga S (11 January 2017) "The Rights of Children in Biomedicine: Challenges posed by scientific advances and uncertainties", Commissioned by the Committee on Bioethics for the Council of Europe

Presentations/Papers

Agius S (26 September 2012) "Trans and intersex people: Discrimination on grounds of sex, gender identity and gender expression", for Trans and Intersex People: Challenges for EU law, European Parliament
Andrew A (2009) Intersexed, intertext: a critique of limited gender identity in Herculine Barbin and Middlesex. Clemson University. https://tigerprints.clemson.edu/cgi/viewcontent.cgi?article=1585&context=all_theses

Audry Sofian, "Summary of Judith Butler 2004 "Gender Regulations" in Undoing Gender" http://interdisciplinarities.orangeseeds.net/system/files/attachments/Presentation-Butler.pdf
Gonzalez Andres Diego, "The Colombia Constitutional Court: Building Legitimacy in its First Period", Constitutional Court of Colombia, Universidad Externado https://www.law.uchicago.edu/files/Session%20VI_Gonzalez.pdf
Hahm SC (2010) Striving to survive: human security of the Hijra of Pakistan. International Institute of Social Studies, The Hague
Lear J (2007) "Unnecessary surgery on intersex infants: Problems of theory become problems in practice", Master's Thesis in Applied Ethics Centre for Applied Ethics Linköpings universitet, presented May 2007
Piantato G (2016) "How has queer theory influenced the ways we think about gender?", Working Paper of Public Health nr. 12/2016, Azienda Ospedaliera Nazionale "SS. Antonio e Biagio e Cesare Arrigo"
Prof. Dr. Danny Pieters (2017) Functions of comparative law and practical methodology of comparing, or how the goal determines the road! University KU Leuven. https://www.law.kuleuven.be/personal/mstorme/Functions%20of%20comparative%20law%20and%20practical%20methodology%20of%20comparing.pdf
Shawkat SS (2016) Construction of the Hijra Identity. BRAC University, Dhaka. http://dspace.bracu.ac.bd/xmlui/bitstream/handle/10361/7804/16217005_ESS.pdf?sequence=1&isAllowed=y
Sledzinska-Simon A. Transgressing gender-gender identity in EU discrimination law. University of Wroclaw
Stenqvist T (Spring 2015) The social struggle of being HIJRA in Bangladesh-cultural aspiration between inclusion and illegitimacy. Malmö University. https://muep.mau.se/bitstream/handle/2043/18568/Stenqvist-T-DP15%20final.pdf

Internet

ABC News, "ACT to make it easier for transgender people to alter birth certificate" http://www.abc.net.au/news/2014-03-17/easier-for-transgender-people-to-change-birth-certificate/5324952
American Convention on Human Rights "Pact of San Jose, Costa Rica", Signatories and Ratifications https://www.oas.org/dil/treaties_b-32_american_convention_on_human_rights_sign.htm
Anne Tamar-Mattis (2008) "Medical decision-making and the child with a DSD", Healio Endocrine Today, https://www.healio.com/endocrinology/pediatric-endocrinology/news/print/endocrine-today/%7B17caf5fa-433f-4bc6-8d12-4b2a299f3e1a%7D/medical-decision-making-and-the-child-with-a-dsd
Archivo Prensa INADI, "Intersexualidad: el INADI contra la violencia del Sistema binario de sexo y de género" http://www.inadi.gob.ar/archivo/?p=16061
Australian Government Attorney General's Department "Same-sex reforms: Overview of the Australian Government's same-sex law reforms". https://web.archive.org/web/20150523133259/http://www.ag.gov.au/RightsAndProtections/HumanRights/Pages/Samesexreforms.aspx
Australian Government, "Australian Government Guidelines on the Recognition of Sex and Gender" https://www.ag.gov.au/Publications/Pages/AustralianGovernmentGuidelinesontheRecognitionofSexandGender.aspx
BBC, "Portugal's president vetoes new gender-change law" https://www.bbc.com/news/world-europe-44063016
Beury Manon. "The CJEU's judgment in Coman: a small step for the recognition of same-sex couples underlying European divides over LGBT rights" https://strasbourgobservers.

com/2018/07/24/the-cjeus-judgment-in-coman-a-small-step-for-the-recognition-of-same-sex-couples-underlying-european-divides-over-lgbt-rights/#more-4202
Carpenter M (2015) Intersex: intersectionality, epistemic and structural violence. http://morgan-carpenter.com/wp-content/uploads/2015/08/MNC-intersectionalities-epistemic-structural.pdf
Child Rights International Network, "Bodily Integrity" https://www.crin.org/en/home/what-we-do/policy/bodily-integrity
Council of Europe, "Values: Human rights, Democracy, Rule of Law" https://www.coe.int/en/web/about-us/values
Court of Arbitration for Sport, The application of the IAAF Hyperandrogenism Regulations remains suspended http://www.sportsintegrityinitiative.com/application-iaaf-hyperandrogenism-regulations-remains-suspended/
CNN, "Uganda's President Museveni signs controversial anti-gay bill into law" https://edition.cnn.com/2014/02/24/world/africa/uganda-anti-gay-bill
CNN, "Hundreds have changed genders on NYC birth certificates" https://edition.cnn.com/2017/03/10/health/new-york-birth-certificate-gender-marker-change/index.html
Dalli Miriam, "Transgender Europe applauds Malta for naming gender identity" https://www.maltatoday.com.mt/news/national/38027/transgender_europe_applauds_malta_for_naming_gender_identity#.W8R8HBMzagS
Dalli Miriami, "Male, Female or X: the new gender options on identification documents" https://www.maltatoday.com.mt/news/national/49185/male_female_or_x_the_new_gender_options_on_identification_documents#.W8XeRxMza8U
Deutsche Welle, "German president signs gay marriage bill into law" https://www.dw.com/en/german-president-signs-gay-marriage-bill-into-law/a-39795137
Dittrich Boris, "Dutch Court Signals Need for Gender Neutral Option" https://www.hrw.org/news/2018/06/01/dutch-court-signals-need-gender-neutral-option
Efsyn.gr, "First time, equal before the law" (in Greek) http://www.efsyn.gr/arthro/proti-fora-isoi-apenanti-ston-nomo
ETCSL The Electronic Text Corpus of Sumerian Literature, "Enki and Ninmah" available on http://etcsl.orinst.ox.ac.uk/cgi-bin/etcsl.cgi?text=t.1.1.2#
Encyclopaedia of the Hellenistic World, Asia Minor: Hermaphroditus available on http://asiaminor.ehw.gr/Forms/fLemmaBody.aspx?lemmaid=8130#chapter_2
European Centre for Law & Justice, "Council of Europe Adopted Resolution Creating New Controversial Rights on Gender Identity" https://eclj.org/family/pace/council-of-europe-adopted-resolution-creating-new-controversial-rights-on-gender-identity-
European Parliament, "Values" https://europarlamentti.info/en/values-and-objectives/values/
European Union, The EU in brief "Goals and values of the EU" https://europa.eu/european-union/about-eu/eu-in-brief_en
Equaldex, "LGBT Rights in Oceania" https://www.equaldex.com/directory/regions/oceania
Gabriela García, "Identidad Forzada" http://www.paula.cl/reportajes-y-entrevistas/reportajes/identidad-forzada/
Gardham Magnus, "Scotland to give legal recognition to people who are neither male nor female" https://www.heraldscotland.com/news/14396678.scotland-to-give-legal-recognition-to-people-who-are-neither-male-nor-female/
Gary Juneau and Rubin S. Neal, "Are LGBT rights human rights? Recent devopments at the United Nations" http://www.apa.org/international/pi/2012/06/un-matters.aspx
GayLawNet, "Laws, Austria" http://www.gaylawnet.com/laws/at.htm
Gaystarnews, "Trans people in Chile can now change their name and gender, without surgery" https://www.gaystarnews.com/article/transgender-chile/#gs.x0IPzZI
Giuseppe Zago, "Oliari and Others v. Italy: a stepping stone towards full legal recognition of same-sex relationships in Europe" https://strasbourgobservers.com/2015/09/16/oliari-and-others-v-italy-a-stepping-stone-towards-full-legal-recognition-of-same-sex-relationships-in-europe/
GLBTQ an encyclopedia of gay, lesbian, bisexual, transgender & queer culture, "Genderqueer" available on https://web.archive.org/web/20120425081046/http://www.glbtq.com/social-sciences/genderqueer.html

Global Legal Monitor, "Sweden: Court Says Previous Sex Change Not a Bar to Second Change of Legal Gender Identity" http://www.loc.gov/law/foreign-news/article/sweden-court-says-previous-sex-change-not-a-bar-to-second-change-of-legal-gender-identity/

Grégor Puppinck, "The ECHR Unanimously Confirms the Non-existence of a Right to Gay Marriage" https://eclj.org/marriage/the-echr-unanimously-confirms-the-non-existence-of-a-right-to-gay-marriage

Harley Robin, "Gender Trouble by Judith Butler: Summary & Concept" http://study.com/academy/lesson/gender-trouble-by-judith-butler-summary-lesson-quiz.html

Hannah Barnes, "How many redheads are there in the world?" http://www.bbc.com/news/magazine-24331615

Hembach Legal, "Physical and psychological integrity pursuant to article 8 ECHR" https://human-rights-law.eu/echr/article-8-echr-right-to-private-life-family-life-correspondence-and-home/physical-psychological-integrity-pursuant-article-8-echr/

Human Fertilisation & Embryology Authority, "PGD conditions" https://www.hfea.gov.uk/pgd-conditions/

Human Rights Watch, "Lawrence v. Texas, Constitutional right to privacy of gays and lesbians in the United States" https://www.hrw.org/news/2003/07/01/lawrence-v-texas

Human Rights Watch, United States Events of 2016 https://www.hrw.org/world-report/2017/country-chapters/united-states#e81181

Human Rights Watch, "Vietnam: Positive Step for Transgender Rights Vietnamese parliament adopts new transgender legislation" https://www.hrw.org/news/2015/11/30/vietnam-positive-step-transgender-rights

Human Rights Watch, "The Netherlands: Victory for Transgender Rights" https://www.hrw.org/news/2013/12/19/netherlands-victory-transgender-rights

Human Rights Watch, "A History of Intersex Activism and Evolution of Medical Protocol" https://www.hrw.org/video-photos/interactive/2017/07/25/history-intersex-activism-and-evolution-medical-protocol

Human Rights Law Centre, "NSW delivers marriage equality for trans people" https://www.hrlc.org.au/news/2018/6/6/nsw-delivers-marriage-equality-for-trans-people

Human Rights Law Center, "Australia now has adoption equality" https://www.hrlc.org.au/news/2018/4/20/australia-now-has-adoption-equality

ICD-11 for Mortality and Morbidity Statistics (2018) World Health Organization https://icd.who.int/browse11/l-m/en

Identity and Passports, "Information about Changing Sex/Gender Identity" https://www.passports.govt.nz/what-you-need-to-renew-or-apply-for-a-passport/information/

Identidad & Diversidad, Ley 26.618-Matrimonio Igualtorio (2010) https://identidadydiversidad.adc.org.ar/normativa/ley-26-618-matrimonio-igualitario-2010/

ihra, "Tony Briffa writes on "Disorders of Sex Development" https://ihra.org.au/26808/tony-briffa-on-dsd/

ILGA Europe, Rainbow Map, https://rainbow-europe.org/

ILGA Europe, "Intersex" http://www.diva-portal.org/smash/get/diva2:649875/FULLTEXT01.pdf

ILGA Europe, "European Union and LGBT rights" https://web.archive.org/web/20130130103555/http://www.ilga-europe.org/home/guide/eu/lgbt_rights

ILGA Europe, "Anti-discrimination law" https://www.ilga-europe.org/what-we-do/our-advocacy-work/anti-discrimination-law

ILGA Europe, "Employment" https://ilga-europe.org/what-we-do/our-advocacy-work/employment

See ILGA Europe, "Equality for All" https://ilga-europe.org/equalityforall

ILO, "10. Gender Equality and Non-Discrimination" http://www.ilo.org/global/topics/dw4sd/themes/gender-equality/lang%2D%2Den/index.htm

Independent, "Pakistan passes law guaranteeing transgender rights" https://www.independent.co.uk/news/world/asia/pakistan-transgender-rights-lgbt-national-assembly-law-drivers-license-passport-a8343321.html

Institute for Studies of Society, Economics and Environment (iSEE), "10 things you need to know about the recognition of transgender rights in Viet Nam" http://isee.org.vn/en/blog/Article/10-things-you-need-to-know-about-the-recognization-of-transgender-rights-in-viet-nam
InterAct, "New UN Special Rapporteur on Torture Report addresses Intersex issues among others" https://interactadvocates.org/new-un-special-rapporteur-on-torture-report-addresses-intersex-issues-among-others/
InterAct, "Federal Government Bans Discrimination Against Intersex People in Health Care" http://interactadvocates.org/federal-government-bans-discrimination-against-intersex-people-in-health-care/
International Models Project on Women's Rights, "Current Legal Framework: Transgender Issues in Germany" https://www.impowr.org/content/current-legal-framework-transgender-issues-germany
International Justice Resource Center, "Regional System" https://ijrcenter.org/regional/
International Justice Resource Center, "In X. and Others v. Austria, ECtHR Finds Discriminatory Restriction on Same-Sex Couple Adoption Violates Convention" https://ijrcenter.org/2013/02/20/in-x-and-others-v-austria-ecthr-finds-discriminatory-restriction-on-same-sex-couple-adoption-violates-convention/
Intersex Human Rights Australia, "Ten years of "X" passports, and no protection from discrimination" https://ihra.org.au/21597/
Intersex Human Rights Australia, "The Yogyakarta Principles +10 launched" https://ihra.org.au/31780/the-yogyakarta-principles-10-launched/
Intersex Human Rights Australia, "Intersex people and marriage, an analysis by Gina Wilson" https://ihra.org.au/21183/intersex-people-and-marriage-analysis/
Intersex Day, "Statement of Intersex Asia and Asian intersex forum" https://intersexday.org/en/intersex-asia-2018/
ISNA, "What's the difference between being transgender or transsexual and having an intersex condition?" http://www.isna.org/faq/transgender
ISNA, "Is a person who is intersex an hermaphrodite?", http://www.isna.org/faq/hermaphrodite
ISNA, "How common is intersex?", http://www.isna.org/faq/frequency
ISNA, "What's wrong with the way intersex has traditionally been treated?", http://www.isna.org/faq/concealment
ISNA, "Who was David Reimer (also sadly known as "John/Joan")?, http://www.isna.org/faq/reimer
ISNA, "What's the history behind the intersex rights movement?" http://www.isna.org/faq/history
Independent, "India's supreme court could be about to decriminalize gay sex in major victory for LGBT rights" https://www.independent.co.uk/news/world/asia/india-homosexuality-legalise-law-gay-lgbt-couples-supreme-court-ruling-a8148896.html
Independent, "India's Supreme Court rules gay sex is no longer a crime in historic Section 377 judgment" https://www.independent.co.uk/news/world/asia/india-gay-sex-crime-supreme-court-section-377-decision-lgbt-rights-illegal-a8524971.html
InterAct, "Interact FAQ" https://interactadvocates.org/faq/
InterAct, "Statement on Terminology" https://interactadvocates.org/interact-statement-on-intersex-terminology/
InterAct, "Tips for intersex inclusive language" https://thebridgesweburn.com/tips-for-intersex-inclusive-language/
InterAct, "What is intersex? https://interactadvocates.org/intersex-definitions/
Ivana Isailovic, "The Y.Y. v. Turkey case and trans individuals' gender recognition" https://strasbourgobservers.com/2015/04/24/the-y-y-v-turkey-case-and-trans-individuals-gender-recognition/
Koyama Emi, Intersex Initiative "Adding the "I": Does Intersex Belong in the LGBT Movement?" http://www.intersexinitiative.org/articles/lgbti.html
Lambda Legal, "Lambda Legal Sues U.S. State Department on Behalf of Intersex Citizen Denied Passport" https://www.lambdalegal.org/blog/20151026_zzyym-intersex-denied-passport
Library of Congress, Global Legal Monitor "Costa Rica/OAS: Inter-American Court of Human Rights Declares Right to Marry Should Be Extended to Same-Sex Couples" http://www.loc.

gov/law/foreign-news/article/costa-rica-oas-inter-american-court-of-human-rights-declares-right-to-marry-should-be-extended-to-same-sex-couples/

Library of Congress, Global Legal Monitor "Austria: Court Allows Intersex Individuals to Register Third Gender Other Than Male or Female" http://www.loc.gov/law/foreign-news/article/austria-court-allows-intersex-individuals-to-register-third-gender-other-than-male-or-female/

Luxembourg Times, "New law facilitates transgender, intersex name and gender change" https://luxtimes.lu/archives/2282-new-law-facilitates-transgender-intersex-name-and-gender-change

Matos Daniel Angel, "Towards Livable Mode of Existence: Judith Butler's (Undoing Gender)" http://angelmatos.net/2013/11/26/judith-butlers-undoing-gender/

McAvan Emily, "Why Australia's gender recognition laws need to change" https://www.sbs.com.au/topics/sexuality/agenda/article/2016/08/11/why-australias-gender-recognition-laws-need-change

McDonald Henry and agencies (2015) The Guardian, "Ireland passes law allowing trans people to choose their legal gender", https://www.theguardian.com/world/2015/jul/16/ireland-transgender-law-gender-recognition-bill-passed

Mind The Gap, "Intersexuality and Injustice: Examining Gender Identity and Reassignment via Butler and David Reimer" http://www.zuzutadeushuk.com/home/2016/10/27/intersexuality-and-injustice

MOVILH, "Cámara de Diputados aprueba incorporar a niños y niñas LGBTI en proyecto de ley sobre derechos de la infancia" http://www.movilh.cl/camara-de-diputados-aprueba-incorporar-a-ninos-y-ninas-lgbti-en-proyecto-de-ley-sobre-derechos-de-la-infancia/

Netherlands Network Intersex/DSD, "Eerste Nederlandse paspoort zonder geslachtsregistratie'" https://www.facebook.com/nnid.nl/posts/eerste-nederlandse-paspoort-zonder-geslachtsregistratiegoed-nieuws-een-kind-van-/1087213044691304/

New York Times, "The Peculiar Position of India's Third Gender" https://www.nytimes.com/2018/02/17/style/india-third-gender-hijras-transgender.html

NHS, "Female Genital Mutilation (FGM)" https://www.nhs.uk/conditions/female-genital-mutilation-fgm/

OII, "Intersex resolution adopted by the Parliamentary Assembly of the Council of Europe" https://oiieurope.org/paceresolution/

OII Australia, "On the number of intersex people" available on https://oii.org.au/16601/intersex-numbers/

OII Europe, "Sham package for intersex: Leaving sex entry open is not an option" https://oiieurope.org/bluff-package-for-inter-leaving-sex-entry-open-is-not-an-option/

OII Europe, "WHO published ICD-11- and no end in sight for pathologisation of intersex people" https://oiieurope.org/who-publishes-icd-11-and-no-end-in-sight-for-pathologisation-of-intersex-people/

OII Europe, "Press Release: OII-Europe applauds Malta's Gender Identity, Gender Expression and Sex Characteristics Act" https://oiieurope.org/press-release-oii-europe-applauds-maltas-gender-identity-gender-expression-and-sex-characteristics-act/

OII Europe, "Portugal adopts law protecting intersex people" https://oiieurope.org/portugal-adopts-law-protecting-intersex-people/

OII Europe, "Really Germany? Germany misses the chance for basing its third gender marker law on human rights" https://www.facebook.com/oiieurope/photos/a.501145923278968/2264328880293988/?type=3&theater

OII Intersex-Europe, "What is intersex?" http://oiiinternational.com/intersex-library/intersex-articles/what-is-intersex/

OII Intersex Network, "Intersex Genital Mutilation- IGM: The Fourteen Days of Intersex" http://oiiinternational.com/2574/intersex-genital-mutilation-igm-fourteen-days-intersex/

OII United States, "How common is Intersex? An explanation of the stats" http://oii-usa.org/2563/how-common-is-intersex-in-humans/

Online Psychology "How Does Science Explain Transgenderism?". https://www.reuters.com/article/us-usa-lgbt-biology/born-this-way-researchers-explore-the-science-of-gender-identity-idUSKBN1AJ0F0

Oxford Human Rights Hub (2013) "Equality v Human Rights?: Same sex marriage and religious liberty" http://ohrh.law.ox.ac.uk/equality-v-human-rights-same-sex-marriage-and-religious-liberty/
Oxford Reference, "Queer Theory", http://www.oxfordreference.com/view/10.1093/oi/authority.20110803100358573
Pakistan Today, "Don't we count? Transgender Pakistanis feel sidelined by census" https://www.pakistantoday.com.pk/2017/10/07/dont-we-count-transgender-pakistanis-feel-sidelined-by-census/
Pieter Cannoot, "A.P., Garçon and Nicot v. France: the Court draws a line for trans rights" https://strasbourgobservers.com/2017/05/05/a-p-garcon-and-nicot-v-france-the-court-draws-a-line-for-trans-rights/
Queer.de, "Österreich: Adoptionsverbot für Homo-Paare verfassungswidrig" https://www.queer.de/detail.php?article_id=23025
Ramirez Berezowsky Daniel, Human Rights Watch, "Latin America Could Lead the Way for LGBT Rights in 2018" https://www.hrw.org/news/2018/02/06/latin-america-could-lead-way-lgbt-rights-2018
Rehbein Consuelo, "Conoce los detalles de la ley de matrimonio igualitario" https://www.publimetro.cl/cl/noticias/2017/08/28/detalles-ley-matrimonio-igualitario.html
Reuters, "German high court rejects 'intersex' as third gender category" https://www.reuters.com/article/us-germany-gender/german-high-court-rejects-intersex-as-third-gender-category-idUSKCN10F2FB
Reuters, "Pakistan counts transgender people in national census for first time" https://www.reuters.com/article/us-pakistan-transgender-census/pakistan-counts-transgender-people-in-national-census-for-first-time-idUSKBN14T1XK
Reuters, "Born this way? Researchers explore the science of gender identity" https://www.reuters.com/article/us-usa-lgbt-biology/born-this-way-researchers-explore-the-science-of-gender-identity-idUSKBN1AJ0F0
Reuters, "Portugal approves law to boost transgender rights, protect intersex infants" https://www.reuters.com/article/portugal-lgbt-lawmaking/portugal-approves-law-to-boost-transgender-rights-protect-intersex-infants-idUSL1N1RQ0ZP
Roosevelt Kermit, "Judicial Activism" https://www.britannica.com/topic/judicial-activism
Sainty Lane, "A Tale of Two Bills: SA Passes Trans Reform, Victoria Cans It" https://www.buzzfeed.com/lanesainty/landmark-transgender-rights-bill-passes-in-south-australia-n?utm_term=.mg059P8ZY#.vcpWLb79X
SBC, "On Transgender Identity", Resolution 2250, 2014 http://www.sbc.net/resolutions/2250/on-transgender-identity
Smith Harriet, "Australia's marriage-equality debate reverberates through the Pacific" https://www.lowyinstitute.org/the-interpreter/australias-marriage-equality-debate-reverberates-through-pacific
Société, "Vincent Guillot: Il faut cesser les mutilations des enfants intersexes en France" https://www.lemonde.fr/societe/article/2017/03/21/vincent-guillot-il-faut-cesser-les-mutilations-des-enfants-intersexes-en-france_5098554_3224.html
SOGIE Unit, "Fact sheet on intersex persons" http://www.chr.up.ac.za/index.php/model-law-on-intersex-persons.html
SPLC Southern Poverty Law Center, "M.C. v. Aaronson" https://www.splcenter.org/seeking-justice/case-docket/mc-v-aaronson
Stanford Encyclopedia of Philosophy, "Feminist Perspectives on Sex and Gender", 2011 http://plato.stanford.edu/entries/feminism-gender/#GenSoc
StopIGM.org, "Portugal: New Law Fails to Protect Intersex Children from IGM" http://stop.genitalmutilation.org/post/Portugal-New-law-fails-to-protect-intersex-children
StopIGM.org, "Denamrk: UN slams intersex genital mutilation-again!" http://stop.genitalmutilation.org/post/Denmark-UN-slams-intersex-genital-mutilation-CRC-2017
StopIGM.org, "The Netherlands questioned over Intersex Genital Mutilations- Gov promises "discussions"- Reprimands expected today" http://stop.genitalmutilation.org/post/CEDAW65-Netherlands-questioned-Intersex-Genital-Mutilations-Gov-promises-discussions

StopIGM.org., "There we go (2): France condemns "mutilation of intersex children", proposes "prohibition" http://stop.genitalmutilation.org/post/France-condemns-mutilations-of-intersex-children-proposes-prohibition
Swedish Secretariat for Gender Research, "Government inquiry leaves out intersex people" https://www.genus.se/en/newspost/government-inquiry-leaves-out-intersex-people/
Taryn Knox and Lynley Anderson, "Fairness and Inclusion: Is it time to replace the gender binary in elite sport?" http://aabhlconference.com/2341
TGEU, map on "Criminalisation and Prosecution of Trans People" https://transrespect.org/en/map/criminalization-and-prosecution-of-trans-people/#
The World Bank (2016) Investing in a research revolution for LGBTI inclusion http://documents.worldbank.org/curated/en/196241478752872781/pdf/110035-WP-InvestinginaResearchRevolutionforLGBTIInclusion-PUBLIC-ABSTRACT-SENT.pdf
Transgender Europe, "Germany introduces Third Gender – fails Trans People" https://tgeu.org/germany-introduces-third-gender-fails-trans-people/?fbclid=IwAR0QqPvEy45oE8yg_U_2LpKgHt9rgGNLm-IQlnzNXQMGc5FusTPvy8W3X9U
The Guardian, "Queensland scraps law forcing married transgender people to divorce" https://www.theguardian.com/australia-news/2018/jun/14/queensland-scraps-law-forcing-married-transgender-people-to-divorce
The Department of Internal Affairs, "Information for Transgender Applicants" https://www.dia.govt.nz/diawebsite.nsf/wpg_URL/Services-Births-Deaths-and-Marriages-Information-for-Transgender-Applicants?OpenDocument
The Queer Dictionary, "Definition of Cisnormativity" http://queerdictionary.blogspot.gr/2014/09/definition-of-cisnormativity.html
The Local, "Sweden to modernize law on changing gender" https://www.thelocal.se/20170316/sweden-to-modernize-law-on-changing-gender
The Telegraph, "India's top court upholds law criminalising gay sex" https://www.telegraph.co.uk/news/worldnews/asia/india/10509952/Indias-top-court-upholds-law-criminalising-gay-sex.html
The Times of India, "In a first, Gurgaon court recognizes lesbian marriage" https://timesofindia.indiatimes.com/city/gurgaon/In-a-first-Gurgaon-court-recognizes-lesbian-marriage/articleshow/9401421.cms
Transgender Europe, "German Experts demand urgent Action for Trans Rights" https://tgeu.org/german-expert-commission-demands-urgent-action-trans-rights/
Transgender Europe, "Malta Adopts Ground-breaking Trans and Intersex Law" https://tgeu.org/malta-adopts-ground-breaking-trans-intersex-law/
Transgender Europe, "New Greek Gender Recognition law fails human rights" https://tgeu.org/greece_lgr/
Transgender Europe, "Belgium-New Gender Recognition Law with obstacles" https://tgeu.org/belgium-new-gender-recognition-law-with-obstacles/
Transgender Europe, "Belgium: Legal Gender Recognition Law (2017)" https://tgeu.org/belgium-legal-gender-recognition-law-2017/
Transgender Europe, "Historic Danish Gender Recognition Law comes into Force" https://tgeu.org/tgeu-statement-historic-danish-gender-recognition-law-comes-into-force/
Transgender Europe, "Denmark: X in Passports and New Trans Law Works" https://tgeu.org/denmark-x-in-passports-and-new-trans-law-work/
Transgender Europe, "More equality for trans persons in Finland" https://tgeu.org/more-equality-for-trans-persons-in-finland/
Transgender Europe, "Third Party Intervention X v Romania and Y v Romania" https://tgeu.org/third-party-intervention-x-v-romania-and-y-v-romania/
Jones Jesse, "Victoria Moves to End Forced Divorce for Trans People under Marriage Equality" http://www.starobserver.com.au/news/national-news/victoria-news/victoria-trans-birth-certificate/167529
ZeeNews, "Pakistan court allows woman to change sex" http://zeenews.india.com/news/south-asia/pakistan-court-allows-woman-to-change-sex_439951.html

Zwischengeschlecht, "Nuremberg Hermaphrodite Lawsuit: Michaela "Micha" Raab Wins Damages and Compensation for Intersex Genital Mutilations". http://stop.genitalmutilation.org/post/Nuremberg-Hermaphrodite-Lawsuit-Damages-and-Compensation-for-Intersex-Genital-Mutilations

Uladzislau Belavusau and Ivana Isailović, "Gay Blood: Bad Blood? A Brief Analysis of the Léger Case [2015] C-528/13" https://europeanlawblog.eu/2015/08/26/gay-blood-bad-blood-a-brief-analysis-of-the-leger-case-2015-c-52813/

UN and the Rule of Law, "Rule of Law and Human Rights" https://www.un.org/ruleoflaw/rule-of-law-and-human-rights/

UN News, "UN Official welcomes ASEAN commitment to human rights, but concerned over declaration wording" https://news.un.org/en/story/2012/11/426012#.UPgVKGckSOI

UNESCO, "Communication and Information" http://www.unesco.org/new/en/communication-and-information/freedom-of-expression/freedom-of-information/

United Nations Human Rights Office of the High Commissioner, "UN expert commends Argentina's "progressive laws and policies" but urges action to stop attacks on LGBT people" http://www.ohchr.org/en/NewsEvents/Pages/DisplayNews.aspx?NewsID=21348&LangID=E

United Nations and the Rule of Law, "Equality and Non-discrimination" https://www.un.org/ruleoflaw/thematic-areas/human-rights/equality-and-non-discrimination/

UN Sustainable Development Goals, "Goal 5: Achieve gender equality and empower all women and girls" https://www.un.org/sustainabledevelopment/gender-equality/

United Nations, Office on Sport for Development and Peace "Overview" https://www.un.org/sport/content/why-sport/overview

UN Women, "Short History of CEDAW Convention" http://www.un.org/womenwatch/daw/cedaw/history.htm

UN Women, "A brief history of the Commission on the Status of Women" http://www.unwomen.org/en/csw/brief-history

University of Minnesota, Study Guide: Sexual Orientation and Human Rights available on http://hrlibrary.umn.edu/edumat/studyguides/sexualorientation.html

U.S. Department of State, "ASEAN Declaration on Human Rights" https://2009-2017.state.gov/r/pa/prs/ps/2012/11/200915.htm

U.S National Library of Medicine, "Androgen Insensitivity Syndrome" available on https://ghr.nlm.nih.gov/condition/androgen-insensitivity-syndrome

U.S National Library of Medicine, "Congenital adrenal hyperplasia due to 11-beta-hydroxylase deficiency" available on https://ghr.nlm.nih.gov/condition/congenital-adrenal-hyperplasia-due-to-11-beta-hydroxylase-deficiency

U.S National Library of Medicine, "Turner Syndrome" available on https://ghr.nlm.nih.gov/condition/turner-syndrome

Washington Blade, "Chilean House of Deputies approves transgender rights bill" http://www.washingtonblade.com/2018/01/23/chilean-house-deputies-approves-transgender-rights-bill/

WHO, "Female genital mutilation" http://www.who.int/mediacentre/factsheets/fs241/en/

WHO, "Gender" available on http://www.who.int/gender-equity-rights/understanding/gender-definition/en/

World Health Organisation (WHO), "Gender and Genetics, Genetics Components of Sex and Gender" available on http://www.who.int/genomics/gender/en/index1.html

WHO, "Gender and Human Rights" available on http://www.who.int/reproductivehealth/topics/gender_rights/sexual_health/en/

WHO, "Gender and Genetics: Sex selection and discrimination" http://www.who.int/genomics/gender/en/index4.html

WHO, "Gender and Reproductive rights" https://web.archive.org/web/20090726150133/http://www.who.int//reproductive-health/gender/index.html

WHO, "Male circumcision for HIV prevention" http://www.who.int/hiv/topics/malecircumcision/en/

Winq, "Eindelijk: officieel verbod op transgenderdiscriminatie" https://winq.nl/articles/229143/eindelijk-officieel-verbod-op-transgenderdiscriminatie/

Printed by Printforce, the Netherlands